BYZANTINE LEGAL CULTURE AND THE ROMAN LEGAL TRADITION, 867–1056

This social history of Byzantine law offers an introduction to one of the world's richest yet hitherto understudied legal traditions. In the first study of its kind, Chitwood explores and reinterprets the seminal legal-historical events of the Byzantine Empire under the Macedonian dynasty, including the re-appropriation and refashioning of the Justinianic legal corpus and the founding of a law school in Constantinople. During this last phase of Byzantine secular law, momentous changes in law and legal culture were underway: the patronage of the elite was reflected in the legal system; theological terms from Orthodox Christianity entered the vocabulary of Byzantine jurisprudence; and private legal collections of uncertain origins began to circulate in manuscripts alongside official redactions of Justinianic law. By using the heuristic device of exploring legal culture, this book examines the interplay in law between the Roman political heritage, Orthodox Christianity and Hellenic culture.

ZACHARY CHITWOOD is a Research and Teaching Associate in Byzantine Studies at the Johannes Gutenberg University of Mainz. He has published on Byzantine law, including the legal status of Byzantine Jews, and foundations/endowments. His scholarship has appeared in the journals *Byzantine and Modern Greek Studies*, *Greek, Roman, and Byzantine Studies* and *Viator*, as well as in *The Late Antique World of Early Islam* (edited by Robert G. Hoyland, 2015) and the first two of the planned three volumes of the *Enzyklopädie des Stiftungswesens in mittelalterlichen Gesellschaften* (2014, 2016).

BYZANTINE LEGAL CULTURE AND THE ROMAN LEGAL TRADITION, 867–1056

ZACHARY CHITWOOD

CAMBRIDGE
UNIVERSITY PRESS

CAMBRIDGE
UNIVERSITY PRESS

University Printing House, Cambridge CB2 8BS, United Kingdom
One Liberty Plaza, 20th Floor, New York, NY 10006, USA
477 Williamstown Road, Port Melbourne, VIC 3207, Australia
4843/24, 2nd Floor, Ansari Road, Daryaganj, Delhi – 110002, India
79 Anson Road, #06-04/06, Singapore 079906

Cambridge University Press is part of the University of Cambridge.
It furthers the University's mission by disseminating knowledge in the pursuit of education, learning, and research at the highest international levels of excellence.

www.cambridge.org
Information on this title: www.cambridge.org/9781107182561

10.1017/9781316861547

First published 2017

Printed in the United States of America by Sheridan Books, Inc.

A catalogue record for this publication is available from the British Library.

Library of Congress Cataloging-in-Publication Data
Names: Chitwood, Zachary, author.
Title: Byzantine legal culture and the Roman legal tradition, 867–1056 / Zachary Chitwood, Johannes Gutenberg University of Mainz.
Description: Cambridge, United Kingdom; New York, NY, USA: Cambridge University Press, 2017. | Based on author's thesis (doctoral – Princeton University, 2012) issued under title: Byzantine legal culture under the Macedonian dynasty, 867–1056, |
Includes bibliographical references and index.
Identifiers: LCCN 2016053922 | ISBN 9781107182561 (hardback)
Subjects: LCSH: Law, Byzantine–Roman influences. | Byzantine Empire–History–527–1081.
Classification: LCC KJA1350.C48 2017 | DDC 340.5/4–dc23
LC record available at https://lccn.loc.gov/2016053922

ISBN 978-1-107-18256-1 Hardback

In Loving Memory of My Father, Gregory Bryant Chitwood
(1954–2010)

Cesare fui e son Iustinïano
che, per voler del primo amor ch'i' sento,
d'entro le leggi trassi il troppo e 'l vano.
I was Caesar and am Justinian
Who, by the will of the first love which I feel,
Removed the superfluous and vain from the law.
Dante, *Paradiso*, Canto VI, lines 10–12

Contents

Acknowledgments *page* viii
Note on Naming, Translation and Transliteration x
List of Abbreviations xi

Introduction: Reciting Homer in the Courtroom – Byzantine Legal Culture 1
1 The "Cleansing of the Ancient Laws" under Basil I and Leo VI 16
2 Gift-Giving and Patronage in Middle Byzantine Courts 45
3 Paradigms of Justice and Jurisprudence 76
4 The Function of "Private" Law Collections in the Byzantine Empire and Neighboring Cultures 103
5 Law and Heresy in the Edicts of the Patriarch Alexios Stoudites 133
6 Legal Education and the Law School of Constantinople 150
Conclusions: The End of Secular Law in Byzantium? 184

Appendix: Translation of the Novella constitutio 193
Bibliography 204
Index 231

Acknowledgments

Over the course of writing this book I have incurred many debts both intellectual and personal. This monograph was first conceived, albeit in a different form, as a dissertation at Princeton University. I owe a debt of gratitude both to the intellectual community there, and in particular to John Haldon and William Chester Jordan, my scholarly role models, as well as to the institutional support I received from the Department of History and in particular from the Seeger Center for Hellenic Studies, which granted me a Stanley J. Seeger Fellowship. Dimitri Gondicas, the center's director, has long hosted a marvelous atmosphere at the center for scholars of Classical, Byzantine and Modern Greek Studies alike. Caroline Humfress, as the external reader of the dissertation, made many valuable suggestions which I implemented in this book.

Beyond Princeton I received invaluable critique and commentary on early versions of this book in various oases of scholarship. At Stanford University, Amalia Kessler introduced me to the Anglo-American tradition of legal history. The Department for Byzantine and Modern Greek Studies at the University of Vienna and its scholars, in particular Johannes Koder and Yannis Stouraitis, were very kind in hosting me for two years. The Max Planck Institute for European Legal History, and in particular the cadre of scholars (Wolfram Brandes, Ludwig Burgmann, and Andreas Schminck) working there on the editing and analysis of Byzantine legal texts, proved a wonderful venue to explore specialized questions of Byzantine law. It is a great sadness that Andreas Schminck, with whom I had corresponded concerning many points of the present monograph until the last months of 2015, did not get to witness the publication of this book, having passed away on December 15, 2015.

Over the last four years I have had the honor of working within the venerable tradition of German Byzantine and Medieval Studies as a post-doctoral scholar on the European Research Council Project "Foundations in medieval societies: Cross-cultural comparisons," hosted by the

Humboldt University of Berlin. I am profoundly indebted to Michael Borgolte, the project's director, who has shown unflagging care and patience in my development as a scholar. Johannes Pahlitzsch, a rare fellow traveler in matters of Middle Byzantine law, and the Byzantinist community at the University of Mainz have provided valuable insights for this project.

I would like to thank Michael Sharp and Cambridge University Press for seeing *Byzantine Legal Culture* through to publication. The ample comments and critique of the anonymous reviewers were vital in improving the initial version of this book.

Last but not least I would like to praise my wife and *słoneczko*, Iga, and our three wonderful children, Gregory, Gabriel and Olivia, for their forebearance and love on nights and weekends I spent away from them to finish this book.

Note on Naming, Translation and Transliteration

The spelling of names in this study follows that of the *Oxford Dictionary of Byzantium*. Transliteration from Medieval Greek to the Roman alphabet is done according to the method prescribed by the Library of Congress. As in the *Oxford Dictionary of Byzantium*, names with a well-established anglicization are presented in their anglicized rather than transliterated form, so Constantine instead of Kōnstantinos, John instead of Iōhannēs, etc. In the interest of readability I completely avoid diacritical marks in the text (no ē for the letter eta, ō for omega, etc.). Given that in the Middle Byzantine administration as well as in Middle Byzantine law there were a great many terms borrowed from Latin, at some points in this study it has proved simpler to use the original Latin term rather than the Greek equivalent, not least of all because these Hellenisms often varied considerably, as the bilingual Greek–Latin lexica from the period demonstrate.

By and large I have attempted to keep quotations in Greek and other ancient and medieval languages confined to footnotes. All Greek words in the main text are transliterated for the benefit of the non-specialist. All translations in the text are my own unless otherwise noted.

For the bibliography I have transliterated Modern Greek and Russian names according to the Library of Congress system while keeping the titles of such authors' work in the original language.

Abbreviations

The use of abbreviations in this work conforms for the most part to their forms found in the *ODB*, vol. I, pp. xix–xlv. Abbreviations for journals are where possible those used in *L'année philologique.*

APF	*Archiv für Papyrusforschung und verwandte Gebiete*
BMGS	*Byzantine and Modern Greek Studies*
ByzF	*Byzantinische Forschungen*
ByzSlav	*Byzantinoslavica*
ByzZ	*Byzantinische Zeitschrift*
CArch	*Cahiers archéologiques*
CFHB	*Corpus fontium historiae byzantinae*
CSHB	*Corpus scriptorum historiae byzantinae*
DOP	*Dumbarton Oaks Papers*
EEBS	Επετηρίς Εταιρείας Βυζαντινών Σπουδών
FM	*Fontes Minores*
GRBS	*Greek, Roman and Byzantine Studies*
JEH	*Journal of Ecclesiastical History*
JGR	*Jus graecoromanum*
JHS	*The Journal of Hellenic Studies*
JÖByz	*Jahrbuch der österreichischen Byzantinistik*
MGH	*Monumenta Germaniae historica*
NG	*Nomos Georgikos*
NM	*Nomos Mosaikos*
NN	*Nomos Nautikos*
NS	*Nomos Stratiotikos*
Nov.	*Novels of Justinian. CIC*, vol. III
Peira	*JGR*, vol 4. pp. 11–260. A reprint of *Jus graeco-romanum*, ed. Karl Eduard Zachariä von Lingenthal, 5 vols. (Leipzig: T. O. Weigel, 1856–69, vol. I (1856).
PG	*Patrologia Graeca*

Pitra	*Iuris ecclesiastici graecorum historia et monumenta iussu Pii IX. Pont. Max.*, ed. I. B. Pitra. Rome: Typis Collegii urbani, 1864–8.
PmbZ	Ralph-Johannes Lilie *et al.* (eds), *Prosopographie der mittelbyzantinischen Zeit.* (8 vols.) Berlin, 1998–2013.
REByz	*Revue des études byzantines*
RHBR	*Repertorium der Handschriften des byzantinischen Rechts.* Forschungen zur byzantinischen Rechtsgeschichte 20, 28. Teil 1. Die Handschriften des weltlichen Rechts (Nr. 1–327) / von Ludwig Burgmann, Marie Theres Fögen, Andreas Schminck, Dieter Simon; Teil 2. Die Handschriften des kirchlichen Rechts I (Nr. 328–427) / von Andreas Schminck und Dorotei Getov; mit Unterstützung mehrerer Fachkollegen. Frankfurt: Löwenklau – Gesellschaft e.V. Frankfurt Am Main, 1995–2011.
Rh.-P.	Σύνταγμα των θείων και ιερών κανόνων [...], ed. G. A. Rhalles and M. Potles. (6 vols.) Athens, 1852–9.
RJ	*Rechtshistorisches Journal*
SG	*Subseciva Groningana*
TIB	*Tabula Imperii byzantini*, ed. H. Hunger. Vienna, 1976–.
Tijdschrift	*Tijdschrift voor rechtsgeschiedenis*
TM	*Travaux et mémoires/Centre de recherche d'histoire et civilisation de Byzance*
ZRVI	*Zbornik Radova Vizantološkog Instituta*
ZRG	*Zeitschrift der Savigny-Stiftung für Rechtsgeschichte. Romanistische Abteilung*

Introduction: Reciting Homer in the Courtroom – Byzantine Legal Culture

Likely sometime in the second quarter of the eleventh century, a widow living in the Byzantine Empire was accused of having a lover. The indignant trustees of her deceased husband's estate charged her with adultery and took her to court. If convicted, the widow stood to lose her share of her first husband's estate. Surprisingly, the judge argued that the law did not prohibit an adulteress from enjoying the estate of her husband, but rather those who marry twice. While the woman who marries twice clearly casts aside her husband's memory and dishonors the children of her first husband by introducing the children of her second husband, the judge reasoned, a woman who has sex outside of marriage merely sins in secret. Having already invoked the law to make his point, the Byzantine judge finalized his decision to dismiss the charge of adultery by quoting some lines of Homer. The context for these verses from the *Odyssey* is Athena urging Telemachus to return home to Ithaca before his mother Penelope chose a new husband in place of Odysseus: "But you know what kind of spirit is in the breast of a women – she resolves to make prosper the house of the man who marries her, and no longer remembers the children of her first husband after he is dead."[1] Upon further examination it was found that her lover was a priest residing in her household in the guise of a servant. Although the ecclesiastical authorities were alerted, the priest was not defrocked.[2]

[1] *Peira* 25.25; *Odyssey* 15.20–3. This passage is discussed in Macrides 2005: 134–6. Although the passage does not explicitly state that the first husband had died, the eventual verdict otherwise makes little sense. The fact that the executors of her husband's estate brought the suit forward suggests the legal incapacity of her husband, due to death, minority or mental illness.

[2] A very similar case (Grumel 1989: n. 883) – I would argue in fact the one described above – was addressed by a decision issued by the patriarch Michael I Keroularios (1043–59). In it the patriarch was asked to clarify the status of a priest named John who claimed that his wife had committed adultery: was he still allowed to celebrate the liturgy? The patriarch answered that, although a candidate for the priesthood married to an adulteress could not be ordained, since John was already ordained and had discovered that she had committed adultery and as a result had separated from

This case, incidentally, was judged by the most renowned Middle Byzantine jurist, Eustathios Rhomaios, and it is recorded along with numerous other verdicts, perhaps around 300 in total, in an anonymously compiled collection, the so-called *Peira*. Eustathios' judgment serves as an excellent entree into the subject of this book, Byzantine legal culture, because it exemplifies its three salient characteristics: (1) a Roman legal and political framework, which extended far beyond the state to encompass the commonweal, the *politeia*;[3] (2) the ethical and moral perspective of Orthodox Christianity; and (3) a Hellenic cultural and linguistic orientation. To Byzantinists, it is the combination of these three aspects which is thought to embody what we term Byzantium.[4] The present study thus follows these three lines of inquiry to argue that together they represent a unique legal culture, a way of thinking about, rationalizing and practicing the law. This book is an examination of this mechanism at a unique moment in Byzantine history, namely during the Macedonian dynasty (867–1056). It analyzes how Byzantines during this period – emperors, judges, intellectuals and (to the meager extent to which it is possible) the non-elite – used, emphasized, downplayed and interwove these three threads of Byzantine legal culture. It is to be hoped that the reader will at the end of this examination not only be convinced that Byzantine legal culture existed, corresponding to some extent to its presentation here, but that it is a phenomenon worthy of further study.

To elucidate why legal culture, a concept that has developed at the intersection of anthropology and legal studies, is a useful heuristic device for this period, it is worth first outlining in some detail the history of scholarship on Byzantine law and exploring the interrelated question of the sources available to the historians who study it. Like any historical sub-field, the quantity and type of sources have dictated to a large extent the sorts of studies that have been produced. For reasons outlined below, the distribution of sources for Byzantine law has led to an unusually sharp

her, then he was still allowed to celebrate the liturgy. This act of adultery also had property implications. Two-thirds of the dowry of John's wife was to stay with their child, and a further third was to go to the convent where the wife would now reside. The main difference between the two cases – whether the priest and the woman were actually married – could possibly have reflected conflicting testimony. The patriarchal decision seems to be based solely on the word of the priest, indicated by the telling phrase "if John is telling the truth." I have consulted the longer version of the decision in *PG* 120: 749, which gives many details lacking in the highly abbreviated summary of the decision in *PG* 119: 852 = *Rh.-P.* 5: 46.

3 On the Byzantine conception of *politeia*, which has been mistranslated as "state," see now Kaldellis 2015: 1–61.

4 Discussed in Rapp 2008: 134; Kaldellis 2015: pp. x–xi.

divide in training, interests and methods between Byzantine legal scholars on the one hand and historians on the other.[5]

A New History of Byzantine Law?

From a constitutional perspective Byzantium had a codified legal system – based on the application and interpretation of a written set of laws, such as is the case today with the majority of European countries – rather than a so-called common law system, a feature of the English legal tradition as well as its former colonies and dependencies around the world, based on case law and precedent.[6] The upshot of having a codified legal system is that the normative laws – the "law in the lawbooks" – generally do not adapt to reflect changing political, social and economic circumstances.[7] Though the Byzantine Empire was hardly unique by medieval or modern standards in this regard, its codified laws were technically valid for an unusually long period of time. The compilation of Roman law commissioned by the Emperor Justinian I (527–65) – a body of law which is now commonly referred to as the *Corpus Iuris Civilis* (*CIC*) – cast a long shadow. In theory, this compilation of Roman law, in the form of its Greek redactions, particularly the so-called "imperial" books (*Basilika*), remained the law of the land throughout the entire political existence of the Byzantine Empire.

This façade of legal continuity has long proved a major impediment for examining Byzantine law in its contemporaneous societal context, since the sources for its actual implementation and societal praxis are to a large extent lacking. Indeed, until the first part of the twentieth century it was assumed that Roman law had not only remained in force but was scrupulously observed throughout Byzantine history. It was a not a legal historian or historian as such but rather an Austrian papyrologist, Artur Steinwenter, who on the basis of papyri from Late Antique Egypt first questioned the actual implementation of Justinianic law. The divergence between Roman law and societal praxis was particularly noteworthy

[5] Stolte 1998 contains a useful discussion of the different approaches to the study of Byzantine law utilized by historians and by legal scholars.

[6] The notion that Byzantium had a civil-law system is not uncontroversial, although it still represents the scholarly *opinio communis*. However, Oikonomides 1986 presented an impressive argument on the basis of the *Peira* that by the eleventh century Byzantium was well on its way to developing a legal system based on precedent, more along the lines of a common law system, although in his narrative this reform failed.

[7] Stolte 1998: 270–2.

in an area where Justinian had enthusiastically legislated, namely on the status of church and monastic property, yet Steinwenter proved that Justinian's provisions had been widely ignored at the time they were issued and indeed well afterward. In Late Antique Egypt church and monastic property was alienated to laypersons; monks could own and dispose of property in a will; and churches, monasteries and pious foundations were treated as private property.[8] All these practices undercut basic principles of Roman and Byzantine law. Steinwenter was thus the first to propose a new history of Byzantine legal institutions (*Institutionengeschichte*) which would not only be based on normative legal sources – which he had demonstrated did not represent the reality on the ground – but would take into account evidence reflecting their implementation.[9]

Though Steinwenter's work on the legal status of ecclesiastical property in Late Antique Egypt garnered much attention at the time it was written, his exhortation for a new history of Byzantine legal institutions remained mostly unheeded until it was made again in the 1980s by the Russian émigré Byzantinist Alexander Kazhdan, who arrived at the same conclusions of the shortcomings of studying Byzantine law solely through normative legal texts, without however explicitly referencing Steinwenter.[10] Harshly criticizing Byzantine legal historians, Kazhdan called for a new history of Byzantine law which would examine law as it was actually practiced in Byzantine society, with such an examination to be made on the basis of a wide range of sources instead of documents representing the official legal regime. Responses to Kazhdan's proposal have been mostly lukewarm or pessimistic, with legal historians in particular critical of the feasibility of writing a history of legal institutions or *Institutionengeschichte*.[11]

Legal Culture as a Heuristic Paradigm

The approach adopted in this book of examining Byzantine law in its wider historical and societal context, although certainly conditioned by the debate surrounding Kazhdan's proposal, is altogether different. Rather

[8] Alienation of church and monastic property: Steinwenter 1958: 32–4; full property rights of individual monks: Steinwenter 1932; foundations as private property Steinwenter 1930: 36.

[9] Steinwenter 1932: 64.

[10] Kazhdan 1989. An earlier version of his argument was published in Italian but attracted less attention: Kazhdan 1988.

[11] Burgmann 1991a: 198–200; Simon 2005: 1–4. Bernard Stolte has penned one of the most thoughtful responses to this debate by contextualizing Kazhdan's critique amidst the historical development of the study of Byzantine law as a field; see Stolte 1998.

than attempting to write a new history of Byzantine legal institutions, a Herculean task that could in this day and age not be undertaken by a single individual, this monograph has made use of the heuristic device known as *legal culture*.[12] *Legal culture* is a somewhat amorphous concept, the theoretical origins of which lie in comparative law, legal anthropology and the sociology of the law.[13] One basic definition runs "it presupposes and invites us to explore the existence of systematic variations in patterns in 'law in the books,' in 'law in action,' and above all, in the relation between them."[14] The idea of legal culture can be traced back to the early days of the field of legal anthropology and is based on the notion that law cannot be understood apart from its wider cultural and societal environment.[15] Initially, legal anthropology was developed as a means of analyzing oral cultures which did not possess a written legal tradition. Lawrence Friedman introduced the term legal culture into the field of the sociology of the law as the amalgamation of a society's legal ideology, practices and social pressures. He distinguished between *inner* and *external legal culture*. Within Friedman's schema, *inner legal culture* encompassed legal professionals, while *external legal culture* referred to the rest of society; the influence of the former, according to Friedman, is often exaggerated by legal scholars.[16] Recently, legal culture has been used with reference to the modern nation-state, to describe for instance the cultural factors which account for differing rates of litigation among various contemporary European countries.[17]

In this study I have refrained from distinguishing between an inner and an external legal culture because, above all, it does not reflect the way law was practiced in the Byzantine Empire. The vast majority of persons who were invested with some degree of juridical power were not professional jurists. Both military governors and the heads of imperial bureaux,

[12] The standard reference work on Byzantine legal institutions remains Karl Eduard Zachariä von Lingenthal's *Geschichte des griechisch-römischen Rechts*, 3rd edn (1892). Although Zachariä's history is still indispensable for anyone interested in Byzantine law, it is a history based on normative legal sources. Archival documents, particularly the acts of the Athonite monasteries, were only just beginning to be published in Zachariä's day, and he understandably therefore made no use of them. A new history of Byzantine law based on archival documents would present a very different picture of how the legal institutions Zachariä surveyed functioned in Byzantine society.

[13] Merry 2012: 58–62.

[14] Definition from Nelken 2007. Nelken 2007: 4–11 discusses the various meanings as well as the relative drawbacks and advantages of using the term legal culture; in short, despite its occasional vagueness, it is preferable to alternatives such as "legal system," "legal tradition," etc.

[15] Goodale and Mertz 2007.

[16] Nelken 2007.

[17] E.g. Bell 2001; Blankenburg and Bruinsma 1994.

to say nothing of the more *ad hoc* forms of justice meted out by large landowners and monasteries (of which we know very little for the period under examination), judged cases as part of their broader administrative duties. Although those who were forced to render judgment without legal training apparently did so with the assistance of *symponoi* (administrative functionaries with some knowledge of the law), ultimately justice and the functioning of the law lay in the hands of those who had, at least for the most part, never formally studied either.

A professional juridical cadre, to the extent that one existed, was confined during the period under examination to the realm of high judges, jurists, lawyers and upper-level legal functionaries. This stratum of Byzantine legal culture was, in its legal orientation, almost completely dominated by its interaction with the Roman legal tradition, not directly via the Justinianic corpus of law, but rather through the medium of the paraphrases and didactic writings of Late Antique jurists, the various Macedonian redactions of the *CIC*, as well as the special treatises and textbooks authored in the tenth and eleventh centuries. In general, these professional jurists were capable of engaging with the Roman legal tradition at a sophisticated level; this much is clear from the jurisprudence of the greatest Middle Byzantine legal scholar, Eustathios Rhomaios, as practiced in the *Peira* and legal treatises like the *Meditatio de nudis pactis*; in both works, despite occasional errors, to a large extent Roman law was correctly interpreted. This relatively small cadre of legal professionals, confined essentially to the capital, drew on its knowledge of the Roman legal tradition as a source of prestige and social status. Middle Byzantine jurists had a professional obsession centered not only on practical knowledge, but also, as is particularly evident in the juristic writings of Michael Psellos, on legal arcana, a state of affairs which has long been a source of bafflement and frustration to historians of Byzantine law. Perhaps the greatest source of cultural cachet it possessed was its claim to know Latin; this skill, which was demanded of the "guardian of the laws" instituted by Constantine IX Monomachos' (r. 1042–55) founding of the Law School in Constantinople, allowed these Byzantine jurists to trumpet a special connection with Byzantium's late Roman political legacy.

Despite the usefulness of legal culture as a heuristic tool of historical analysis, its use has been criticized for its vagueness: "[a]ll too often, legal culture is a term used to account for that which cannot be accounted for in any other way – that is, culture becomes the beneficiary of the residual term in explanatory equations."[18] Along these lines, other scholars have

[18] Gibson and Caldeira 1996: 56.

suggested dividing legal culture into smaller and more specific discrete categories, such as a culture's "attitudes," "expectations," "knowledge" and "values" with regard to law.[19] While duly acknowledging the drawbacks of using the concept "legal culture," its utility as a shorthand way of collectively referring to different aspects of the interaction between Byzantine law and society outweighs its potential drawbacks. In this study as well, the term Byzantine legal culture is employed in a general way as referring to any aspect of the interaction between the official legal regime and various phenomena – be they ideas about justice, customs and practices of a particular social group, or the influence of unofficial legal texts – of Middle Byzantine society.[20] The principal objection of the sociologist of law to defining a modern legal culture in such an open-ended way – that such a definition impairs quantification – is in this case unfounded, since quantification of legal cultural phenomena (e.g. the percentage of the population which was regularly involved in civil suits) is in any case impossible because of the paucity of the sources.

Sources

Why then is the concept of legal culture particularly suited to the study of law in the Middle Byzantine period? This approach was chosen, in part, because it can be employed with the types and quantities of sources, particularly legal sources, which are available to the historian for this era, about which more shall be said later in the introduction, but which can be broadly characterized as follows: an abundance of lawbooks, imperial novels (new legislation issued from the time of Justinian onwards) and legal textbooks (which will be referred to as *official legal sources*), but relatively few records of cases or examples of what legal historians like to call "the law in action." This imbalance has impinged upon the type of work which most Byzantine legal historians have undertaken in the past, which is primarily *Quellenkritik*.

Although it is worth going into greater detail as to the official legal sources which this study utilizes, it should be noted that there exist numerous and much more exhaustive studies of Byzantine official legal sources.[21]

[19] This is essentially the critique of Von Benda-Beckmann and Von Benda-Beckmann 2012.

[20] This study is not the first to use the term "Byzantine legal culture." It has been used, among others, by the Russian Byzantinist I. P. Medvedev, in his monograph *The Legal Culture of the Byzantine Empire* (in Russian); see Medvedev 2001.

[21] The modern pioneer of this type of study was once again Zachariä von Lingenthal 1839. Pieler 1994 is a much-updated Greek translation of Pieler 1978, though the latter remains the perhaps common

Here, official legal sources include the following: lawbooks, imperial novels, legal textbooks, scholia and commentaries on other legal sources and legal treatises.[22] Among lawbooks a distinction is to be made between *official* or imperially sanctioned collections of law and so-called *private* collections. The former were compiled and sanctioned by the imperial regime and represented the official law of the land. The chronology and content of the major imperially sanctioned lawbooks of this period, which include the *Prochiron*, *Eisagoge*, Leo VI's *Sixty Books/Basilika*, and the *Epitome* are explored in detail in Chapter 1. It is important to note that the most important of these codifications, that of the *Basilika*, has not survived in its entirety; sixteen of its sixty books are not directly transmitted.[23] Private collections of law, such as the Farmer's Law, Mosaic Law and Rhodian Sea-Law for the most part have unclear origins and were not imperially sanctioned, although sometimes forged histories of imperial promulgation were appended to these texts. The chronology and content of these private laws is presented in Chapter 4. The major collection of post-Justinianic imperial novels, that of Leo VI, is examined in Chapter 1.

This study makes major use of legal textbooks from this period, particularly the so-called *Peira*, an anonymously compiled casebook consisting of the judgments and verdicts of Eustathios Rhomaios, a jurist whose activity as a judge spanned the last quarter of the tenth and the first two quarters of the eleventh century.[24] Of the 200 to 300 decisions (*hypomnemata*)

basic reference for Middle Byzantine official legal sources. Troianos 2011 is the up-to-date and most thorough reference, though it is inaccessible to those without a reading knowledge of Modern Greek. The portions of Troianos' work which treat canon law are however now available in English translation, see Troianos 2012a (to 1100) and 2012b (twelfth to fourteenth centuries). The overview of Van der Wal and Lokin 1985 has much to recommend itself due to its brevity and clarity. Mostly concerned with Roman law but with some treatment of the Middle Byzantine period as well is Wenger 1953.

[22] An exhaustive discussion of the history (from around the year 1500 to the present day) of the editions of imperial novels issued from the time of Justinian onward can be found in Burgmann 2005a. As Burgmann points out, only a small portion (around one-fifth) of the novels issued from 912 to 1204 are in editions which meet contemporary standards of textual criticism (ibid. 126–7). Regarding the twenty-three surviving novels issued by emperors of the Macedonian dynasty after Leo VI, see Andreas Schminck 2005b.

[23] On this see Van der Wal 1989.

[24] There are no hard and fast dates for Eustathios' life; Nicholas Oikonomides conjectured that he was born around 970 and died sometime in the early 1030s (see Oikonomides 1986). Arguing for a somewhat older Eustathios Rhomaios, Andreas Schminck believes that the Byzantine jurist was born no later than the early years of the 960s (Schminck 2005b: 305–6) and possibly considerably earlier than that. I would argue based on the case presented at the beginning of this chapter that he lived until at least 1043. There are numerous articles and studies of the *Peira*, but relatively few of them have attempted to place the work within its wider historical and societal context.

which Eustathios wrote and which were used along with his shorter pronouncements of a verdict (*semeiomata*) as the basis for the *Peira*, only six decisions have survived in their entirety.[25] Very soon after the composition of the *Peira* in the middle of the eleventh century it was used as a legal textbook, as a school text stemming from the first half of the twelfth century testifies.[26] Eustathios also wrote a legal treatise on the bride-gift (*hypobolon*), referred to in the secondary literature as the *De hypobolo* ("On the bride-gift").[27] Finally, later tradition identifies Eustathios as the author of a text on the property acquired or delegated to those who under Roman and Byzantine law did not theoretically have the right of ownership (such as slaves or minors), the so-called *peculium* (Gr. *pekoulion*).[28]

The *Peira* is one of the few sources which allow historians to see how the law was applied and interpreted by Byzantine jurists at the higher Constantinopolitan courts of the Hippodrome and Velum. In analyzing the *Peira*, one must be careful to distinguish, where it is possible, between the work's anonymous redactor, who added the references to the *Basilika*, and the oeuvre of Eustathios himself.[29] Despite its obvious importance, the *Peira* remains in many ways a source which is underutilized by Middle Byzantine historians. A number of reasons have contributed to this state of affairs. Zachariä's edition is imperfect, although given that the entire *Peira* survives only in a single manuscript, it is not to be assumed that a

Among the exceptions are Oiknomides 1986 and Vryonis 1974. The broad outlines of Eustathios' jurisprudence are presented in Simon 1973 as well as Weiss 1973a. In general, analyses of the *Peira* and of Eustathios' other writings tend to be specialist examinations of particular legal institutions. Marriage law, for example, has been extensively studied: see Burgmann 2003; Papagianne 2008; Simon 1987; Troianos 1986. Two articles of Antonio d'Emilia (see d'Emilia 1965–6 and 1967) treated the law of sale and inheritance law respectively. Other aspects of the *Peira* which have recently been examined include slavery (Köpstein 1993) as well as the sale of office (Tsourka-Papasthathe 2001; 2002). The text has even been used as an indicator of economic data; see Laiou 2003. For a detailed analysis of the terminology employed for the various documents mentioned in the *Peira*, see Burgmann 2005b.

25 Four of these decisions are edited in Eustathios Rhomaios, *Hyponemata on Marriage Law*. The other two were for many years ascribed to the patriarch Alexios Stoudites (1025–43), but were in fact the work of Eustathios as well (see ibid. 222).

26 Treu 1893. Treu dated this text to the end of the eleventh century on the basis of a mention of the *Tipoukeitos*, but, as Schminck observed, it was more likely composed in the first half of the twelfth century; see Schminck 1979: 221, n. 2.

27 Eustathios Rhomaios, *De hypoblo*.

28 Eustathios Rhomaios, *Tractatus de peculiis*. On the authorship of the tract, see ibid. 294–6.

29 A very good point recently made by Sirks 2010: 198–9. In general, when the jurisprudence of Eustathios can be discerned, then it conforms to Justinianic law, see Sirks 2009: 590: "The conclusion is that in the early 11th century the law on the legitimate portion as collected in Peira 41 did not differ much or at all from the law in the 6th century and was applied in a way, basically consistent with 6th century law."

new edition would correct all of the ambiguities of the current printed text. The lack of a translation or commentary in any modern language hinders access to the text for non-specialists. The new edition, translation and commentary currently being undertaken by Lorena Atzeri will remove many of these obstacles when it is completed.[30]

This study also makes use of scholia, particularly the scholia to the *Basilika*.[31] These scholia are agreed to exist in two main divisions: "old" scholia dating from the sixth century and "new" scholia dating mainly from the eleventh and twelfth centuries.[32] Oftentimes a name at the beginning of the scholion indicates the author. Unfortunately, not all of the scholia to the *Basilika* can be dated: many are anonymous and dating them by other means, such as vocabulary, is a very tricky proposition. Additionally, some scholars have bemoaned, quite rightly, the practice of categorizing scholia into "new" and "old" in general, as oftentimes the scholia themselves are written in a much more complex fashion. For instance, a sixth-century scholion to the Justinianic corpus could be continually reworked by later scholiasts: in such a case does one classify the scholion as "new" or "old"?[33]

There are differing views as to whether when these scholia, particularly the "old" scholia, were attached to the text of the *Basilika* itself, and whether these scholia constituted a catena-style commentary.[34] According to one view, the surviving manuscripts indicate that there never existed any archetypal or standard collection of scholia; it appears as though scholia were selected and written *sui generis* for each manuscript.[35] According

[30] Atzeri is completing a project began by Ludwig Burgmann, who has published a sample of the work, a translation and commentary of *Peira*, chapter 51 "On Judges"; see Burgmann 2008.

[31] Contained in vols. 9–16 of the Groningen edition of the *Basilika*. For a detailed discussion of the *Basilika* scholia, see Pringsheim 1963. Since the publication of the Groningen edition of the *Basilika*, a number of new *Basilika* scholia have been discovered in manuscripts. Marie Theres Fögen brought to light two manuscripts which contained fragments of *Bas.* 37.1–2 (which is only reconstructed to a very small degree in the Groningen edition); see Fögen 1979 178–93. Somewhat later Fögen and Burgmann published scholia on books 2, 7–8 of the *Basilika*; see Burgmann and Fögen 1982. In 1993 fifty-one passages from the *Basilika* which to that point had not been directly transmitted (that is, only transmitted through direct quotations from later legal compilations) along with forty-four new *Basilika* scholia were published (see Tiftixoglu and Troianos 1993). Scholia from books 35–45 were edited in that same volume of *Fontes Minores*; see Dittrich 1993. Quite recently, two new *Basilika* manuscripts from the Austrian National Library were discovered. While they add little to the reconstructed text (mainly some better readings for book 19), they are important examples of the process of translating Latin legal terms into Greek in the *Basilika*; see Stolte 2010.

[32] See Schminck 1991a.

[33] Burgmann and Fögen 1982: 127.

[34] For a concise summary of these issues, see Troianos 2011: 281–4.

[35] See Scheltema 1960.

to another view, a catena-style commentary to the *Basilika*, consisting of both "old" as well as many "new" scholia, was completed in the middle of the eleventh century, perhaps during the reign of Constantine IX Monomachos.[36] Last but not least among official legal sources, there are a number of legal treatises on special subjects, especially from the eleventh century. Chief among them are the *Meditatio de nudis pactis* ("Treatise on open pacts") and the *Tractatus de peculiis* ("On the property of minors").

For the purposes of this study, unofficial legal sources include the various types of documents found in surviving monastic acts, such as wills, deeds of sale, gifts and agreements. These sources are given little or no coverage in most surveys of Byzantine law. Most of the surviving monastic acts from the time of the Macedonian dynasty stem from the various Athonite monasteries, although a few documents from elsewhere in the Balkans as well as Asia Minor and Southern Italy survive from this period as well.[37] This examination also makes extensive use of sources which are not generally the preserve of Byzantine legal historians, including chronicles, epistolary collections, histories, orations and – despite the well-known problems they present the historian – saints' lives.[38] Lead seals, although incredibly useful for administrative and prosopographic studies, are less informative regarding Byzantine legal culture.

Plan of Study

This book is an analysis of Byzantine Legal Culture during the period of the Macedonian dynasty (867–1056). The rule of the Macedonian dynasty frames this study of Byzantine legal culture because while there are certain features of Byzantine legal culture which are *diachronic*, there are particular *synchronic* features of Byzantine legal culture under the Macedonian dynasty which distinguish it from other epochs of Byzantine history.[39]

[36] Schminck 1986: 47–52, but see now the comments of van Bochove 2014. I discuss the problem of the addition of scholia to the *Basilika* in Ch. 6.

[37] For an introduction to documents stemming from the monasteries of Mount Athos, see Morris 2008. Although the focus of the chapter is prosopography, Vera von Falkenhausen has written a comprehensive overview of South Italian monastic acts in the Middle Byzantine period; see von Falkenhausen 2007.

[38] Conceptions of justice and the basis of the law in Middle Byzantine hagiography have been studied by Bourdara 1987; 2000; 2004. For the use of hagiography as a genre see the excellent introduction to Byzantine hagiography (including hagiography in other languages as well) in Efthymiades 2011.

[39] Various periodizations of Byzantine law exist, and they are discussed in detail by Dieter Simon; see Simon 1988. Simon notes that Byzantine legal history can be periodized according to "inner" and "outer" legal history. In Simon's schema, "outer" legal history corresponds to legal sources (*Quellengeschichte*), while "inner" legal history is a history of legal institutions

First, many historians have in the past have identified a so-called "classicizing" tendency in the culture of the period, including art, law and literature, and thus some have described it as a "Macedonian Renaissance" or, to borrow Paul Lemerle's designation, "the first Byzantine humanism."[40] In many literary and scientific genres, the age was characterized by attempts at collection and systemization or "encyclopedism,“ efforts sanctioned above all by the dynasty's two famous scholar-emperors, Leo VI (r. 886–912) and Constantine VII (r. 945–59). The "classical" past that the artists, jurists and writers of the Macedonian period evoked was often late Roman, particularly the reigns of Constantine I and Justinian I.[41] However, the "Macedonian Renaissance" was also marked by a rapprochement with the pagan heritage of Antiquity. This classicizing tendency in law is reflected in the recapitulation of late Roman law, by which Byzantine law was Hellenized via a "cleansing" (*anakatharsis*) of the Justinianic corpus of laws. Second, the Macedonian emperors, more so than any other Byzantine rulers after Justinian, chose to legitimate their rule by presenting themselves as guardians, patrons and protectors of the law. One can apply Alexis de Tocqueville's oft-cited observation about American politics in the early nineteenth century, that "there is hardly a political question in the United States which does not sooner or later turn into a judicial one," to the way in which the Macedonian dynasty conducted its social policies. Indeed, the Macedonian dynasty's principal attempt at internal reform, the protection of "poor" peasants against the "powerful," predatory large landowners, was construed as a legal question. Nor was the resolution of this legal question a one-way dynamic: the "powerful" managed to combat these regulations by interpolations in imperial novels.[42] The

(*Institutionengeschichte*). If one accepts 1453 as an endpoint for the history of Byzantine law (which is itself debatable, but space does not permit a discussion of this here), then the history of Byzantine legal sources can be divided, like Gaul, relatively unproblematically into three parts: Early (330–842), Middle (842–1261) and Late (1261–1453) Byzantine (Simon 1988: 93–4). Periodization is trickier for "inner" legal history, but Simon notes that it can utilize the same periodization as "outer" legal history if one adopts the Middle Byzantine period as a starting point (Simon 1988: 105). This tripartite schema is the one used in this study.

40 On the Macedonian Renaissance, see Magdalino 1999; Treadgold 1984 as well as a number of articles by Speck. For "the first Byzantine humanism", see Lemerle 1986. The idea of a revival of classical artistic taste and techniques, made immensely influential by the work of Kurt Weitzmann, has been problematized by more recent art historical scholarship; see Hanson 2010.

41 Magdalino 1999: 127–9.

42 This has been maintained by Nicholas Svoronos for a novel of Basil II issued to combat predatory land practices by the "powerful." The novel was originally promulgated in January 996 but was reworked at the end of the eleventh century. The second version of the novel in Svoronos' view evidences interpolations by redactors sympathetic to the "powerful"; see *Land Legislation of the Macedonian Emperors* 190–8 as well as Svoronos 1964b.

Macedonian dynasty's policies on "military lands" (*stratiotika ktemata*) can also be seen as the implementation of social policy via legislation and the legal system.[43] Third, the legal reforms of the Macedonian emperors coincided with the last great flowering of Byzantine secular law. As this study is a study of secular or civil law, it must be noted that, for this period, a clear distinction between canon and civil law is not always possible. From the time of Justinian, canon law had been granted the force of secular law, and canonists throughout the Byzantine period drew upon secular law, particularly the *CIC*. Nonetheless, during this period both the prominent jurists, such as Eustathios Rhomaios, Michael Attaleiates and Michael Psellos, and legal achievements, such as the completion of the *Basilika*, the writing of secular legal treatises and the foundation of a "law school" in the eleventh century, were secular. The following centuries, particularly in the twelfth and again in the fourteenth century, would be marked by a golden age of Byzantine canonists and canon law.

In the pages that follow, it will be argued that a unique "Macedonian" synthesis of Byzantine legal culture arose during the period of the dynasty's rule. It was throughout very much a "top-down" phenomenon, in which the impetus for legal reform, the refinement or reformulation of existing law or its political use, stemmed from the emperor and a handful of his confidants. As with so many questions of origins, the reasons for the sudden rekindling of interest in the empire's legal tradition are murky. Nonetheless, in Chapter 1 I attempt to contextualize the impetus for the Macedonian dynasty's program of legal reform as an instrument of political ideology and a reaction to very specific political circumstances in the second half of the ninth century. While Basil I's and Leo VI's reform of Roman law was prompted by and directed at external powers, the internal dynamic of legal culture is examined in Chapter 2, namely how influence and friendship were expressed via the legal system.

Chapter 3 is an exploration of Byzantine jurisprudence. Previous studies have explored Byzantine jurisprudence and legal thought largely through the prism of the surviving excerpts of the writings of the Byzantine jurist Eustathios Rhomaios. Yet his own writings as well as those of other jurists of the period represent the legal thought of a mere handful of legal professionals; their ideas about the law were by no means necessarily representative of the Byzantine society as a whole. By casting a wide net amidst the sources of the period, a more representative picture of Middle Byzantine

[43] Górecki 1998; 2009.

legal thinking emerges. Key to our understanding of Byzantine jurisprudence is the question of which legal collections were used Byzantine officials with juridical powers – the vast majority of whom probably had only a passing familiarity with Roman law. Thus in Chapter 4 a new interpretation of the function of a number of "private" law collections is advanced, arguing that the popularity of legal collections like the Farmer's Law, the Mosaic Law and the Rhodian Sea-Law in Byzantium and neighboring cultures was due to the inaccessibility of the Roman legal tradition as represented by the *Basilika*.

The next two chapters, Chapters 5 and 6, narrate how expertise in Roman law enjoyed ever greater social prestige status and played an ever more important role in the state administration and church, as well as in the empire's political ideology. These chapters complete the arc of the story of the development of the Macedonian synthesis of Byzantine legal culture begun in Chapter 1. In the dynasty's waning decades, particularly after the death of Basil II in 1025, professional jurists reached the pinnacle of their power. After the passing of Basil's aged brother Constantine VIII (r. 1025–8), the continuation of the dynasty's rule depended upon Constantine's three daughters: Eudokia, Theodora and Zoe. The next four Byzantine emperors laid claim to the Macedonian inheritance through Zoe, either via marriage (Romanos III Argyros (r. 1028–34), Michael IV Paphlagon (r. 1034–41) and Constantine IX Monomachos (r. 1042–55)) or adoption (Michael V (r. 1041–2)). These emperors, with only a tenuous hold on power and unable to match the military exploits of Basil II and his two soldier-emperor predecessors, Nikephoros II Phokas (r. 963–9) and John I Tzimiskes (r. 969–76), allowed this newly prominent cadre of Byzantine jurists to play an increasingly prominent societal role. Chapter 5 examines the edicts of the patriarch Alexios Stoudites (1025–43), which were directed against the West Syrian community in Melitene and brought back into force Justinianic legislation against heretics. These edicts, which were the result of a commission of jurists working in the 1030s, evidence the waxing influence of legal professionals in Byzantine society and their role in shaping Byzantine identity. Chapter 6 chronicles the apogee of Byzantine secular law, represented by the "law school" founded by Constantine IX Monomachos, which, rather than initiating a renaissance in legal studies, as has often been assumed, instead is to be seen as both the culmination of a two-century-long revival of Roman law as well as fitting the proclivities of Monomachos himself, who privileged law and legal studies more than any emperor since Justinian.

The preeminence of this cadre of professional jurists and the efflorescence of Roman law were, however, short-lived. The political chaos and civil strife which lasted from the end of the Macedonian dynasty to the accession of Alexios I Komnenos (r. 1081–1118), disrupted the hitherto growing influence of professional jurists. The "Komnenian Revolution" in government, which created an exclusive ruling class connected by blood or marriage to the Komenenoi themselves, effectively excluded these Byzantine lawyers from undertaking the political roles they had performed during their eleventh-century heyday. Moreover, the increasing role of the church was mirrored by the growing importance of canon law. The terminus of this study thus constitutes the last gasp, as it were, of the civil or secular law tradition in Byzantium.

CHAPTER 1

The "Cleansing of the Ancient Laws" under Basil I and Leo VI

Hellenizing the Twelve Tables

The Romans considered the Twelve Tables (written down around 450 BCE), the first codification of Roman law, to be among their greatest achievements. Cicero relates that children were required to memorize them by heart; the brief excerpts of the law code which have been haphazardly preserved via quotations from later authors convey the laconic, direct style of the archaic Latin in which the laws were written. The great Roman jurists of later centuries, such as Gaius and Pomponius, still acknowledged the Twelve Tables as the basis of the *ius civile* centuries after the law code had ceased to be of any practical use.[1]

Long after even the ability to read Latin had become rare, at least in Byzantium, this story of the origins of Roman law was expounded upon by another jurist, Symbatios. Symbatios, whom we would designate as Byzantine but who would have thought of himself as no less Roman – despite the Hellenized form of his Armenian name – than Cicero or Julius Caesar, writing in the first decades of the tenth century, used Pomponius' account of the history of Roman law, including the Twelve Tables, in the introduction to his legal collection, the *Epitome* (*legum*).

Symbatios did not simply regurgitate Pomponius' account of the Twelve Tables via his likely source, *Digest* 1.2.2.4. Rather than simply stating, as Pomponius does, that some relate that the author of the Twelve Tables was Hermodorus, an Ephesian exile living in Italy, Symbatios made his own inference about the original language of the Twelve Tables. The Twelve Tables, according to Symbatios, were written originally in Greek before, some say, "a certain Hermodorus, an Ephesian exile in Italy, translated the Twelve Tables from Greek into Latin."[2] Thus Symbatios, who

[1] For general information on the Twelve Tables as well as further bibliography, see Crawford 2012; Schiemann 2001.

[2] *Epitome*, proem. 29–31.

was probably working exclusively from Greek sources to compile the *Epitome*, underlined that the origins of Roman law were likewise written in the Greek language. Though no direct transmission need be posited, an emphasis on the Greek origin of Roman law is found in later texts, particularly from the eleventh century.[3] Thus a uniquely Byzantine interpolation in the legend of the Twelve Tables – namely that they had originally been written in Greek rather than Latin – took root.

Symbatios' rewriting of Roman legal history has not received the attention it deserves: why did Symbatios and later Byzantine jurists think it necessary to claim that the first codification of Roman law had been written in Greek rather than Latin?[4] Rather than being some antiquarian's jest, Symbatios' act is to be read within a context of a reassertion of Byzantine imperial ideology which began after the end of the Second Iconoclasm in 843. The contours of this reassertion can be detected in a debate which occurred in the middle of the ninth century. This discussion, evidenced via an exchange of letters between emperors – both Byzantine and as well as Carolingian – and popes, arose in a new political climate in which the Byzantine Empire attempted to reassert its claim to the late Roman ecumenical and imperial heritage. The defense of Byzantine claims to this legacy was advanced via a number of massive encyclopedic projects directed by the Macedonian dynasty in a number of genres (court ceremony, hagiography, historiography), the most important of which was law.[5]

Byzantine historians often characterize the two hundred-year period from around 850 until around 1050 CE, roughly the time during which the Macedonian dynasty ruled, not only as a time of cultural, economic and political revival, but indeed as the empire's post-Justinianic apogee.[6] After the massive territorial losses of the seventh century and the conflict over Iconoclasm which dominated much of the eighth and first half of the ninth century, the subsequent period was marked by demographic

[3] *Legal History Treatise* 82; Michael Attalieates, *Legal Textbook* 415–16.

[4] Pitsakes 2000 is an excellent examination of the history of Roman law in later legal handbooks (particularly the *Hexabiblos* of Harmenopoulos and the *Syntagma kata Stoicheion* of Blastares), including post-Byzantine ones, yet does not discuss this interpolation in the *Epitome* (brief discussion of the *Epitome* in Pitsakes 2000: 401, n. 5).

[5] The impetus and implementation of Macedonian "encyclopedism" not only in law but other genres as well has been expertly examined by Magdalino 1999. Burgmann 1999a: 598–605 offers a more technical analysis of how the legal texts stemming from this project were composed, while Pieler 1989 and Troianos 2001a each offer the legal historian's perspective on the "Cleansing of the Ancient Laws."

[6] For general surveys of this period in Byzantine history, see Gregory 2010: 242–89; Ostrogorsky 1980: 233–350; Treadgold 1997: 446–579; Vasiliev 1961: vol. I, 300–74.

and economic expansion, military successes, territorial growth, administrative reform and a revival of scholarship. The reasons for this stunning reversal of fortune are still disputed, though some credit is surely due to the much-maligned but effective rulers of the Isaurian dynasty, Leo III (r. 717–41) and Constantine V (r. 741–75), who stabilized the empire's borders after the catastrophic losses of the seventh century.[7] Since the founder of the Macedonian dynasty, Basil I (r. 867–86), was a Thracian peasant of Armenian origin, the term "Macedonian dynasty" is something of a misnomer, but it is used so ubiquitously in secondary scholarship and in the sources themselves as well that it is pointless to attempt to replace it with something else.[8]

Territorially, this period is marked by a number of important conquests and military victories. The Paulicians, heretics in eastern Asia Minor who set up their own army and state, were defeated during Basil I's reign. The First Bulgarian Empire, which had for several centuries been Byzantium's most dangerous rival, was conquered fleetingly during the reign of John I Tzimiskes (r. 969–76) and more durably during the reign of Basil II (r. 976–1025). At sea, despite the sacking of Thessaloniki during the reign of Leo VI, the Byzantines managed to retake Crete (961) and Cyprus (965) later in the century. Expansion into eastern Asia Minor and Northern Syria also occurred: Antioch was taken in 969, Vaspurakan in 1021/2, Ani in 1045. By the end of Basil II's reign the empire had reached its greatest territorial extent since the time of Justinian I. The only major territorial loss during the period of Macedonian rule was the gradual erosion of Byzantine authority in southern Italy over the course of the eleventh century.

Economic expansion accompanied these territorial gains. From an economic standpoint, the inauguration of the Macedonian dynasty coincides with the beginning of a long period of growth in population, land under

[7] Treadgold 1988, for instance, emphasizes the importance of the post-Isaurian rulers, the emperors of the Amorian dynasty.

[8] The ethnic origin of Basil I's family is comprehensively treated by Tobias 2007: 1–24. Tobias proves convincingly that Basil was of Armenian birth and humble origin. Claims that Basil was of Slavic origin, as adamantly maintained by Arab historians, rest on a conflation of the ethnonyms "Macedonian"/"Thracian"/"Slav." Schminck 2001 has more recently rejected the Armenian origin of Basil I. Schminck's argument is based on the report, found in the *Vita Ignatii*, that Photios fabricated the elaborate Arsacid lineage of the first Macedonian emperor. The fact that Basil fabricated his connection with an Armenian noble house (something he almost certainly did), however, does not necessarily mean that he was ethnically Greek; this fabrication addressed more his lack of social status rather than his ethnic origin.

cultivation and trade extending to the end of the eleventh century.[9] The stabilization of the Balkans facilitated the emergence of powerful new monasteries with substantial landholdings, particularly on and around Mount Athos.[10] The interior of Asia Minor was freed from the prospect of annual raids for the first time in centuries, allowing the formation of huge aristocratic estates.

The Macedonian dynasty, perhaps more than any other in Byzantine history, employed law and particularly legal reform as a means of legitimation. Although all Byzantine emperors recognized that the maintenance of the law and the legal order was an imperial prerogative and duty,[11] the first two emperors of the Macedonian dynasty, Basil I (r. 867–86) and Leo VI (r. 886–912) chose to present legal reform, particularly the codification project which would eventually culminate in the completion of the *Sixty Books/Basilika*, the so-called "Cleansing of the Ancient Laws," as one of the principal achievements of their reigns.

This chapter will demonstrate that the recapitulation of Justinianic law was a component of a larger political program directed at the recovery of "Romanness" or *Romanitas* in the face of new threats to imperial legitimacy, represented in the West by the rising power of the Carolingians and the Papacy and in the Balkans by the First Bulgarian Empire. While the Arab invasions of the seventh century and nearly continual warfare with the Umayyad and then Abbasid Caliphates had resulted in the empire adopting an introspective worldview, which emphasized the Orthodox Christian rather than Roman imperial portion of the late Roman political legacy, this trend had abated by the ninth century due to the changing political situation.[12]

The Byzantine Empire's eastern frontier was stabilized under the Macedonian dynasty, but it was confronted now by the Carolingian Empire claiming imperial authority in the West, a series of popes who

[9] The case for significant economic growth during this period is made convincingly by Harvey 1989. For an overview of economic activity from the early eighth to the tenth century, see Laiou and Morrisson 2007: 43–89.

[10] For the role of monks and monasticism in this period, see in particular Morris 1995. On the substantial economic importance of monasteries in Middle and Late Byzantine history, see Smyrlis 2006.

[11] For this *topos* in imperial documents see Hunger 1964: 103–22. Laiou 1994b in her examination of the law and justice by Middle Byzantine historians shows that the period of Macedonian rule witnessed some important innovations. The tenth century in particular saw a serious preoccupation with justice in the sense of "impartiality, good government, protection of the poor, and to some extent – and it is a limited extent – good laws as well" (Laiou 1994b: 183).

[12] The best analysis of this process is Haldon 1997. See now as well Humphreys 2015.

challenged the Byzantine emperor's ecumenical leadership, as well as a new Bulgarian state which, by adopting Orthodox Christianity, attempted to supplant Byzantine suzerainty in the Balkans. These three powers from an ideological standpoint presented fundamentally different challenges to Byzantine authority than that of the caliphates. While the latter constituted a rival state with superior resources, neither the Umayyads nor the Abbasids challenged the Byzantines as heirs to the late Roman political legacy, choosing instead to lay claim to the philosophical and scientific traditions of Antiquity.[13] The Carolingians and the Bulgarians, by contrast, sought to appropriate certain aspects of the Roman imperial legacy itself, including the title of emperor and much of its attendant symbolism. Tsar Symeon of Bulgaria (r. 893–927), who himself was educated in Constantinople and steeped in Byzantine culture, attempted to fuse his Bulgarian realm with the Byzantine Empire.[14] The Carolingians and the Papacy could challenge the *Romanitas* of the Byzantines on linguistic grounds: how, they asked, can you call yourselves Romans when you don't even speak Latin? Symbatios' reimagining of the Twelve Tables as composed in Greek is best understood as a response to these Western challenges.

Evidence of this challenge to the *Romanitas* of the Byzantines is especially noticeable in the sources of the second half of the ninth century. Amidst the controversy of the Photian schism a letter of Pope Nicholas I (858–67) addressed to Michael III (r. 843–67), the predecessor and eventual victim of Basil I, contained a scathing response to the charge that the Greek language was preferable to Latin. Although the epistle of Michael III has not survived, apparently he had described Latin as both "barbaric" (*barbaram*) as well as "Scythian" (*Scythicam*).[15] Pope Nicholas, obviously offended by such an assertion, defended the use of Latin and then proceeded to ridicule the absurdity of the Byzantines calling themselves Romans, stating "if you thus call the Latin language barbarous, because you do not understand it, then keep in mind that it is ridiculous to call yourselves emperors of the Romans and not even know the Roman language."[16] Continuing in this vein, Pope Nicholas urged Michael to "stop calling yourselves emperors of the Romans, because according to your

[13] As presented in the impressive study of Gutas 1998.

[14] The bibliography in Kazhdan 1991g includes important older works on his life and reign. On Symeon's formative years in Constantinople, see Sergheraert 1960: 15–48.

[15] Nicholas I, *Letter to Michael III* 459.5–7.

[16] Ibid. 459.19–21.

opinion you are barbarians ... the Romans, however, use this language, which you call barbaric and Scythian."[17]

A letter of Louis II (r. 876–82) addressed to Basil I, likely written by the bilingual Carolingian intellectual Anastasius Bibliothecarius, also contested the claim to Byzantine *Romanitas* along much the same lines. Writing on behalf of the Carolingian emperor, Anastasius asserted that the Franks were worthier successors of the Roman imperial legacy than the "Graeci" over whom Basil ruled. In an elaborate metaphor, Anastasius reasoned that just as Christians were more worthy of being God's chosen people than the Jews, the descendants of Abraham, because of their belief in Christ, for the same reason the Franks were worthier heirs of the Roman imperial legacy than the Byzantines: "therefore we have undertaken the office of the Roman imperium because of our good belief, *orthodosia*; the Greeks, because of their *kacodosia*, that is bad belief, have ceased to be Roman emperors, deserting the only city and capital of the empire, but also utterly parting with both the Roman people and the very Roman language, and transplanting themselves to another city, capital, people and language in all respects."[18] Additionally, Basil had claimed in his letter, now lost, that the title of emperor (Gr. *basileus*, Lat. *rex*) was reserved for the Byzantine emperor alone. However, "rex" had apparently been rendered "rix" in his epistle, a source of great amusement to Anastasius.[19]

As Marie Theres Fögen has likewise emphasized, these two letters, which contain respectively papal and Carolingian attempts to undercut Byzantine *Romanitas*, definitely shaped, and indeed probably in some respects were a cause of, the "Cleansing of the Ancient Laws" undertaken by the Macedonian dynasty.[20] In her view "the reanimation of Roman law in the time of the emperor Basil I and the patriarch Photios looks like the answer to Nicholas's letter, an attempt to regain the mighty symbol of Roman power and to demonstrate that the Byzantines were still and forever true Romans."[21] This program of legal reform was, therefore, as much an exercise in reasserting the Roman identity of the Byzantine Empire under the Macedonian dynasty as it was a more practical matter of restoring Justinianic law.[22] Indeed, one cannot separate the "Cleansing of the

[17] Ibid. 459.30–2.
[18] Louis II, *Letter to Basil I* 390.10–15.
[19] Ibid. 390.34–391.6.
[20] See Fögen 1998.
[21] Fögen 1998: 22.
[22] As Troianos 2001a: 243–6 points out, these two aims (restoring Justinianic law and reasserting the empire's Roman character respectively) are complementary and by no means mutually exclusive.

Ancient Laws" from the wider political and social context – it cannot simply be seen as a "correction" of a flawed legal system, but rather a hearkening back to the power and glory of the Justinianic age.[23] This chapter will examine in detail the legal reforms of the first two Macedonian emperors, Basil I and Leo VI, and the fruits of their codification projects: the *Prochiron*, the *Eisagoge*, and the *Sixty Books/Basilika*. While these three works mainly consisted of the rearrangement as well as the Hellenization of Justinianic law, the emperor Leo VI also composed 113 novels, which comprise the largest single instance of imperial legislative activity in Byzantine history after that of the Justinian himself. His legislation, penned in order to correct what he deemed to be flaws in Roman law, represents an attempt to adapt Roman law to a distinctly Middle Byzantine context. Finally, the proem to the *Epitome* bookends the program of the "Cleansing of the Ancient Laws" and was the culmination of an effort to link the Macedonian dynasty with the Roman past, not only in its imperial but also its republican iteration.

The *Prochiron*

The program of legal reform initiated by the first Macedonian emperors cannot be understood without contextualizing the development of Byzantine secular law from the time after Justinian until the middle of the ninth century. Through the reign of Heraclius (r. 610–41), himself a legislator of some importance, the study and teaching of Roman law remained quite strong. Already in the half century after Justinian's death one of the enduring characteristics of Byzantine law, namely the analysis and logical reordering of his *Novels*, is evidenced by the so-called *Syntagma* of Athanasios of Emesa, a legal scholar active in the second half of the sixth century. To this period also belong the first redactions of the most popular collection of Byzantine canon law, the *Nomokanon in Fourteen Titles* – since Justinian's *Novels* became the basis of much of Byzantine canon law, and he himself had given the first four ecumenical councils the authority of secular law, it is more difficult to separate church and secular law in Late Antiquity and the Early Byzantine period than in later centuries.[24]

[23] Pieler 1989: 69.

[24] The relationship between canon and secular law is discussed throughout Wagschal 2015, who examines the language of the canons during the first centuries of Byzantine canon law.

Little is known of either secular or canon law during the "dark centuries" of Byzantine law, from roughly 650 to 850.[25] Simply put, there is an appalling paucity of evidence as to how the law was interpreted and applied between the end of the reign of Heraclius and the advent of the Macedonian dynasty: there are no casebooks (such as the *Peira* for the eleventh century) and no monastic records, which appear only slightly later, particularly from Mount Athos. The first transmitted document among the acts of the archives of the Athonite monasteries, which in total contain some 1,200 legal documents (primarily property demarcations, donations, sales and exchanges) stemming from the medieval period, was a *sigillion* issued in 883 during the reign of Basil I.[26]

The Justinianic corpus of Roman law was still certainly in force at this time. However, if a remark from the most important of the lawbook of the period is to be believed, it could be used only with great difficulty even in the capital, likely through the medium of translations and commentaries into Greek made by the legal scholars during the time of Justinian and immediately afterward, the so-called *antecessores* and *scholastikoi*.[27] From the lawbook in question, the *Ecloga*, promulgated by Leo III (r. 717–41) and Constantine V (r. 741–75) in 741, we learn that particularly in the provinces the Justinianic corpus was nearly impossible to use.[28] Historians of Byzantine law postulate that the increasing inaccessibility of the Roman law may have led to the use of compact and relatively simple lawbooks termed the *leges speciales*, such as the *Nomos Georgikos* and *Nomos Mosaikos*, which did not presuppose an extensive knowledge of Roman law.[29]

At first glance, the *Ecloga* itself seems suited to solve the problem of the inaccessibility of Roman law cited by its promulgators. Running to

[25] For legal literature during the "dark centuries," see Pieler 1994: 302–23; Troianos 2011: 160–212; Van der Wal and Lokin, 1985: 71–7; Wenger 1953: 695–9. For more general remarks on the role of law during this period see Signes Codoñer and Andrés Santos 2007: 53–68 and Haldon 1997: 254–80.

[26] For the first Athonite document see Kaplan 1993: 486. On the Athonite monastic archives as sources, see Morris 2008.

[27] On the *antecessores* and *scholastikoi* see Ch. 6.

[28] *Ecloga*, proem 36–40: "[The emperors Leo III and Constantine V] being mindful that the matters legislated by previous emperors are written in many books and that knowing their intent is difficult to understand, and for some quite indiscernible, especially for those outside of this divinely protected and queenly city of ours [Constantinople]."

[29] Unlike the authors of most traditional overviews of Byzantine law, I think there is no compelling reason to date the appearance of the *leges speciales* to the seventh and eighth centuries. In light of their diachronic popularity, even in (by the standards of Byzantine law) relatively "enlightened" epochs like the period of the Macedonian dynasty's rule, it is clear that they never completely replaced the Justinianic corpus of Roman law and its various adaptations. They instead filled a particular niche for easily accessible lawbooks among those invested with juridical authority yet at the same time lacking training in Roman law. I discuss these points at greater length in Ch. 4

eighteen titles and overwhelmingly concerned with private law, the *Ecloga* also reflects the ever increasing importance of Orthodox Christianity in secular law; the heading of its proem proclaims it as a "correction towards greater humanity" (*epidiorthosis eis to philanthropoteron*).[30] This phrase is the leitmotif of the entire work and is especially evident in its amelioration of punishments, for instance substituting mutilation for crimes that under Roman law would have been merited the death penalty.[31] The marriage provisions of the *Ecloga*, also innovations, were especially popular and were adopted into later compilations of Justinianic law. Another plausible interpretation of the meaning of the Eclogian phrase *epidiorthosis eis to philanthropoteron* is that the language of the law was simplified and made easier to understand, and was thus a stylistic rather than a substantive "correction."[32]

Far more important than the (in the grand scheme of things quite minor) changes to the substance of Justinianic law was the completely different ideological perspective, and correspondingly a sea change in the way the law was articulated, of the *Ecloga*. The Isaurian emperors saw themselves as but the latest in a long line of lawgivers extending back to Moses, Solomon, the Old Testament prophets and the New Testament apostles.[33] The subjects of the emperor are not described as "Roman" a single time in the entire text, and are instead designated "marked as Christians" (*christosemeiotoi*).[34] This stark emphasis on the Orthodox Christian thread of Byzantine legal culture was in a sense counteracted by the program of the "Cleansing of the Ancient Laws", which instead sought to highlight the Roman political legacy and Hellenic orientation of the Macedonian dynasts.

Despite the popularity of the *Ecloga*, attested both by its translation into other languages (Armenian, Arabic and Church Slavonic) and its extensive manuscript tradition, within the Byzantine Empire itself the lawbook was tainted by the religious policies of its promulgators.[35] As the initiators of the First Iconoclasm, the legacy of both Leo III and Constantine V was condemned after the eventual triumph of the iconophile faction in 843. Rather than being subjected to a *damnatio memoriae*, these iconoclastic

[30] *Ecloga*, proem 6.
[31] Humphreys 2015: 118–25.
[32] Schminck 2015a: 469–74. I would like to express my thanks to Andreas Schminck for sharing this article with me.
[33] Humphreys 2015: 128.
[34] Humphreys 2015: 255.
[35] On the translation of the *Ecloga* into other languages see Burgmann 2005c: 50–1.

emperors occupied center stage in the iconophile narrative of their victorious struggle against them; Leo and Constantine became analogues to past heretical emperors such as Valens, with the former's Iconoclasm playing the same role as the latter's Arianism.[36]

Though in the first half of the ninth century some reworkings of the *Ecloga* attest to a continued interest in secular law, the so-called Amorian dynasty, including Basil I's immediate predecessor Michael III (r. 842–67), appears to have had no serious interest in law.[37] The decades that followed Michael's demise witnessed a rapid and unexpected period of engagement with the secular legal tradition. The impetus for the "Cleansing of the Ancient Laws," undertaken by Basil I and continued by his son, is described by the anonymous author of one of the principal histories of the period, the so-called *Vita Basilii*, a hagiographic whitewashing of the unscrupulous first emperor of the Macedonian dynasty. The characterization of the state of contemporaneous secular law in the *Vita Basilii* is very similar to that in the proem to the *Ecloga*, and indeed the phenomenon of a legal reformer finding the laws in a state of confusion and then correcting them is a well-known Byzantine *topos*.[38]

> Upon finding that the secular laws contained much obscurity and confusion because of the juxtaposition of good as well as wicked laws, that is the indistinguishable and joint listing of valid and abrogated [laws], he fittingly corrected them according to what was suitable and what was possible, by removing the uselessness of the abrogated [laws] and cleansing the multitude of the valid [laws], and by placing the former infinity [of the laws] in chapters, just as in a summary, so that they could be remembered easily.[39]

According to the traditional dating schema, the first text published as part of the Macedonian codification effort, and likely the text which Basil commissioned in the aforementioned *Vita Basilii*, was the *Procheiros Nomos* (*ho procheiros nomos*/"The Law Ready at Hand"); it is referred to as the *Prochiron* in much of the secondary literature.[40] The first promulgation of the *Prochiron* is dated by most scholars to the "reign of the three emperors", that is, Basil along with his sons Constantine and Leo (870–9),

36 Magdalino 1999: 145–6.

37 Troianos 2001a: 241–2.

38 The same *topos* of "correction" (*epanorthosis*) is used as well as the eleventh-century *Novella constitutio*; in general see Hunger 1964: 103–9.

39 *Vita Basilii*, §33.

40 The only existing English translation of the *Prochiron* is that of Freshfield 1928, which is essentially a paraphrase of the text.

and a newer interpretation suggests that a second version of it was distributed towards the end of the reign of Leo VI.[41]

The proem to the *Prochiron* is mainly a rationale for its creation. Its first thirty-two lines contain a number of commonplaces in Byzantine legal texts, supported by biblical citations. Justice is the best means by which a ruler can give benefit to his subjects and by which they are uplifted.[42] Law has been given by God to humankind as an aid.[43] While attempting to implement the divine injunctions for justice, the emperors undertook the present work. However, they realized that a comprehensive lawbook would be almost boundless.[44] The character of the work is further elaborated upon in the following lines: much of the law was clarified, while other portions were deemed worthy of proper correction, still other regulations were passed over in silence.[45] The didactic purpose of the handbook is then emphasized: "Since instruction [in the law] is necessary for all, what should we have intended, in order to put away men's hesitation and to make instruction in the law easy to comprehend? Nothing other than to closely examine the mass of the legal writings and to select together that which is most necessary and important and to write them up by chapter in this law ready-at-hand, without omitting almost anything, which most ought to have knowledge of."[46] Perhaps with the didactic purpose of the

[41] The traditional dating schema for the *Prochiron* was challenged by Schminck 1986: 55–107, who argued that it postdated rather than predated the *Eisagoge*, and that the unnamed work which is attacked in the proem was the *Eisagoge* and not the *Ecloga* (see the discussion of the *Eisagoge* below) as most scholars had assumed. Schminck's arguments hinge on the assumption that the *Eisagoge*, generally believed to have been authored by the patriarch Photios, was anathematized because of its expansive views on the role of the patriarch and his relationship to the emperor, a topic he has expounded upon in other publications (e.g. Schminck 1985 links Photios' views on the roles of the patriarch and emperor to contemporaneous mosaics in Hagia Sophia). Schminck's views on the dating of the *Prochiron* were criticized ten years later by van Bochove 1996: 29–56, who upheld the traditional dating. Van Bochove subordinated the other relevant issues discussed by Schminck, such as the dynastic aspirations of Basil and Leo, to the question of the rubrics, and maintained strongly that the presence of Basil's name was genuine and not an interpolation. The most recent examination of the authorship and dating of the *Prochiron* and *Eisagoge* for the most part maintains the traditional dating: affirming Photian authorship, Signes Codoñer and Andrés Santos 2007 argue that the *Prochiron* was promulgated in the period 870–9 and was then revised after the death of Leo VI during the second decade of the tenth century, while the *Eisagoge* was written by Photios between 880 and 888 as a revision of the *Prochiron*. For recent overview of the scholarly debate regarding the dating of the legal codifications stemming from the first few decades of the Macedonian dynasty, see van Bochove 2011.

[42] *Prochiron*, proem, lines 9–10.

[43] Ibid., lines 26–7.

[44] Ibid., lines 33–41.

[45] Ibid., lines 42–5.

[46] Ibid., lines 45–51.

work in mind, terms in Latin were rendered into Greek, therefore creating what are known as *exhellenismoi* in the secondary literature.[47]

Although the vast majority of the *Prochiron* is based on the Justinianic corpus, the proem also states that in areas where there existed no law, new constitutions were introduced.[48] In a reference to the ongoing codification effort, the proem then states that if someone needs to find a solution to a problem which is not found in the *Prochiron*, then he must diligently search through "the breadth of the laws which we have recently cleansed."[49] All Justinianic law which remained valid was to be found in sixty books, while the abrogated portion was to be found in a single volume, "so that its clear and manifest lack of validity would be known to all."[50]

Transitioning from presenting the rationale for its composition, in the proem a previous attempt at compiling a handbook similar in format to the *Prochiron* is vehemently criticized. This passage is given in full below:

> Since those before us undertook something similar in this way, one might say, why were we not content with that summary and instead proceeded to introduce a second? It is necessary to know, that the so-called "handbook" constituted not so much a selection as an overturning of good legislation according to the will of the redactor, which was not of benefit to the commonweal, and [it is necessary] to be on guard against its fraudulence. For why would someone of sound mind think it just to remember a law which effects so great an overthrow of legislation piously written by many emperors and teachers, both reverent and great, who for the most part instituted reverence for the law? For one who accepts such a law shall be shamed by pride against the earlier pious legislators rather than receiving instruction. For this reason the earlier handbook was untouchable even by those before us, not the whole thing entirely so, but rather that part that should have been. And that which has been recently redacted and put together by us is intended for the support of good legislation and the facilitation of knowing it.[51]

[47] Ibid., lines 52–3.

[48] Ibid., lines 57–9.

[49] Ibid., lines 59–62. It has also been argued that "The Breadth of the Laws" referred to a standardized Greek translation of the *CIC*, based on the *indices* (translations and paraphrases) of the *antecessores*, at least until the end of the ninth century; see Signes Codoñer and Andrés Santos 2007: 246–67. The evidence for such a project is tenuous and indirect, and the use of the phrase "The Breadth of the Laws" does not appear to have this narrow technical sense in later sources. Signes Codoñer and Andrés Santos do not however (quite understandably given the scope of the book, which is mainly concerned with the *Eisagoge*) claim to present a complete discussion, examining how the term is used in other sources which are analyzed in this study, particularly the *Peira* and the *Edicts* of the patriarch Alexios Stoudites.

[50] *Prochiron*, proem, lines 77–83.

[51] Ibid., lines 63–76.

In the last thirty years conflicting views have emerged as to the object of the proem's attack. Traditionally scholars believed that the *Ecloga* was clearly the target of this diatribe, yet this lawbook's continuing popularity and indeed the incorporation of some of its provisions (especially regarding marriage) into the other legal works of this period renders this interpretation in some respects problematic.[52] Another possibility is that it is in fact an attack on the patriarch Photios and his *Eisagoge*, and particularly the expansive powers delegated to the patriarch in the latter (see below).[53]

In view of the general thrust of the program of the "Cleansing of the Ancient Laws," the traditional view that the proem refers to the *Ecloga* is the most plausible interpretation. Law was not the only genre in which the emperors after the restoration of Orthodoxy in 843 sought to condemn the iconoclastic legacy while at the same time reemphasize the essential continuity of imperial authority before and after Iconoclasm.[54] An attack upon the *Ecloga* in the proem of the *Prochiron* conforms to the larger agenda of the founders of the Macedonian dynasty, whose rulers took great pains to present themselves as the restorers of an imperial legacy tarnished by the iconoclast emperors.

More relevant to the present study is the relation of the *Prochiron* to the general Macedonian codification effort: what was the purpose of the work? According to the preface, the *Prochiron*'s function was primarily didactic – it constituted the absolute minimum amount of law which an unspecified group of people was required to know. Based on the relevant provisions in the *Book of the Eparch*, it was intended for, among other groups, the guild of notaries in Constantinople. It should be noted here that by no means did the *Prochiron* represent the minimum familiarity with the law which any legal functionary was required to have – mid-level legal officials like thematic judges, for instance, were primarily administrators who were not necessarily expected to have a legal background, much as in the late Roman context. At the same time many thematic judges would have been themselves notaries at an earlier stage in their careers.

Intertwined of course with the practical intent of the *Prochiron* as a didactic handbook is the underlying political theme of the text found in the proem of the *Prochiron*. Related to the Macedonian codification effort, this is the reappropriation of Roman (i.e. Justinianic) law, and thus

[52] Signes Codoñer and Andrés Santos 2007 and Van Bochove 1996 are the contemporary representatives of this opinion.

[53] This is the view of Schminck 1986.

[54] This point is especially conspicuous in the wide-ranging study of Magdalino 1999.

an important part of the late Roman heritage, by honoring the "legislation piously written by many emperors and teachers, both reverent and great." The primary fault of the "handbook" mentioned in the proem was not that it did in fact constitute a selection (*ekloge*) of past legislation so much as an overthrow (*anatrope*) of this same legislation. Therefore the users of such a handbook were guilty of pride (*hybris*) against these emperors and teachers, rather than receiving instruction (*didaskalia*).

In the *Prochiron* are found all of the hallmarks of the Macedonian "Cleansing of the Ancient Laws." On a practical level, the *Prochiron* was to improve the clarity and instruction of the law. From a political standpoint, the creation of the *Prochiron* was part of the Macedonian dynasty's reappropriation of *Romanitas*; by excerpting the laws of past pre-iconoclastic emperors, the creators of the *Prochiron* were in effect cementing the continuity of the Macedonian emperors with their pious predecessors. Later lawbooks of the period built upon the *Prochiron*'s themes of rapprochement with the Roman past and the Hellenization of Roman law, two of the three strands of Byzantine legal culture as defined in this study. Yet it is the next lawbook according to the traditional dating schema, the *Eisagoge*, in which the role of Orthodox Christianity, the third thread of Byzantine legal culture, comes to the fore.

The *Eisagoge*

Traditionally, the second recapitulation of Justinianic law issued by the Macedonian dynasty is the *Eisagoge*, a shortened form of *Eisagoge tou nomou* ("introduction to the law"), incorrectly referred to within older literature as the *Epanagoge* ("return [to the law]").[55] All of the proposed datings for the work fall within the period 880 to 888.[56] The *Eisagoge*, or at least the proem and titles two and three, is generally assumed to have been authored by the patriarch Photios.[57] As is the case with the *Prochiron*,

[55] Schminck 1986: 12–14.

[56] Schminck 1986 presents his case for the issuing of the *Eisagoge* in 886; van Bochove 1996: 1–27 argues for the beginning of the period 880–3. Signes Codoñer and Andrés Santos 2007: 160–278, who thoroughly evaluate the relative merits of both Schminck's and van Bochove's arguments, adopt the broader period 880–8.

[57] On the issue of Photian authorship, see especially the pioneering studies of Scharf 1956; 1959. See also Dagron 2003: 236–42. Aerts et al. 2001: 138–40 rightly points out that it is difficult to reconcile Photios' authorship of the *Eisagoge* with that of a revision of *Nomokanon in Fourteen Titles*, some of the provisions of which contradict those of the *Eisagoge*. The latter attribution is probably not valid, or at least the case for Photian authorship of the *Eisagoge* is much stronger than that for the *Nomokanon in Fourteen Titles*.

an examination of the proem of the *Eisagoge* highlights the impetus behind the creation of the text and its role in the Macedonian codification process.[58]

In contrast to other proems from the Middle Byzantine period, such as the *Ecloga* and *Prochiron*, the rationale and justification for law is strongly philosophical, itself a strong indication of Photian authorship. Indeed, biblical justification for the law, which is such a strong component in other proems, is completely absent from the introduction to the *Eisagoge*. The value of the present work, Photios states, is proven by its "most holy nobility."[59] Even in these first lines, the Macedonian dynasty's underlying goal of reaffirming the Byzantine Empire's connection with its late Roman past is affirmed – the validity of the lawbook lies not *ipso facto* in its utility, but rather in its pedigree as a correct recapitulation of the ancient laws. Photios continues by explaining the divine origin of the law, in strongly Platonic rather than biblical terms. God is here described as the "ruler and steward of all good things" who gave man a mixed constitution composed of two opposing and antithetical natures, the "knowable" (*noeta*) and "perceptible" (*aistheta*). He introduced the "good law" to restrain and order his condition.[60] God did this, according to Photios, not so that one would suppose that these natures were separated and delineated within their own boundaries by one source or another, but rather so that one would recognize that that their source, God, is good and not wicked.[61] God gave the "good law" to teach man that God had banished the impiety of the sacrilegious "Manichaeans" – clearly a reference to the iconoclastic emperors – and introduced the power of the uniform monarchy.[62] God did not intend this monarchy to be embodied in any one person, but rather three aspects: the knowable, the perceptible, and the law, which binds and holds them together, in imitation of the Trinity.[63] The content of these opening lines of the *Eisagoge* mirrors the *Prochiron*'s narrative of a reestablishment of legitimate, law-abiding and divine governance after a period of misrule.

The means by which the new dynasty sought to reestablish the law are related in the next lines. First they "cleansed everything remaining in the

[58] There is now also the very useful English translation and commentary of the proem in Aerts et al. 2001.

[59] *Eisagoge*, proem, lines 5–7. Cf. Aerts et al. 2001: 106–10.

[60] *Eisagoge*, proem, lines 7–12. Cf. Aerts et al. 2001: 109–11.

[61] *Eisagoge*, proem, lines 13–16. Cf. Aerts et al. 2001: 111.

[62] *Eisagoge*, proem, lines 17–23. Cf. Aerts et al. 2001: 111–12.

[63] *Eisagoge*, proem, lines 23–7. Cf. Aerts et al. 2001: 112–13.

breadth of the ancient laws, and mixed the mass of the law clearly and purely into forty books like a divine draught."[64] The *Eisagoge* then directly confronts the legacy of the *Ecloga* by lambasting the "babblings of the Isaurians."[65] Traditionally viewed as a condemnation of the content of the *Ecloga*, it has now been convincingly argued that this is in fact an attack on the caesaropapist tendencies of the proem of the *Ecloga*.[66] The *Eisagoge* via its clear delineation of the powers of the emperor and patriarch thus eliminated the dangerous precedent of the Isaurian priest-kings and their policy of iconoclasm. Unlike the *Prochiron*, the *Eisagoge* appears to have been given the force of law.[67] The legitimacy of the Isaurians is questioned further in a section which questions the rule of unorthodox emperors; "therefore the emperor is descended also from emperors, who did not [merely] become emperors, but who were remembered and praised for their orthodoxy and justice."[68]

The narrative presented by the *Eisagoge* outlines in brief the ideology behind the Macedonian codification project. Photios presents the law in powerful neo-Platonic terms: God, as Demiurge, gave law to humankind as a way of ordering its two natures, that of the knowable and the perceptible. Together, the knowable, the perceptible and the law constitute the three aspects of the uniform monarchy, corresponding to the three emperors (Basil, Constantine and Leo) mentioned in the rubric. The Isaurians represented a terrible caesura in imperial history: their laws were anathema and they were guilty of separating humankind's two natures. The *Eisagoge*, the result of a cleansing of the ancient laws, is given the force of law by the new dynasty: this corresponds to the neo-Platonic "good law" in the text, the law which was given by God to aid humankind. Although there are strong elements of continuity, it is important to note that Photios presents the Macedonian dynasty as representing a distinctly new type of governance; God "has introduced the lordship and power of one rule and unitary monarchy."[69] The Macedonian dynasty is thus innovative and traditional at the same time – past emperors are honored for their orthodoxy and justice, the ancient laws are purified, but these

[64] *Eisagoge*, proem, lines 31–3. Cf. Aerts et al. 2001: 115–17.

[65] *Eisagoge*, proem, lines 33–6.

[66] Schminck 2015a: 474–8. Once again I would like to thank Andreas Schminck for this reference.

[67] Schminck 1986: 73–4; *Eisagoge*, proem, lines 41–2. Signes Codoñer and Andrés Santos 2007: 165–82, by contrast argue that the *Eisagoge* was not in fact promulgated, a conclusion they base mainly on the limited number of *Eisagoge* manuscripts.

[68] *Eisagoge*, proem, lines 45–6. Cf. Aerts et al. 2001: 120.

[69] *Eisagoge*, proem, lines 22-2.

activities are subordinated to a very new political project. "Novelty" was also a motif of Basil I's building program in the capital, highlighted by the construction of his magnificent "New Church" (*nea ekklesia*).[70]

The strongly neo-Platonic overtones of the proem to the *Eisagoge* also play a role in the presentation of the Macedonian dynasty's codification process. While one could possibly ascribe the neo-Platonic rather than biblical presentation of the law to the proclivities of Photios himself, such a view is undercut by the fact that Photios was writing an officially promulgated text, or at the very least a text he intended to be promulgated, at the behest of the empire's rulers. Likewise, viewing the text solely as a legal analogue to the classicizing trend in Byzantine art under culture under the rubric "Macedonian Renaissance" is also problematic: at least among officially promulgated texts, the neo-Platonic overtones of the proem to the *Eisagoge* are exceptional, and are not found in similar texts from the same period like, for instance, the eleventh-century *Novella constitutio* (in which the more traditional biblical justification of law is utilized).

While the neo-Platonic turn of the proem of the *Eisagoge* offers a stark contrast to not only the legislation of the Isaurian dynasty but indeed all previous secular law, some of the content of the work is quite exceptional. Most noteworthy are the second ("On the Emperor") and the third titles ("On the Patriarch") of the *Eisagoge*, which present a unique Middle Byzantine schema for government.[71] While the vast majority of the provisions of both the *Prochiron* and the *Eisagoge* was based on Justinianic law, much of the second and all of the third titles are interpolations, written expressly for the *Eisagoge*. In the *Eisagoge*, the emperor and patriarch are figures of almost equal authority, the former possessing the highest authority in temporal and the latter in spiritual matters.

The *Sixty Books* of Leo VI

Moving now to the reign of Leo VI (r. 886–912), the son and successor of Basil I, the Macedonian codification effort reached its climax with the publication of the so-called *Sixty Books*.[72] The *Sixty Books* in essentially the

[70] Magdalino 1987.

[71] The Spanish translation and extensive notes of Signes Codoñer and Andrés Santos 2007: 288–93 are extremely useful and discuss the more recent literature's views of these two titles.

[72] On the reign of Leo VI in general see Tougher 1997. The *Sixty Books* is a term coined by Andreas Schminck to designate the forerunner to the code which would later, in the eleventh century, become known as the *Basilika*; Schminck 1986: 27–33; 1991a; Troianos 2011: 185–8. Schminck believes that the first use of the term *Basilika* comes from document authored by one John during the reign of the patriarch Alexios Studites, which is dated to September 1039 (this document is

same form would later become known as the *Basilika* (so-called because they are the "imperial" lawbooks), although the term *Basilika* did not gain currency until the eleventh century.[73] In this study the term *Sixty Books* will be used to distinguish Leo's codification from the *Basilika*, because even if they did not differ in content it is nonetheless useful to distinguish the legal reform project of Leo VI from the later *Basilika*, which were supplied with extensive scholia that played a vital role in the text's interpretation.

The *Sixty Books* were promulgated early in Leo's reign on Christmas Day 888.[74] The preface to the *Sixty Books*, which was not included by the editors of the new Groningen edition of the *Basilika*, but is accepted by other scholars as genuine, gives further evidence of the continuing codification process. As a sign of the growing concern to compare and connect the Macedonian codification effort with that of Justinian, the first lines of the proem recount Justinian's own legal reforms and list the various components of the Justinianic corpus: the *Digest*, *Institutes*, *Codex* and *Novels*.[75] Justinian's *magnum opus*, however, was not without its flaws: "thus our Majesty thought the state of the laws as it has been apportioned to be lacking with regard to both the elimination of the difficulty of studying the laws as well as to a clarification of their order."[76] Towards that goal, all of the useful portions of the law were gathered into six volumes; the way the *Basilika* is transmitted, either in six or (later) in four manuscripts, confirms the veracity of this information in the proem.[77] The parts

analyzed in Ch. 5) – probably John Xiphilinos, future patriarch and *nomophylax* of the "law school" founded by Constantine IX Monomachos; see Schminck 1986: 30–2.

[73] According to Schminck's theory, the *Sixty Books* were not exactly the same as the *Basilika* without the accompanying scholia (which in his schema were attached in the eleventh century), but actually contained some differences (particularly in book 60), and that textual witnesses to the *Sixty Books* can be found in the earliest manuscripts, including the so-called *Florilegium Ambrosianum*, an early tenth-century anthology of passages taken from all the books of the *Basilika*. Van Bochove 1996: 107–39 disputed whether there was any difference between what Schminck designated as the *Sixty Books* and the *Basilika*, while at the same time acknowledging that the term *Basilika* was not the original title Leo used for his sixty-book law code (ibid. 204). More recently, Van Bochove 2011: 262–6 has argued that the term τὰ βασιλικά was used in at least one case before the eleventh century, in the scholia transmitted by cod. Taur. B I 20. This would undercut Schminck's argument that the term τὰ βασιλικά was used as a noun only starting in the eleventh century.

[74] Schminck 1989: 92–4. Schminck also believed that Leo VI's novels were promulgated at exactly the same time, but meanwhile Signes Codoñer 2009 has advanced some convincing arguments that the collection of 113 novels that has been transmitted to us is a very accidental and ad hoc assemblage of his legislation; see below.

[75] *Sixty Books*, proem, lines 5–15.

[76] Ibid., lines 15–17.

[77] Ibid, lines 19–20; cf. Burgmann 2002: 90.

of the Justinianic corpus which were not included in this collection were grouped into two categories: that which was contradictory and that which seemed superfluous.[78] The useful matter was divided thematically into sixty books, so that Leo could proudly proclaim "we have offered through our diligence concerning the laws an easy study, and a final answer for any sort of pressing matter, with not a single piece of legislation which bears a correct judgment from the earliest times until the legislation of our Majesty omitted."[79]

The proem to the *Sixty Books*, in contrast to the *Prochiron* and *Eisagoge*, is much more explicit about the law which is being reworked: it is not merely the "old laws" but the laws of the emperor Justinian. Furthermore, Justinian's massive codification is implicitly compared, by juxtaposition, with that of the Macedonian emperors. Whereas emperors from earlier periods, such as Leo III and Constantine V in the *Ecloga*, felt no need to state their affinity with Justinian and to situate their own legal reform efforts with regard to his, this had clearly changed by the end of the ninth and beginning of the tenth century.

It is worth discussing what the *Sixty Books/Basilika* were as well as what they were not. They represented an almost completely Hellenized (though not absolutely so – they were still numerous Latin words and phrases) redaction of the *CIC* divided in sixty books (*biblia*), then further into titles (*titloi*) and chapters (*kephalaia*). More important is the realization of what the *Basilika* were not: in general surveys as well as in some of the secondary literature on the subject, the official law of the Byzantine Empire during the period of Macedonian rule is sometimes assumed to have been the *Basilika*.[80] Yet it is at best only partially correct and at worst misleading to state that the *Basilika* constituted the official law of the Byzantine Empire during this period, because there is no firm basis for this and normative legal texts from this epoch tend to support a broader definition of what valid law actually was. Notwithstanding some opinions to the contrary, it also does not appear as though the publication of Leo VI's *Sixty Books*/the *Basilika* invalidated older Justinianic law.[81] The

78 *Sixty Books*, proem, lines 21–4.

79 Ibid., lines 28–31.

80 See Kazhdan 1991b: 265–6: "The *Basilika* was considered the official collection of actual law"; this is the assumption of much of Kazhdan's work on Byzantine law, including his "Do We Need a New History of Byzantine Law?" While it is true that the *Basilika* became the official compilation of Justinianic law after the middle of the twelfth century, this was not the case for much of the Middle Byzantine period, including the epoch of Macedonian rule.

81 This is the opinion of Berger 1954. Berger's contention that the *Basilika* invalidated Justinianic law was extensively refuted by Scheltema 1942.

Basilika was, after all, valid law only insofar as it was assumed to represent, in paraphrased Greek, the *Corpus Iuris Civilis* of the emperor Justinian.[82]

In short, although the publication of the *Sixty Books/Basilika* represents the greatest achievement of the "Cleansing of the Ancient Laws," it was not an exclusivist endeavor: Byzantine legal manuscripts show that jurists continued to consult the Greek paraphrases and commentaries stemming from the age of Justinian alongside the *Basilika*.[83] It was not until considerably later, in a novel of Manuel I Komnenos (r. 1143–80) issued in 1166, that the *Basilika* were granted exclusive legal force. In the same vein the titular patriarch of Antioch and consummate canonist Theodore Balsamon (died after 1195) stated in a canonical response to the Greek Orthodox Patriarch of Alexandria Mark III that the Melkite community in Egypt was obliged to use the *Basilika*, even though they apparently had no access to it. These twelfth-century opinions on the absolute authority of the *Basilika* are outliers within the wider Byzantine secular law tradition in general, and do not reflect the understanding of the role of the *Sixty Books/Basilika* through the end of the eleventh century.

The *Novels* of Leo VI

To this point the program of the "Cleansing of the Ancient Laws" has delimited aspects of Byzantine legal culture for the most part indirectly. While the proems of the *Prochiron*, *Eisagoge* and the *Sixty Books* offer strong justifications for their composition (better organization and standardization of the written laws, translation into Greek), their contents by contrast differ little from the Justinianic corpus, the *Eisagoge* being only a very minor partial exception. The patrons of this codification project, Basil I and Leo VI, intent on appropriating the empire's legal legacy, generally avoided introducing new constitutions into these lawbooks. This conservatism corresponded to evolving sensibilities in theology, which were then applied to law, regarding the negative connotations of innovation or *kainotomia*.[84] This state of affairs changed drastically however during Leo VI's reign, as he issued perhaps as many 120 novels, although only 113 novels have been transmitted to us.[85]

82 Scheltema 1935: 341.

83 Burgmann 1999a: 598–9.

84 See Ch. 3.

85 Signes Codoñer 2009: 8–13 discusses the problem of the numbering of the novels and demonstrates that they were likely only given numbers in the tenth century or so. For the *Novels of Leo VI* in general surveys of Byzantine law for this period, see Pieler 1994: 330–3; *Novels of Leo VI*, 17–37;

The precise chronology of the novels is disputed; until recently most legal historians believed that Leo promulgated all his novels in a collection along with the *Sixty Books* on Christmas Day 888.[86] Several years ago a convincing study demonstrated that the *Novels of Leo VI* as they have been transmitted to us are in fact a heterogeneous collection of his legislation that was composed at different points in his reign.[87] This flurry of legislative activity was the most extensive of any emperor after Justinian.

While the works stemming from the "Cleansing of the Ancient Laws" to this point for the most part did not actually comment on the content of Roman law, the *Novels of Leo VI* specify what particular portions of the Justinianic corpus Leo found objectionable, and, in a limited number of cases, one finds corresponding reworkings in the *Basilika*.[88] The working formula of the vast majority of the novels is to begin with an inconsistency or problem in the Justinianic corpus, canon law or both and then to present a solution, via an abrogation, new legislation or both. Generally, Leo is far more critical of past emperors, who are referenced in a general sense, than he is of canon law. It is treated as a given that the divine canons are perfect, "since the holy and divine canons and other acts which govern the priesthood and the ordination of bishops have regulated excellently and most accurately – how could they not have been pronounced

Troianos 2011: 219–32; van der Wal and Lokin (1985): 86–7; Wenger 1953: 705–7. The only monograph dedicated to the novels, now almost a century old but nonetheless quite useful and often insightful, is that of Monnier 1923.

86 This is the view of (among others) Fögen 1989; Lokin 1997; and Schminck 1989.

87 According to Signes Codoñer 2009, who argues quite convincingly that Leo VI's *Novels* consist of four components: Part A (the proem and Novel 1) consists of two versions of an introductory constitution written at different points in his reign; Part B (Novels 2–68) is thematically organized, addressed for the most part to Leo's trusted advisor and father-in-law Stylianos Zaoutzes and was likely composed between 886 and 893; Part C (Novels 69–104) has no discernable order and was probably written in the period 893–9; Part D (Novels 105–13) has no addressees except Zaoutzes (Novel 111, which Signes Codoñer suggests was only a draft) and was the last section of the novels to be written. Note that the edition of the *Novels* cited in this study is the new edition of Troianos, which it is based primarily on the older edition of P. Noailles and A. Dain, although with some corrections as well as reference to Zachariä von Lingenthal's nineteenth-centry edition.

88 Whether these interpolations were actually prompted by Leo's novels depends to a large degree on which chronology one accepts for the composition of the novels. Fögen 1989 makes the case that the composition of the novels accompanied the final stages of the completion of the *Sixty Books*. In total, Fögen found that of the seventy-two novels which criticize the Justinianic corpus, in twenty of these cases Leo's *Novels* indisputably led to interpolations in the *Basilika* (Fögen 1989: 28–9). The comparatively incomplete implementation of Leo's reforms is ascribed by Fögen to the realization of later jurists of Leo's haphazard grasp of Roman law and, more plausibly, the supposition that when faced with the contradictory regulations of various emperors, in this case Justinian and Leo VI, the redactors of the *Basilika* could freely choose which regulations to adopt and thus often chose those of Justinian over Leo (Fögen 1989: 33–5). Signes Codoñer 2009: 1–8, however, casts significant (and well-founded) doubt on this theory.

accurately when the Divine Intent worked among their authors?"[89] Leo's imperial predecessors, by contrast, are by no means immune from critique. Justinian for example, who is only mentioned by name twice in the entire work, is criticized by Leo for having issued one novel which forbade a woman from contracting a second marriage (Novel 22.16), then issuing another novel (Novel 117.8) which Leo read (incorrectly) as making certain exceptions to this rule.[90] Yet even in this context the Late Antique ruler is described as "that Justinian, whose piety and attentiveness toward his subjects honored [his] diadem."[91]

The *raison d'être* of the *Novels*, and its relation to the Macedonian codification effort, is most evident in the proem and in Novel 1.[92] Leo compares the laws to doctors, who hinder the coming of maladies and uproot evil.[93] As is common in human affairs, however, many of the laws had been forgotten, neglected or become contradictory.[94] Finding this unfortunate situation unacceptable, Leo then details how that he will rectify it. Although the word "cleansing" (*anakatharsis*) is not used, the methods Leo employs to correct the laws are consistent with the *modus operandi* of the Macedonian codification program which has been examined above. First, the mass of laws was submitted to a careful examination, and the laws which were judged "useful" (*lusiteles*) were granted the force of law again by imperial degree.[95] Those laws which by contrast were considered without benefit were either explicitly derogated or were left unmentioned.[96] Finally, customs which seemed reasonable were granted the force of law.[97]

The hearkening back to the empire's heyday under Justinian, a leitmotif of the entire program of the "Cleansing of the Ancient Laws," took an unusual turn in Leo's corpus of novels. Novel 1 compares Leo's own

[89] Leo VI, *Novels*, Novel 2, lines 9–12. On the attitude toward canon law in Leo VI, *Novels*, see Monnier 1923: 23–30.

[90] Leo VI, *Novels*, Novel 30.

[91] Ibid., lines 17–18.

[92] According to Signes Codoñer 2009: 16–18 the proem and Novel 1 constitute Part A of the *Novels* of Leo VI.

[93] Leo VI, *Novels*, proem, lines 10–14.

[94] Ibid., lines 14–25.

[95] Ibid., lines 26–32.

[96] Ibid., lines 32–6.

[97] Ibid., lines 36–40. Kaldellis 2015: 9–14 has argued that Leo's granting of the status of official law to certain customs somehow represents the exercise of constitutional power by the common populace. Leo's recognition of the legally binding precedent of custom is, of course, merely a Middle Byzantine example of a longstanding principle, in both Roman and Byzantine law, which gave custom legal force in certain circumstances. Yet since custom could only acquire legal force where no written law existed, one cannot plausibly argue, as Kaldellis does, that this represented an instance of popular will trumping imperial legislation.

efforts at legal reform with those of his illustrious predecessor, Justinian. Like Justinian, Leo issued a new redaction of Roman law along with a collection of novels. Leo himself, however, saw at least one crucial difference between his own legislative activity and that of Justinian. He at first praises Justinian for his legal achievements, for "he thus perfectly rendered the dispersed substance of the laws into one body."[98] Yet Leo then criticizes the sixth-century emperor for having sullied the completion of the *CIC* by later issuing a second redaction of his work, so that "thus Justinian himself was shamed through his own efforts,"[99] a reference is to the *Novels* of Justinian, which were issued after the completion of the initial codification effort. Thus Leo could present himself to have surpassed Justinian's legal achievements, at least in this respect.[100]

Legal historians have for the most part viewed the *Novels of Leo VI* as a curiosity that had a minimal impact on Byzantine society.[101] The testimony of Michael Attaleiates would seem to confirm the limited influence of the *Novels*, as he states in his *Legal Textbook* that: "The blessed lord Emperor Leo issued many novels, but they were not in use, excepting only those which were written without other laws already existing, or which were a supplement to the novels enacted by Justinian."[102] Only one of Leo's novels is included in the *Basilika*.[103] An anonymous history of Roman/Byzantine law, which was perhaps authored around the year 1080, likewise notes that few of Leo's *Novels* were actually in use, with the exception of his novels concerning distances between fishing nets (Novel 103) or between a new house and a field boundary (Novel 71), as well as regulations for houses in Constantinople.[104] What legal historians have judged to be the illogical and erratic nature of the laws has reinforced the notion that Leo's *Novels* were more an academic exercise than a serious attempt

98 *Leo VI, Novels*, Novel 1, line 22–4.

99 Ibid., lines 33–4.

100 Lokin 1997: 138–9.

101 This tendency of the secondary scholarship to minimize the impact of Leo's novels was expressed already in the middle of the nineteenth century by Jean-Anselme-Bernard Montreuil, who stated that "ces Novelles n'ont eu dans la législation d'Orient qu'une autorité très secondaire, sans influence sur les principes généraux du droit." Montreuil 1843–6: vol. II, 290.

102 Michael Attaleiates, *Legal Textbook*, proem, §6.

103 *Basil.* 58.11.16 (Novel 71).

104 *Legal History Treatise* 61–4: "Such was the state of affairs, until the sixty imperial books came into being. For [the emperor] united the 50 books of the *Digest*, the 12 books of the *Codex* and the *Novels* of Justinian, and there were 60 books. Lord Leon also composed 120 novels, but they are not all in use. Valid however is that which concerns [the distances between] fishing nets and pieces of land." The novels of Leo VI referenced by the anonymous author of the treatise are nos. 71, 102–4 and 113.

at legislation.[105] The content of Leo's legislation, which treats some admittedly arcane subjects, likewise did little to dispel this notion: some of the topics include the consumption of blood (Novel 58) as well as precise building regulations and spacing requirements.

The negative verdict of legal historians on the relevance of Leo's novels illustrates the danger of examining legislation without taking into account the wider societal context. In fact, the *Novels of Leo VI* reflect this emperor's attempts to adapt the late Roman heritage to a Middle Byzantine context. Laws which restricted the use of clergy (Novel 4) and baptism (Novel 15) in private chapels were overturned, reflecting the increasing importance of privately endowed churches and monasteries.[106] Leo's legislation in this regard is reflected in the interplay between Middle Byzantine architecture and liturgy, as both became more private and closed in contrast to the public and processional nature of both in Late Antiquity.[107]

Leo's monastic legislation represents an attempt to make Justinianic law conform to the empire of his day.[108] It was precisely at this time that the Athonite monasteries began to become large landholders, mainly by acquiring and cultivating fiscally unproductive (*klasma*) land.[109] Byzantine society itself was much more monasticized in Leo's than in Justinian's epoch, with monks playing a more prominent role in the church, the economy, intellectual life and politics.[110] Although Leo did not attempt a comprehensive reform of Justinian's monastic legislation, he made some nods to contemporary monastic practice, for instance legalizing (under certain conditions) the acquisition of property after a monk was tonsured (Novel 5).[111] Monks and clerics were also given the legal capacity to serve as the guardians (*epitropoi*) of orphans, thus administering their property until the orphaned children became adults (Novel 68).[112]

Other innovations which Leo introduced grappled with more recent forms of Roman law, including the provisions which the Isaurian dynasty

105 Monnier 1923: 204–7. Pieler 1994: 332 surmised that from a legal perspective Leo VI only in a few cases solved the problems he presents. Fögen 1987: 149–53, in her comparison of the function of legislation of Justinian I, Leo VI, and the Palaiologoi, found that the *Novels of Leo VI* had a mainly symbolic role. Recently, Signes Codoñer 2011: 320–1 has underlined the importance of examining the novels in the wider context of Leo's literary oeuvre.

106 Thomas 1987: 139–43.

107 Mathews 1982.

108 On Leo's monastic legislation see Granić 1931.

109 Kaplan 1993: 485–6.

110 Brilliantly analyzed for this period in Morris 1995.

111 Granić 1931: 67–8.

112 Granić 1931: 68–9.

introduced into marriage law via their lawbook, the *Ecloga*. Though the Isaurian dynasty and the *Ecloga* are not mentioned explicitly by Leo in his *Novels*, he did indirectly refer to some of the latter's regulations.[113] Novel 20 attacks some of innovations in marriage law found in the *Ecloga*, claiming that "These [regulations concerning prenuptial gifts], which seemed good to the ancients, were overturned by [their] successors."[114] Leo goes on to criticize these Eclogian provisions and later in the novel mentions that his father, Basil, overturned Eclogian marriage law with a novel.[115] Yet he praises Eclogian marriage law elsewhere in his legislation.[116] Notwithstanding the portrayal of the Isaurian emperors as despicable heretics by post-iconoclastic hagiography and historiography, Leo still thought it acceptable to enact some of the *Ecloga*'s provisions. Novel 32 concerns the punishment that should be meted out to adulterers caught *in flagrante delicto*, for which a constitution of Constantine I ordered that adulterers in question be put to death.[117] Though Leo admits that adultery merits a punishment, in his opinion, no less than that of murder, he finds the aforementioned constitution too harsh.[118] He then orders that a more humane provision (*philanthropotera psephon*), perhaps a reference to the *Ecloga*, which its promulgators touted as a selection of laws "with a more humane tendency" (*eis to philanthropoteron*), be enacted which mandates the amputation of the offender's nose.[119] Another novel (Novel 41) which reduces the number of witnesses required for a will in rural areas from five to three coincides with a provision of the *Ecloga*, but Leo appears to have been unaware of it.[120]

Bridging the orthodoxy of the late Roman emperors with that of the Macedonian dynasts also meant confirming the validity of canons issued after Justinian's legal reforms. In the *CIC* the first ecumenical councils up to Chalcedon (451) were given the force of secular law by Justinian's

[113] Monnier 1923: 16.
[114] Leo VI, *Novels*, Novel 20, lines 23–4.
[115] Ibid., lines 54–8.
[116] Leo VI, *Novels*, Novel 110, which says that a wife only has a claim on the property of her deceased husband if her prenuptial possessions have been diminished over the course of the marriage; she must also produce an inventory which lists her prenuptial possessions. The novel refers to *Ecloga* 2.5.
[117] *Cod*. 9.9.29.4: "Sacrilegos autem nuptiarum gladio puniri oportet."
[118] Apparently unknown to Leo was Justinian's *Nov*. 134.10, which had already abolished the death penalty for adultery.
[119] *Ecloga* 17.27. The *Ecloga* tends to proscribe amputation for offences which would have been met with the death penalty under Roman law.
[120] Leo VI, *Novels*, Novel 41; *Ecloga* 5.8.

Novel 131.1, yet there was no obvious provision within the Justinianic corpus which allowed the incorporation of canons from later councils. The *Novels of Leo VI* thus aimed at harmonizing post-Chalcedonian canon law, including Constantinople II (553) and III (680–1), for which no canons were issued until the Council in Trullo (691–2), Nicaea II (787) and the Apostolic Canons, the validity of which was confirmed by the second act of the canons of the Council in Trullo, with Byzantine civil law.[121] It is possible that the *Novels of Leo VI* led to an interpolation in the *Basilika*, since Justinian's Novel 131 was reworked so that the three post-Chalcedonian ecumenical councils were also given the authority of law.[122]

The actual content of the *Novels* demonstrates that the Macedonian codification program was not a mere regurgitation of Roman law. The "Cleansing of the Ancient Laws" was both a mimetic and creative act; the new legal regime was substantially like the old one but the Macedonian dynasty presented it as a betterment in certain respects. Though a connection between the Macedonian dynasty's reappropriation of *Romanitas* and Leo's efforts to bring canon law into line with more recent councils may appear tenuous at first glance, further examination allows the link to be much more clearly seen. The states that challenged Byzantine claims to the late Roman Imperial heritage, including the Papacy, the Carolingians and the Bulgarian Empire, differed from the threat of the Arab invaders and Islamic successor polities in that they challenged the emperor's spiritual leadership of the Christian peoples. The empire's claim to doctrinal orthodoxy and leadership of the *oikoumene* had been undercut, in the view of later writers, by the policies of the iconoclastic emperors. Part of the Macedonian dynasty's program of legitimation was to reassert its role as a defender of orthodoxy and rehabilitate the emperor's spiritual authority. Thus although the Macedonian dynasty's codification project was primarily a recapitulation of Justinianic law, in Leo's novels one can deduce some of the importance which was attached to rehabilitating the spiritual authority of the emperor.

Unlike the law codes which have been examined in this chapter (the *Prochiron*, the *Eisagoge* and the *Sixty Books*), which for the most part represented recapitulations of Justinianic law, Leo's *Novels* represent an attempt to critically engage with the empire's Roman legal tradition and to harmonize seeming contradictions and obsolete rules as well as to legitimize

[121] Such is the conclusion of Troianos 1990 and 1997a: esp. 148–9, who has combed through the Leo VI's *Novels* and identified the influence of post-Chalcedonian canons.

[122] *Basil.* 5.3.2.

post-Chalcedonian canon law. Both of these aims were congruent with the Macedonian Dynasty's "Cleansing of the Ancient Laws," which was itself a part of a larger program of dynastic legitimation that included the reappropriation and renewal of *Romanitas*.

The *Epitome* (*Legum*)

The success of the Macedonian dynasty's efforts to reappropriate the Roman past and to place itself within the arc of Roman history can be found in a private lawbook compiled shortly after the death of Leo VI. The so-called *Epitome* (*legum*) ("Extract from the laws") was probably first authored in 912–13 before being extensively reworked in 921 during the reign of the usurper Romanos I Lekapenos (r. 920–44).[123] The designation *Epitome* (*legum*) is not supported by the manuscript tradition but is nonetheless overwhelmingly used in the secondary literature.[124] The *Epitome* appears to be an expanded version of the *Prochiron*. In adding relevant excerpts from the *CIC*, the author of the *Epitome*, Symbatios who is named in the proem (lines 66–7), evidently consulted the writings of the *antecessores* rather than the corresponding passages in the *Sixty Books*.[125] Little is known about this Symbatios and "the other pious and righteous men" mentioned in the proem, other than his rank (*protospatharios*) and likely ethnic origin ("Symbatios" is a Hellenized form of Armenian "Smbat (Սմբատ)". References to a jurist by the name of Symbatios are found in later legal texts.[126]

The proem of the *Epitome* begins with a typical rationalization for law, before Symbatios states that "I shall give a history of the ancient genesis of [the law], whence it received its beginning and some of the laws the Romans put into effect during particular times."[127] The *Epitome* thus begins a trend found in later Middle Byzantine lawbooks, which often give some sketch of Roman legal history and present contemporary legal works as successors to Roman antecedents.[128] Symbatios then offers a brief history of Roman law using *Digest* passages of Gaius and Pomponios, which in his account begins in the time of the Seven Kings and continues

[123] In general see Moulakis 1963; Pieler 1994: 348–99; Troianos 2011: 190–3; van der Waal and Lokin 1985: 90; Wenger 1953: 709.

[124] Schminck 1986: 120–31; 1991b.

[125] Van der Wal and Lokin 1985: 90.

[126] For the case for Symbatios as author, see Schminck 1985: 129–31.

[127] *Epitome*, proem, lines 8–10.

[128] For example, the *Legal Textbook* of Michael Attaleiates and the *Synopsis legum* of Michael Psellos.

through the republican period. The scope of the history is likewise innovative as it stretches back before even Constantine, and indicates a newfound interest in the pre-Christian phase of the Roman Empire. As noted in the introduction to this chapter, in the proem the story of the Twelve Tables is recounted, and via a clever interpolation that they were in fact originally written in Greek, Symbatios underlines Byzantine *Romanitas* – challenged as it was by papal and Carolingian claims that Latin, as the language of the Roman Empire, had long been abandoned by the Byzantines in favor of Greek.[129]

Symbatios gives a very brief synopsis of law during the republican period before moving on to the age of imperial Rome. Like Leo VI, Symbatios describes Justinian's codification effort, which was directed by Tribonian.[130] As in other texts of the Macedonian codification project, the sheer unwieldiness of the laws in their Justinianic redaction is emphasized: "Thus the laws were so extended and multiplied by legislators in their times that they seemed infinite in [their] multitude, and men thought that the advantageous and sweet burden of the law was heavy rather than light and useful."[131] Symbatios then gives an overview of the codification effort: how Leo VI commissioned the *Sixty Books* and issued his *Novels*.[132] The result of the "Cleansing of the Ancient Laws" is the reestablishment of the Roman legal order: "Having related in brief this exercise of the collection of the selection of the law, we have transmitted most of the laws [from] the aforementioned times, in which they were honored and praised."[133] The legal codification project of the first two Macedonian emperors, Basil I and Leo VI, was thus brought to a successful conclusion – and as such sets the stage for the further examination of Byzantine legal culture in the rest of this book.

Conclusion

An analysis of the proems of the various texts associated with the Macedonian codification effort (respectively the *Prochiron*, *Eisagoge*, *Sixty Books* and the *Epitome*) along with the *Novels of Leo VI* has clearly delineated the goals and scope of the "The Cleansing of the Ancient Laws."

[129] Fögen 1998: 17–22.
[130] *Epitome*, proem, lines 56–8.
[131] Ibid., lines 58–61.
[132] Ibid., lines 62–71.
[133] Ibid., lines 72–4.

The impetus for the Macedonian codification effort consisted primarily of the need for dynastic, ecumenical and political legitimation in the face of new powers which challenged the Byzantine Empire's claim to the legacy of Roman imperial authority. Thus, the codification effort can be seen in large part as the reappropriation of *Romanitas*.

This effort to reappropriate the past was not, however, merely mimicry. Resurrecting the Roman legal order was both a creative and emulative act. As the *Novels of Leo VI* in particular demonstrate, the codification effort was legitimate because it was based on Roman law, but it many respects the new Macedonian redactions of primarily Justinianic law were presented as an improvement: more humane and more in line with contemporary canon law. Even the great Justinian was not spared from criticism.

"The Cleansing of the Ancient Laws" is important for our understanding of Middle Byzantine legal culture both because it both frames the entire period with which this study is concerned and also because the ideological impetus of the Macedonian codification project – the reappropriation of the Roman legal past as a means of legitimizing dynastic, ecumenical and political authority – permeates all the juristic works written during this period as well as what we know of Middle Byzantine jurisprudence. The effort to strengthen the link with the past at the behest of the present was applied not merely to legal compilations which we would call Byzantine rather than Roman, as in texts like the Rhodian Sea-Law or the Farmer's Law, but also to elements of the Christian, and particularly Old Testament, legal tradition, as is the case with the *Nomos Mosaikos*.[134]

[134] In general see Ch. 4.

CHAPTER 2

Gift-Giving and Patronage in Middle Byzantine Courts

Introduction

While the first chapter focused on the origins and implementation of the program of "Cleansing the Ancient Laws," this chapter will examine how law functioned in practice. The focus here is on the empire's civil courts, and in particular how gift-giving and patronage were exercised within them. Both "gift-giving" and "patronage" encompassed a range of practices, including the payment of judges and their staffs by litigants and the exercise of influence or friendship to obtain a favorable verdict for oneself or one's friends. The legality or the degree to which these practices were favorably or unfavorably viewed varied considerably in both normative and non-normative legal texts for the entirety of the Middle Byzantine period. As such the considerable span of responses to gift-giving and patronage within Byzantine legal culture reflect the legal gray area which these phenomena occupied.

While within Byzantine Studies the importance of patronage has long been recognized in subfields such as Byzantine art, no study dedicated to the practices of gift-giving and patronage in Byzantine law has appeared. More general studies which examine Byzantine courts have tended to condemn these practices as symptoms of a corrupt legal system. Thus the most comprehensive study to date has highlighted the susceptibility of Byzantine judges to bribery, the recognition of this fact by Byzantine emperors and their subsequent attempts to combat corruption within the legal system.[1] Presented in this way, the imperial administration was in a constant struggle to attenuate corruption within the legal system. Although it is true that emperors and certain authors of the Middle Byzantine period, most notably Kekaumenos, viewed corruption of judges and legal officials as a serious problem, what modern scholars often

[1] Saradi 1995.

describe as "bribery" or "corruption" does not adequately encompass the relevant phenomena: a more heuristically useful way to approach these concepts is to contextualize them within the broader categories of gift-giving and patronage and their function within Byzantine legal culture.

Recent work on the study of the legal system and legal culture of the later Roman Empire offers instructive paradigms for examining corruption, gift-giving and patronage in the Middle Byzantine period.[2] These studies have cautioned against an over-simplistic reading of condemnations of bribery and corruption in the legal system and have sought to examine these phenomena within their broader societal context. In many ways the interpretation offered in the following pages is inspired by these recent reappraisals of the legal system of Late Antiquity.

Factors such as the customary payment by litigants for legal services, the important role of patronage and the value placed upon friendship within the Byzantine elite all contrived to obscure the line between licit and illicit, between gift and bribe, between assistance and personal favor. That is not to say that bribery and corruption did not exist or that Byzantine authors did not possess a conception of what these phenomena looked like in practice, rather that the line between legal and illegal influence was not clearly distinguished, or even if it was delineated in certain instances by the law these regulations appear to have been largely ignored or sporadically enforced. Although there is no medieval Greek word which adequately expresses this style of patronage, its features within Middle Byzantine courts included: the importance of knowing the right people, of cultivating relationships with people in positions of power through gifts and of asking for and rendering favors which were either illegal or which occupied a legal gray area.[3]

[2] Particularly relevant work includes problematization of "the corrupt judge" in Late Antiquity in Harries 1999: 153–71. Immensely important for the examination of legal fees in this chapter is the discussion of "purchasing power" in the legal system by Kelly 2004: 138–85.

[3] Harries 1999: 158–63 offers a useful analysis of the terms *iniuria*, which denoted judicial incompetence but not deliberate wrongdoing, and *gratia*, which underlined that a judge had committed a corrupt act. With regard to the broader phenomenon of patronage, there existed a term for this in Late Antiquity (Lat. *patrocinium*, Gr. προτασία), but by the Middle Byzantine period no single word was employed for describing patronal relationships: see Cappel and Kazhdan 1991c. Saradi 1994 in another study has attempted to find traces of Late Antique patronage practices in Byzantium. The approach employed in this chapter with regard to Middle Byzantine patronage differs from that of Saradi in that it does not attempt to categorize patron–client relationships according to Late Antique paradigms of patronage. The way patronage was exercised was, after all, quite fluid and depended on the social status, wealth and influence of the patron and client, with varying degrees of equality and dependence. In any case, as is evident from Saradi's investigation, there does not appear to have been a standard set of recognized obligations for patrons and clients, nor even an agreed-upon term by which such a relationship was designated.

Although gift-giving and patronage were diachronic phenomena within Byzantine history, the Middle Byzantine phase of the role of gift-giving and patronage is significant, not least because – especially compared with the immediate preceding period – courts, and in particular secular courts – grew in their societal importance as provincial legal officials, particular thematic judges, saw their powers increase within the administrative system. Alongside these thematic courts, the creation of higher Constantinopolitan courts during this period, such as that of the Hippodrome and Velum – the activity of which is well-documented in the *Peira* – meant that courtrooms inevitably became another arena where elites exercised their patronage and influence.

Imperial patronage as well as the patronage of the power elite, or what one might call "state patronage," is a well-studied phenomenon in Byzantium, not least because of its conspicuous presence in sources concerned with court ceremony like the *De ceremoniis*.[4] Indeed, as Paul Magdalino puts it "as much as, if not more than, other royal courts from Cordoba to Beijing, that of the Byzantine emperor was society's main hub for the concentration and redistribution of wealth, the performance and communication of government buisness, decision-making and dispute-settlement, the interface between rulers and ruled, social mobility both upward and downward, the group consciousness of the elite and their competition for individual status within the group."[5] In contrast with state patronage, private patronage, or patronage not carried out only by the power elite, has been less studied by Byzantinists. This is at least partially because Byzantium has long been seen as an intensely bureaucratic state, especially by the standards of its "feudal" Western medieval counterparts. A step in correcting this notion was taken in the 1960s by the eminent Byzantinist Hans-Georg Beck. Drawing on examples from the ninth through eleventh centuries, Beck demonstrated that the existence of retinues loyal to a powerful individual (*hetaireiai* or *phratriai*) played a key role in the accession of usurpers to the imperial throne. Time and time again, ambitious and lucky young men, often of humble origins, were able to advance to the highest levels of the Byzantine administration by participation in and use of these *hetaireiai*.[6]

[4] For an introduction to the role of court society and its relationship with the rest of the elite, Magdalino 2009. See also the articles in Maguire 1997, particularly the contributions of Kazhdan and McCormick 1997 and Oikonomides 1997.

[5] Magdalino 2009: 212.

[6] Beck 1965.

Leonora Neville in her study on authority in the Byzantine "core" provinces articulated a powerful and convincing refutation of the traditional notion of Byzantium as a centralized, bureaucratic state.[7] Drawing from a wide variety of sources, Neville demonstrated the essential apathy of the imperial administration in Constantinople toward provincial matters, outside of tax collection; if no overt display of power threatened the emperor, he largely left the provinces alone as long as their fiscal obligations were met.[8] This benign neglect was exploited by powerful provincial households (*oikoi*), which could and did create and maintain spheres of local influence.[9] Obviously, although loyalty to friends and family was prized, loyalty to one's *oikos* was not necessarily seen as inimical to serving the emperor.[10] Friendship and patronage networks were entwined within the fabric of Byzantine society, and evidence for the existence of these networks can be evinced throughout the empire's existence at every level of the administration and in the church. The Byzantine legal system and Byzantine legal culture did not constitute exceptions to the general prevalence of friendship and patronage networks: on the contrary, it is in these areas that it was especially noticeable.[11]

Byzantinists and legal historians, when confronted by the existence of these friendship networks tend to group them under the rubrics of "bribery" and "corruption." By modern standards, of course, actions like paying a judge for his services or aiding a friend by handing down a favorable judgment undoubtedly constitute instances of bribery and corruption. Like most contemporary legal systems, these practices were condemned at an official level; as we shall see below, as the only legitimate legislators of the Byzantine state, emperors attempted to regulate gift-giving. Further down the social scale, members of the power elite likewise imagined an ideal judge as completely free of corruption. Yet Psellos, among others, could both condemn corruption in general while at the same time courting his friends for legal favors.[12]

Rather than examining corruption and bribery as problems which prevented the Byzantine legal system from operating effectively and

7 Neville 2004; many of these same themes have been more recently highlighted in the studies collected together in Herrin 2013a.

8 Neville 2004: 39.

9 Neville 2004: 66–135.

10 Magdalino 1989.

11 The importance of patronage in the Byzantine legal system is especially evident Weiss 1973b.

12 Saradi 1995: 185–6. On Psellos' use of friendship (*philia*) in currying legal favors from his friends in his letters, see Kazhdan 1994: 206–12.

efficiently, the interpretation presented here emphasizes how networks of gift-giving and patronage were legitimated through the legal system and legal culture.[13] The tension between the ideal of the incorruptible judge and the reality of judges who utilized the same practices of gift-giving and patronage as the rest of the elite was not contradictory to contemporary Byzantine writers. After briefing sketching how the secular courts functioned in the Middle Byzantine period, an examination of imperial legislation from Late Antiquity into the time of Macedonian rule will show that judges accepted fees from litigants as a matter of course, and it was the undue abuse of this practice, not the custom of accepting fees *per se*, which garnered imperial condemnation. Moreover, the provincial judge's function as the collector of secondary taxes reinforced his image as a fiscal official.[14] The views of Middle Byzantine writers will then be scrutinized with regard to the qualities they looked for in the ideal judge, and how they legitimated the practices of gift-giving and patronage. Lastly, an examination of surviving legal documents, the majority of which are found within the various Athonite archives as well as cases referenced within the *Peira*, will show how patronage and gift-giving functioned in practice.

Thus, the practices of gift-giving and patronage were carried out as effectively and enthusiastically by officials with judicial powers as in any other area of the Byzantine administration. Moreover, a heuristically useful examination of these practices should not underline that they were venal and corrupt, but rather emphasize that gift-giving and patronage were so basic to the Byzantine conception of state and society, and thus were replicated at every level of the administration from the emperor on down, that a completely impartial and incorruptible judiciary would have been utterly antithetical to the reality of Byzantine governance. Although one is unable in this instance to answer that age-old conundrum of whether a society develops laws and customs to best suit its mores or whether laws and customs order the society that utilizes them, nonetheless it can be stated with conviction that the Middle Byzantine legal system and legal culture were well-suited to accommodate the *prima facie* surprising coupling of Roman law and Orthodox Christian ethics.

[13] On the function of gift-giving in letters between Byzantine intellectuals in the eleventh century, see Bernard 2011.

[14] As Magdalino 1994 has shown, justice and revenue were closely entwined within Byzantine legal culture.

The Legal-Administrative System

Before examining how gift-giving and patronage were practiced within Byzantine legal culture and in particular the legal system, it is worth giving an overview of the latter. In briefly sketching the Byzantine legal-administrative system of the ninth to eleventh centuries, it is heuristically useful to at all times to distinguish between the imperial capital, Constantinople, and the provinces. Particularly with regard to the way the legal system was organized, the capital was in many respects *sui generis* and it is difficult to disentangle the numerous overlapping jurisdictions of its administrators, in contrast to the relatively simple way the administration of justice in the provinces appears to have been structured.[15]

Beginning then in the provinces, the administrative system during the period of Macedonian rule was the so-called *theme* system.[16] Although scholars have long debated the origin of the theme system, a consensus now holds that it was the result of organic administrative developments, as imperial armies moved east to combat Persian and then Arab invaders in the seventh century, rather than a onetime administrative innovation.[17] From the time of Leo III (r. 717–41), the commands of these provincial armies, or *strategides*, began to be associated with the districts from which they were supplied.

Very little is known about the administration of justice in the eighth century. The *Ecloga* mentions three classes of legal officials: magistrates (*archontes*), judges (*dikastai*) and *akroatai*.[18] The last of these is a designation not found on lead seals of the period, and thus M. T. G. Humphreys has plausibly argued that *akroatai* were synonymous with *archontes*, that is, magistrates with juridical powers.[19] These *akroatai* also play a prominent

[15] For general comments on the legal-administrative system see most recently Burgmann 1997; Puliatti 2011 and Saradi 1995. Gkoutzioukostas 2004 has examined the courts of the capital in great detail. For justice in the provinces one can consult the long-term overview of Sarris 2011 with profit. Though based on the Athonite evidence and thus geographically limited to Macedonia, the studies of Morris 1986; 2010; 2011; 2013; are the best analyses of provincial juridical administration in the Middle Byzantine period.

[16] On the administrative system the dated but still valuable study of Bury 1911 is useful; more recently see Hélène Glykatzi-Ahrweiler 1960 and Oikonomides 1976.

[17] For the most complete overview of the development of the theme system, see Haldon 1997: 208–53; Haldon 1993: 7–11. The organic theory of theme development was originally championed by Karayannopulos 1959 and Pertusi 1958. It was confirmed later by Lilie 1984.

[18] Humphreys 2015: 105–13.

[19] Ibid.

role in the Farmer's Law (Nomos Georgikos), in that they judged disputes within and between villages.[20]

Although the development of the theme system in some respects took several centuries, the reign of Nikephoros I (r. 802–11), with its numerous administrative and fiscal reforms, represents a major turning point. This was the time in which the main features of the theme system came into being, including the actual use of the term *themata* to refer to territorial units as well as the armies they supported.[21] In fact, one can even go as far as to call Nikephoros I the founder of the theme system. There were five main characteristics of a theme in the early ninth century.

(1) It was a territory where an army was based and where poorer soldiers were supported by local taxpayers.
(2) It was a fiscally distinct unit managed by a *protonotarios*.
(3) Officials within the theme maintained the military registers and the tax assessments of the soldiers' families on those registers.
(4) Its judicial administration was headed by a *praitor* (later called a *krites*).
(5) The governor of a theme was a *strategos*, who was aided by a clerical department under a *kagkellarios*.[22]

As outlined above, each theme was governed by a *strategos* or military governor.[23] In earlier conceptions of the theme system, particularly that of the influential mid-twentieth-century doyen of Byzantine Studies Georg Ostrogorsky, in the first centuries of its existence the *strategos* had absolute civil and military powers within his theme. Newer research on the Byzantine administration has completely overturned this notion, and it is unlikely that the *strategos* ever possessed any sort of comprehensive civil authority before the reign of Leo VI (r. 886–912).[24] From the standpoint of judicial administration officials called *anthypatoi*, who had been diocesan functionaries in the administration during Late Antiquity, appear to have retained their judicial powers throughout the eighth century and into the early ninth century.[25] If one accepts the newly proposed dating of *c.*811–13 for the earliest Middle Byzantine list of precedence for dignitaries and

[20] Humphreys 2015: 219–20.
[21] Brubaker and Haldon 2011: 723–71.
[22] Brubaker and Haldon 2011: 752–3.
[23] Glykatzi-Ahrweiler 1960: 36–52.
[24] Haldon 1993: 9–11.
[25] Brubaker and Haldon 2011: 671–9.

functionaries, the so-called *Taktikon Uspenskij*, then new officials charged with judicial administration appear for the first time at the beginning of the ninth century.[26]

It is only during a roughly one hundred-year period, from *c.*850 to *c.*950, that a *strategos* corresponded to an Ostrogorskian *generalissimo* with ultimate military and civil powers within his theme. The primary duty of a *strategos* was his role as a military commander; his ability and/or propensity to involve himself in civil affairs not directly related to the functioning of the army with his theme varied considerably and were probably restricted.[27] Yet as the highest authority in the theme until around the eleventh century or so, he had judicial duties as well, at least in theory.[28] A *strategos* performed his juridical duties, most likely exclusively, without the aid of legal training: *strategoi* were first and foremost military men, and the background of the most well-known *strategoi* clearly shows that they were career soldiers, often foreigners drawn to imperial service, for whom even rudimentary literacy, much less literacy of the sort necessary to read and interpret Roman law, would have been rare. It is assumed that other judicial functionaries, so-called *symponoi*, could have been assigned to the *strategos* to assist him in judging.

The vesting of ultimate civil and military powers in a single official was gradually eroded over the course of the tenth and eleventh centuries by the increasing power of a theme's chief civil official, the judge (variously described as a *krites*, *dikastes* or *praitor*).[29] By the eleventh century thematic judges had become the civil administrators of themes, and were the highest judicial officials within their jurisdictions. The central administration appears to have taken for granted that the decisions of these provincial courts would be imperfect, and therefore allowed appeal of their decisions to the emperor, patriarch and other officials in Constantinople.[30] Two novels of Constantine VII (r. 944–59) demonstrate that these thematic judges and their staffs were paid legal fees (Lat. *sportulae*, Gr. *ektagiatika*) by both parties in court.[31] Constantine IX Monomachos (r. 1042–55)

[26] *Taktikon Uspenskij* 53, line 3. The *Taktikon Uspenskij* has been dated to 842–3 almost exclusively on the basis of a title which is found in the manuscript, which was probably added later. Živkovič 2005 presents a convincing argument that the *Taktikon Uspenskij* was originally authored in *c.*811–13 and then was reworked and edited afterward.

[27] Brubaker and Haldon 2011: 769.

[28] Leo VI, *Taktika* 1.9: "The *strategos* is the person who, after the emperor, has greater authority than anyone else over the entire province subject to him."

[29] Glykatzi-Ahrweiler 1960: 67–78; Gkoutzioukostas 2004: 101–2.

[30] *Eisagoge* 11.9.

[31] See the discussion below.

created a judicial office, the *epi ton kriseon*, to verify and correct the decisions of thematic courts.[32]

In the imperial capital of Constantinople, the eparch (*eparchos*) was the highest-ranking legal official,[33] with the quaestor as well having considerable legal authority.[34] But the *Peira* makes it clear that the various imperial departments or *sekreta* of the administration in the capital had their own internal jurisdictions.[35] Thus legal disputes involving a member of a particular *sekreton* would be judged by the head of that *sekreton*. Also in the capital were the so-called *politikoi* or "city" judges, judges with a relatively high level of legal training, who were assigned cases by the emperor and other higher level administrators with juridical powers. According to the most recent work on the subject, the two main groups of these judges, the judges of the Hippodrome and the judges of the Velum, respectively, formed tribunals which took place in the covered Hippodrome.[36] These city judges could also be assigned as *symponoi* to other officials. The aforementioned novels of Constantine VII on legal fees state that these judges and their staffs were forbidden from receiving customary legal fees rendered by both parties in court.

The Practices of Paying *Sportulae*, Bribery and Patronage in Imperial Legislation

> It is nowadays generally expected of a judge that he should not only be learned in the law but honest and independent, yielding neither to bribes nor to intimidation or social pressure. In the later Roman empire legal learning was, as we have seen, not expected of a judge. Honesty and fearless independence were highly esteemed, but they were rather ideals than normal requirements. Judicial corruption was an endemic evil which the emperors were powerless to overcome. It is attested not only by the denunciations of the moralists, Christian and pagan, but by many constitutions in the codes, and even more strikingly by the praise given to honest governors. An age in which it was a high compliment to a retiring judge to say that he left office as poor as when he entered upon it must have had low standards of judicial honesty.[37]

[32] Oikonomides 1976: 134.
[33] *Eisagoge* 11.7; cf. Gkoutzioukostas 2004: 103–7.
[34] *Eisagoge* 11.8; cf. Gkoutzioukostas 2004: 107–10.
[35] *Peira* 51.29.
[36] Gkoutzioukostas 2004: 119–81.
[37] Jones 1964: 502.

As this quotation from A. H. M. Jones' section on "Justice" in his classic study *The Later Roman Empire* emphasizes, judges, who were seen primarily as administrators with judiciary powers rather than legal specialists, were constantly subjected to attempts at "bribery."[38] The term "bribery" here tends, however, to conflate two related phenomena: the customary payment of fees by litigants to legal officials for cases tried in their courts (Lat. *sportulae*, Gr. *ektagiatika*) and the purchasing of influence with legal officials by paying a sum above and beyond these fees.[39] The problem in distinguishing between the two both in the later Roman Empire as well as in the Middle Byzantine Empire is that imperial legislation alternated between banning and regulating *sportulae*. Nonetheless, it is clear that whatever the official imperial position regarding *sportulae* was, within Byzantine legal culture legal officials expected to be paid for their services and that these fees were to be provided by the litigants. While the customary amounts paid by litigants fluctuated, there was also a recognition that at some point a litigant crossed a line between paying these *sportulae* and purchasing undue influence in a case; the use of the term "bribery" will be confined in this chapter to the latter occurrence.

The Middle Byzantine custom of paying legal fees had its roots in the practice of paying legal officials *sportulae* in the Roman Empire; as in the Middle Byzantine period, imperial regulation or outright abolition of *sportulae* does not seem to have seriously impeded the continuity of the practice. One extreme reaction was that of Constantine I (r. 306–37), who issued a constitution which threatened bribe-takers with death.[40] Despite the legal prohibitions against *sportulae*, they appear to have become institutionally accepted by the end of Late Antiquity. A list of *sportulae*, a so-called *ordo salutionis*, for the province of Numidia during the reign of Julian (r. 361–3) has survived and the emperor Justinian I set a schedule for *sportulae* which is referenced frequently in the *CIC*, but it has unfortunately not been transmitted.[41] The historian of Late Antiquity Chistopher Kelly has offered an interesting interpretation of the persistence of these *sportulae*, namely that they worked as self-sorting gatekeeper mechanism which prevented late Roman legal officials from being overwhelmed with

[38] Jones 1964: 470–522.

[39] Dölger 1940 remains the best introduction to *sportulae*.

[40] Jones 1964: 496; *Cod. Theod.* 1.16.7 (Nov. 1, 331).

[41] Jones 1964: 496–8. Kelly 2004: 138–40 offers a fascinating analysis of the Numidian schedule of *sportulae*, particularly with regard to average person's – to say to nothing of the poor's – (lack of) access to the Roman legal system.

requests for legal action and deterred frivolous suits.[42] There is no reason to suppose that the practice did not continue into the seventh century and later despite considerable economic, military and political upheaval.

The bribery of judges is addressed again as a problem in the eighth century during the rule of the Isaurian dynasty. The emperors Leo III (r. 717–41) and Constantine V (r. 741–75) in their *Ecloga* chose to condemn bribery as a moral failing – like much of the *Ecloga*, venality is condemned in biblical terms:

> For our Lord and Savior Jesus Christ has said "Judge not according to appearance, but judge righteous judgment" (John 7:24), [therefore] it is just to refrain from all bribery. For it is written: "Which justify the wicked for reward, and take away the righteousness of the righteous from him!" (Isaiah 5:23) and "Turn away the way of the meek" (Amos 2:7); "so their root shall be as rottenness, and their blossom shall go up as dust: because they have cast away the law of the Lord" (Isaiah 5:24). "For a gift doth blind the eyes of the wise, and pervert the words of the righteous." (Deuteronomy 16:19). Therefore we have endeavored to entirely suppress such disgraceful venality, and we have determined that the most glorious quaestor, the *antigrapheis*, and all of those serving in the principal courts are to receive their wages from our pious treasury, so that they are unable to receive anything at all from anyone who is being judged by them, lest the saying of the prophet be fulfilled for us: "They sold the righteous for silver" (Amos 2:6), and [lest] we desire to receive divine censure as trespassers of His commandments.[43]

Thus we see quite clearly in the first major collection of post-Justinianic legislation that the bribery of judges and legal officials aroused imperial scrutiny. The quaestor, the *antigrapheis* and the officials serving in the principal courts were prohibited from receiving payment of any sort. However, just because these legal officials were precluded from receiving *sportulae* does not necessarily lead to the conclusion that all judges were forbidden from doing so or that the practice stopped during this period.[44] Indeed, the fact that these officials are enumerated as salaried and forbidden from accepting *sportulae* in place of a general prohibition against accepting *sportulae* tends to support the idea that they were exceptional and such an assumption would explain the same prohibition against accepting *sportulae* which applied to the "city judges" (*politikoi dikastai*), who appear in imperial novels of the tenth century. The period of Isaurian

[42] Kelly 2004: 144.
[43] *Ecloga*, proem, lines 96–109.
[44] *Pace* Humphreys 2015: 61; Saradi 1995: 177.

rule for the most part constitutes unknown territory for legal historians, and particularly for the legal administration we have a far more complete picture before and after rather than during this epoch.

The major contribution of the *Ecloga* to the Byzantine understanding of judicial corruption was that bribery of legal officials began to be construed as a moral problem. Thus, from the period of issuance of the *Ecloga* until the eleventh century, for writers like Kekaumenos bribery of legal officials was thought to originate out of character failings: as shall be shown, this notion was repeated time and time again by Byzantine writers. The efficiency of the legal administration did not constitute a secondary concern *per se*, since in Middle Byzantine legal culture a morally upright judge was a necessary component of an efficient legal-administrative system. Nonetheless, whatever the perceived shortcomings of the legal system, both problem and solution were construed morally.

There are several regulations regarding judges in the *Eisagoge*.[45] Like most of the *Eisagoge*, these regulations represent a reworking of material in the *CIC*. Concerning the practice of *sportulae*, the relevant passage in the *Eisagoge* represents either a misreading/mistranslation of the original text or a deliberate omission. *Eisagoge* 7.1 states that magistrates in the provinces (*archontes*)[46] should not allow judges to receive anything of any sort when judging cases, not even in the name of custom, and that they are liable to penalties if they knowingly do this.[47] However, Justinian's *Nov.* 8.6, on which *Eisagoge* 7.1 is based, states that judges are not to collect any fees beyond the regulated *sportulae*. Thus a reworking of the original text led to a very different regulation; judges were not to receive any *sportulae* whatsoever. Magistrates were also not allowed to appoint a guardian or a judge.[48]

Judicial corruption is next indirectly referenced in the *Novels* of Leo VI.[49] Novel 84 overturns Justinianic regulations which prohibited

[45] Saradi 1995: 177.

[46] *Archon* (ἄρχων) being a blanket designation for any of the various high-ranking provincial magistrates; see *Eisagoge* 6.1: "*Archon* is a general term which denotes the *strategos*, the *anthypatos* and all of the provincial officials if they are of senatorial [rank]."

[47] *Eisagoge* 7.1: "The magistrates are not to suffer those of any court taking something in any way in the name of custom, since they know that if this is so they bring about all manner of neglectful harm to Our subjects."

[48] *Eisagoge* 6.4: "A magistrate cannot appoint his own special guardian or judge."

[49] Saradi 1995: 178. There is no compelling reason to accept Saradi's interpretation of the *katakrisis* of judges issuing decisions without any basis in the law (included among the παραλειπόμενα of Noailles and Dain's edition) as referring to the bribery or undue swaying of judges. This *katakrisis* was most probably simply a standardized form of the curses and condemnations found in

magistrates in the capital from constructing private buildings and purchasing movable or immovable property without the permission of the emperor; additionally, any gift given to a magistrate while in office had to be confirmed in writing by the donor after the end of the magistrate's term of office or if five years had passed since the magistrate's term of office ended. In Leo's view, these regulations had been issued to limit coercion (*bia*), but were now unnecessary because of the ability of every citizen, rich or poor, to appeal to the emperor.[50] While lifting the regulations for magistrates in the capital, Leo adds that magistrates in the provinces, namely the *strategos*, are likewise not allowed to begin the construction of buildings nor to purchase or enjoy the use of anything nor to accept gifts while in office; officials working under the *strategos* involved in similar activities had to refer them to him.[51] The *strategos* during the period in which the *Eisagoge* was written, at the end of the ninth and the beginning of the tenth century, was the *generalissimo* of his province or theme and within it represented it the highest civil and military authority. As the chief civil official in a theme, he naturally had judicial powers as well,[52] so that the provisions of this novel can be taken as evidence of an imperial effort to curb judicial corruption.

A century and a half after the appearance of the *Eisagoge*, the activity of judges again attracted imperial attention, and with it renewed evidence of the payment of *sportulae*, in the form of two novels of Constantine VII.[53] The payment of these legal fees had been a custom which was granted the force of law by Constantine VII. According to the earlier of the two novels, a thematic judge (*thematikos dikastes*) could not receive more than 3 *nomismata* per pound of gold under dispute,[54] up to a maximum of 100 *nomismata*. This worked out to a rate of a little over 4 percent. Litigants designated as "poor" were to pay only 1 *nomisma*, which corresponded to a rather miserly 1.4 percent. In cases involving the contestation of ownership of land between "powerful" and "poor," the judge was to receive 1 *nomisma* from the "powerful", and nothing from the "poor." These fees

Byzantine legal acts, serving as a formula which a notary could insert into the document he was writing.

50 Leo VI, *Novels*, Novel 84, 1–13.

51 Ibid. 18–24.

52 It is, however, questionable to what extent the *strategos* ever actually exercised his civil authority in matters not directly related to the upkeep and functioning of the army: see Brubaker and Haldon 2011: 769.

53 Constantine VII, *Novel I on Legal Fees*; cf. Dölger 1940: 241–4.

54 NB: The novel does not explicitly state what is measured: Dölger conjectures "Streitwert."

did not include expenses incurred for the travel and lodging of the judges. This amount was intended not only for the thematic judge but also his subordinates. The effect of this first novel seems to have been chaotic, as judges split the pleading of the litigants' cases so that multiple judges could collect fees from one case.[55] Thereafter, a second novel was issued which attempted to correct these abuses.

The upshot of these regulations regarding legal fees was to create an incentive for thematic judges to judge as many cases as possible. This was apparently intentional, as the second novel of Constantine VII states that the subordinates of the thematic judge would encourage him and work all the harder because they knew that they would be paid for each case which resulted in a final verdict.[56] Additionally, the schedule of legal fees doubtless affected the types of suits which were judged, as both thematic judges and their subordinates were paid much more for judging cases involving two wealthy parties. Not only were amounts under dispute much higher, but judges were paid at a rate of three times that of poorer litigants. And in those cases which involved a contestation of ownership between parties designated as "powerful" and "poor," judges and their retinues received nothing at all from the "poor" party. Aside from the considerable wealth and influence which the "powerful" already had over thematic judges, the system of legal fees created substantial incentives for their cases to be judged and the cases of "poor" litigants to be consigned to the back burner. Likewise, lower level legal functionaries stood to make much more money under a judge who regularly presided over suits with wealthy litigants, as opposed to a judge who mainly judged suits between poor farmers disputing their field boundaries: a Middle Byzantine analogue to a contemporary Harvard Law School graduate's choice between making six figures in a boutique Wall Street firm or doing public interest work.

55 Constantine VII, *Novel II on Legal Fees* 227: "For they [the thematic judges] reasoned that it would not be beneficial for one of the judges to make a profit from the loss of another, and so thus they split the presentation of evidence (by the litigants), so that oftentimes they did not abide the exposition [of evidence] of the litigants. And before the necessary examination and hearing they effected a transfer of the case [to another judge]. And oftentimes it happened that from the proceedings of meddling judges and from the successive transfer [of cases] they overshot the value of the established value of the estate through bribery."

56 Constantine VII, *Novel II on Legal Fees* 228: "Thus the judge shall be roused more diligently toward a final verdict of the [parties] seeking it, and his subordinates shall urge him on and encourage him in his duty and shall exhort him and serve more enthusiastically, knowing that there will otherwise be no income outside of the final resolution of the case, and if he makes one verdict and judgment each day, then they will certainly carry away over three hundred *nomismata* in profit over the course of a year."

Crucially, these regulations were intended for thematic judges, the legal officials who were entrusted with the maintenance of the Byzantine legal system outside of the capital. As mentioned above, thematic judges, in addition to their substantial judicial powers, were the highest civil officials within the regional Byzantine administrative unit, the theme (*thema*), at least by the eleventh century. The increasing power of judges reflected a devolution of authority from the military governor (*strategos*), who for a roughly 100-year period from the mid-ninth to the mid-tenth century had been invested with supreme civil and military power within his theme. Indeed, one should not understate the fiscal role of these officials: the thematic judge was also responsible for the collection of taxes within his theme.[57] The public fisc also collected revenue from judges in the form of fees collected from fines and forfeits in certain types of private lawsuits, which included contracts, dowries, inheritances and sales, as well as confiscations from criminal cases.[58] It is difficult to establish what percentage of a judge's income came from his public maintenance as opposed to his legal fees, but the potential obviously existed for a judge to substantially augment his public salary by judging enough cases.

While the novel of Constantine VII countenances the collection of legal fees by judges in the provinces, it condemns any similar activity by the "city judges," that is those judges who made up the higher courts of the capital.[59] For these high judges, the novel allowed no collection of "customary" fees: "For these [city judges] it is incumbent, not only that they govern with clean hands, but that they also possess subordinates who are above any disgraceful profit [i.e. bribe]."[60] This prohibition is repeated later in the novel in even less uncertain terms: "None of the city judges [is allowed] to receive anything for any sort of reason, but they [must] instead have clean hands and disdain all money."[61] The supervisory and appellate role of the city judges meant that their rulings needed to be above suspicion. The thematic judges, on the other hand, perhaps understandably

[57] Oikonomides 1976: 148–9.

[58] Magdalino 1994: 96.

[59] In fact, the preceding line states that the extraordinary staff (*apaitetai*) and executors of sentences (*ekbibastai*) working under the "city judges" (*politikoi dikastoi*) are to be paid at the aforementioned rates in the novel. However, the "city judges" themselves and their regular subordinates (the two previously mentioned groups were considered outside the normal staff of the "city judges") were not to receive *sportulae*. Saradi 1995: 183.

[60] Constantine VII, *Novel I on Legal Fees* 219.

[61] Constantine VII, *Novel II on Legal Fees* 220.

given their other rather considerable administrative duties and presumably low level of legal expertise, were not held to the same standard.

Thus imperial policy toward *sportulae* oscillated between condemnation and acceptance; it is hard to ascertain what the official stance toward the practice of *sportulae* at any given time actually was. To maintain that judicial corruption was a problem which Byzantine emperors consistently sought to combat, as Saradi does, fails to accurately convey the generally ambiguous, and in the case of Constantine VII even encouraging, attitude of Byzantine rulers towards *sportulae*. A more nuanced view would be that, since efforts to completely ban the payment of customary legal fees by litigants were impracticable, Middle Byzantine emperors typically allowed the payment of *sportulae* in lower courts, that is the courts outside of Constantinople like the thematic courts, while banning the payment of *sportulae* to higher legal officials, such as the eparch, the quaestor and the "city judges." The professionalism of the latter was held to a high standard; the decisions of the eparch and of the quaestor could not be appealed and were subject only to the emperor himself.[62] It seems to have been taken for granted that provincial courts would require the correction of the higher courts in Constantinople; thus a passage in the *Eisagoge* states: "The magisterial courts are subject to appeal, and [their cases] can be retried by both the emperor and the patriarch, as well as the eparch and quaestor. For the further they are separated from the center of rule, the more they are in need of greater help and further corrections and retrials."[63] Interestingly, these passages on the hierarchy of courts found in *Eisagoge* 11.1–9 have no antecedent in the *CIC* nor were they later incorporated in the *Basilika*. They represent a "snapshot" as it were of the legal system at the turn of the ninth century.

There does seem to have been a feeling or in some cases even admissions of helplessness of the imperial administration concerning the mid- and lower levels of the legal system, a conclusion congruent with recent studies of the Middle Byzantine Empire which have emphasized the limited reach of the central government in the periphery as well as the central provinces.[64] The Byzantine Empire, like any pre-modern state, did

[62] *Eisagoge* 11.7: "The decision of the eparch is not subject to appeal, except to that of the emperor alone"; *Eisagoge* 11.8: "The decision of the quaestor is not subject to appeal, but is also only scrutinized by the emperor alone."

[63] *Eisagoge* 11.9.

[64] Neville 2004: 5–38 in her incisive study Neville convincingly demonstrates the considerable authority retained by local authorities in areas such as dispute resolution and policing. Stephenson 2000 likewise argues for a deliberate imperial policy of indirect governance in Byzantine territories lining the Danube River.

not possess the resources to comprehensively direct every facet of governance at a polity-wide, provincial or local level. On the other hand the administration of justice in the provinces was by no means completely neglected. The studies of Rosemary Morris have nuanced this picture of benign neglect by showing that, at least in Macedonia during the tenth and eleventh centuries, peripatetic provincial judges conducted business throughout the theme in *kathismata* (temporary administrative centers, often on private property, set up to house visiting officials, including judges).[65] Yet the practice of paying and collecting *sportulae*, even when it attracted imperial attention during periods of imperial condemnation, seems to have continued relatively unhindered throughout the Middle Byzantine epoch.

A Culture of Reciprocity: The Embedding of Gift-Giving and Patronage Networks

At this point in the chapter imperial responses to the practice of paying *sportulae* and bribery have been explored, but the question remains to what extent did official opprobrium of bribery find support among Byzantine elites. Certainly at some level, as in the imperial legislation examined above, censure of the practices of bribery and of granting favors for friends can be ascertained across the spectrum of Middle Byzantine writers. Even the practice of *sportulae*, as common as they were, could be condemned in other contexts. The patriarch Nicholas I Mystikos (901–7, 912–25), in a text which ordered that patriarchal letters be made available free of charge, likened the archivist's (Gr. *ostiarios*, Lat. *ostiarius*) practice of collecting fees in exchange for access to the letters to a chronic bodily ailment.[66] Nicholas corrected the practice by giving the *ostiarios* a salary and forbidding him from collecting fees in the future.

Concurrently, however, the frequent mention of these practices suggests their prevalence and acceptance within the Byzantine legal system. Having sketched the inconsistent imperial condemnation of *sportulae*, we shall now embark on an exploration of how Byzantine writers of the

[65] Morris 2013.

[66] Nicholas I Mystikos, *Miscellaneous Writings*, Text 201, 84–7. According to Westerink's translation of this text, copies of patriarchal letters were given out as requested free of charge: "Its keeper, who bears the Latin title of *ostiarius*, used to demand fees from those who requested patriarchal letters in payment for the copy, a thing he should not have done." At least given the context, according to my own reading of the passage the *ostiarius* is in fact asking for fees for access to the letters, not for copies of the letters (a very expensive proposition).

period construed the problematic dynamic of balancing legal ideals against the pervasive practices of gift-giving and granting favors to friends. As a counterpart to the imperial novels discussed above, it is first of all worth discussing whether judicial impartiality existed at all in Byzantium. There are certainly statements from normative legal texts that law was supposed to be rendered impartially; it is stated in the *Basilika* that "justice is a fixed and constant aim which renders to each [person] what is fitting."[67] Yet not only was the idea of impartial justice far removed from the everyday reality of Byzantine law, but within Byzantine legal culture judicial impartiality, as it is understood in modern legal systems, was completely unknown. Judges were supposed to consider the character and past history of the litigants; not only that, but the personal relationship of the judge to the litigants was also a factor in jurisprudence.[68] A discussion of judicial impartiality or in this case the lack thereof is extremely important for our understanding of the legitimation of gift-giving and patronage within Byzantine legal culture, because judicial partiality aided and abetted these two practices of the Byzantine elite.

No less an authority than the ninth-century patriarch Photios (858–67, 877–86) lists the traits an ideal judge should possess in a letter to Michael, the then recently baptized ruler of Bulgaria, around the year 865:

> Consider the best judge to be he who seeks after the nature of the just by the swiftness of his thoughts, and after seeking it out produces [a verdict] correctly. He is quick to provide relief to the wronged, and slow to punish wrong-doers. He is above gold, and is not overcome by love of power. He retains control of his anger, and is not swayed by undue influence (*sympatheia*). He knows that in judging kinship, friendship and good repute alone [are components of] justice, while estrangement, enmity and ill-repute alone [constitute] injustice.[69]

Photios, like the emperors of the Middle Byzantine Period, underlined that an ideal judge should not be susceptible to bribery. Note again here however that condemnations of bribery are not necessarily condemnations of *sportulae*. In the passage above, what modern legal scholars would define as impartiality clearly did not constitute one of the qualities of the ideal judge – on the contrary, the patriarch states that kinship (*syngeneia*), friendship (*philia*) and good reputation (*doxa*) were components of justice. Conversely, negative preconceptions towards the parties at court,

[67] *Basil.* 2.1.10.
[68] Byzantine jurisprudence is discussed more extensively in Ch. 3.
[69] Photios, *Letters*, vol. I, Letter 1, lines 844–50.

such as estrangement (*allotriosis*), enmity (*echthra*) and ill-repute (*adoxia*), were associated with injustice. Since the importance of mercy (*philanthropia*) within Middle Byzantine legal culture continually prodded legal officials to soften the application of the law, feelings of friendship toward litigants were not discouraged; thus the prescription that the ideal judge is slow to punish wrong-doers.

Drawing the line between due and undue influence was a trickier proposition. Byzantine authors often denoted undue influence with the Greek word *sympatheia*, which does not possess the same connotations as the English word sympathy, at least in a legal context. *Sympatheia* instead meant an inordinate leaning toward one of the parties within a case. Returning again to the oeuvre of Photios, in his *Bibliotheca* the story of Original Sin is recounted, and Adam, when asked why he had eaten the fruit from the Tree of Knowledge, responded that Eve had given it to him. Photios writes that at that moment Adam had a merciful (*philanthropos*) judge, as well as a convenient (*sympathes*) excuse. Of course Photios was not here implying that God was an illegitimate judge, but rather that Adam, through his mendacity, had attempted to subvert the righteousness of God's judgment.[70] As these two examples from the works of Photios suggest, the idea of complete judicial impartiality as understood in the modern sense, and evident at times in texts like the *Basilika*, did not exist in Byzantine legal culture. The judge's relationship to the litigants was a legitimate component of jurisprudence.

Another catalogue of the qualities which good judges were to possess can be found in the roughly contemporary text *De re strategica*. Once thought to be the work of the so-called "Anonymus Byzantinus," it is now accepted to have been written by one Syrianos Magistros, who previously had been credited with the composition of a treatise on naval warfare, and it was likely authored sometime in the ninth century, perhaps during the reign of Theophilos (r. 829–42).[71] In a section concerning magistrates, Syrianos describes the characteristics of an ideal judge:

[70] Photios, *Bib.* vol. VIII, Codex 272, 100–11. This section is a summary of two works of Leontios, bishop of Arabissos, who lived during the seventh or eighth century.

[71] The proposal for Syrianos' authorship of the *De re strategica* as well as the *Rhetorica militaris* and his *Naumachica*, so that the three texts can be viewed as a "military compendium," was advanced by Zuckerman 1990. Syrianos' authorship is now accepted as the scholarly *communis opinio*, although the dating for the composition of the text varies: Zuckerman believes it was authored in a late sixth-/early seventh-century context. Rance 2007 has advanced a convincing argument that there is no compelling evidence to assume that *De re strategica* was written around the time of the emperor Justinian, as had hitherto been assumed, and that it was probably not authored before around 790. Cosentino 2000: 262–75 argues that Syrianos wrote his military compendium in the second third of the ninth century, perhaps during the reign of Theophilos, as the emperor mentioned in the text

> Judges must be discerning by nature – for many abound in good ideas, yet err in selecting which one is best. Judges must be knowledgeable about the laws, with which they are directly concerned, but also the other matters which may have some bearing upon the interpretation of the laws. They should have control over their actions, their emotions and their pleasures. They must not be terrified by fear. They should not indulge friendship (*philia*), nor be overcome by enmity (*echthra*), nor should money entice them. They are to be stern with those who despise the laws and gentle with those who follow them.[72]

As in Photios' description of the ideal judge, Syrianos Magistros likewise underscores the need for judges to avoid having enmity (*echthra*) color their judgment. On the other hand, Syrianos, in contrast to Photios, recognizes that friendship (*philia*) can also have a negative impact on a judge. Though Syrianos' description of the ideal judge is closer to the modern concept of judicial impartiality, Photios and Syrianos were in agreement about one commonplace of Byzantine jurisprudence, namely that knowledge of the law did not constitute the sole or even the primary prerequisite for judging.

The constant tension between rewarding one's friends while at the same time refraining from allowing undue influence in the courts is especially evident in the *Strategikon* of the eleventh-century aristocrat Kekaumenos. The *Strategikon* is a supremely informative source regarding the functioning of the legal system, since it contains two sections of advice for provincial judges and notaries, respectively. In his advice to provincial judges, Kekaumenos first of all warns them to avoid judging their friends, at the risk of censure by the city judges in Constantinople: "Do not feel compassion for anyone in judgment because of *philanthropia*, but if someone is a dear friend of yours and he is about to be judged, beg leave of judging such a case so that you do not judge unjustly. Far be it from you that you disgrace yourself, and your friend will be judged by the city judges."[73] As the two novels above of Constantine VII above demonstrate, provincial judges expected to receive *sportulae* from litigants, and this practice was sometimes abused. This passage from Kekaumenos, interestingly, reflects the imperial position regarding the different levels of the legal system: namely, that the thematic courts, subject as they were to the practice

is not praised or named, which could signal his dubious reputation after the end of the Second Iconoclasm.

[72] Syrianos Magistros, *De re strategica* 3.30–7.

[73] Kekaumenos, *Strategikon* 6.8–12.

of *sportulae*, were easily subjected to bribery and were therefore in need of correction by the city judges, who were of course forbidden from receiving *sportulae*. Consequently, within this same section Kekaumenos also pens perhaps the most emphatic condemnation of bribery written in the Middle Byzantine period:

> And if you are a thematic judge, do not extend your eye and hands toward the acquisition of gifts. For someone who is wholly absorbed in the [acquisition] of gifts goes into the darkness of ignorance, even he is exceedingly learned and full of all discernment and knowledge. Instead be satisfied with what you are allocated. Do not let them send money to enrich you, but render justice to those who have been wronged ... If you look toward the acquisition [of gifts], those who did not bribe you shall not seem good in your eyes, even if they are exceedingly excellent men, but those who bribed you shall seem good and your spirit shall give repose to them, though they be murderers. For it is the habit of those who appropriate bribes for themselves to imprint on their souls that "I am going to take these bribes from this person." Should he accept [the bribe], and he looks away and receives them a second and third time, and if he doesn't receive them, because he has been deprived of his own [due] he shall become filled with black bile, and the just shall turn into the impious.[74]

The important conclusion to garner from this quotation is the extent to which gift-giving and friendship networks permeated the Middle Byzantine legal system and Byzantine legal culture. As Kekaumenos surmises, some provincial judges did not selectively practice bribery; on the contrary, they *expected* to receive gifts from all litigants. Therefore particularly at the provincial level of the legal system, as described in Kekaumenos, the cultural practices of the Byzantine elite emitted an especially powerful resonance. Given the widespread understanding that provincial judges expected to receive payment for their services, it is understandable that testators ensured that legal officials received payment from their estates in order to ensure that their wishes were carried out (discussed below).

Kekaumenos is hardly the only source which attests to the prevalence of bribery in the Byzantine period. One field which demonstrates how networks of friendship were mediated through the legal system is Byzantine epistolography.[75] The writing of letters throughout the Middle Byzantine Empire served both a pragmatic and literary function for the Byzantine elite. Byzantine officials in the administration as well as the church used

[74] Kekaumenos, *Strategikon* 6.4–8, 12–19.

[75] For an introduction to Byzantine epistolography, see Papaioannou 2010.

official correspondence to compose epistles which underlined their own erudition and cleverness. The letters themselves were often rhetorical exercises, while more mundane news was usually delivered orally by the messenger. The messenger also often bore a gift; fish seems to have been particularly popular.

These letters deal with a variety of topics of interest to this study: among them is the condemnation of officials for bribery or mishandling of justice and appeals for clemency. For example, returning once again to the patriarch Photios, in one of his letters to the quaestor Basil he expresses dismay at what others have said about Basil's style of justice: "But now they say that you'll do anything for gold, and I do not believe it. Golden, they say, are your hands, your tongue and your justice."[76] Note that as a quaestor Basil was likely excluded from receiving *sportulae*.

The correspondence of John Mauropous, an eleventh-century intellectual educated in Constantinople who became bishop of Euchaïta in Asia Minor, is of particular interest to this inquiry.[77] Echoing a point made earlier in this chapter about the importance of the character of the litigants in a case, Mauropous maintains that the laws must "examine the differences and the characters of people, who is capable of treachery and knavery and who is most unlikely to be guilty of such a charge."[78] In another letter Mauropous discusses the difficulty of maintaining one's friendships as a judge. Despite all the wonderful aspects of true friendship, "when it comes to the judgment of friends it is viewed with suspicion and it is not easily conceded as trustworthy to act as either a witness or a judge [on the behalf of friends]."[79] Mauropous goes on to recommend that the judge be less eager to praise his friends, lest suspicion arise that he is favoring them too much in his judgments. At another point the bishop asks for "a more clear interpretation (*ekdelotera saphenia*)" – i.e. for a more favorable decision – from a judge who had already rendered a decision against one of

[76] Photios, *Letters*, vol. I, Letter 154, lines 6–8.

[77] Unlike many other epistolary collections from the Middle Byzantine period, there are no recipients listed for the letters of John Mauropous. According to Karpozilos, Mauropous intentionally omitted the recipients' names in the course of selecting texts to demonstrate the literary quality of his oeuvre: "The names of the addressees must have been omitted by Mauropus intentionally. As he explains in the epigram with which he prefaced his collected works, his intention was to give to the public only a small part of his writings. The letters he chose for his collection represent only a fraction of his correspondence. The selection he made, however, he wanted primarily to be read as literary pieces. It was for this reason that the names of the actual addressees were withheld." (John Mauropous, *Letters*, 29).

[78] John Mauropous, *Letters*, Letter 11, lines 5–7.

[79] John Mauropous, *Letters*, Letter 28, lines 21–2.

his friends.[80] The tension between the maintenance of friendships and at the same time appearing to be impartial and just is manifest in all of these letters.

Among Middle Byzantine epistolary collections, the richest in content with regard to Middle Byzantine legal culture and the functioning of the legal system is that of the court intellectual Michael Psellos.[81] Of Psellos' surviving letters, well over 150 of them were addressed to officials with judicial powers (above all *kritai*). Though not all of these letters are concerned with legal cases, and even letters describing such affairs usually often give the barest of details, in total Psellos' letters constitute one of the two most important sources for Byzantine legal culture in the eleventh century, along with the *Peira*. As in Kekaumenos, the importance of friendship and patronage in Middle Byzantine society immediately strike the reader. In the letters of Psellos, however, unlike in the *Strategikon* of Kekaumenos, one can see how patronage was actually exercised within the legal system.[82]

Although like other contemporary Byzantine writers Psellos pays lip service to the notion of impartial justice, his letters more often play upon its mutability. For Psellos the strict letter of the law and the application of justice are either to be softened or molded in his own favor. While in order to do this he often invokes Orthodox Christian notions of mercy and compassion, his preferred device for seeking legal influence is friendship or *philia*. In Psellos' worldview the pursuit of justice and the influence of *philia* are not contradictory aims: since the former is an obligation and the latter a voluntary act, it is better that a judge investigate a crime because of *philia*.[83] Justice and *philia* were to reinforce each other.[84] In one

[80] John Mauropous, *Letters*, Letter 31.

[81] There is still no standard edition of Psellos' letters, though one is in preparation by Stratis Papaioannou (see Papaioannou 1998). The letters I have cited here are all from the editions of Sathas or Drexel and Kurtz, where the majority of the letters are to be found. I would like to thank Michael Jeffreys for asking me to be a reader for his soon-to-be published summaries of the Psellos' letters, which allowed me to verify and in some cases correct some of my earlier interpretations of particular letters.

[82] Letters which reference legal disputes, attempt to garner favor with legal officials, or other such acts are found in the following letters: Michael Psellos, *Letters of Psellos S*, Letters 20, 24, 41, 43, 45, 47, 49, 55, 65, 76, 77, 78, 103, 119, 131, 134, 135, 146, 151, 158, 180, 192, 195, 200; and Michael Psellos, *Letters of Psellos KD*, Letters 24, 28, 31, 35, 39, 41, 42, 47, 50, 51, 52, 55, 60, 63, 64, 65, 66, 69, 73, 74, 77, 79, 81, 82, 83, 84, 89, 90, 92, 99, 100, 106, 107, 108, 109, 117, 118, 119, 127, 140, 142, 152, 162, 163, 166, 171, 181, 182, 184, 200, 221, 222, 227, 243, 248, 250, 251.

[83] Michael Psellos, *Letters of Psellos KD*, Letter 107, in which a client of Psellos had had his mulberry trees and the grove in which they grew stolen by his neighbor. The thematic judge (*krites*) was to put this situation to rights. Though he might have already received a request to do so from the emperor, it was better for the *krites* to properly investigate the matter because of his *philia* with Psellos.

[84] Ibid., Letter 99.

letter to the thematic judge of Boleron, Psellos asks the *krites* to consider the monastery for which Psellos served as a trustee as their common property: "Supervise and preserve another's property as your own, for it is thus also yours because of [our] shared *philia*."[85]

In another letter to the thematic judge of Philadelphia Psellos, attempting to aid some villagers in the theme who had shown him hospitality in the past, noted that the initial verdict of the judge in the villagers' case had not been favorable. To Psellos, an initially unfavorable sentence, if the matter were considered with Psellos' *philia* in mind, could be changed to a favorable one, just as the philosophers Plato and Aristotle had not been afraid to reconsider their initially incorrect beliefs:

> Therefore I know that you would recognize everything that is just, and it seems to me to fit with the law. And if I somehow endanger our friendship, this would not be less just or merciful, lest you decide this wrongly. But by mixing my friendship with the arbitration of the case, perhaps you might recognize something more lawful and just that what has already been decided. For second and third approaches to matters change earlier diagnoses, [when] they had not arrived at the depth of the matter, but rather only the surface of it. Thus Aristotle and Plato thought differently earlier, and were not ashamed to change their ideas.[86]

To Psellos, serving as a just judge meant carefully considering the various relationships that the litigants and the judge himself had; thus Psellos often exercised influence on behalf of one of the parties in court via his friendship with a judge or other legal official. In a letter to the thematic judge of Anatolikon, Psellos, writing on behalf of a bishop of Sozopolis, ends his letter by stating: "And I would say in summation to be the sort of judge to him, who is an arbitrator of our friendship."[87] Being a friend and a judge were seen by Psellos as complementary rather than competing influences. In order to court favor with legal officials, Psellos would call upon a judge to play both roles adequately. In a letter to judge concerning a man who had committed a violent act, Psellos construed the official's responsibility to act in the following way: "Since you are a friend and a judge, as a judge you should supply the laws to the unjust and as a friend you should not delay the matter, but swiftly you should bring forth a

[85] Ibid., Letter 89.
[86] Michael Psellos, *Letters of Psellos S*, Letter 180.
[87] Ibid., Letter 41.

verdict."[88] Likewise, a judge who did not render justice dishonored both the laws and friendship.[89]

Serving as a judge was clearly a financially lucrative office; numerous letters emphasize the importance of making money as a *krites*. One addressee of Psellos' letters was praised as having mastered the twin responsibilities of being a thematic judge: performing his prestigious duties openly (*lamproteron*), while secretly (*kryptomenon*) enriching himself.[90] In a very entrepreneurial spirit he wished another judge first good health and second that he might profit from his cases.[91] Woe to the judge assigned to a poor theme – perhaps it was wealthier than it appeared at first glance.[92]

Bribery, understood here as the illicit courting of influence beyond customary gifts or *sportulae*, seems to have been a common occurrence, at least judging by how frequently Psellos mentions it in his letters. He singles out judges who do not accept bribes for praise.[93] A wronged party erred by attacking the integrity of an "unbribed" (*adekastos*) judge, even if they were Psellos' own clients.[94] In a letter to the judge Nikephoritzes asking to aid a bishop, Psellos notes that "for other judges either the hand that gives or a huge stream of tears from the eyelids will do, but for you noble reason suffices."[95] Though refusing bribes was a noble act, it is worth emphasizing again that bribes and the legitimate collection of *sportulae* were not the same thing. In one letter Psellos recommends that a judge take a *notarios* in his service, despite the fact that "the present times are difficult for help and for the thematic judges and their servants. For the exactitude of our emperor checks the hands of all."[96]

The letters of Psellos also make clear that knowing the right people was the best way for a notary or judge to advance his career. A large number of his letters are introductions for notaries, clients of Psellos, looking for a lucrative post under a thematic judge. Yet the importance of patronage was not restricted to the lower levels of the legal system; a judge in the provinces might ask Psellos for a more prestigious posting in a bigger theme or even in the capital.[97] A *semeioma* (a report of a judicial verdict)

88 Michael Psellos, *Letters of Psellos KD*, Letter 243.
89 Ibid., Letter 142.
90 Michael Psellos, *Letters of Psellos KD*, Letter 35.
91 Ibid., Letter 90.
92 Ibid., Letter 96.
93 Ibid., Letter 166.
94 Ibid., Letter 77.
95 Michael Psellos, *Letters of Psellos S*, Letter 103.
96 Michael Psellos, *Letters of Psellos KD*, Letter 109.
97 Ibid., Letter 255.

of Psellos has survived in which he attempted to recover the dowry of his daughter upon breaking her engagement to one Elpidios.[98] In recounting the numerous favors with which Psellos graced his presumptive future son-in-law, he mentions that he succeeded in having Elpidios appointed as one of the judges of the Hippodrome – the Byzantine equivalent of becoming a Supreme Court judge – by petitioning the emperor. Clearly knowing the right people and having their support at the right time was crucial for a successful career as a judge in the Middle Byzantine period. The patronage systems which permeated the legal system were openly called upon during the arbitration of legal disputes. As Kekaumenos emphasized, a judge had to walk a fine line between aiding his friends and potentially attracting scrutiny from higher courts.

Legal Patronage in Monastic Foundation Charters

Among the surviving written sources which demonstrate the pervasiveness of patronage and personal relationships within Byzantine legal culture are the testaments of monastic founders (*ktetorika typika*). These monastic charters, which date from the end of Late Antiquity, contain the stipulations and regulations of the founder for his or her monastery.[99] For the most part *typika* consist of regulations governing the commemorative and philanthropic functions to be performed by the monastic community, the composition and governance of the endowment, as well as more quotidian rules for the lives of the monks and nuns, but some of these charters also give detailed information on the legal status of these monastic foundations.[100] Therefore these documents provide legal historians with an excellent approximation of how legal relationships were construed in practice, and it is here, within the Byzantine legal *Alltag*, that the importance of personal patronage among the Byzantine elite supersedes any institutional relationship that a monastic foundation may have had with an imperial office or department. Many monastic founders felt that their interests were best served by entrusting their foundations to particular

[98] Michael Psellos, *Orationes, forenses et acta* 143–55. English translation in Kaldellis 2006: 147–56. On other translations see Kaldellis 2006: 146. This verdict is analyzed, along with Psellos' other legal writings, in Dennis 1994: 193–4.

[99] For the basic characteristics of *ktetorika typika*, see in particular the excellent overview of Galatariotou 1987.

[100] *Ktetorika typika* is a designation used by researchers for documents spanning a whole range of genres (testaments, hagiography, founding inscriptions, letters), not all of which had legal authority in the strictest sense. For *typika* as legal documents, see Stolte 2007.

powerful individuals, and though these officials were oftentimes bound by the privileges which these monastic institutions had received to protect and support them, the authors of these *typika* nonetheless preferred to emphasize the personal friendship they had cultivated together rather than the legal obligation of the official to intervene in particular instances. This pattern of patronage further underlines the importance of *philia*, which as we have already seen played an important role in the letters of Michael Psellos. Furthermore, invocations of a particular office, such as a thematic judge or eparch, to protect a monastic foundation were sweetened with testamentary bequests, both monetary and otherwise. Thus in this area also the importance of gift-giving and patronage was paramount.

In examining how monastic founders went about ensuring that their institutions would last after the founder's death, it is necessary to underline the degree to which these testators were on guard concerning potential threats to their foundations. Founders in the period stretching from the ninth to the eleventh century denounced any attempts whatsoever by relatives, ecclesiastical authorities, the patriarch of Constantinople, powerful officials or landowners, or even the emperor himself to appropriate any measure of authority or confiscate any property from these monastic foundations. John Thomas has seen this deep distrust of outside authority as culminating in an "Ecclesiastical Reform Movement," whereby founders sought to ensure that their monasteries attained and retained complete independence, especially in response to the practice of purportedly rapacious lay trusteeship, the *charistike*.[101] Nor was this wariness unfounded; the *Peira* contains examples of ecclesiastical authorities attempting to acquire ownership of monastic foundations. For instance, *Peira* 15.4 has the patriarch Nicholas I Mystikos of Constantinople attempting to acquire jurisdiction over the monastery Tou Piperatou, an attempt which was rebuffed by the Court of the Hippodrome.[102] Sometimes this paranoia manifested itself as a deep mistrust of all temporal authority. For instance, John of Rila, who founded what became the most famous monastery of medieval Bulgaria, enjoined to the surviving monks to spurn all worldly patronage: "Do not rely on temporal authorities to preserve you: Nor look to be recognized and beloved by earthly kings and princes, nor put your hope in them, leaving the heavenly King, with whom you enlisted to be soldiers and 'wrestle not against flesh and blood,' but 'against the ruler of

[101] John Thomas has postulated the existence of a Byzantine "Ecclessiastical Reform Movement" both in his monograph (Thomas 1987: 214–43) as well as in several articles (Thomas 1984; 1986).

[102] Thomas 1984: 263; Thomas 1987: 154–5.

the darkness of this world.' "[103] More often, however, a general declaration of hostility towards any attempts at outside interference was balanced by a reliance on particular notables to help preserve the independence of a monastery.

As a counterweight to potential outside interference, monastic testators often invoked local officials to help maintain the independence of a foundation. Two examples from the Peloponnese demonstrate the trust that monastic founders placed in particular officials, and both of these examples also rely upon the future holders of two offices, that of the military governor and that of the provincial judge. In the late tenth- or early eleventh-century testament of Nikon Metanoeite for the Church and Monastery of the Savior, the Mother of God and St Kyriake in Lakedaimon, both the military governor and judge of the province were to receive five measures of wine and one measure of apples. Moreover, the military governor and judge, along with the emperor, were to be commemorated by the monks. These privileges were tempered by caution, as any bequests left to the foundation were to be given to the monks and priests, and the Nikon explicitly forbids the military governor, judge or any other official from appropriating said bequests.[104] The second example is unusual in that it has survived as an inscription, with which one Nikodemos endowed a monastery church to maintain a then recently built bridge over the Eurotas River in 1027. Again, the military governor and judge are enjoined to care for and protect the monastery church. The testament is unusually deferential to these officials, and it invests them with the power not only to select a superior but to do to the monastery whatever they (and the emperor) see fit.[105] The respect which both of these testaments display toward the highest-ranking military and civil official respectively in the province underline just how much power these officials possessed at a local level. Additionally, since by the time of the Macedonian dynasty it was rare for either a military governor or provincial judge to serve in any province long-term, it behooved these monastic testators to refer to the offices rather than particular individuals. A last point is to be kept in mind as well: within the provincial milieu, in stark contrast to the capital, there was only one jurisdiction, that of the provincial judge, outside of the exceptional circumstance when an emperor empowered a higher judicial

[103] John of Rila, *Testament*. English translation by Ilija Iliev in *BMFD*, vol. I, 125–34, here 131.
[104] Nikon Metanoite, *Testament* 255–6. English translation by Anastasius Bandy in *BMFD*, vol. I, 313–22. Cf. Chitwood 2013: 56.
[105] Nikodemos, *Testament*. English translation by Stephen Reinert in *BMFD*, vol. I, 323–5.

functionary to resolve a particular dispute. While there were many overlapping jurisdictions in Constantinople, a provincial judge possessed practically unlimited power in his jurisdiction. The novel of Constantine VII regarding *sportulae*, discussed above, is a reflection of just how easily a provincial judge could augment his salary through accepting gifts. The five measures of wine and one measure of apples given yearly to the provincial judge in the testament of Nikon *Metanoeite* might have been multiplied dozens if not hundreds of times even in a relative economic backwater like the Peloponnese.

Another example of invoking the protection of an office for a foundation is the testament of Michael Attaleiates for his almshouse at Rhaidestos and for the Monastery of Christ Panoiktirmon in Constantinople. Michael Attaleiates was himself a judge, and he authored a "textbook" consisting of a brief introduction to Roman and Byzantine law followed by thematically organized excerpts from the *Basilika*. Compared to the aforementioned foundations in the Peloponnese, Attaleiates endowed what was a very large fortune, at least judging from the personal effects and sums listed in his testament. Mindful of potential interference by officials and relatives, Attaleiates chose to appeal to the most powerful legal official, other than the emperor, within Constantinople: namely, the eparch of Constantinople. Historians know a great deal about the office of the eparch because a tenth-century treatise details the regulations he was to enforce over the various guilds of the city. In a section of the testament describing what course of action is to be taken when a lawsuit is advanced against the almshouse or monastery, Attaleiates requests that such a lawsuit should be judged "with his knowledge and assistance." For example, if the abbot of the Stoudios Monastery, the most powerful and influential monastic institution in the capital at that time, were to attempt to acquire ownership rights or guardianship of the monastery or almshouse, the eparch was commanded to intervene.[106] In return for his services, the eparch was to have his name inscribed in the holy diptychs and commemorated, and he was also to receive 5 *nomismata*. The latter demonstrates just how embedded gift-giving was within Byzantine legal culture; moreover, to our knowledge, giving such a gift to the eparch was not an illegal act. According to the aforementioned novel of Constantine VII, city judges were not allowed to accept any

[106] Michael Attaleiates, *Diataxis* 75; English translation by Alice-Mary Talbot in *BMFD*, vol. I, 326–76, here 351–2.

gifts, but there is no similar surviving regulation for the eparch. In the three monastic testaments discussed to this point, all of them from the tenth or eleventh century, the aid of the highest-ranking legal official within a particular jurisdiction is invoked, in two out of three cases in exchange for bequests. Nor were the bequests always worldly. Athanasios of Athos, the founder of the Great Lavra on Mount Athos, which today hosts the largest Orthodox monastic community in the world, promised spiritual rewords to the imperial official (an *epitropos*, later an *ephoros*) entrusted with supervising Athos.[107] Demonstrably so in this monastic milieu, gift-giving and patronage ensured the independence of the testators' foundations.

A case from the *Peira* illustrates the role the thematic judge played in the execution of testaments. In this instance, a testator left behind a bequest for the judge in his will. However, since he did not mention the judge by name, both the thematic judge who was in office at the time of the making of the will as well as the thematic judge who next took the office and opened the will took the bequest, causing the heirs of the testator to sue the judges. Upon the case being brought to Eustathios Rhomaios' attention, he decided that the judge who had been in office at the time that the will had been made needed to be questioned before the case could come to a resolution.[108] Again, this *Peira* case demonstrates how legal officials, particularly the thematic judge, were called upon to safeguard the testator's wishes.

[107] Athanasios of Athos, *Testament* 125; English translation by George Dennis in *BMFD*, vol. I, 271–80, here 275.

[108] *Peira* 43.5: "Someone in Mesopotamia wrote a will, and he wrote in it concerning a bequest specifically thus: 'I leave by my authority a sum of so many *nomismata* to the [thematic] judge.' While the testator was still living the judge ended his term in office, and another one was put forward. The testator died, and the [first] judge took the bequest before the opening of the will. And he left office, and the other judge came, and he performed the opening of the will and the summary of the estate. And he [the second judge] took the bequest. However, the heirs brought suit, claiming that the two judges had requested two bequests, and the [first judge] said 'the bequest was left to me. For I was in office at the time of his death.' And the other replied, 'But I opened the will and made the division [of the estate], so I was right to take the bequest.' And such were the statements. And I asked the *magistros*, and he said the following: 'The testator seems to have left the bequest to the thematic judge who was in office after his death and who disposed of his estate, since he did not specifically write down the name of the judge, which would indicate his intention to us. But we should examine the judge at the time of the making of the will, whether it was to him. For if we find that he disposed of it to him, and he made a promise to him about a bequest or trustee, and after his term of office if he came to him about the estate and if he shared it with him, then from this evidence the judge who is in the document of the bequest is the one at the time of the making of the will and he should receive the bequest.' Cf. Chitwood 2013: 59–60.

Conclusion

Over the course of this chapter evidence from imperial novels, epistolography and monastic testaments has demonstrated that the practices of gift-giving and patronage were deeply embedded within Byzantine legal culture. The novels of Constantine VII concerning judges' salaries make it clear that it was customary for provincial judges to receive sums proportionate to the size of the cases which they were judging, and in fact his legislation merely regulates the amount that provincial judges were to receive, without outlawing the practice.

Kekaumenos writes that thematic judges expected to be bribed as a matter of course. Although such practices would be linked today with bribery and corruption in modern legal thought, they were essential for the creation and maintenance of relationships among the elite in the Middle Byzantine period. As shown above, there was no consistent definition of "bribery" in the normative legal sources, and therefore the practice occupied a gray area between the customary fees paid to legal officials, the so-called *sportulae* or *ektagiatika*, and illicit gifts which were in any case often demanded under the pretext of custom. *Sportulae* were only completely outlawed for the higher Constantinopolitan courts, such as the Court of the Hippodrome.

An examination of epistolography as well as testaments yielded further insights. Legal matters are occasionally featured in Byzantine letters, and the examples from this genre make clear that patronage constituted an important component of Byzantine legal culture. The analysis of Byzantine testaments revealed that both gift-giving and personal relationships were crucial for implementing a testator's wishes. Thus the highest-ranking legal official in a particular jurisdiction was often supplied with either money or goods to ensure that a foundation suffered no outside interference.

CHAPTER 3

Paradigms of Justice and Jurisprudence

Introduction

> The greatest contrast between 'classical' Roman and Byzantine legal literature lies in the intellectual quality of the legal thinking that speaks from them. With the exception of the Justinianic age, in which Tribonian was the directing genius behind the codification, Byzantine lawyers did not reach the level of legal sophistication of their Roman predecessors. To that extent our interpretation of Byzantine legal literature probably suffers from the difficulty we experience when trying to place ourselves in the position of these Byzantine lawyers, who apparently found it harder to grapple with a Roman legal heritage than, for example, the Italian lawyers of the high Middle Ages. It is not easy to ascertain to what extent they understood and put to good use the rich material at their disposal in, for instance, the *Basilica*. When dealing with Byzantine law it is probably best to abandon the modern habit of thinking too much of law as a system, an approach advocated in any case by the eclectic way the Byzantines have mostly proceeded in legal questions. At the end of the day, they lacked the legal mind characteristic of the ancient Romans.[1]

As the remarks of Bernard Stolte in the quotation above underline, it is clear to anyone who has compared Roman with Byzantine jurisprudence that the Byzantines interpreted and understood the law quite differently from their classical forebears. Though codified law was theoretically the basis of Byzantine jurisprudence, a whole range of other factors influenced the legal thinking not only of the typical Byzantine, but also of the Byzantine jurist. The variegated and complex way in which Byzantine jurisprudence functioned has led to various attempts to explain how it functioned. By far the most influential study of Byzantine jurisprudence, Dieter Simon's classic *Rechtsfindung am byzantinischen Reichsgericht* (published in 1973), an examination of the *Peira*, an anonymously compiled

[1] Stolte 2008: 691. Similar comments in Stolte 2009: 89.

work consisting of the decisions of the high-court judge Eustathios Rhomaios, highlighted the (by the standards of modern jurisprudence) highly eclectic way by which Eustathios reached his verdicts.[2] Simon proved, convincingly, that Byzantine judges practiced a style of jurisprudence which suited their Orthodox Christian worldview, in explicit contrast to the modern judge who supposedly reaches a decision without personal bias. Therefore these judges would justify a particular decision with reference both to Roman law as well as to concepts and paradigms outside of the classical Roman legal tradition, such as notions of Christian clemency, biblical conceptions of justice and even anecdotes from the literature of the Byzantine educational curriculum. Byzantine legal texts thus constituted, in words of the Austrian legal historian Peter Pieler, "collections of topoi" (*Topoisammlungen*), which could be deployed as needed to justify a particular decision or position.[3] Simon himself concluded, somewhat facetiously, that Michael Psellos' claim that it was sufficient for a Byzantine jurist to study only rhetoric had perhaps been true.[4]

Since the publication of *Rechtsfindung*, a truly groundbreaking study in many respects and by far the most influential essay on Byzantine jurisprudence ever written, Middle Byzantine jurisprudence in particular has received only the barest of scrutiny from scholars.[5] Most scholars have continued to more or less accept Simon's interpretation of Byzantine jurisprudence as an essentially rhetorical exercise.[6] Though *Rechtsfindung* is an excellent study of the jurisprudence of one high-ranking Byzantine jurist, to extrapolate a societal conception of Byzantine legal thought from only the redacted writings of Eustathios Rhomaios is analogous to describing eighteenth-century English legal thought solely via the writings

[2] Simon 1973, translated as well into Modern Greek by Konidares 1982.

[3] Pieler 1978: 348–9.

[4] Simon 1973: 32.

[5] To my knowledge there is exists only one monograph on Byzantine jurisprudence, that of Lipshits 1981; due to the pernicious tenacity of *russica non leguntur* among Byzantinists, myself included, Lipshits' (as well as the work of Russian Byzantine scholarship more generally) contributions to the study of Middle Byzantine jurisprudence have not been evaluated by most specialists, especially legal historians. Oikonomides 1986 (discussed below) represents another way at looking at Eustathios' jurisprudence.

[6] Weiss 1973a reaches conclusions regarding Eustathios' jurisprudence similar to those of Simon. As John Haldon wrote in his study of the seventh-century transformation of Byzantine society, "Byzantine judges worked within a widely respected normative judicial framework only at the most general level. They did not order and interpret their case material within a pre-existing normative system according to which the correct interpretation and the solution to a given problem could be read off. Their activity was seen instead as determined by moral-ethical considerations within a Christian framework, drawing upon the accepted principles of an orthodox culture and the accepted 'common-sense' understanding of the society as a whole." (Haldon 1997: 278).

of William Blackstone. Eustathios Rhomaios represented the pinnacle of Middle Byzantine legal learning; more recent studies of the *Peira* have, moreover, confirmed that he interpreted Byzantine law correctly, in contrast to his characterization in *Rechtsfindung*.[7] Nor were the plaintiffs and defendants of the *Peira* representative of Byzantine society: they were clearly the empire's elite, able to afford the rather considerable costs of using the system of secular courts.[8]

Any description of Middle Byzantine jurisprudence and legal thought must of course reckon with an outlier, in terms of the depth of his knowledge of Roman law, like Eustathios Rhomaios. However, as this book is an analysis of Byzantine legal culture, this chapter will range widely between different sources from various genres to present, to the extent that such an undertaking is possible, a representative picture of legal thought in Middle Byzantine society. In the following pages jurisprudence will be explored via the three threads of Byzantine legal culture used throughout this study: (1) the Roman legal and political heritage; (2) the ethical and moral perspective of Orthodox Christianity; and (3) a Hellenic cultural and linguistic orientation.

The Roman Legal and Political Heritage

> Byzantine law was in principle a codified system. In such a system the sentence of a judge must be based on one or more passages, 'articles', of a code of a law previously issued by the legislator. In other words, the judge needs the authority of the legislator and is unable to 'create' law on his own or to build on previous judgements only, so-called 'precedents'. It is this aspect that distinguishes Anglo-American common law from continental, codified law.[9]

Legal scholars have long classified Middle Byzantine law as a codified system, or a legal system within which the law is applied from a discrete set of written rules. In a general sense this classification is correct. Whatever its deviations from the letter of Roman law, there is no doubt that the grounding for any legal decision was Roman law, at least as it was preserved

[7] Many of Eustathios' presumed idiosyncrasies are, moreover, actually those of the *Peira*'s anonymous redactor, a jurist of considerably lesser skill than his master. Sirks 2009 and 2010 shows that Eustathios correctly applied Roman/Byzantine law in his cases.

[8] For the fees associated with Byzantine secular courts, see in general Ch. 2. Simon 1973: 9–10 on the Court of the Hippodrome as a *Klassengericht*.

[9] Stolte 1998: 270–1.

in the various Macedonian redactions or Late Antique commentaries and paraphrases of Justinianic law. Well into the twentieth century, legal scholars postulated an essentially uninterrupted continuity of the Roman legal tradition into the Byzantine period.[10] Since that time there have arisen reasons to doubt the strength of this continuity, as shall be shown later in this chapter. Nonetheless, it is important to emphasize that, of the examples of jurisprudence which survive from the Middle Byzantine period, almost all decisions or verdicts were framed within the compass of Roman law. The seeming constraints of a legal system based on fixed set of codified laws should not suggest that the Byzantine law was static; much like countries today which employ a civil law system, in the Middle Byzantine case outward stasis masked surprising inner adaptability.[11]

If Roman law was the basis of the Byzantine jurisprudence, did the Byzantines understand Roman law in the same way modern jurists understand a civil code, as a discrete set of laws sanctioned by the state (in this case the emperor)? In this regard describing the legal system of the Byzantine Empire as a codified system is a misleading comparison, because Byzantine jurists had a much more expansive view of what law actually was than legal scholars working within a civil law country today. Indicative of the expansive Byzantine understanding is the phrase "The Breadth of the Laws" (*to platos ton nomon*), often employed by Middle Byzantine jurists, to refer to all of the valid law in existence.[12] Individual jurists would have disagreed as to what it encompassed. Depending on the definition, "The Breadth of the Laws" included the *Corpus Iuris Civilis*, the various didactic materials of the *antecessores* and *scholastikoi* as well as post-Justinianic legislation. It is possible that private legal collections of the period may have also fallen in this category in certain cases.[13] Some scholars have seen didactic juristic works and imperially sanctioned law as

[10] Edwin Hammond Freshfield, a translator of several Byzantine legal collections into English, opined in 1928 that "I must again remind the student that there was no break in the continuity of Roman law" (Freshfield 1928: p. vii). Fifty years later Peter Pieler expressed essentially the same sentiment in his overview of Byzantine legal literature (Pieler 1978: 343). On the degree to which Byzantine law was Roman law see Stolte 2003–4. In the scholarship on Byzantine law, the question of the importance of Roman law in Byzantine law has understandably dominated scholarship for centuries, the traditional view being that the Byzantines acted as conservators, albeit at times flawed ones, of the Roman legal tradition: cf. Stolte 1998: 268.

[11] Stolte 1998: 276–7.

[12] It has also been argued that "The Breadth of the Laws" referred to a standardized Greek translation of the *CIC*, based on the *indices* (translations and paraphrases) of the *antecessores*, at least until the end of the ninth century; see Signes Codoñer and Andrés Santos 2007: 246–67.

[13] See Ch. 4.

sets of competing norms within Byzantine law.[14] The two sets of sources were occasionally presented as representing different points of view, as in the so-called *Medidatio de nudis pactis* ("Treatise on Open Pacts"), an eleventh-century legal tract in which the author argued for the superiority of the interpretation of the late Roman jurist Stephan over passages in the *Basilika* concerning whether the parties to an open pact were subject to any obligations.[15] More often they played complementary roles, with didactic materials such as commentaries and paraphrases serving to elucidate difficult and even contradictory passages in the *Basilika*. The synodal edicts of the patriarch Alexios Stoudites (1025–43) are an illustration of this phenomenon, in which contradictory ordinances regarding the legal status of heretics and Jews in the Justinianic legislation were clarified via the *scholia* of Byzantine jurists.[16]

Outside of the *Basilika*, there existed two other legitimate sources of legal authority: custom and the emperor himself. Within Roman law, custom acquired legal sanction where there existed no written law.[17] This principle is stated in the *Basilika* as follows: "From Ulpian: Longstanding custom takes precedent in place of law in those situations where there is no written [law]."[18] A longer passage elaborates:

> From Ulpian: Concerning matters where there is no written law, one must observe tradition and custom. Failing this, one must follow what is fitting and appropriate in the matter under investigation. And if none of these [methods] yields a result, then the ordinance which Rome utilizes must be observed. For ancient custom is observed in place of law. Just as the establishment of the law is either written or unwritten, thus also its repeal can come about through law written or unwritten, that is in the case of disuse.[19]

In classical Roman legal thought, the difference between law (*nomos*) and custom (*synetheia* or *ethos*) was between written and unwritten law. As an anonymous scholiast to the *Basilika* explained, "Law and custom differ in this one respect only: law happens to be written custom, and custom is unwritten law."[20] Custom continued to play an important role throughout the period of Macedonian rule as well, at least to judge by frequency with

[14] Notably Scheltema 1958a: 41.
[15] The *Meditatio de nudis pactis* is discussed more thoroughly in Ch. 6.
[16] See Ch. 5.
[17] Kazhdan and Bartusis 1991.
[18] *Basil.* 2.1.42.
[19] *Basil.* 2.1.41.
[20] *Basil. Schol.* 2.1.1.1.

which custom was granted the force of law in the legislation of Leo VI and other emperors.[21] It has recently been argued that the use of custom was attenuated in the ninth and tenth centuries by legislatively inclined emperors as well as by changing social conditions in the countryside, such as the conflict between the "poor" and "powerful."[22]

The other main source of legitimate legal authority, indeed the highest authority beneath God himself, was the emperor; a Byzantine expression of the Platonic *nomos empsychos* or "law incarnate."[23] The scholarship on Byzantine political thought has traditionally been awed by the power allocated to the emperor by normative legal texts: one would certainly draw this conclusion from reading the relevant passages in the *Basilika*. Theoretically, the emperor was not subject to the laws of his empire.[24] The extent of imperial control over the written law was stated bluntly as "Whatever pleases the emperor is law … "[25] This power to change the written laws was exercised in the form of edicts or novels, which often addressed particular abuses of the legal system. The edicts against the "powerful" (*dynatoi*), enacted by the Macedonian emperors, are an

[21] The discussion of Silvestrova 2011 on the use of custom in the *Novels of Leo VI* (via the example of fishing rights) gives a good overview of the problem. More recently Kaldellis 2015: 9–14 has interpreted Leo's elevation of custom to law as indicative of the constitutional power of the common populace. While this is an interesting view, it is undercut by two considerations: first, that custom was accorded the power of written law only where no legislation was already in place; and secondly, that Leo's actions were well within the parameters of the importance granted to custom by Roman and Byzantine law.

[22] Sarris 2011. Sarris makes a number of incisive points in this article, including the pervasiveness of legal knowledge at all levels of Byzantine society, even the peasantry. However, an increasing use of documents in legal disputes cited by Sarris does not necessarily imply an increased familiarity with the written law. Indeed, most disputes described in the various surviving monastic archives were settled without actually referring to the legal texts of any sort. Even when normative legal texts like the *Basilika* were cited, for instance in the *Peira* (added by the text's anonymous redactor and not part of the original *hypomnemata* of Eustathios Rhomaios), it is interesting to see just what was considered valid law. Indeed, even one of the examples cited by Sarris 2011: 58, *Peira* 15.3, to show the importance of using "codified" law in legal disputes, is in fact yet another example of the importance of the writings of the *antecessores* in Byzantine jurisprudence ("ἑρμηνεύει δὲ εἰς τοῦτο καὶ ὁ στέφανος"). That the writings of the antecessor Stephan were the basis of the decision would explain the *Peira* editor's (i.e. Zachariä von Lingenthal's) perplexity at the mention of the Justinianic *Codex* in connection with Stephan's writings: the references to the *Basilika* and *Codex* were added later by the *Peira*'s redactor, in many cases without a clear connection to the cases themselves.

[23] Kaldellis 2015: 70–82 offers a convincing and at the same time highly revisionist take on the *nomos empsychos*. For the origins of the idea in Greek philosophy, see Ramelli 2006, who however does not explore the Late Antique and then Byzantine appropriation of the idea.

[24] *Basil.* 2.6.1: "The emperor is not subject to the laws. The empress is subject to them. However, the emperor gives her his privileges."

[25] *Basil.* 2.6.2.

excellent example of the corrective power Byzantine emperors exercised upon the legal system.

Yet it would be misleading to overemphasize the emperor's role as the *nomos empsychos* or to somehow conclude that he was above the law in practice, as Anthony Kaldellis has shown in his impressive *Byzantine Republic*.[26] The dynamic that arose between the emperor exercising his opinion as law and the law itself is demonstrated by some cases from the Court of the Hippodrome which are documented in the *Peira*. One case, revolving around the confiscation of property of those who assist in bride-kidnapping, highlights a contradiction between an ordinance of Romanos III Argyros (r. 1028–34), himself a former judge, and the *Basilika*.[27] In this instance, the intent of the emperor is important: whether he meant to exercise authority only in a particular case or meant to apply it to the whole empire. If he had intended his prescriptions as a new law, then the judges reminded the emperor that there already existed provisions concerning those who assisted in bride-kidnapping.[28]

In addition to the written evidence of imperial legislation, one case in the *Peira* demonstrates the fascinating phenomenon of the transmission of unwritten imperial opinion. *Peira* 15.2 states:

> The *Bestes* [i.e. Eustathios Rhomaios] said that an owner cannot legally eject *paroikoi* [peasant tenants] who are found to have been granted the lands of their tenancy without interruption and to have paid rent for a thirty-year period. These ones are like owners through the length of their possession, but they have the obligation to pay rent. And he [the *Bestes*] said that he heard this, that the blessed Lord Basil [i.e. Basil II, r. 976–1025] had said that one should [only] eject one's own *paroikoi* for well-founded reasons.[29]

[26] Kaldellis 2015: 32–61.

[27] This case is discussed and provided with a German translation in Weiss 1973a: 128–9. *Peira* 61.3: "The Magistros [maintained] that the emperor Romanos wrote that the possessions of those who assist in bride-kidnapping [Gr. *haparge* /Lat. *raptio*] are to be confiscated by the state. But the judges answered, that if this was written for his personal power or assertion thereof, it requires no correction. But if he wrote it for the law, his holy majesty ought to recognize the law ordains that the possessions of those who participate in bride-kidnapping and those who aid in the seizure of women shall belong to the women who were attacked. It subjects those who knew about it or those serving them or those who in some way incited them to the bride-kidnapping only to certain penalties, and does not cause their property to be lost."

[28] Namely *Basil.* 60.58.1. This law is richly commented upon by the scholia tradition, with three scholia (*Basil. Schol.* 60.58.1.9–11) making explicit reference to the *Peira*'s handling of the case. On the practice of bride-kidnapping in Byzantine law, see Deles 2005.

[29] Weiss 1973a: 130–1. *Peira* 15.2.

As this passage demonstrates, even the transmission of imperial oral opinion, in function practically a Byzantine *hadith*, could be invoked as a source of legitimate law.

This *Peira* case alludes to a further legacy of Roman society which played an important role in Byzantine jurisprudence, namely that of social class. Although there are various schemas for describing the class structure of Middle Byzantine society, the one used in this study, which in fact very well fits the way the legal system was used by various societal groups, is one recently advanced by John Haldon.[30] In his social breakdown of Byzantine society, there are two overlapping groups of elites, namely a power elite and an elite in general. The larger of these two elite groups, the elite in general, sometimes also called the ruling or dominant class, consists of "those who, broadly speaking, occupied a social and economic situation which either reflected, or ensured access to, senior positions in state and church, social esteem from their peers, the ability to transmit their social, economic, and cultural capital to their offspring, and the ability to control resources in terms of land and its products, manpower, and movable wealth."[31] A subset of the ruling class is that of the power elite, which is "the leading fraction of the economically dominant social strata, those who shared a situation in respect of access to political/ideological power and influence, in particular at Constantinople and in the various branches of the imperial administration."[32] One can therefore delineate a third group as an *Unterschicht* consisting of everyone excluded from the elite or power elite, which will be referred to here as the "lower classes" or "lower social strata."[33]

Many of the novels of the Macedonian emperors starting at the beginning of the tenth century during the reign of Romanos I Lekapenos (r. 920–44) make provisions for the protection of "poor" (*ptochoi* or *penetes*) peasants against the incursions of "powerful" (*dynatoi*) predatory landowners.[34] The ability to designate parties in court as "poor" or "powerful"

[30] Haldon 2009c. In that same edited volume he has also written an excellent overview of the various approaches to social history in Byzantium as well as many of the broader methodological and theoretical issues with which it is intertwined; see Haldon 2009c. The role that social class played in identity and ideology, hitherto downplayed by Byzantinists, has recently been explored in the wide-ranging study of Stouraitis 2014. Grünbart 2015 represents the latest comprehensive attempt to define the elite, which he defines instead as the aristocracy (Grünbart 2015: 14–15).

[31] Haldon 2009b: 171.

[32] Haldon 2009b: 172.

[33] Note that Haldon restricts his analysis to the two respective groups of elites; this third category is used here for the sake of convenience.

[34] See Cappel 1991a; 1991b; Kaplan 1992: 359–444; Morris 1976. Note however that Cappel's definition, with reference to *Prochiron* 27.13 as supposedly defining "poor" as someone who had a

had no exact precedent in Justinianic law (terms for the "poor" and "powerful" are used in the *CIC*, but usually in a more general way), although offices like the Late Antique *defensor civitatis* demonstrate that the government certainly had shown concern for the poor in the legal sphere.[35]

Besides the description of the "powerful" found in the novel of Romanos Lekapenos which first announced the measures which were to be taken against them, one also finds a number of criteria used to determine whether someone could be counted as a "powerful" person in lawbooks of the period. At the end of the ninth century poverty was defined in the *Prochiron*, whereby someone who is "poor" (*penetes*) was unable to serve as a witness if he possessed an estate (*periousia*) worth less than 50 *nomismata*.[36] This definition is found within the *Peira* as well, although in a slightly different context. Here, the conditions for prosperity (*euporia*), and thus the capacity to serve as a witness, are listed: a witness must either possess a title, his own *strateia* (which by the eleventh century was a fiscal obligation to equip a soldier), a trade/business or an estate of 50 *nomismata*.[37] The *Peira* passage would suggest that a person was defined as "poor" only in the absence of other potential poverty-negating criteria; that is, by no means was every person with an estate of less than 50 *nomismata* considered "poor," but only those people who did not possess a livelihood (*epitedeuma*), a *strateia* or title.[38]

Outside of this (admittedly not widespread in the sources) 50-*nomismata* definition of poverty as a qualification to serve as a witness,

property valued at less than 50 *nomismata* should instead be *Prochrion* 27.22; the former passage cited concerns witnesses and what to do if they disagree with one another. For the use of "poor" and "rich" in Late Antique/Early Byzantine legal texts, see Patlagean 1977: 9–35.

35 Jones 1964: 480–2.

36 *Prochiron* 27.22: "The poor are not to serve as witnesses. A poor person does not possess an estate of [at least] 50 *nomismata*." This regulation is repeated in the *Eisagoge* as well (*Eisagoge* 22.8). This definition of poverty is based on *Dig.* 48.2.10: "Some [are unable to accuse others of a criminal offense] on account of poverty, such as those those who have less than 50 *aurei*." Interestingly, the *Digest* passage concerns a completely different matter, that of making accusations in criminal cases, rather than rendering testimony in general, which is the case in the relevant passages in the *Eisagoge* and *Prochiron*.

37 *Peira* 30.2.

38 Morris' rejection of the possibility that this definition of poverty was ever actually used (Morris 1977: 22, n. 55), is, I think, unwarranted. The limited context in which this 50 *nomismata* definition of poverty is discussed, that is concerning the qualifications of witnesses, tends to broadly agree with other qualifications witnesses were supposed to possess. In general, and this is confirmed by a perusal of the surviving monastic documents from this period, witnesses were almost always of high social standing: officials of various rank, village elders, churchmen, etc. Whether or not this definition of poverty was used in other contexts is more of an open question, but as a qualification to serve as a witness it would certainly not have been out of tune with other regulations regarding the characteristics witnesses were supposed to possess.

there appears to have been no officially accepted definition of what conditions were necessary to designate a party "poor" or "powerful"; it was probably left to the discretion of the judge. In cases deigned to be between "poor" and "powerful" parties, the party designated as "poor" paid a lower schedule of legal fees and was supposedly protected from predatory land acquisition by "powerful" parties.[39]

The imperial legislation regarding the "poor" and "powerful" seems to have been followed by judges. In fact, Title 9 of the *Peira* concerns among other things, the "poor." One case mentions a novel of Basil II which states that the sale of a "poor" person's farm to a "powerful" person is not valid unless there is a great famine, as there was in the time of Romanos I, or if the transaction precedes the time of the legislation.[40] "Poor" possessors of "poor" or "rich" property could gain ownership of it after a thirty-year period through the so-called *longi temporis praescriptio*; "powerful" persons could not.[41] Persons designated as "powerful" were condemned for buying land illegally.[42] The monastic record likewise confirms that Macedonian legislation against the "powerful" was enforced. In a verdict of the judge Samonas dated to the year 952, which confirmed the validity of a sale and then donation of a brickworks to the Monastery of Peristerai, it is mentioned that the brickworks was surrounded by "powerful" persons, and that no "poor" neighbor could be found to invoke the right of first offer of sale or preemption (*protimesis*).[43]

The protections accorded to the "poor" seemed to have been occasioned by a situation in which the "powerful" often resorted to violent means to acquire the properties of the "poor." This was the case in the aforementioned sale and then donation of the brickworks, as its neighboring landowners, led by the *droungarios* John, even used force to contest the monastery's claim to the property.[44] Although the terms "powerful" and "poor" are not mentioned in it, the following case clearly describes the type of occurrence which the Macedonian dynasty's legislation against the "powerful" was meant to prevent:

39 See Ch. 2.

40 *Peira* 9.1. On Romanos I's program of social welfare to alleviate the suffering caused by this famine, see Kresten 2002.

41 *Peira* 8.1. On the *longi temporis praescriptio* see Fögen 1991b and Nörr 1969. Note that the conclusion of Sarris 2011: 60 that Basil II, in his novel of 996, abolished the *longi temporis praescriptio* is incorrect, as he actually quite specifically states that this provision is only invalid for "powerful" persons acquiring the property of the "poor."

42 E.g. *Peira* 9.2.

43 *Lavra*, vol. I, no. 4 (952), lines 23–4.

44 *Lavra*, vol. I, no. 4 (952), lines 15–18.

> The *protospatharios* Romanos Skleros roughed up some villagers and came to their residence, then he forced them to make an agreement with him whereby they would offer gold to him, and a transaction was made. But the villagers afterward brought suit, [claiming] that they made the settlement under duress, and that the [thematic] judge had compelled them [to agree to the settlement].[45]

Another legacy of the Roman social order in Byzantine jurisprudence was the penal system.[46] In this regard Roman law was an essentially unfair institution. While different penalties for the rich and poor are understandable for levying fines for misdemeanor offences, Roman law also proscribed different penalties for each group for more serious crimes, often to the detriment of the poor. A major shift in penal law was brought about by the eighth-century *Ecloga*, which under the leitmotif of making law more humane (*epidiorthosis eis to philanthropoteron*) not only mandated more lenient penalties for capital offenses (e.g. amputation instead of the death penalty in many cases), but also set punishments which would be enacted upon the rich and poor alike.[47] Though the penal provisions of the *Ecloga* were enthusiastically adopted by the Macedonian redactions of Byzantine law, in the *Basilika* the older Justinianic provisions were not excised.[48] Byzantine judges thus had to deal with penal provisions which occasionally contradicted one other.

Orthodox Christianity

The diachronic changes in the role of social class in differentiating between different types of punishments underline the fact that the Roman legal and social heritage did not remain static during the Middle Byzantine period. In particular Orthodox Christianity, the second thread of Byzantine jurisprudence and of Byzantine legal culture in general, had an enormous impact in shaping how judges, jurists and indeed typical Byzantines thought about and interpreted the law. Although Roman law had been Christianized since the time of Constantine I, to a significant extent these two strands of Middle Byzantine jurisprudence remained

[45] *Peira* 42.18.

[46] As in so many other areas the summary of Zachariä 1892: 330–4 is still unsurpassed.

[47] On the penal law of the *Ecloga*, see Sinogowitz 1956; Bibikov 2007; Humphreys 2015: 118–25. The study of Troianos 1980 on the penal law of the *Eklogadion* is a very useful discussion of the changes in penal law from the *CIC* to the *Basilika*. For the interpretation that this Eclogian "betterment" was a stylistic rather than substantive change in the law, see Schminck 2015a: 469–74.

[48] Zachariä von Lingenthal 1892: 333–4.

contradictory. If one were to generalize this dynamic in the simplest way, then it could be characterized as the tension between the role of the law as an impartial instrument of justice and objective seeker of truth (Roman law) and its function as a societal necessity which had to be ameliorated and softened in its application (Orthodox Christianity). This was a complex and multifaceted interaction: Byzantine jurists adopted Orthodox theological concepts like *philanthropia* ("mercy"), *oikonomia* ("dispensation") and *kainotomia* ("innovation") and applied them to legal texts and the exercise of jurisprudence; notions of divine retribution for illegal acts influenced legal practice; and the influence and importance of Byzantine canon law became greater, foreshadowing the eventual subsuming of Byzantine secular law itself within canon law and the golden age of the Byzantine canonists.

Philanthropia, itself a leitmotif of Byzantine civilization, is a good place to begin exploring the role of Orthodox Christian precepts in Byzantine jurisprudence.[49] In Classical Greek *philanthropia* was an important component of Hellenistic kingship, in which context it could be translated as "benevolence."[50] As the Roman Empire was Christianized, so was *philanthropia*.[51] Though in the New Testament the Greek word *agape* is used for Christian charity (I Cor. 13:4–8), *philanthropia* began to replace it already in the first centuries of Christianity to become the predominant term for Christian charity.[52] From there it became a trait of an ideal Christian emperor, the Byzantine *basileus*.[53] Agapetos the Deacon, the sixth-century author of the most influential Byzantine *Mirror of Princes*, recommended that the emperor confront his enemies with force and his subjects with *philanthropia*, which he described as "weaponless charity" (*aoplos agape*).[54]

From its status as an imperial virtue the drive to practice *philanthropia* was disseminated throughout the Byzantine administration, and there are abundant references to it in a legal context. Within Middle Byzantine jurisprudence, the Orthodox Christian imperative to judge mercifully and humanely, that is with *philanthropia*, was considered to be among the most important traits of a good judge. The eleventh-century aristocrat

[49] The classic essay on *philanthropia* is Hunger 1963.

[50] See Schubart 1937.

[51] Constantelos 1991: 3–9 discusses the antique origins of Christian *philanthropia*, though he overemphasizes the diachronic Hellenic nature of the term. Cf. Herrin 2013b: 271.

[52] Constantelos 1991: 26–7 ascribes this shift in vocabulary to the theologians of the Alexandrian School.

[53] On this transformation see Rapp 2009.

[54] Agapetos the Deacon, *Mirror of Princes*, §20.

Kekaumenos admonished one tasked with judging a case to render a verdict with *philanthropia*, even if a multitude urging the prosecution had been proved right.[55] This statement is prefaced by the story of Christ before Pontius Pilate; though Pilate had the power to release Christ, he chose not to do, instead giving in to the demands of the crowd. For this error he himself would be judged harshly.[56]

The eleventh-century bishop of Euchaïta, John Mauropous, in a letter to a judge on behalf of a friend likewise emphasizes the importance of *philanthropia* in judgment: "If disputed matters are resolved by others in the spirit of *philanthropia*, I suppose for you it is more fitting to show greater humanity than any other in your deliberations and to include much benevolence in your decisions … "[57] Likewise, Mauropous in another letter asks for clemency for a friend who was accused of smuggling. Though the bishop knows the unbending harshness of the law, he maintains that, even if the accused is guilty, it is nonetheless the duty of the judge to imitate God's mercy: "In summary, if they appear to be completely free of guilt, deliver them, o upright guardian of the laws, to the laws and to justice. But if not, then it is commanded by Merciful God, to imitate the fatherly *philanthropia* of God, just as He Himself is merciful."[58] In this case the act of applying clemency by the judge was imagined as an emulation of God's love toward mankind. In these contexts, the intransigency of the law required the mitigation of love and mercy.

Though Middle Byzantine texts evince a strong preference for showing *philanthropia*, its exercise was not completely unchecked. True, the *Basilika* commands that "it is necessary to interpret the laws humanely."[59] Yet judging a case humanely still had to occur within the framework of the Roman law. Eustathios Rhomaios remarked upon this dichotomy in *Peira* 51.22, where he notes one law which says to give milder verdicts and another law which states that judges should not depart from the prescribed boundaries of the law. His solution was the following: "A judge who follows this legal rule, where he finds two fitting punishments, one harsh and one milder, thinks to give a legal verdict by especially favoring the milder."[60] Nonetheless, even the milder sentence had to have a legal basis.

[55] Kekaumenos, *Strategikon* 2.29.
[56] Ibid. 2.16–26.
[57] John Mauropous, *Letters*, Letter 31, lines 23–7.
[58] Ibid., Letter 11, lines 18–21.
[59] *Basil.* 2.1.18.
[60] *Peira* 51.22.

Eustathios in the aforementioned case hints at another concept which was imported from Orthodox theology into the realm of Middle Byzantine jurisprudence: *oikonomia*. In Classical Greek *oikonomia* was associated with first and foremost with the management of estates and households, and indeed it continued to have these connotations in Byzantine Greek as well, with the *oikonomos* being the manager of a monastery's fiscal and economic affairs.[61] As is the case with *philanthropia*, *oikonomia* is a theological term rich in meaning, which one could perhaps translate as "dispensation."[62] As a legal concept, *oikonomia* became a commonplace of Middle and Late Byzantine jurisprudence, as well as the entire Orthodox canon law tradition.[63]

Oikonomia was a fluid notion, the precise uses of which were rarely delimited by Byzantine authors, with Theodore the Stoudite, who advocated its use only in rare circumstances, constituting a notable exception.[64] Essentially, a judge could invoke *oikonomia* when confronted with a legal contradiction or impasse: two contradictory laws, say, or an unduly harsh penalty. *Oikonomia* allowed the judge to find some sort of accommodation: in the case of the two contradictory laws, by picking provisions from each which would allow him to reach a verdict, or, in the case of the unduly harsh penalty, by arbitrarily reducing it to something that seemed more reasonable.

Invoking *oikonomia* really had no antecedent in Roman law: the term itself or related forms (like the verb *oikonomeo*) do not appear in the main text of the *Basilika*. Yet the increasing acceptance of *oikonomia* as a concept that could be invoked in a secular law context is demonstrated by its limited appearance in the scholia to the *Basilika*.[65] In two cases the scholiasts cite Basilian canons (*Basil. Schol.* 60.39.4.3; 60.39.22.3) while commenting upon a law which forbids magistrates from murdering people on a whim.

Yet it is the use of the term of *oikonomia* that marks a paradigm shift in jurisprudence, from a Roman to a distinctly mode of Byzantine mode of

[61] Dagron 1990: 2–3.

[62] An excellent overview of the development of *oikonomia* as a theological concept in Dagron 1990. Until recently there was no comprehensive study of *oikonomia* in Byzantine theology, and one had to instead consult, among others, the essays of Cupane 1988 and Erickson 1977. The massive study of Richter 2005: 453–574 has changed this state of affairs.

[63] Dagron 1990: 17, with a brief discussion of its use by the jurists Eustathios Rhomaios and Demetrios Chomatenos.

[64] Dagron 1990: 6–7.

[65] *Basil. Schol.* 28.5.7.1 (an "old" or sixth-century scholion from Enantiophanes); 60.39.4.3 (citing the 65th canon of Basil of Caesarea); 60.39.22.3 (citing the 56th canon of Basil of Caesarea).

legal reasoning.[66] It is mentioned seven times in the *Peira*, yet even where it is not invoked the same principle of seeking some sort of accommodation by bending the exact letter of the law is discernable throughout the text.[67] Oftentimes these accommodations amounted to rendering lighter sentences for crimes than what the law mandated. Thus a nobleman who had had sexual relations with a woman and then refused to marry her was fined five pounds (*litrai*) of gold instead of suffering a harsher penalty.[68] Likewise a man who had married a girl of 8 (her father had lied to him about her age) and was thus convicted of raping a minor, was severely flogged and tonsured, with half of his property being allocated to the girl.[69] The penalty prescribed had been the amputation of the nose and giving half his property to the victim; again, the letter of the law was not followed.

The penalties for murder as well were ameliorated by the judges of the *Peria*. For instance, someone who had murdered an official (a *skeptophoros*) claimed sanctuary by running into a church.[70] The judges of the Velum, employing more merciful reasoning (*oikonomoteros logos*), sent a directive to the resident thematic judge, instructing him to take his estate and, after removing his outstanding obligations, to give two-thirds of it to the heirs of the murdered man and to leave one-third to the murderer. This was a remarkable act of mercy, as the murderer himself was not a rich man (with the implication that this settlement did not bring much money to the murdered man's family). In another case the *magklabites* Skeuenas had not himself murdered someone but rather had his men carry out the deed for him. If his estate (excluding outstanding obligations) exceeded ten pounds of gold, he was to give ten to the victim's wife and children.[71] If he did not have this amount then he would have to come to some sort of accommodation (*pros ten oikonomian elthein*).

The scholar who has written one of the most perceptive analyses of the *Peira*, Nicholas Oikonomides, saw the flexibility of Eustathios Rhomaios and his colleagues, notably through the invocation of *oikonomia*, as a daring and ultimately failed attempt to adapt Roman law to the conditions of eleventh-century Byzantine society.[72] For him as well as for many other

[66] Oikonomides 1986: 185, 191–2.

[67] *Peira* 1.14; 19.1; 41.11; 42.20; 45.7; 66.24; 66.25.

[68] *Peira* 49.4; cf. Oikonomides 1986: 184.

[69] *Peira* 49.22; cf. Oikonomides 1986: 184.

[70] *Peira* 66.24.

[71] *Peira* 66.25.

[72] Oikonomides 1986: 190–2.

scholars, the question of how a legal system, which had been codified in the sixth century under the auspices of the emperor Justinian, managed to adapt to the completely changed social, political and economic circumstances of the succeeding millennium proved extremely problematic. While imperial legislation as well as custom may have played a role in adapting the legal system to new challenges, nonetheless no introduction of a completely new set of written laws, à la Code Napoléon, was promulgated after the *CIC* during the entire political existence of the Byzantine Empire. This legal stasis prompted Oikonomides to suggest that the anonymous compiler of the *Peira* had intended that this textbook based on the writings of Eustathios Rhomaios would constitute a new source of law, thereby alleviating the need to refer to outdated law codes.

One does not have to search far and wide to find bizarre anachronisms in the *Basilika*. It contains titles, such as that of the late Roman *illustris*, which had long since fallen out of use.[73] References to lost provinces like those in Africa, Italy and Syria were without a second thought brought from the *CIC* to the *Basilika*. Nor were these unconscious borrowings: both the *Peira* and scholia to the *Basilika* show that Byzantine jurists earnestly struggled to interpret and apply these obsolete laws. In the case of the aforementioned title of *illustris*, they helpfully noted that it actually corresponded to the contemporaneous title of *protospatharios*.[74] *Peira* 16.10, for example, concerns a passage of the *Basilika* (*Bas*il. 37.2.15) granting a guardian a ward's property in Africa or Syria:

> There is a law which says "A guardian [*epitropos*] is able to be validly granted with matters in Syria or Africa of the ward." And [this] appears to contradict what is said earlier. But Stephan and the *magistros* interpreted it [thus], that the property of the ward in Africa and Syria is inviolate. At the same time a guardian of a child [i.e. ward] in Byzantium is unable to competently look after the ward's affairs in Africa because of the length of the road [there]. And for this reason a testator knows that he indeed can allow another guardian for the property in another territory; it [the property] is granted validly to the new [guardian].[75]

The difficulty of the above rule is that it refers to territories (Africa and Syria) which had been completely lost by the seventh century; this passage more than likely did not refer to any existing case. Even though the chances of a ward having property both in the Byzantine Empire and

[73] Kazhdan 1989: 8; Oikonomides 1986: 186–7.
[74] Oikonomides 1986: 186–7.
[75] *Peira* 16.10.

North Africa by the early eleventh century were practically nonexistent (though given the reconquest of Northern Syria in the second half of the tenth century, a ward owning property in both Byzantium and Syria is not inconceivable), Eustathios still felt compelled to solve a legal problem which likely had nothing to do with any of the cases he worked with by advocating that a testator could appoint a new guardian if a ward had property a great distance away from the original guardian.

This conscientious preservation and continuing use of anachronistic legal provisions should not only be ascribed to that inimitable conservatism in all things which the Byzantines are often accused of, but rather to a third theological concept alongside *philanthropia* and *oikonomia* which appeared in Middle Byzantine jurisprudence, that of *kainotomia* or "innovation."[76] In Orthodox theology, *kainotomia* came to be viewed in a very negative light, in the sense of introducing something new and therefore by implication heretical and contrary to received doctrine. Before the end of the ninth century there is no evidence that *kainotomia* was used in this sense in a legal context.[77]

Yet from its first appearance in the *Eisagoge*, *kainotomia* rapidly became another fixture of Byzantine jurisprudence with its origins in Orthodox theology. It is frequently used in the *Peira* to designate an irregular legal practice as illegal. Two short *Peira* cases will illustrate this point, with the first case explicitly rejecting innovation and the second implicitly condoning it. *Peira* 14.5 rejects an innovation regarding the number of witnesses needed to certify a will:

> For the security of a will, when of the seven undersigned witnesses two die, is valid through the remaining five. But if they all live, the security is not valid, unless all of them come and testify. And the *patrikios* Alopos did this. For he presented fifteen witnesses, that is fewer than those living who were undersigned in the will, and thus gave security to the will. But the *magistros* contradicted this, [saying] that it was instituting a legal innovation (*kainotomia*).[78]

According to Byzantine law, a will was invalidated unless it was attested by either five or seven witnesses.[79] Within the Justinianic legislation, wills

[76] Lampe 1961: 693; Trapp 1994: 734.

[77] Here I would like to thank Andreas Schminck for sharing with me work on *kainotomia* (Schminck 2015b: 140–4), in which he suggests that the introduction of the theological term into Byzantine jurisprudence is connected with Photios' authorship of the proem of the *Eisagoge* and his mention there of "sinful *kainotomia*," which was misunderstood by his collaborator Stylianos Zaoutzes and in this way entered the Byzantine juristic lexicon.

[78] *Peira* 14.5.

[79] *Basil.* 35.1.24.

were considered valid if a will was attested by seven witnesses. In the *Ecloga* the number of witnesses was reduced to five, thus explaining the allowance for five or seven witnesses in later redactions of Roman law.[80] A novel of Leo VI even allowed for three witnesses in places where there was a scarcity of men worthy enough to be called forth in this capacity.[81] For whatever reason, the provision allowing for three witnesses found in Leo VI's Novel 43 is not cited, which is either a deliberate omission or indicates an ignorance of Leo's legislation.[82] As is to be expected, legal innovation (*kainotomia*), in this case by having a large number of witnesses appear, more than the five or seven required, is rejected because not all of the living witnesses undersigned in the will appeared.

A last feature of Orthodox Christianity which played a role in Middle Byzantine jurisprudence consisted of conceptions of the afterlife and particularly the Last Judgment. While Byzantine and Orthodox ideas about the end times never became as doctrinally fixed as in the medieval West, in a way this allowed a great deal of freedom for the development of vastly different conceptions of what the hereafter would look like.[83] Given that so many other aspects of Byzantine society were projected onto the afterlife – a heavenly court reminiscent of the imperial one, tollbooths for sins and record bureaux which recorded virtuous and evil deeds instead of tax obligations – it is unsurprising that aspects of the courtroom experience can be found in Byzantine imaginings too.

Judges both good and bad made their way into this liminal space between life and death. The *Apocalypse of Anastasia*, composed around the year 1000, is the tale of a pious nun who suddenly died, and then over the course of three days journeyed through the afterlife before being called back to life by God. Right after visiting Paradise and the Heavenly

[80] On the number of witnesses needed to certify the validity of a will in Byzantine law, see Lokin 2010: 229–31.

[81] Leo VI, *Novels*, Novel 43: "We therefore decree that in every territory and city for the most part inhabited by the unlearned that for testaments, as is customary, witnesses [must] be trustworthy. And we do not set the limit to the number [of witnesses] to five, but in those places where, as it is likely, there is a scarcity of men worthy to serve as witnesses, then to three, since it is acceptable and better than annulment [of a testament]."

[82] See also e.g. *Peira* 14.6: "Neither in the political law nor in the praetorian law nor in the breadth of the novels does a testament signed by only three witnesses hold force ... " In addition *Peira* 14.23: "The *magistros* found a testament sealed by three witnesses, and he did not accept it, writing thus: Neither in the political nor the praetorian law nor in the breadth of the novels is the testament as it appears now valid. For it does not contain a sufficient number of witnesses, nor were they undersigned in it, but only three seals are affixed to the document."

[83] On the Byzantines and their conception of the hereafter, see Baun 2008; Beck 1979; Brubaker 2009; Constas 2001; Dagron 1980; Ombres 1984.

Records Office, she is taken to the equivalent of Dante's Ninth Circle of Hell, where especially wicked sinners are subjected to special punishment (including the emperor John I Tzimiskes (r. 969–76)). Here she encounters a high-ranking official (a *protospatharios*), Peter of Corinth, who had lived a truly wicked life. He admits to Anastasia that he had stolen lands, mistreated orphans and widows, had many people murdered and had judged unjustly for money.[84]

In the same era Theodora, a pious follower of the St Basil the Younger, recounted her own vision of the afterlife in the latter's *vita*, and was able to glimpse the polar opposite of judges like Peter of Corinth. The righteous judges, radiant, clad in cloaks in all the colors of the rainbow and wearing crowns not made by human hands, were able to enter the heavenly city through a special gate. They had hungered and thirsted after righteousness, refused bribes and judged rich and poor alike with the same unbending justice.[85] Both visions of the afterlife demonstrate that the Byzantine judge could not expect that the consequences of his conduct would be confined to this mortal sphere; his actions would have consequences in the hereafter.

The Byzantine judge, conscious of the post-temporal implications of his earthly behavior, certainly took the long-term behavior of his litigants into account as well. A litigant's history of moral rectitude or immorality clearly influenced the verdict of the judge. Individual lapses or violations of the law could be extremely leniently punished as long as they did not indicate more serious perceived failings of character. Once again, the general impulse toward clemency characteristic of Orthodox Christian theology was evident in the evaluation of crimes and moral failings. This was the case even in instances in which Byzantine canon law sternly punished individual lapses, such as adultery. When discussing the reasons whereby a wife could lose her dowry and be forcibly divorced from her husband, Eustathios Rhomaios lists among them drinking, bathing or going to the chariot races and theatre with other men, all of which raised the suspicion of adultery.[86] However, Eustathios is adamant that individual instances of these offenses are not to be punished by the law. He cleverly deduces this interpretation from the use of the present rather than aorist subjunctive in the words for "drinking together" (*symposiaze*) and "bathing together"

[84] *Apocalypse of Anastasia* 29–30. English translation in Baun 2008: 411, 423.
[85] *Life of Basil the Younger* 41.
[86] *Peira* 25.23.

(*sullouetai*). It is only, Eustathios insists, repeated instances of these offenses which necessitate divorce and the loss of a wife's dowry.

Likewise, repeated bad behavior could result in a judge giving preference to the opposing party. *Peira* 23.7 illustrates how the Byzantine judicial principle of partiality functioned in practice.

> Many suits were issued against the *magistros* Skleros, saying that he had effected the theft of some of their possessions, attacked their guards, and struck them. When the Magistros and the Droungarios [i.e. Eustathios Rhomaios] found out that someone had wrought vengeance, mistreated the guard, and that gold had been lost, this weighed only on him [i.e. *magistros* Skleros] to show that he could be excluded [as a suspect] or that the guard had been struck, and then [Eustathios Rhomaios] preferred that he take the oath [first], stating his logic as such: "Since you imprisoned him and struck him and mistreated him [in the past], there is an assumption [of guilt] (*prolepsis*), that you also committed that which was inflicted, and for that reason I prefer that he [the *magistros* Skleros] take an oath. For the presumption [of guilt] (*prolepsis*) is present." Normally, if no [past] violence or misdeed [of the defendant] can be demonstrated, then the Magistros refuses [to convict him], and it weighs on the plaintiff to demonstrate [that some violence or misdeed occurred]; if doubt exists an oath is to be rendered to the Magistros.[87]

The case is also mentioned in *Peira* 69.5:

> When [someone] struggles against a presumption [of guilt] (*prolepsis*), the defendant and the one contesting [the case] is not to be preferred [i.e. to take an oath first] to take an oath, but rather the plaintiff. And the Magistros ruled this. For many suits had been set in motion against the *magistros* Skleros, that he had taken away some of their gold and had inflicted wrongdoings on them and their guards. The Magistros [said], that if someone had inflicted some evil and imprisonments [upon others], then the plaintiff was received to swear, as to what he had lost. For he [Eustathios] said, that the *magistros* [Skleros] was struggling against a presumption of guilt (*prolepsis*). For since he struck a man or imprisoned him or inflicted some other evil, then it is likely that the crime was carried either by this very man [Skleros] or his men, on account of which the plaintiff is trustworthy.[88]

In the preceding passages, the *magistros* Skleros, who had been accused of attacking and striking guards in the past, is presumed to be guilty

[87] *Peira* 23.7.
[88] *Peira* 69.5.

when a similar case arises. Eustathios explains that because of his past behavior there exists a presumption (*prolepsis*) of guilt, and therefore he would have Skleros take an oath in the first case (*Peira* 23.7) in order to prove his innocence, while in the second case (*Peira* 69.5) he would have the accuser take the oath first as to what he had lost, thus more or less obligating Skleros to repay what had been stolen. Continuing in this line of reasoning, Eustathios writes that normally if the defendant has not demonstrated any past behavior of misdeeds then it is incumbent upon the plaintiff to prove the guilt of the accused; in cases of doubt oaths are still resorted to. In the same passage Eustathios elaborates further that, presumably in cases where the plaintiff's case has not been sufficiently proven by evidence, the judge can call the plaintiff to take an oath. Yet when *prolepsis* exists, the defendant can be compelled by the judged to take an oath. Within Byzantine legal culture, giving an oath was considered the deciding factor in a case and usually trumped all other evidence.[89] It is quite clear from this case and others that a defendant's reputation was an extremely important factor within Byzantine jurisprudence, and it also hints at a possible motive as to why people accused of even very minor offenses chose to contest them, often acting against their financial best interest: the maintenance of one's reputation was vital to being favorably looked upon by the presiding judge, and could easily sway the verdict.

The increasing influence of Orthodox belief on Byzantine jurisprudence during the time of the Macedonian dynasty presages the eventual subsuming of the tradition of Roman secular or civil law into Byzantine canon law. The eleventh century, the time of Eustathios Rhomaios' exercise of jurisprudence at the Court of the Hippodrome, is the period in which historians possess substantial evidence for the practices of "secular" jurists and jurisprudence in the Greek-speaking world. Eustathios Rhomaios is one of the last representatives of this tradition: he is in some sense to be counted among the last *antecessores*, a twilight example of a species of remarkable legal scholars going back to the age of Justinian. Yet it is here, in Eustathios' oeuvre, that one clearly sees the sudden and remarkable impact of Orthodox theological concepts on Byzantine jurisprudence.

[89] See Burgmann 1991d.

Hellenic Culture

The third strand of Byzantine jurisprudence, Hellenic culture, is in some ways more difficult to discern than the first two.[90] From a chronological perspective, Hellenic culture for the Byzantines had first been Romanized and then Christianized. Nonetheless, there is a distinct trend from the ninth to the eleventh century of Byzantine emperors and jurists consciously attempting to Hellenize their legal tradition. The most noteworthy example of this, as discussed in Chapter 1, was the rewriting of the history of Roman law in the prologues to Byzantine lawbooks, which is to be read in the context of a broader imperially sponsored program dedicated to the "Cleansing of the Ancient Laws." In that instance the story of the Twelve Tables was reworked so that they were believed to have originally been written in Greek rather than Latin: a subtle but unmistakable interpolation aimed at Hellenizing the Roman legal tradition.

Echoes of the ancient Greek past are found elsewhere in Middle Byzantine texts. As in the case of the rewriting of the story of the Twelve Tables, a special effort was made to connect contemporary Byzantine legal ideas or institutions to classical and even pagan antecedents. Such is the case in a remarkable passage from his otherwise unremarkable *Legal Textbook*, in which Michael Attaleiates underlines the continuity of the doctrine of *res sacrae* ("sacred things") from pagan temples to Christian churches, monasteries and philanthropic institutions: "And in the ancient laws these things [*res sacrae*] had a distinction of this sort. For they said that the temples or the sanctuaries were *res sacrae*. This [distinction] was adopted by the Orthodox faith: the divine churches, monasteries and the reverend houses have, as it were, veritably inherited the status of the [pagan] *res sacrae*."[91]

Even where a legal doctrine or institution had been changed over the course of time, Antiquity still served as the starting point for its discussion.

[90] For a thought-provoking analysis on how to define Hellenic culture or Hellenism for this period and what it meant in the context of Byzantine identity, see Kaldellis 2007. His approach, which downplays of the role of Orthodoxy as a component of Byzantine identity and over-privileges the vantage point of the part of the Constantinopolitan elite which was not part of the church, runs against the general thrust of the scholarly literature on Byzantine identity. To my knowledge this work has not provoked debate among Byzantinists with the exception of Stouraitis 2014, who criticizes Kaldellis' characterization of Byzantine identity as that of a pre-modern nation-state. Rapp 2008 is a more traditional overview, though unfortunately, because of the gap between composition and publication, it was in fact written before the publication of Kaldellis' book and thus does not take it into account.

[91] Michael Attaleiates, *Legal Textbook* 2.5. This passage is discussed and translated in Stolte 2007: 126.

While Attaleiates noted that Christian religious institutions had simply inherited the special status of *res sacrae* from pagan temples and sanctuaries, Eustathios Rhomaios in the *Peira* with reference to endowments underlined that the Byzantines of his day really did have different concerns than their pagan forebears. The case, *Peira* 67.1, concerns a problematic clause in a will: a man had named his son as his heir in his will, but did not change the will after his son's death. Once the testator himself passed away, leaving behind only his wife, the implementation of the provisions of the will proved problematic because his deceased son was still technically the heir. Though the thought process at work here is not entirely clear from the text, it appears the judge was left with either trying to invalidate this particular part of the will or to interpret the clause as a *psychikon*, that is as a pious bequest for the soul of his son.[92] In order to define what a *psychikon* was, the endowment practices of pagan antiquity are contrasted with those of the Orthodox Christianity: "For in Antiquity it was customary for those dying to bequeath money so that the horse races of Thessaloniki take place, or that baths be built or some amusement for the people occur. Once Christianity came these things ceased and a concern for the soul rather than the body took hold."[93]

Not only Antiquity in general but also particular classical texts were also occasionally invoked in the *Peira*. Thus *Peira* 48.12 quotes Dionysios of Halikarnassos to define an *assarion*. The most prominent citation of a classical text, in which Eustathios quoted Homer's *Odyssey* to justify one of his decisions, is discussed in the introduction to this book. Though an exceptional jurist, Eustathios was not an outlier in quoting classical texts in his legal decisions. A *hypomnema* written in 1062 by another judge of the Hippodrome and Velum, Nicholas Serblias, likewise resorts to a literary reference, stating that the Persians' love for aquiline noses is like the reciprocal love of justice for the law.[94] This urbane literary reference comes from Xenophon, *Cyropaedia* 8.4.21, which mentions that Cyrus was admired by the Persians for his extremely aquiline nose, as aquiline noses in general were highly prized among them. The judge probably encountered it via Plutarch's *Moralia*, as the editor of the act notes.

92 There is no comprehensive study on the *psychikon* in Byzantium; Zepos 1981 gives a useful overview of the its development as a legal institution, especially in the imperial legislation, while Evangelatou-Notara 2005 discusses some of the difficulties of instances where *psychika* overlapped with investment annuities or *adelphata*.

93 *Peira* 67.1.

94 *Ivir.*, vol. I, no. 34 (1062), lines 1–3.

It is interesting to note that literary references in surviving legal records are found within cases judged by high judges, judges of the Hippodrome and Velum.[95] The manner in which the decisions of these high judges were written supports the notion that the rendering of justice at this level was framed in certain respects as a literary exercise; *hypomnemata*, the part of a judge's decision which explained the legal reasoning behind the verdict, seem to have been the venue of choice for the citation of classical texts. This is at a certain level unsurprising, given that the expansive way in which Byzantine writers understood literature as *logoi*; that is, not in the narrow sense of *belles lettres*. Rather, the writer of any text, even one stemming from a technical or more formal genre like law, could aspire to the composition of a work of literature.

The extent to which a *hypomnema* could turn into a literary composition is exemplarily demonstrated by a text composed by the court *philosophe* Michael Psellos, who himself was a lawyer and teacher of law.[96] Psellos was given to transforming the legal texts he composed into displays of his wealth of classical learning and rhetoric, yet even so his description of the resolution of a legal dispute via so-called "Usual Miracle" at the Blachernai Church is a unique text.[97] Indeed, there has been much debate as to which genre this composition belongs. Though other scholars have doubted the veracity of the claim, Psellos himself relates in the text that, acting at the behest of the emperor Michael VII Doukas (1071–8), for whom Psellos served as a tutor and who had taken a personal interest in the case, he had written a text which served as the official *hypomnema* for the case as well as panegyric to the Virgin.[98] Though an extreme example of other literary genres appearing in legal documents, Psellos' claim for the dual purpose of the text is likely accurate and conforms to how other jurists of the period like Eustathios Rhomaios or Nicholas Serblias peppered their own *hypomnemata* with references to literary works.[99]

95 The types of works referenced by judges would put them within the "high style" of Byzantine prose writers. For the classic article on the subject of levels of style in Byzantine literature, see Ševčenko 1981.

96 *The Usual Miracle at Blacharnai* is well-studied, and a number of important contributions on it have appeared in the last fifteen years, especially Fisher 2012; Papaioannou 2001; and Pentcheva 2000; 2006: 145–63. On Psellos as a lawyer and teacher of law see Dennis 1994, with a discussion of the Usual Miracle at 194–6.

97 Discussion of other legal cases argued or recorded by Psellos in Dennis 1994: 190–4.

98 Michael Psellos, *Usual Miracle at Blacharnai* 756–7.

99 Fisher 2012: 192, 202–3 makes a convincing case for accepting Psellos' assertion of the dual purpose of the composition.

Psellos begins his *hypomnema*/panegyric to the Virgin by describing a well-known miracle which occurred in the Blachernai Church of the imperial capital, Constantinople.[100] As works like the *Akathistos Hymn* attest, the Virgin was viewed as the divine protectress of Constantinople, and the Blachernai Church contained the most important icon of the Virgin in the city, that of the Virgin "Hodegetria" ("Guide").[101] Every Friday evening priests would close the church and conduct special rituals where the icon of the Virgin Hodegetria was housed, apparently in a small rotunda connected to the main church. Once the church was again opened to worshippers, they then witnessed (usually but not always at the expected time) a silk veil covering the lower part of the icon miraculously rise and stay suspended in midair until Saturday morning. The icon during this period became *empsychos* or "animate", so that it to its viewers it appeared either to change color or to move.[102]

This "Usual Miracle" then became an unusual means of arbitration: "It was not a civil court of a civil case, but rather a mystical and ineffable place of judgment for the stated problem through the Virgin Mother of God. Nor was it a mortal finding, but rather it was a mystical choice, a judgment and sentence not from the lips of a judge, but a verdict and resolution from supernatural signs."[103] The case in question revolved around the ownership of a watermill in the theme or province of Thrakesion in western Asia Minor. This watermill stood on the border between two properties, the owners of which were respectively the monks of the monastery Tou Kalliou and the military governor or *strategos* Leo Mandalos. According to Psellos, given the importance of watermills in this period, disputes over mills and the water which powered them were extremely common, a statement confirmed by the numerous cases concerning the ownership or use of mills in the surviving Athonite monastic acts.[104] Both sides brought forth documentation which they believed would prove their ownership of the land, as disputed boundaries were supposed to be adjudicated on the basis of boundary markers and public records. Multiple

[100] Psellos' actual description of the miracle is very short (encompassing only thirty-four lines of the 757-line oration, as noted by Fisher 2012: 188). Anonymous as well as contemporaneous descriptions of the miracle by Western travelers, discussed in Fisher 2012: 189–91, are valuable complements to Psellos' own account of how the miracle occurred.

[101] The history of this icon, tied as it is the development of the notion that the Virgin succored and defended the capital, is ably discussed by Pentcheva 2006: 109–92.

[102] Opinions differ among scholars, as discussed in Fisher 2012: 188.

[103] Michael Psellos, *Usual Miracle at Blacharnai* 3–8.

[104] Ibid. 166–73; cases of disputes over watermills in e.g. *Lavra*, vol. I, no. 14 (1008) and no. 30 (1037).

judges attempted to settle the matter, bribery was even attempted, but no final verdict to the satisfaction of both parties could be reached.[105] Finally, the two litigants decided that they would seek a resolution outside of the courts, by selecting the Mother of God as a "special judge" (*hairetos dikastes*).[106] The monastery Tou Kalliou and the *strategos* Leo Mandalos agreed that the Virgin would arbitrate the case in the following way. At a time when the miracle did not customarily happen, the two parties would stand in front of the icon holding their legal documents and beseech the icon by wailing and rending their clothes. If the cloth which covered the icon did not move, then the monks of the monastery Tou Kalliou would win the case. If, however, the cloth moved, then the *strategos* Leo would receive full control of the watermill. Both parties came to the Blachernai Church at the appointed time and awaited the arbitration of the Virgin. For a long time, the cloth did not move. Finally, the monks started to become excited that they had won the case, and the *strategos* Leo gloomily prepared to hand over his documents of ownership to the monks. However, at the very moment when Leo handed over the documents, the cloth moved and remained stationary in mid-air. Now the *strategos* Leo appeared to have won the case, as the cloth had moved. The monks disputed this because, even though the cloth had moved, it had taken an extraordinarily long time to do so. Psellos gives his own opinion on the matter, saying that the *strategos* had clearly won, and the monks had lost because they had acted shamelessly when it had appeared that victory was theirs.[107]

Though at first blush Orthodox Christianity rather than the Hellenic culture appears to have played the major role in the resolution of the case, in fact Psellos used his description of the dispute to advocate the use of his neo-Platonic ideas. Psellos himself seems to have recognized that employing an icon as a judge in this way could have been interpreted as contravening canon law.[108] He thus sought classical as well as well as biblical precedents for the case; as a neo-Platonist, Psellos acknowledged that while lesser divinities or *daimones* had been able to give rather more vague and less useful prophecies, such as those of the Delphic Oracle, the Virgin's divine intervention was clear, unerring and not subject to appeal.[109] Psellos even suggested that the successful resolution of the case

[105] Michael Psellos, *Usual Miracle at Blacharnai* 174–201.
[106] Ibid. 209–21.
[107] Ibid. 272–305.
[108] Fisher 2012: 196–7.
[109] Fisher 2012: 194–6.

could become a model, a "paradigm for future innovations" (*mellouson kainotomion … paradeigma*) for other disputes bogged down in civil courts.[110] The normally negative connotations of *kainotomia* found elsewhere in Byzantine legal texts are absent from Psellos' *hypomnema*.

Conclusion

Middle Byzantine jurisprudence, as demonstrated in the preceding pages, consisted of the complex interaction of the components of Byzantine legal culture, namely the Roman legal and political legacy, Orthodox Christianity and Hellenic culture. It represented a transitional phase, in which the nominally secular though Christianized legacy of Justinianic law was further Christianized via the introduction of theological concepts into jurisprudence, while at the same time links to the Roman past and the Hellenic cultural legacy were further reinforced. It is, from the standpoint of the legal historian, essentially the last phase of the secular Roman legal tradition. The incipient use of theological concepts like *kainotomia*, *oikonomia* and *philanthropia* in the texts of the ninth through the eleventh centuries foreshadows the Late and post-Byzantine dominance of canon law.

The eclectic way in which the Byzantines approached legal questions is further explored in the next chapter, in which the role of a number of "private" legal collections is discussed. Unlike the official texts stemming from the "Cleansing of the Ancient Laws" explored in Chapter 1, these works, whose origins and dates of composition are shrouded in mystery, achieved great popularity without official sanction. Instead, they attained acceptance via their bundling with more official collections of Byzantine law and through the inevitable result of the copyist's predilection for including them in legal manuscripts.

110 Psellos, *Usual Miracle at Blachernai* 348–55.

CHAPTER 4

The Function of "Private" Law Collections in the Byzantine Empire and Neighboring Cultures

Introduction

To this point, the legal basis for Byzantine legal culture has been, above all, Justinianic law. The lawbooks produced during this epoch, like the *Basilika*, *Eisagoge* and *Prochiron*, were likewise essentially Hellenized and Christianized versions of Justinianic law: Late Antique laws passing through the filter of Middle Byzantine culture. Yet the legal texts stemming from the time of the Macedonian dynasty (or perhaps somewhat earlier) which have most profoundly influenced law and legal culture not only in the Greek-speaking cultural sphere but also the wider Byzantine Commonwealth (Eastern Europe, the Balkans and the Caucasus) were not lawbooks based on Justinianic law, but rather a triad of enigmatic legal texts known as the Farmer's Law or *Nomos Georgikos* (NG), the Mosaic Law or *Nomos Mosaikos* (NM) and the Rhodian Sea-Law or *Nomos Nautikos* (NN). Their origin, function and most importantly how they came to viewed as part of the tradition of Roman/Byzantine law is the subject of this chapter.

A useful paradigm for exploring this question is that of the dualism *Reichsrecht* and *Volksrecht*, a dichotomy made famous by the consummate historian of Roman law Ludwig Mitteis.[1] Mitteis, writing at the end of the nineteenth century, felt compelled to author a book on the gap between imperial law (*Reichsrecht*) and provincial law (*Volksrecht*) because of the discovery of many new sources that did not fit neatly within the received canon of imperial novels and constitutions. In addition to the finds which were accumulating in the new field of papyrology, the rediscovery and publication of the *Syro-Roman Lawbook* by the Dutch theologian and orientalist Jan Pieter Nicolaas Land in 1858 in a manuscript of the British Museum radically changed how legal historians viewed Roman law.[2] The

[1] Mitteis 1891.

[2] Previous to the mid-nineteenth century, the *Syro-Roman Lawbook* had been mentioned, edited and translated by orientalists and church historians who nonetheless did not realize what the work

work contains regulations on slave, family and inheritance law and does not correspond to the supposedly dominant Roman legal precepts of the time when it was authored, perhaps in the fourth or fifth century CE, and it confounded the contemporary legal-historical community.[3] Above all, these newly discovered legal texts forced Mitteis and his contemporaries to reevaluate just how influential the law of the land, namely Roman law, actually was in places where there obviously existed private legal collections.

Mitteis' dichotomy of the terms *Reichsrecht* and *Volksrecht* has had a long, powerful and not always unproblematic resonance.[4] Nonetheless, Mitteis' understanding of *Volksrecht* can still profitably be understood as a deviation in law or legal practice from normative Roman law.[5] Among more recent work, Dieter Simon has demonstrated how provincial norms, very much *Volksrecht* in the way Mitteis used it, may have been incorporated into "official" legal collections, not only in the *Ecloga*, which has long been thought to have been substantially influenced by eighth-century customary law, but also the *Prochiron*.[6] One of course need not insinuate connotations of decline or decay when using this definition of *Volksrecht*; the merit of this concept is that it recognizes that manifestations of "unofficial" law or legal practices do not draw upon an entirely different system of legal values.[7] Rather, *Volksrecht* at its core, as Mitteis defined it, is still based on Roman law. Within the framework of Byzantine law, and more specifically Byzantine legal culture, *Volksrecht* can be understood not simply as the later development of Roman law, but rather as instances in

actually was. Land edited and translated the work into Latin in his *Anecdota Syriaca* in 1862, giving the text the title *Leges saeculares e lingua Romana in Aramaeam versae*. On its history in modern scholarship, see *Syro-Roman Lawbook*, vol. I, 27–32.

3 Mitteis 1891: 1.

4 An example would be the much-criticized reappropriation of Mitteis' concept over half a century later by the legal historian Franz Wieacker, who posited that throughout the history of Roman law there existed two oppositional "styles" of law, *Vulgarismus* and *Klassizismus*; see Wieacker 1955. On the history of this debate, see Simon 1978b.

5 Mitteis 1891: 4; Wieacker 1955: 10.

6 Simon 1976.

7 Indeed, for the period which Mitteis and Wieacker examined, Late Antiquity, there is no basis for postulating a decline in legal practice or thinking, as has been proven by Humfress 2007. Yet the idea of *Volksrecht* as a degradation of Roman law in its classical iteration can still be found among some scholars, e.g. Górecki 2009: 140: "The subsequent surge and rapid spread of vulgar law, during post-classical times, became a menace to the integrity of the official Roman legal system … Law and customs of peoples inhabiting the Roman provinces found their way into official legislation through judicial verdicts, which eventually became part of official law. The continuing accumulation of such verdicts, being in conflict with the philosophy and objectives of the official legal system, gradually distorted and degraded that system."

which law was formulated or applied outside of the framework of what we, as well as most Byzantine jurists, would have understood as valid law.

At first glance, the various redactions of Justinianic law which were written at the end of the ninth century would indicate that *Reichsrecht* was steadily growing in importance. The *Basilika*, particularly from the middle of eleventh century onward, started to be consulted as the standard collection of Justinianic law, at least from the standpoint of the legal textbooks stemming from this period. The *Peira* as well as the *Legal Textbook* of Michael Attaleiates, for instance, when providing justification for the rendering of a particular case merely state "the law (says)," the law being the *Basilika*.[8] Even an aid to finding where particular topics are treated in the *Basilika*, titled *Tipoukeitos* ("What is found where?"), attributed to a judge named Patzes who lived toward the end of the eleventh century, has survived.[9] In summation, an examination of the official legal sources alone would indicate that Roman law (*Reichsrecht*) survived relatively unchallenged into the eleventh century, after which the golden age of Byzantine canon law begins, or to use the words of Nicolaas van der Wal and J. H. A. Lokin, "Le grand siècle de la science du droit canonique (1110–1204)."[10] Nor is the predominance of *Reichsrecht* in this period necessarily confined to the official legal sources; Peter Sarris has also argued that the surviving monastic records demonstrate an increasing predominance of "official" law.[11]

On the other hand, some historians, notably Alexander Kazhdan and Nicholas Oikonomides, have drawn attention to the obsolescence of the Justinianic corpus in the Middle Byzantine period and have tried to explain how Middle Byzantine society coped with what were antiquated, essentially sixth-century laws.[12] The *Basilika* and its antecedents, being almost entirely composed of extracts from the *CIC*, contained provisions and regulations which were definitely obsolete by the time of the Macedonian dynasty. Moreover, most surviving records of legal cases, stemming primarily from the monasteries of Mount Athos, South Italy and western Asia Minor, only rarely invoke Roman law.[13] Excluding the

[8] Note that even thoughe the relevant references to the *Basilika* were added to the rulings of Eustathios Rhomaios, there is reason to believe that Eustathios himself utilized the *Synopsis Basilicorum Major*.

[9] See Burgmann 1991e.

[10] Van der Wal and Lokin 1985: 107. The eleventh century was arguably the start of the golden age of Byzantine canon law: see Pitsakes 2003.

[11] Sarris 2011.

[12] Kazhdan 1989: 7–10; 1991a; Oikonomides 1986.

[13] See the examples in Morris 1986; 2010.

activity of the high court judges recorded in the *Peira*, can one still posit the widespread use and acceptance of Roman law?

To ascertain how collections of private law like the *NG*, *NM* and *NN* might have functioned in Byzantium, it is worth exploring some instances in which a conscious decision was made – or not – to apply Roman law. In *Peira* 14.16, an unnamed *patrikios* deprived a daughter from a first marriage of her full due under Roman law, according to the custom of his unnamed people, and was subsequently chastised for it:

> A certain *patrikios* made a will, and wrote that the wife of his second marriage should be the possessor of all his fortune. But he had a daughter from his first marriage, who was found to have taken much less from [her father's estate] than from her mother's estate. And the *Magistros* ruled thus: For someone who makes a will, even if he is from a foreign people, but has come to the Roman Empire and been honored with a great rank and showered with many gifts, it is necessary than he follow the laws of the Romans and [therefore] not make a testament according to ethnic customs. For although he does not know the correct content of the laws, he is nonetheless able to ask those who ought to teach him what is necessary. And on account of this, in regard to its legal accuracy and [his] decision the provisions of the testament were corrected.[14]

This *patrikios* was not Greek and had made a will according to the customs of his own people, which apparently allowed for a daughter to receive less than a half-share of her father's estate. Eustathios Rhomaios had his will corrected so that its provisions would instead follow the inheritance practices prescribed by Roman law. The case is resolved largely as one would have expected.

Yet another case, from the *Peira* 54.6, finds Eustathios Rhomaios allowing unusual provisions in a will to stand because a potential heir was a foreigner (*ethnikos*), more specifically a member of the Armeno-Georgian Chalcedonian elite which played such a prominent role in Middle Byzantine history.[15] The *patrikios* David the Iberian made a will which

[14] *Peira* 14.16; cf. Laiou 1994a: 79–80.

[15] *Peira* 54.6: "The *Patrikios* David the Iberian left behind a child, and wrote [in his will], that if the child should die childless and intestate, then his uncles should be established as heirs. And once the child died and his uncles came into the inheritance, a suit was brought forth and the *Bestes* ruled, that since the son had died at the age of 20, the mother should receive one-third of the estate, and the uncles should receive the rest. He said that a substitution is prevented by minority status according to the law which says 'If there is substitution it ought to be given to the furthest extent, unless it is prevented by minority status.' [He also said] that the son was able to dispose of the entire inheritance via a will, since he was no longer a minor. Since the son was a foreigner, he made an accommodation for this." Cf. Laiou 1994a: 78.

stated that his only son would inherit his whole estate, but that if the son died childless and made no will, then his uncles (presumably the brothers of the *patrikios*) would inherit his estate. When his son died childless and intestate, the uncles came into the inheritance, but someone sued (probably the mother of the deceased son), and Eustathios ruled that the mother was entitled to a one-third share of the estate, and the uncles were allowed to have the rest. Yet according to Roman inheritance law, the uncles would not have been entitled to any share of the estate since the son died at the age of 20, and thus was no longer a minor.[16] It is then stated that this arrangement was made because the deceased son was a foreigner, and that Eustathios invoked *oikonomia* to arrive at a solution. Thus in this instance non-Roman inheritance customs were allowed to be realized.

Outside of the *Peira*, there are few but nonetheless tantalizing clues that Roman/Byzantine law was not always followed to the letter. Stemming from the same Armeno-Georgian Chalcedonian elite as David the Iberian, Gregory Pakourianos, the founder of the still-functioning monastery in what is now Bačkovo, Bulgaria, had received a chrysobull which allowed him to transmit his estate even to his family members of the "Armenian" (i.e. Monophysite/Miaphysite) faith.[17] This blatantly contradicted Justinianic provisions against heretics, which did not allow non-Orthodox to inherit from Orthodox. In a similar vein, the synodal Edicts of the patriarch Alexios Stoudites (1025–43), for instance, note that at least in Melitene Justinianic provisions against heretics were ignored by the judges there, practices which included the omission of Orthodox heirs in the wills of non-Orthodox, allowing non-Orthodox to testify against Orthodox in court and even the intermarriage of Orthodox and non-Orthodox.[18]

A somewhat different area where the hold of Roman law appears to have not been absolute are the Russo-Byzantine treaties preserved in the *Russian Primary Chronicle*, or as it also known the *Tale of Bygone Years* (*Povest' vremennych let*). These treaties, stemming from the years 907, 911, 944 and 971, regulate the conduct of and resolution of conflicts between Byzantine and Rus' merchants. The Treaty of 911, still a half-century before the conversion of Rus', allows Rus' who died while serving the Byzantine emperor in the empire to have their property transmitted to their relatives in Rus', if they died intestate.[19] A Muslim community of merchants and

[16] Kaser 1971–5: vol. II, pp. 497–512; Simon 1991b.
[17] Gregory Pakourianos, *Typikon* 129, lines 1813–15. Cf. Laiou 1994a: 77.
[18] See Chitwood 2014 and Ch. 5.
[19] *Russo-Byzantine Treaties* 4–7 (Treaty of 911), here 6.

prisoners, predominantly in the capital but also in the provinces as well, was allowed to maintain mosques, again violating the spirt if not the letter of Justinianic law.[20]

Nonetheless, the above examples all were admittedly somewhat exceptional situations: foreigners in Byzantine service, a recently reconquered city on the eastern frontier and reciprocal agreements with foreign powers. At the very least they suggest that contexts did exist where Roman law was either ignored or was used in synthesis with other forms of law. The difficulty with assessing the importance of private legal collections like the *NG*, *NM* and *NN* is that no acts or cases have been transmitted from the Middle Byzantine period in which they were cited as law. This is a paradoxical state of affairs, as from the time after the emperor Justinian until the end of the eleventh century, and at least judging by the number of manuscripts which have survived that contain these private collections, they were at least as popular as their imperially sanctioned counterparts.

Within this chapter the manuscript tradition of these private legal collections will be dealt with in some detail, which will highlight the popularity of these texts in comparison with their imperially sanctioned counterparts.[21] A comparison is possible because of the recent publication of a catalogue listing all of the "secular" manuscripts of Byzantine law.[22] The popularity of Byzantine private law collections is also a feature of the *Nachleben* of Byzantine law, particularly in its Armenian and Slavic iterations. Taken in conjunction with the Byzantine manuscript tradition, the reasons why these private law collections suited the peoples who later employed Byzantine law much more than the Macedonian emperors' recapitulation of Justinianic law suggest a possible *raison d'être* for the creation, maintenance and transmission of these legal collections. Above all, three factors facilitated the composition, use and spread of these private law collections: (1) their lack of untranslated Latin legal terminology, allowing judges and lawyers to utilize these legal texts without a mastery of Roman legal vocabulary; (2) the brevity and conciseness of these private legal collections in comparison to the *Basilika* as well as the Greek paraphrases/translations and commentaries of the Justinianic corpus; (3) the

[20] On the Muslim community in Constantinople see Anderson 2009; Reinert 1998.

[21] An excellent and concise introduction to Byzantine juridical manuscripts can be found in Burgmann 2011. This article is a translated, slightly revised and bibliographically updated version of Burgmann 2002.

[22] The *RHBR*. This inventory of manuscripts is based on the extensive collection of Byzantine juridical manuscripts, in microfilm as well as increasingly in digital format, at the Max Planck-Institut für europäische Rechtsgeschichte in Frankfurt.

complementary as opposed to adversarial function of these texts, which supported rather than undermined the official framework of Roman law.

Before an examination of private law collections and their function in the Middle Byzantine Empire can be undertaken, the definition of "private" law needs to be clarified. Private law will be used throughout this chapter mainly to denote that which it is not, namely, imperially sanctioned law which was incorporated into what would eventually in the twelfth century become, according to the views of some jurists and canonists, the official redaction of the Roman law used in the Byzantine Empire, the *Basilika*. A partial exception here is the so-called Rhodian Sea-Law which was inserted as an appendix into the fifty-third book of the *Basilika*.[23] Even this definition is fraught with difficulties, as a number of "official" law codes, such as the *Eisagoge*, were perhaps never promulgated. Discussion here will therefore be confined to three legal collections: (I) the Farmer's Law or *Nomos Georgikos* (*NG*); (II) the Mosaic Law or *Nomos Mosaikos* (*NM*); and (III) the Rhodian Sea-Law or *Nomos Nautikos* (*NN*). Two of these three legal collections, the *NG* and *NN*, are often designated in secondary scholarship, along with the Soldier's Law or *Nomos Stratiotikos* (*NS*), as the *leges speciales*, reflecting both the fact that these legal collections are often grouped together in the manuscript tradition as well the assumption that they were authored in the same period, from the seventh to the eighth century.[24]

The *NS* is excluded from this examination, however, because most of its regulations stem from the *CIC* as well the *Strategikon* of Maurice. Moreover, as a text which was probably authored at the in middle of the seventh century, it stems from a different period than most generally accepted datings of the *NG* and *NN*.[25] To the best of our knowledge, none of these laws was imperially promulgated (although in the case of the *NG* and *NN* compilers and copyists claimed that these legal collections were

[23] The process by which this was achieved has been extensively studied by Rodolakes 2007. Rodolakes' study is useful in a number of respects, as it addresses all the pertinent issues regarding the incorporation of the *NN* into the *Basilika*. Additionally, it contains an edition of *NN* as it appears in the *Basilika* (Rodolakes 2007: 213–60). He also, however, advances some views in this study which I find less convincing, such as postulating the existence of an actual written *Rhodian Sea-Law* at Rome in the Early Empire.

[24] See the bibliography in Verri's edition of the *Nomos Stratiotikos* as well as Burgmann and McGeer 1991. Verri's study contains the various editions of the *NS* as appendices. English translation of the *NS* Freshfield 1926: 122–9.

[25] Burgmann 2009: 53–64. Humphreys 2015: 152–65, however, has argued, in my opinion without convincing evidence, that the final recension of the text was completed in the 740s or 750s and is to be seen, like the *Appendix Eclogae*, as a supplement to the *Ecloga*.

imperially sanctioned).[26] Since so little is known about the provenance of these three legal collections it is easy to confine oneself to *Quellenkritik*, but the goal of this chapter is to try and ascertain the function of these laws within Byzantine legal culture.

The *Nomos Georgikos* (*NG*)

The so-called Farmer's Law or *Nomos Georgikos* (*NG*)[27] is one of the most controversial texts within Byzantine history and has been the subject of numerous analyses.[28] The text consists of eighty-five provisions governing what appears to be a free peasantry practicing agriculture and animal husbandry. During the twentieth century many scholars postulated a Slavic origin of the *NG*, a theory which has been overturned, as the *NG* does not contain any words of indisputably Slavic origin.[29] Certain features of the text, such as the lack of a mention of olive trees, has led some scholars to attempt to localize the *NG* to, for instance, Asia Minor, Thessaloniki or Italy. None of these attempts has found widespread acceptance among Byzantinists, and there is an argument to be made against inferring too much about the region of the text's composition from the terse information of the *NG*'s articles.[30]

Equally elusive is the date the *NG* was composed. The eminent nineteenth-century legal historian Karl Eduard Zachariä von Lingenthal initially believed that the law originated in a ninth- or tenth-century context before deciding on a date of composition around the time of the Isaurian emperors Leo III (r. 717–41) and Constantine V (r. 741–75), a

[26] By contrast Humphreys 2015 argues that the *leges speciales* were the result of a conscious program of legal reform over the course of the eighth century. This is an interesting theory but there is no good evidence for it. Moreover, it downplays the agency of jurists and the copyists of Byzantine legal manuscripts, who hardly needed imperial directives to collect, edit and copy the legal collections they found useful.

[27] Although most secondary literature written in English uses the designation *Farmer's Law*, in this study the acronym *NG* is used both for convenience as well as to correspond to the numerous publications of the Frankfurt team.

[28] The most recent edition of the *NG* includes a Russian translation as well as the Old Church Slavonic version of the text. Walter Ashburner's English translation of the *NG* based on his older edition is still useful for non-Byzantinists: see Ashburner 1910; 1912. Note the corrections to ch. 67 in Ashburner's edition suggested by Laiou 1971. One cannot here comprehensively list all of the interpretations of the *NG*, as such a study could easily occupy the space of a monograph. The *NG* has been discussed in detail most recently by Humphreys 2015: 195–232. The overview of Troianos 2011: 170–4 is the most concise recent survey of the literature. In addition, for general information on the *NG* see Kazhdan 1991e; Pieler 1994: 317–19; Van der Wal and Lokin 1985: 73–5.

[29] Humphreys 2015: 197–8; Karayannopulos 1958: 380, n. 1; Kazhdan 1991e.

[30] Köpstein 1995.

view which was at first supported by the author of the first reliable critical edition of the text, Walter Ashburner, and then later refuted.[31] George Vernadsky postulated a date of composition during the first regnal period of Justinian II (r. 685–95, 705–11), a view which gained considerable currency among non-specialists when it was taken up by Georg Ostrogorsky.[32] Later in the twentieth century Franz Dölger challenged Vernadsky's thesis, instead proposing that the *NG* originated as a private collection of law from the time of Justinian I.[33] Additionally, an oft-refuted but persistent strain of scholarship has insisted on the pre-Justinianic, even ancient Greek origin of the law.[34] More recent evaluations of the *NG* have argued for a date of composition in the eighth or even the end of the ninth century, two theories which ironically correspond to Zachariä's original hypotheses, showing that this scholarly guessing game has over the course of a century come full circle.[35] A quite provocative new theory of M. T. G. Humphreys is that the text is an official composition of an Isaurian legal reform, and thus stems from the generation of jurists after the promulgation of the *Ecloga* in 741.[36]

These sundry theories regarding the geographic origin and date of composition of the *NG* demonstrate the futility of attempting to date a text of such popularity without a context for its use in societal praxis.[37] In fact, one of the few certainties of the *NG* is the remarkable prevalence of its

[31] Zachariä von Lingenthal 1892: 249–57; Ashburner 1910: 85.

[32] Vernadsky 1925: 178–80. Cf. Humphreys 2015: 198. Given what he thought were similarities between the *NG* and the law in Late Roman/Byzantine Egypt, Vernadsky ascribed what he described as a *tendance orientale* of the *NG* to the influence of refugees from the former Byzantine territories arriving in Constantinople in the seventh century. Vernadsky also emphasized a particular lexical feature, namely the use of the word *idios* ("his own"), in papyrus documents from Egypt as well as in the *NG*.

[33] Dölger 1945; cf. Humphreys 2015: 198–9.

[34] Svoronos 1981 proposed that the *NG* contained pre-Justinianic Roman law rather than local law, as well as borrowed provisions from the *NM*. Pantazopoulos 1971 saw Greek and Near Eastern origins for the *NG*'s institutions of *antitopia* (exchanging one piece of land, crop or tree for another) and *dendroktesia* (owning trees or crops on someone else's property), both of which violate the Roman legal principle of *superficies solo cedit*, i.e. whatever is on your land belongs to you. Though Pieler 2008 likewise affirms that these legal institutions are foreign to Justinianic law, he sees the *NG* stemming from the period after, rather than before, the *CIC*. Burgmann 1982, written as a response to Svoronos 1981, refuted the theory of the *NG*'s pre-Justinianic origins.

[35] Pieler 2007 has confirmed that, despite the influence of the Old Testament, the work is substantially based on Roman law; overall, he prefers a time of composition during the "dark centuries" of Isaurian rule. Schminck 2005a: 261 by contrast dates the *NG* to the end of the Photios' first patriarchate (September 25, 867).

[36] Humphreys 2015: 223–4, 228–31.

[37] A *nomos georgikos* is mentioned in the correspondence of Ignatios the Deacon, but it is far from clear that this is a reference to the *NG* under discussion here: see Humphreys 2015: 224.

manuscripts. Johannes Karayannopulos counted over eighty manuscripts of the *NG* from the eleventh to seventeenth centuries in his 1958 overview.[38] Since that time the editors of the *RHBR* have counted a total of 104 Greek manuscripts, two of which are excerpted. If one includes later copies, the *NG* is transmitted in over 120 Greek manuscripts in total. Of that number, more than four-fifths are from the fourteenth–sixteenth centuries. Within this subgroup, the majority are found in conjunction with the *Hexabiblos* (*c.*1345), a compilation of secular law written by fourteenth-century jurist Constantine Harmenopoulos. The *Hexabiblos* proved to be tremendously influential within both the last century of the Byzantine Empire's political existence as well as *Byzance après Byzance.* According to the famous Royal Decree of February 23 [March 7], 1835, promulgated during the regency of King Otto (r. 1832–62), Byzantine law, as represented by the *Hexabiblos,* was to be the law of the new Kingdom of Greece until the completion of a new civil code, which was not achieved until precisely 111 years later on the same date in 1946.[39] However, these later, "Harmenopoulian" manuscripts are not relevant to this inquiry.[40] It is the tenth- to thirteenth-century grouping of manuscripts which is of greater interest, given that they reflect which other legal works were typically grouped with the *NG* at the beginning of the manuscript tradition.[41] It is this group of seventeen or possibly eighteen manuscripts which can speak to how the *NG* was used by its copyists, and with what other legal collections it was grouped.

Almost every early manuscript which includes the *NG* also includes a Macedonian redaction of Roman law.[42] Within these manuscripts, the *NG*

[38] Karayannopulos 1958: 369–73, with an excellent discussion of the manuscript tradition.

[39] Scheltema 1970b: 1, n. 1. At the start of the twentieth century, the *Hexabiblos* was the official law of three states (the Kingdom of Greece, the Principality of Samos and of Bessarabia): see Pitsakes 2005: 280.

[40] It is possible that Harmenopoulos, rather than faithfully reproducing the text of the *NG*, interpolated clauses of his own in order to attenuate some aspects of the law which were not easily reconciled with official Roman law: see Pantazopoulos 1971: 544–5.

[41] One of the manuscripts in this tenth/thirteenth-century group, *RHBR* 92, is excluded because although it includes an older copy of the *NG*, it was later found inserted along with works of Armenopoulos.

[42] Including the *Appendix Eclogae, Ecloga privata, Eisagoge aucta, Epitome ad Prochiron mutata, Epitome Marciana, Epitome "Vaticana," Prochiron, Prochironderivat, Prochiron auctum* and the *Prochiron Calabriae.* The exception to the rule here is *Codex Barberinianus* 578 in Rome's Biblioteca Apostolica Vaticana (*RHBR* 251), which contains primarily canon law texts such as the *Nomokanon in Fourteen Titles*, the *Synagoge in 50 Titles*, as well as other canons. This manuscript also contains a florilegium from book 53 of the *Basilika* as well as the *NN*, the latter of which made its way into the *Basilika* as an appendix to book 53. For the interesting story of the discovery of secular law in this manuscript as well as its use as a basis for the Latin translation of book 53 of the *Basilika* by the Florentine scholar Francesco Venturi (fl. fifteenth–sixteenth centuries), see Simon 1978a: 340–3.

is usually circulated with the *NN* as well as the *NS*. In essence, the presence of the *NG* within manuscripts also containing "official" law, especially as an appendix to the *Ecloga* or its later reworkings, demonstrates that imperial and "local" law could exist side by side.[43] The *NG* was probably used by magistrates tasked with juridical duties who employed this compact and succinct code to settle everyday village disputes rather than turning to the more complex regulations found in the many redactions of the *CIC*. This interpretation would dovetail nicely with the *akroatai* mentioned as the legal authorities in the text, who appear to be administrators rather than professional judges.[44]

While modern scholars dismiss the assertion, contained in most rubrics of the *NG*, that it was promulgated by the emperor Justinian, it is not clear to what extent Middle Byzantine judges or officials having recourse to it would have accepted this. In fact, that there was no simple way for a Byzantine reader of judicial manuscript to determine whether a work was genuinely part of the Justinianic corpus or one of its later reworkings or redactions, much less whether a work was imperially promulgated or not. It is therefore common in Byzantine juridical manuscripts to find attestations of imperial, patriarchal or synodal legitimation.[45] Exactly when the belief became widespread that Justinian I had promulgated the *NG* is unclear. The fact that it was not incorporated into the *Basilika* or other Macedonian redactions of Justinianic law would seem to indicate that Middle Byzantine jurists had some doubts concerning its imperial pedigree. The more famous Late Byzantine canonists do not seem to have questioned its legitimacy: Harmenopoulos in his preface to the *Hexabiblos* appears to have regarded the *NG* as part of the "Breadth of the Laws" (*platos ton nomon*).[46] Likewise, early modern jurists who translated or incorporated the *NG* into their own works, especially those of the Danubian principalities, genuinely thought that they were dealing with a work of "the Great Justinian."[47]

It is also within this context that one can invoke Bernard Stolte's observation on how derogation functioned in the Byzantine Empire, namely, that it is far from clear that older imperial legislation, even if it was not included in the redactions of Roman law characteristic of the Macedonian

[43] Karayannopulos 1958: 373.
[44] Humphreys 2015: 219–20.
[45] Burgmann 2011: 93.
[46] Pitsakes 2000: 414–15.
[47] Georgesco 1969: 88.

dynasty, became automatically invalid.[48] Indeed, imperial legislation in the form of constitutions and novels appears to have retained its legal validity until it was specifically revoked. From this standpoint the use of the *NG*, which to the modern scholar is obviously outside the canon of what is considered Roman law since it was not included in the *CIC*, would not have been seen as objectionable to Byzantine judges, whose jurisprudence in any case also recognized paradigms of justice outside of Roman law.[49]

The *NG*, the first of the three texts to be examined in this chapter, was thus, whatever its actual provenance, a product of Middle Byzantine legal culture: it was the jurists and judges of this period who extensively copied and likely used it as well, given the reasonable assumption that their dissemination of the text had a practical purpose. Moreover, they incorporated the *NG* into manuscripts which contained collections of official law. The long-term effect of this legitimacy by association was profound, because it caused later Byzantine jurists and canonists to assume, quite understandably, that the *NG* was a text of imperial pedigree and thus no different from the rest of the Roman legal tradition. The *NG*, especially for those cultures influenced by Byzantium, thus became a quintessential Byzantine lawbook, and a far more familiar representative of Byzantine law than the *Basilika*.

The *Nomos Mosaikos* (*NM*)

While like the *NG* the so-called *Nomos Mosaikos* (*NM*) has an uncertain date of composition, the source of its statutes is not in doubt. The *NM* is a collection of fifty titles (*kephalaia*) of thematically related excerpts from the Pentateuch; each title consists of between one and five excerpts, so that the work in its two recensions consists of seventy (Recension "A") or seventy-one (Recension "B") passages from the books of Exodus, Leviticus, Numbers and Deuteronomy.[50] There is no consensus on when the *NM* was compiled, a shared feature of the legal collections discussed in this chapter: scholars have offered dates ranging from the beginning of eighth to the middle of the ninth century.[51]

[48] Stolte 2005: 68–9.

[49] See Ch. 3.

[50] Although the designation *NM* will be employed here as well, it should be noted that, as with so many other Byzantine legal texts, this is not the title found in most manuscripts, but is rather a shortened form of "A Selection of the Mosaïc Law given by God to the Israelites." For general comments on the *NM* see Brubaker and Haldon 2001: 289–90; Troianos 2011: 178–9.

[51] Burgmann and Troianos, the editors of the text, offer no concrete dating for the composition of the *NM*, instead only noting that the *NM* probably was composed around the same time as the *Ecloga*.

Although like the *NG* the *NM* did not become part of Roman secular law, unlike the *NG*, which perhaps served as a supplement to the Macedonian redactions of Roman law, the *NM* offers a Judeo-Christian legal framework completely unlike that of the *Basilika*. As yet there exists no scholarly consensus on the function of the text, a result mainly of how the *NG* is presented. Although the *NM* somewhat resembles the Late Antique *Collatio legum Mosaicarum et Romanarum*, it does not, unlike the *Collatio*, explicitly compare Roman and biblical law.[52]

Yet according to a plausible recent analysis, the *NM* does in fact constitute an implicit comparison of Roman and biblical law; this can be surmised from the order of chapters.[53] That the compiler of the *NM* must have consulted the *Ecloga* can be deduced from chapters 28–39 of the *NM*, twelve chapters which are excerpted out of their order in Leviticus yet which correspond to the order of thematically related chapters in the *Ecloga*. Thus, the compiler of the *NM* likely used the *Ecloga* as his basis for the Roman law portion of his comparison, and then found and wrote out the corresponding norms in the Pentateuch. According to this view the goal of the *NM* is a critical comparison of the secular norms of the *Ecloga* with the divine ordinances of the Pentateuch.[54] The *NM* has also been read as a complement to the *Ecloga*.[55]

Would the application of an exclusively Old Testament-derived lawbook have been possible in the Byzantine Empire at the time of the Macedonian dynasty, that is at a time and in a place still very much imbued by the Roman legal tradition? The plausibility of such possibility is suggested by a roughly contemporaneous text which offers the perspective of a Middle Byzantine monk on the laws which a Christian nation should adopt, a collection of laws known as the *Nomoi* ("laws") ascribed to the missionary St Gregentios of Taphar. The historicity of St Gregentios

Pieler 1987: 501–3 posited that the creation of the *NM* could be ascribed to the Old Testament tendencies of iconoclasm and the Isaurian dynasty. Due to his belief that the text was possibly authored by Photios, Schminck 2005a: 261–6 dates the *NM* to around 866, more than a century later than the date suggested by the editors of the text. More speculatively, Schminck suggests that the *NM* could have been authored by Photios, since Photios had demonstrated admiration for Moses as a lawgiver. Humphreys 2015: 171–9 has rejected the arguments of Schminck and argues, as he does for every law of unknown provenance from this period, that the law was intended as a complement to the *Ecloga*.

52 Pieler 1987 discusses the importance of Mosaic law in early Christianity as well as both the *Collatio* and the *NM*. See Pieler 1997 for similar remarks.

53 What follows in this paragraph is a summary of Schminck 2005a.

54 Schminck 2005a: 254–5.

55 Humphreys 2015: 171–9.

is extremely problematic, as well as where and when the texts ascribed to him were written. Scholars of pre-Islamic Arabia have shown a particularly keen interest in the texts, as they purport to tell the story of Gregentios' conversion of the Kingdom of the "Homerites" in what is now Yemen to Christianity. After his successful missionary efforts sometime during the sixth century, Gregentios issued a set of laws for the new converts. The editor and translator of the texts ascribed to Gregentios has convincingly argued for a tenth-century date of composition and Constantinopolitan provenance for the *Bios* and *Nomoi* of Gregentios.[56] Particularly for the *Nomoi*, which describe an urban setting more reminiscent of the tenth-century imperial capital than pre-Islamic Arabia and the use of mutilation as punishment, a novelty of the *Ecloga*, a Middle Byzantine dating and provenance make good sense.

Given that the author of the *Nomoi* probably lived in tenth-century Constantinople, the character of the laws enacted by Gregentios for the Kingdom of the Homerites is remarkable for how far it is removed from Roman law. At roughly the same time that the Macedonian emperors Basil I and Leo VI were issuing new redactions of Justinianic law, the anonymous author of the *Nomoi* hearkens to Moses as a legal reformer.[57] The text also prescribes mutilation as punishment for particular offenses, a feature the *Nomoi* shares with the eighth-century *Ecloga*. The authors of the *Ecloga* introduced mutilation as a milder form of punishment for crimes in Roman law which merited the death penalty. In the *Nomoi*, the form of mutilation inflicted often corresponds with the nature of the crime perpetrated. For instance, a man who sleeps with a married woman shall have his penis cut off, while the woman shall have her left breast excised.[58] The justification for this punishment, as with the rest of the legal prescriptions in the *Nomoi*, is biblical: "For it is better, says the Lord, that one of your limbs be lost here and not your whole body be cast into the Gehenna of fire."[59] In contrast to the absolute authority of the Byzantine emperor, the power of the Homerite king to enact and change law is quite limited: "The king must take counsel in weighty matters with holy men and beseech Holy God through them, and [that] is thus better than doing

[56] Berger 2001, but see now Messis 2012, who has however called Berger's dating into question and argues for a fifth- or sixth-century Alexandrian or Ethiopic context. I would like to thank Philipp Winterhager for drawing my attention to this article.

[57] Gregentios of Taphar, *Nomoi*, lines 14–19.

[58] Ibid., lines 69–71.

[59] Ibid., lines 71–2; Matt. 5:29.

what seems right to him. For whoever acts so will not be put to shame eternally."[60] The tenth-century monastic author of the *Nomoi* thus undercuts the legal absolutism of the secular authorities in this text, a notion utterly anathema to the *Basilika*.

The *Nomoi* were emphatically a moral code meant to effect the spiritual salvation of the people living in the Kingdom of the Homerites. Instead of viewing the law as a harsh and unbending institution which necessitated the application of mercy and clemency, the author of the *Nomoi* seems without compunctions regarding the draconian measures prescribed in his code. Indeed, he underlines the essentially antagonistic nature of his legislation:

> We shall honor the oath, which God swore to our father Abraham, fulfilling it, that we shall not cease all the days of our life from exhibiting innumerable calamities to all those committing iniquity and treading upon our God-given law with their feet, unless they cease sinning; nor shall we leave unmentioned their utter eradication. For the wondrous David as well did the same to these ones, and writing to the world he uttered: 'Early I will destroy all the wicked of the land, / That I may cut off all the evildoers from the city of the Lord.' "[61]

Although the *Nomoi* were never enacted or enforced, the moral code contained in the text demonstrates the profound influence of biblical and particularly Mosaic conceptions of law and justice. The tenth-century author of the *Nomoi*, writing in a monastic milieu, composed a legal order with no reference to Roman law. However, one cannot dismiss the *Nomoi* as the harsh ravings of a monk completely detached from his Middle Byzantine milieu. For his newly Christianized Kingdom of the Homerites, the inspiration for law and justice was to be biblical, not Roman.

Set against the imagined though illustrative example of the implementation of Mosiac law depicted in the *Nomoi* ascribed to Gregentios of Taphar, the popularity of the *NM* in the manuscript tradition becomes understandable. Similar to the *NG*, the manuscript tradition of the *NM* offers some insights as to its function. The *NM* manuscripts, of which there are forty, can be divided into two main categories: (1) among manuscripts containing the *Ecloga* as well as the *Appendix Eclogae*, a set of penal regulations; (2) as part of canon law collections. Although both categories contain manuscripts from a period well after when the *NM* was

[60] Gregentios of Taphar, *Nomoi*, lines 345–7. My translation differs somewhat from Berger's as I have tried to retain the sense of the comparative in the original Greek.

[61] Ibid., lines 136–43; Ps. 100[101]:8.

composed, it is the opinion of the textual editors that the first category consists of manuscripts which closely followed the contents of their prototypes, while the second category represents a later reworking of the texts the *NM* was copied with. The *NM*'s early presence in manuscripts with the *Ecloga* and *Appendix Eclogae* forces us to examine the *NM*, in spite of its biblical content, in the context of "secular" legal works. Indeed, the arrangement of topics in the *NM* strongly suggests that its compiler was comparing the *Ecloga* to biblical law.

While the evidence for the direct influence of biblical law on Byzantine law is minute at best,[62] the *NM* would have offered the judge a set of biblical norms which could be used to contextualize a particular decision. As discussed elsewhere, while Byzantine jurisprudence was necessarily framed by an overarching Roman legal tradition, the Bible offered paradigms of justice which the judge could use to justify his decision, much as Eustathios Rhomaios cited some verses from the *Odyssey* in support of his decision not to punish a woman who did marry a second time. Given the *NM* would not have been able to subvert or overturn a Roman legal precedent on its own, its function should be seen as more complementary than subversive. Like the *Nomoi* of Gregentios of Taphar, the existence and indeed prevalence of the *NM* need not be a reason for legal historians to posit its implementation or enforcement. Rather, the popularity of the *NM* should instead point to the variety of texts which judges and lawyers drew upon in approaching legal questions.

The *Nomos Nautikos* (*NN*)

The Rhodian Sea-Law (*nomos Rhodion nautikos*) or *Nomos Nautikos* (*NN*), a collection of maritime regulations divided into three parts, has, perhaps uniquely for a Byzantine legal text, attracted considerable attention outside of the field because of its relevance for the history of commerce and

[62] An example would be the emendation to Ashburner's text of the *NG* proposed by Laiou 1971. According to Laiou's reading of the text, the provision should read that a creditor, once he had held the land of a debtor for a seven-year period, had to apply the whole of the profits from the land after the seven-year period to the principal of the loan, and half of the profits made during the seven-year period. Thus the law was meant to discourage creditors from holding onto debtors' property for long periods of time. The *Ecloga* does not mention interest, which Zachariä von Lingenthal interpreted as a prohibition against interest, but there is no way to say for certain what the Isaurian emperors thought about the practice. Laiou also mentions this ch. 67's similarity to Deut. 15:1–2, which remits all debts after a period of seven years.

merchants.[63] The date and circumstances of composition of the *NN* are, like the *NG* and the *NM*, uncertain. Yet unlike the *NG* and *NM*, the date of the composition of the *NN* is complicated by the fact that the island of Rhodes in Antiquity did possess a well-known body of maritime law. What form the law took (written or unwritten) and its contents are open questions.

The Rhodian Sea-Law is mentioned in two places in the *CIC*, both within *Digest* 14.2 ("De Lege Rhodia de iactu"). The first mention is *Digest* 14.2.1, a fragment from the second book of the *Sententiae*, a work authored by the Roman jurist Paulus.[64] The second mention of the Rhodian Sea-Law is the famous and enigmatic *Digest* 14.2.9. Coming from the authority of the otherwise-unknown Volusius Maecianus, this Greek *Digest* fragment appears already in the *Florentiana* manuscript containing the *Digest* from the year 533/4, thus excluding the possibility that it is a later interpolation.[65] Given the importance of the passage for the history of the Rhodian Sea-Law, it is worth quoting in full: "The petition of Eudaimon of Nikomedia to the emperor Antonius: 'Lord Emperor Antonius, after we were shipwrecked in Italy we were robbed by officials living in the Cyclades Islands.' Antonius said to Eudaimon 'I am the lord of the world, and the law of the sea. Let [the matter] be judged according to Rhodian Sea-Law, in [instances] which none of our own laws contradicts it.' And the most divine Augustus judged the matter thus."[66] As the passage shows, the "Rhodian Sea-Law" (the mention of which here should not be confused with the text under discussion, which was authored much later) was used in those cases in which the Rhodian Sea-Law did not conflict with Roman law. Although of course one cannot definitely say whether or not the Rhodian Sea-Law was a written legal code or rather an unwritten body of customary law, the way the Rhodian Sea-Law is used in this instance closely resembles the way Roman jurists utilized customary law, which allowed a customary rule to be legally valid wherever there existed no written Roman legal precedent.[67]

[63] Ashburner's edition of the *NG* includes an English translation. For information on the *NG* see: Humphreys 2015: 179–93; Letsios 1996: 215–35; Pieler 1994: 319–20; Rodolakes 2007; Troianos 2011: 175–8; Van der Wal and Lokin 1985: 74–5.

[64] *Dig.* 14.2.1: "Lege Rhodia cavetur, ut, si levandae navis gratia iactus mercium factus esset, omnium contributione sarciatur quod pro omnibus datum est."

[65] Schminck 1999: 172.

[66] *Dig.* 14.2.9.

[67] *Basil.* 2.1.42.

This Rhodian Sea-Law of antiquity, which some scholars believe may have served as some kind of incipient maritime international law, must be considered separately from the *NN*, which despite uncertainty concerning its exact provenance, is agreed to be a Byzantine legal text. Byzantine legal historians have given various dates of composition for the *NN*. Zachariä saw considerable similarities between the *NN* and the *Ecloga*, and therefore dated the *NN* to the same period, even believing that the *NN* to have been an official act of Leo III or Constantine V.[68] Zachariä's assignation of the text to the period of Isaurian rule is reflective of his belief that the emperors Leo III and Constantine V were great legal reformers and innovators, a notion which is true to an extent but which later Byzantine legal historians believe was overstated. Ashburner, the editor of the modern critical edition, more conservatively assigned the text to the period 600–800.[69] Nicolaas van der Wal and J. H. A. Lokin propose the period 650–717 for the composition of the three *leges speciales* (the *NG*, *NN* and *NS*); in their view dating the *leges speciales* prior to the beginning of the reign of Leo III would in part explain why Leo felt the need to reassert the most commonly used areas of Roman law in simple and easily understandable language.[70] Later datings of the text have been proposed more recently, with Andreas Schminck arguing for a late ninth-century date of composition, while M. G. T. Humphreys, interpreting the text within his broader thesis of an Isaurian legal renaissance, dates it to perhaps in the third quarter of the eighth century.[71] Thus as is the case with the *NG*, there is no feature of the *NN* which can be used to construct a convincing argument as to its date of composition.

In lieu of attempting an exact dating of the text, it is at least safe to say that its authoring and use better fit an economic context in the second half of the period 600 to 800, if not somewhat later. The economic situation here is vital in determining why a set of regulations regulating ship-borne commerce would have been enacted in a period when most economic historians believe there was hardly any long-distance ship-borne trade at all. The Byzantine economy as well as the Mediterranean economy in general have been the subjects of numerous studies over the past thirty years, and these inquiries have refined our understanding of the Byzantine

[68] Zachariä von Lingenthal 1892: 316.

[69] *NN* lxvi.

[70] Van der Wal and Lokin 1985: 75.

[71] Humphreys 2015: 191–2; Schminck 1999.

economy during the "dark centuries."[72] The date of composition for the *NN* proposed by Ashburner, van der Wal and Lokin, and Zachariä represents the likely nadir of both the Byzantine economy and Mediterranean trade, before economic activity briskly increased starting over the period from *c.*750 to the mid to late ninth century.

The *NN* has been divided by its editor into three parts: Part I is a list of Roman emperors who purportedly sanctioned the *NN*; Part II consists of nineteen chapters of uncertain relation to one another; and Part III contains forty-seven more or less thematically grouped chapters. Ashburner relegated Part I to an appendix in his edition, since it is a later addition to the text. The way the *NN* is arranged, as with every other characteristic of the *NN*, has been subject to much debate. Part III is the most coherent and organized portion of the *NN*. Part II seems to have no organizing principle, and Part I is an obvious forgery transmitted in a draft state. According to Ashburner's outline of the textual history of the *NN*, the *NN* existed in two redactions. An original edition, written by a "private" hand and corresponding both to Part II and Part III, was followed by a later, "vulgate" edition. This "vulgate" edition, which is represented in the earliest manuscripts as well as the *Synopsis Basilicorum Major* (*SBM*, a one-volume abridgement of the *Basilika*), was a reworking of the text in preparation for its insertion into the *Basilika*, and at that time Part II was severed from Part III.[73]

Yet perhaps the most interesting part of the *NN* for this study, and at the same time the section which scholars have dismissed as nonsense, is the forged prologue. While the *NG* and *NM* achieved entry into the broader Byzantine legal tradition mainly by association, that is by being transmitted in manuscripts with more officially recognized codes of law, the *NN* was validated by an enigmatic act of forgery.[74] This prologue of the *NN* was written well after its contents, likely in the tenth or eleventh century.[75] Though undoubtedly a forgery, and transmitted in what appears

[72] Chief among them are Laiou 2002; Hendy 1985; Harvey 1989. In a wider context, there is of course McCormick 2001.

[73] Schminck 1999: 173–4 suggests instead that Part III was written at the behest of Photios around 866, while Part II was authored specifically for the *NN*'s incorporation into the *Sixty Books*, perhaps even by Leo VI himself. Rodolakes 2007 believes that Part II, as well as the prologue, predates the existence of the *CIC*, while Part III was authored before the eighth century.

[74] The prologue, corresponding to Part I of the *NN*, at *NN* 39–41 (Appendix A).

[75] There are two main versions of the prologue, both appearing in manuscripts starting in the twelfth century. The oldest manuscript containing the prologue is *Codex Parisinus graecus* 1384, which is dated to 1165/6 (Schminck 1999: 177–8). Yet a tenth-century manuscript from Southern Italy (according to Cavallo), the *Codex Bodleianus Laudianus* 39, contains the heading: "Νόμος Ῥοδίων ναυτικός, ὃν ἐθέσπισαν οἱ θειότατοι αὐτοκράτορες Ἀδριανός, Ἀντωνῖνος, Τιβέριος, Λούκιος,

to be a draft state, it is certainly possible that it was modelled on actual legislation.[76] Though scholarship on the *NN* has examined in some detail whether and to what extent the prologue to the *NN* was a forgery, hitherto downplayed has been the question of why a prologue, purporting to give *NN* the sanction of early Roman emperors, was authored at all.

The selection of emperors who supposedly promulgated the *NN* according to the prologue is unusual. Instead of Justinian, who was credited with promulgating the *NG*, or some other past Christian emperor of prominence like Constantine, one finds the pagan emperors Hadrian (r. 117–38), Tiberius (r. 14–37), Commodus (?, listed as Lucius, r. 180–92), Septimius Severus (r. 193–211) and Pertinax (r. 193).[77] Other pagan emperors appear in the jumbled narrative of the text as well, including Nero (r. 54–68) and Vespasian (r. 69–79).[78] The criteria by which these particular emperors were chosen are unclear; the forger perhaps simply selected names from a list of Roman emperors, like that of the anonymous *Chronographia brevis*, which was completed during the reign of Leo VI.[79] This attention to the pagan past is a well-recognized phenomenon in Byzantine culture of the period, which shifted around the time of the beginning of the Macedonian dynasty, and particularly in the tenth and eleventh centuries, toward a rapprochement with its classical roots.[80] This "Macedonian Renaissance" has long been posited with regard to the art and literature of the period, but extended as well to matters like the genealogies of influential families.[81] The Phokas family, for instance, adopted an entirely fabricated lineage extending back to the Roman Fabii and Scipii, as recorded by the eleventh-century historian Michael Attaleiates.[82]

Σεπτίμιος Σευῆρος, Περτίναξ Ῥωμαῖοι ἀεισέβαστοι", which is also found at the start of the prologue.

76 Following Zachariä von Lingenthal 1892: 29, Ashburner (*NN* lxxiv) suggested that the prologue could have been a student exercise at the Law School founded by Constantine IX Monomachos (r. 1042–55) at Constantinople. Schminck 1999: 177–8, citing the South Italian provenance of many of the manuscripts, argues for an eleventh-century South Italian context, perhaps Amalfi. In contrast to older scholars like Ashburner who categorically rejected the notion that the prologue of the *NN* could have been based on actual historical documents, Rodolakes 2007: 112–13, *passim* has proposed the prologue is a "layered" composition, with constituent parts ranging from the first to the end of the seventh century. According to Rodolakes, the beginning and end of the prologue contains, with some changes, text from a *constitutio principis* of the emperor Tiberius (r. 14–37). Thereafter the original constitution of Tiberius was successively reworked. This is in keeping with the general thrust of Rodolakes' work, which is that the *NN* contains remnants of authentic Roman law.

77 *NN* 39.

78 *NN* 401.

79 *Chronographia brevis (e cod. Coislin. 193)* 222–3.

80 Kazhdan and Epstein 1985: 133–8.

81 Ibid. 102–4.

82 Michael Attaleiates, *Historia* 158–61. Cf. Krallis 2012: 147–8.

The author of the prologue of the *NN*, like Attaleiates for the Phokades, thus invented or pasted together an illustrious Roman pedigree for his text. These activities evidence a reappropriation of *Romanitas*, a process accelerated by papal and Carolingian challenges to the Byzantines' "Romanness" during the so-called Photian Schism.[83] The codification efforts of the Macedonian emperors, which focused on the recapitulation of the *CIC*, likewise reflect the reappropriation of Roman political heritage.[84] The classicizing tendency of the author of the forgery of the prologue to the *NN* is clearly a sign that it stems from the time of Macedonian dynasty; thus regardless of where the *NN* stems from, it was made to fit the ideological agenda of the "Cleansing of the Ancient Laws."

The Transmission of the *NM* and the *Leges Speciales*

Although at first glance the transmission of Byzantine secular law and the function of the *NM* and the *leges speciales* appear to have little to do with one another, an examination of how Byzantine law was transmitted to Eastern Europe and the Middle East reveals what both the Byzantines and their neighbors considered "Roman law," in the broadest of senses.[85] What is most revealing about an examination of the transmission of the Byzantine secular law is a conspicuous lacuna: the *Basilika*, as well its antecedents like the *Sixty Books*, were simply neither translated nor adopted by foreign cultures; nor were the most classicizing legal compositions of this period, such as the *Legal Textbook* of Michael Attaleiates or the *SBM*, to say nothing of the short yet uniquely Byzantine *Eisagoge*.[86] Instead both the *Prochiron* and *Ecloga* feature much more prominently, and their transmission very much occurred alongside the *NG*, *NM* and *NN*. This state of affairs becomes clear via the consideration of the transmission of these texts into three cultural spheres: that of the Slavic peoples, where Old Church Slavonic was used as a literary and liturgical language in the Balkans and medieval Rus'; the Caucasus and Eastern Asia Minor, containing cultures both in (Georgians) and out of (Armenians) communion

83 Fögen 1998: 17–22.

84 See Ch. 1.

85 On the transmission and influence of Byzantine law in general, see in particular the excellent surveys of Pitsakes 2005 and Burgmann 2005c. Georgesco 1969 traces in great detail the transmission of Byzantine law in the Balkans via a single text, the *NG*.

86 Burgmann 2005c: 49–50.

with the Constantinopolitan patriarchate; and the Near East, where Byzantine texts were translated into Arabic and Roman ones into Syriac.[87]

The ninth-century mission to Moravia by the brothers Constantine/Cyril and Methodios, and their decision to translate the Bible and other theological works into a newly created, Slavic literary language which became Old Church Slavonic (OCS), served as the vehicle of transmission by which Byzantine law, both canon and secular, spread outside the Empire's northern frontier.[88] Without engaging with it too closely, it perhaps best to cite here the idea of an enduring Byzantine sphere of cultural influence in the Balkans and Eastern Europe, the "Byzantine Commonwealth" famously postulated by Dimitry Obolensky.[89] The influence of Byzantine law is evident in one of the earliest legal collections written in OCS, the *Law for Judging the People* (*Zakon Sudnyj Ljudem*).[90] The *Law for Judging the People* is a work of thirty chapters based primarily on the seventeenth chapter of the *Ecloga*, sometimes reproducing the original exactly while at other times reworking it. The Serbian *Nomokanon* of St Sava contained both the *Prochiron* and the *NM*.[91] One Serbian and three Church Slavic translations of *NG* are known, and this text found eventually found its way in the law code promulgated by the fourteenth-century Serbian ruler Stefan Dušan, appearing as the "Law of the Emperor Justinian."[92] The pattern already discernable in the dissemination and translation of Byzantine secular law in the Balkans – namely

[87] Excluded from this study is Italy, and South Italy in particular, as it is a special case for the influence of Byzantine law, complicated by the fact that that the region had both a large Greek-speaking population (it was known as Magna Graecia in antiquity for a reason) as well as a comparatively recent (in contrast in particular to the Arabic-, and Syriac-speaking populations in the Middle East) legacy of Byzantine rule, which only ended at the close of the eleventh century. The continuing linguistic and cultural influence of Greek-speaking monasteries in Calabria and Sicily is likewise a factor not at play in the areas discussed here, with the exception of Palestine for Arabic- and Aramaic-speakers. On Byzantine law in Italy see Pitsakes 2005: 270–1 and Fögen 1991a. The most authoritative monograph on the subject remains Brandileone 1886.

[88] The influence of Byzantine culture on the medieval Slavs has been and is such a heavily studied subject that it constitutes a field all its own. For a good introduction to the subject, see the articles (published between 1954 and 2004) in Shepard 2007. Schminck 2005c sees a connection between the request of Slavic rulers for law codes and the start of the "Cleansing of the Ancient Laws." On the legal works which the Cyril-Methodius mission to Moravia produced, see Papastathes 1978.

[89] Obolensky 1971. Fowden 1993 further developed Obolensky's conception of a Byzantine Commonwealth, arguing that there existed two commonwealths, one in Late Antiquity and a second corresponding Obolensky's mostly Slavic formulation. The downplaying of the Caucasus, and in particular of Orthodox Georgia, in Obolensky's Byzantine Commonwealth has been justifiably highlighted by Rapp 2013.

[90] Burgmann 1991f.

[91] Burgmann 2005c: 60.

[92] Burgmann 2005c: 56; Pitsakes 2005: 268.

an emphasis on the *Ecloga*, *Prochiron*, *leges speciales* and *NM* – can *grosso modo* be applied to the other regions and cultures discussed below.

Medieval Rus' likewise played a prominent role in the transmission of Byzantine law after the conversion of Prince Vladimir in 988.[93] The influence of secular Byzantine law is represented by translations of the *Ecloga*, *Prochiron* and the *NG*. Of the three *leges speciales*, while the *NG* was quite popular and formed the kernel of a manuscript collection known as the *Knigi Zakonnye* ("Law Books"), the *NN* and *NS* were of little interest, although they were sometimes copied anyway.[94] The Old Church Slavonic translation of the *Prochiron* found its way into a series of legal collections known as the *Zakon gradskii* ("City Law").[95] Excerpts from the *Ecloga* and *Prochiron* were included in the earliest version of the *Kormčaya Kniga* ("The Pilot's Book"), an *ad hoc* collection of canon and secular law perhaps intended for the use of ecclesiastical officials.[96] With regard to the *Basilika*, an expert on the transmission of law in medieval Rus' has remarked that: "There are no indications that the *Basilika* ever came to Russia during this period and nobody has ever suggested that it did influence Russian law."[97]

The noteworthy omission of the *Basilika* is likewise the case with Armenian as well as Georgian translations of secular Byzantine lawbooks.[98] Although the Armenian Church already possessed a well-developed canon law tradition dating back to the time of the *kat'ołikos* John of Odzun (718–29), no autochthonous secular legal collection was authored before that of Mkit'ar Gosh.[99] Mkit'ar Gosh himself cited the lack of an Armenian legal tradition, which forced Christian Armenians to utilize Muslim secular courts, as one of the principal motives for the composition of his *Datastanagirk'*.[100] The sources of the *Datastanagirk'*, and particularly the degree to which it is indebted to other legal traditions, particularly Byzantine law, is still not entirely clear.

[93] The two best English-language overviews on the medieval Russian law are Feldbrugge 2009: 59–128 and Kaiser 1980.

[94] Feldbrugge 2009: 71.

[95] Feldbrugge 2009: 75.

[96] Feldbrugge 2009: 90; Burgmann 1991b; Burgmann 2005c: 54–8. In general see Žužek 1964.

[97] Feldbrugge 2009: 74.

[98] A good overview of the transmission of Byzantine law into both Armenian and Georgian can be found in Kaufhold 2012: 314–42. An extensive bibliography on the same subject is contained in Burgmann and Kaufhold 1992: 91–268.

[99] The enormously complex composition and transmission of the main collection of Armenian canon law has been exhaustively analyzed by Mardirossian 2004.

[100] *Datastanagirk'*, Ch. 1.

A more direct case of the transmission of Byzantine law can be found in Mkit'ar Gosh's twelfth-century contemporary, Nerses of Lambron (1153–98).[101] Nerses himself translated a great deal of Byzantine law; in one of his letters he wrote that since, echoing the sentiment of Mkit'ar Gosh, there existed no secular law among the Armenians, he therefore sought out a Greek text and translated: (1) the *Ecloga*; (2) the *NM*; (3) the *NS*.[102] Again, as with the case of Byzantine law translated into OCS, neither Nerses nor any translator attempted to copy what was by then the completed *Basilika*, or any of its antecedents like Leo VI's *Sixty Books*.

The orthodoxy, from the Byzantine point of view, of the Georgian church as well as the large number of medieval Georgian intellectuals who made translations from Greek into Georgian sustained a substantial Georgian interest in translating Byzantine canon law. A smaller and a larger *nomokanon* were compiled on the basis of translated Greek canon law texts at the end of the tenth and eleventh century, respectively.[103] Secular law by contrast was neglected, and it is not until the codification project of King Vakhtang VI of Kartli (r. 1716–24) that we find what is possibly a Georgian translation of a Middle Byzantine lawbook, namely the *NM*, though the *NM* as the source of this Georgian collection of precepts from the Pentateuch has not yet been confirmed by scholarship.[104]

Last but not least Byzantine law was also translated into Arabic and Syriac. The case of Syriac in particular is interesting because certain works of Roman law, like the *Syro-Roman Lawbook* and the *Sententiae Syriacae*, have been preserved in Syriac but not in the language they were originally written in, presumably Greek. Both of the aforementioned compilations are of disputed provenance and their relationship to Roman law has been long debated without resulting in any scholarly consensus. At a later date the *Ecloga* and other works of Middle Byzantine law were translated into Arabic. Within the legal tradition of the Coptic Church, a collection of Byzantine law known as the *Canons of the Emperors* (Ar. *Qawānīn al-mulūk*) demonstrates the texts which were selected for translation.[105] The *Canons of the Emperors* appear in three independent forms by thirteenth- and fourteenth-century scholars: (1) ibn al-'Assāl (died

[101] See Thomson 1991b; list of editions, translations, and secondary literature Thomson 1995: 175–8, to be supplemented by Thomson 2007.

[102] Kaufhold 1976: 596–8.

[103] Kaufhold 2012: 332–8.

[104] Kaufhold 2012: 341.

[105] Kaufhold 2012: 234–6.

before 1260); (2) Abū l-Barakāt (died 1324); and (3) Makarios (Maqārah), a contemporary of Abū l-Barakāt.[106] Their three versions of the text all contain the *Prochiron*, the *Syro-Roman Lawbook* and the *Ecloga* (complete in two of the three versions but excerpted in ibn al-'Assāl). The Arabic *Ecloga* includes excerpts from the *Appendix Eclogae*, the *NS* and the *NN*.[107] Among the Melkites an Arabic translation of the *Prochiron* circulated separately; though the translation cannot be dated with certainly, there is manuscript evidence which suggests that an Arabic translation of the text was planned, if not necessarily carried out, already in the eleventh century.[108] Again, the point to take away from this overview of the transmission of Byzantine law in the Middle East is that the *Basilika* and its antecedents were simply not translated. As the above has demonstrated, the principal achievement of the Macedonian legal reforms, the "Cleansing of the Ancient Laws" which resulted in a substantially correct recapitulation of Justinianic law, the *Basilika*, was simply not appropriated along with other secular legal texts into the cultures influenced by Byzantium.

Conclusion

In this chapter, the manuscript tradition and the transmission of the *NG*, *NM* and *NN* revealed that these legal texts were incredibly popular within and without the Byzantine Empire, despite the fact that there no exists no evidence that these laws were ever legally valid, that is to say, that they complemented or superseded "official" collections of Roman law, such as the Justinianic corpus or the various Macedonian redactions of it. An explanation will now be advanced as to how and why these laws were used.

In order to contextualize the historical period during which these laws appeared, it is necessary to emphasize that, while pronouncing that Roman law was hopelessly outdated as Oikonomides and Kazhdan did is perhaps an overstatement, Roman law in the Justinianic iteration which the Byzantines had inherited it was at the very least unwieldy and, according to isolated anecdotes, unusable. While the statement in the prologue of the *Ecloga* that judges, particularly those outside the capital, had great difficulty understanding Roman law was perhaps a rhetorical

[106] *Arabic Ecloga* 2–3.

[107] Ibid. 18–19.

[108] *Arabic Prochiron* 22–33. I would like to thank Johannes Pahlitzsch for sharing with me the manuscript version of his book.

exaggeration of the actual situation on the ground,[109] there is evidence enough to believe that Justinianic law from the end of the period of the *antecessores* in the sixth century until the completion of the process of *exhellenismos* in the late ninth century required both a mastery of Greek and Latin along with a good corpus of commentaries and lexica which very few jurists in the Byzantine Empire possessed. The question of competence in Latin among Byzantine legal scholars is treated more fully elsewhere,[110] but suffice it to say that until the eleventh century, at which time newer scholia were written to complement the older sixth- and seventh-century scholia, use of the Greek translations of Justinianic law which had been made by the *antecessores* would still have required a limited knowledge of Latin, as many Latin legal terms were maintained in the Greek translations of Justinianic law.[111] The number of legal scholars competent in both Greek and Latin must have been extremely small, rendering the huge corpus of Justinianic law difficult, although certainly not impossible, to utilize. Thus the first advantage of the laws discussed in this chapter was that they could be used by judges and lawyers *without* knowing Latin. This advantage is all the more important when one considers which laws were translated by the peoples neighboring Byzantium, for if a good working knowledge of Latin was rare in the capital, it was even rarer in Armenia, Bulgaria, Rus' and the Middle East. The occasional outlier, like the Armenian *kat'ołikos* Gregory Vkayaser ("Martyrophile" 1065–1105), who translated or commissioned translations of Greek, Latin and Syriac *vitae* into Armenian, is the exception that proves the rule.[112] In addition to its conciseness, the lack of Latin legal terminology in the *Prochiron*, which was also at times translated, was partially due to the fact that its writer(s) had shorn or calqued the Latin legal language of its prototypes. Although one cannot prove how the *NM* and the *leges speciales* were used, at the very least they constituted a kind of "stop-gap" legal code which provided judges and lawyers with a comprehensible set of texts before the process of *exhellenismos* was completed. The lack of Latin in these texts likewise accounted for

[109] *Ecloga*, proem, lines 36–40: "[The emperors] being mindful that the matters legislated by previous emperors are written in many books and that knowing their intent is difficult to understand, and for some indiscernible, especially for those outside of this divinely protected and capital city of ours [Constantinople] … "

[110] See Ch. 5; on knowledge of Latin in Byzantium during this period, see Fögen 1998: 12–17; Michel 1949.

[111] Fögen 1998: 14.

[112] On this Armenian *kat'ołikos* see Kapoian-Kouymjian 1974.

their popularity among those cultures which were influenced by the Byzantine legal tradition.

Besides their lack of untranslated Latin legal terminology, the *NM* and the *leges speciales* had the advantage of being small and therefore economical, especially in comparison with the massive *Basilika.* After Byzantium was cut off from the Egyptian supply of papyrus following the Arab conquests of the seventh century, the price of writing material – parchment and the small amounts of papyrus which could be procured from Southern Italy – became much dearer. There was doubtless access to the Justinianic corpus and its Greek translations in the capital, where the emperor, the courts of appeal, the eparch, as well as the legal officials holding jurisdiction within the various departments (*sekreta*) could refer to the necessary Roman legal texts. It is also possible but by no means certain that access to much of the Justinianic corpus could have been found in some of the other larger cities of the empire like Thessaloniki. The availability of legal texts in the provinces is a much trickier question, and there is no evidence which would allow a comparative analysis of which legal texts were available in a rural milieu as opposed to say Constantinople. Some anecdotes, however, should militate against equating an urban milieu with access to legal texts and a rural milieu with their lack. The mysterious ninth-century polymath and autodidact Leo the Mathematician, for instance, finding no teachers of note in the capital, purportedly found the mathematical and philosophical texts he required for his studies on the island of Andros.[113] From an earlier period, the teacher of the seventh-century Armenian scholar Ananias of Shirak, Tychikos, taught mathematics in strategically important but rather small Trebizond.[114]

As a practical matter, however, the sheer size of the *Basilika* when compared with the *NM* and the *leges speciales* is inescapable in considering the question of access to legal texts. We know that the *Sixty Books*/*Basilika* was at first commonly divided into six volumes or manuscripts, and later into four.[115] A one-volume abridgement of the *Basilika*, the so-called *Synopsis Basilicorum Major*, was made in the tenth century. According to the *TLG*, the Groningen edition of the *Basilika*, which represents only the incomplete text that has been transmitted to modern scholars, runs to 765,405 words. When one considers this number with the length of the received commentary tradition, which runs to 1,282,347 words and

113 See Kazhdan 1991f; Lemerle 1986: 171–204; Wilson 1983: 79–84.

114 See Thomson 1991a.

115 Burgmann 2011: 90.

which would have been indispensable for applying the law in the *Basilika*, the corpus in total constitutes over two million words. By comparison, the *NM* contains 5,628 words, the *Ecloga* 10,514, the *Prochiron* 29,735, the *Eisagoge* 44,063. None of the *leges speciales* is even one hundredth of the length of the *Basilika* with commentaries. The sheer size of the *Basilika* probably limited its regular use only to the courts of the capital. Such a conclusion is warranted by a response of the twelfth-century canonist Balsamon to Mark III, the Melkite patriarch of Alexandria, who asked whether the *Basilika* had to serve as the standard secular lawbook for Orthodox Christians, given the *Basilika* were not in fact available in his patriarchate.[116]

This is probably also a reason why the courts of appeal in Constantinople, like that of the Hippodrome and Velum, were stationary. The court of the thematic judge, by contrast, was peripatetic; a novel of Constantine VII regulating legal fees mentioned that expenses for travelling and upkeep were excluded from the prescribed legal fees that the plaintiff and defendant paid to the thematic judge, but which both parties in court were still obliged to pay for.[117] The fact that thematic courts travelled meant that carrying copies of even abridged versions of the *Basilika* would have been extremely difficult. Again, the brevity of the *NM* and the *leges speciales* must have at least partially contributed to their enormous popularity, for such texts were short enough that they could likely be found in the provinces or could be carried with the peripatetic thematic courts. Thus, the economy of these legal texts, particularly in comparison with the *Basilika*, no doubt contributed to their ubiquity within and without the Byzantine Empire.

With regard to the perceived validity of these texts, it is likely that the *NG*, *NN* and *NS* were recognized as a genuine part of the Roman legal tradition. In this respect scholars have long missed the mark, repeatedly pointing up that the imperial attributions of the *NG* and *NN* were false: yet the key question is not whether these texts' fabricated pedigree was genuine or not, *but when exactly they came to be seen by contemporaneous jurists and judges as genuine*. As we know from the mid-eleventh-century *Meditatio de nudis pactis*, which argued for the superiority of the writings of the *antecessor* Stephan over the *Basilika* with reference to a case concerning the validity of an informal agreement between a *protospatharios*

116 *Theodore Balsamon, Canonical Responses to Mark, the Patriarch of Alexandria*, question 4 (English translation 117–18). Cf. Pitsakes 2003: 251–2.

117 See Ch. 2; Morris 2013.

and a monastery, as well as cases like *Peira* 51.16, which involves a disagreement between two passages from *Digest* and *Novels* of Justinian which made their way into the *Basilika* concerning whether a decision requires unanimity or majority, Byzantine legal scholars acknowledged that the Roman legal tradition was layered. It is within this conceptual framework that one can contextualize the use of the *NG*, *NN* and *NS*. While the most competent legal scholars, like Eustathios Rhomaios, probably recognized that these three laws postdated the Justinianic legal reforms, an individual lawyer, like the author of the *Meditatio de nudis pactis*, would have been able to draw on these laws if by doing so it somehow benefitted his case. This fact once again reflects the eclectic way in which Byzantine judges and lawyers drew upon legal texts.

The *NM*, which by no stretch of the imagination could have been included within the Roman legal tradition, performed a different function that that of the *NG*, *NN* and *NS*. While the legal framework of the Byzantine Empire remained Roman, Christian ideas about justice and jurisprudence profoundly influenced the way the law was interpreted and applied,[118] and in this context the *NM* could have served as a guide as how to provide legal opinions grounded in Roman law with biblical trappings. This would explain why the *NM* contains no explicit comparison between Christian and Roman law, since its function was complementary rather than adversarial. The arrangement of material, which Schminck rightly points out corresponds to its presentation in the *Ecloga*, was thus intended as a side-by-side reading, rather than a comparison of differing opinions. One might object that biblical and Roman law were so radically different that one could not use the other to support a particular decision, but this would belie the way they are effectively intertwined in a number of Byzantine legal texts, most notably the introduction to the *Ecloga*.

As a final consideration, it is worth taking into account the nature of the polities which appropriated parts of the Byzantine legal tradition and which commissioned and supported these translations. By and large, the Macedonian redactions of Justinianic law, understandably given that they were ninth- and tenth-century reworkings of texts which reflected the sixth-century empire, projected the worldview of an autocratic and, by the standards of the period, highly centralized and bureaucratic state. Yet the cultures and states which appropriated these texts, however much they attempted to remake their polities along the lines of the Byzantine model,

[118] In general see Ch. 3.

were organized completely differently, not least of all in that they were much less centralized. It is therefore interesting that it has been proposed that the one state which perhaps did attempt to appropriate Justinianic law was most similar to it in terms of administration and the way in which the state was organized, that of Harun al-Rashid's Abbasid Caliphate.[119] For the decentralized polities which appropriated Byzantine law, the *NG*, *NM* and *NN* were better suited to states with no institutional memory of Roman/Byzantine rule and which did not presuppose a centralized administration. In closing, despite the opaque textual history of the *NG*, *NM* and *NN*, these laws were used and transmitted to neighboring cultures because of their lack of Latin legal terminology; their brevity and conciseness in comparison to the *Basilika*; and the complementary role these texts played within Byzantine legal culture, serving as aids rather than countermeasures to the framework of Roman law.

[119] Jokisch 2007. While the book is extremely ambitious and original, its numerous shortcomings with regard to Byzantine history and Byzantine legal texts in particular render many of Jokisch's theories less plausible; these are detailed in Wolfram Brandes' review of the book. See Brandes 2010.

CHAPTER 5

Law and Heresy in the Edicts of the Patriarch Alexios Stoudites

Introduction

The final two chapters of this study narrate the concluding arc of the Macedonian synthesis of Byzantine legal culture.[1] While the initiation of the program of the "Cleansing of the Ancient Laws," examined in Chapter 1, was clearly a top-down initiative, an enterprise directed by the Basil I (r. 867–86) and Leo VI (r. 886–912), the first emperors of the Macedonian dynasty, its eleventh-century denouement featured a new cadre of jurists that this centuries-long revival of legal studies had produced. Despite their considerable achievements, the identity of most of the Byzantine jurists of the late ninth and early tenth century who produced the *Prochiron*, *Eisagoge* and above all the *Basilika*, a project whose Herculean dimensions favorably compares with the codification exploits of the Justinianic age, will probably forever remain unknown to us. This presents quite a contrast to the Isaurian *Ecloga*, whose collaborators were named and can be to an extent analyzed prosopographically.[2] Moreover, the great legal minds of the age, like Leo VI and the patriarch Photios, were polymaths who used law among many other disciplines to advance their ideological and political aims.

This is not true of the legal scholars of the eleventh century. There were of course many intellectuals who also dabbled in law, with Michael Psellos standing out as the most prominent example of someone particularly adept at peddling his cultural capital as a famed scholar for political influence.[3] Yet in the waning decades of the Macedonian dynasty there were also professional jurists who used their legal expertise to advance their own in some cases quite spectacular political careers. The most talented

1 This chapter is a slightly revised version of Chitwood 2014.

2 In fact this has been done in an exemplary fashion by Pratsch 2001.

3 On Psellos as a lawyer, see Dennis 1994; as a teacher of law, see Fögen 1982.

and respected member of this elite group was Eustathios Rhomaios, yet his role in the power struggles and politics of his day is difficult to follow. The rapid ascension of Eustathios into the upper echelons of the empire's judiciary was facilitated by one of his judicial colleagues, the future emperor Romanos III Argyros (r. 1028–34). Before he ascended to the throne Romanos had been a judge and eparch of the capital. He is mentioned in the *Peira*, at one point praising Eustathios' "admirable judgment,"[4] and his esteem for his onetime colleague was so great that he repurposed a previously military office, that of the *droungarios* of the Vigla, and by assigning it to Eustathios made him essentially the chief justice of the supreme court of the empire.[5]

It is this first prominent generation of professional jurists, that of Eustathios, Romanos and their colleagues, which demonstrates the rise and the increasing political power of a cadre of legal scholars in the capital. Their newfound prominence was occasioned by a power vacuum, as in the decades after the passing of Basil II (r. 976–1025) his successors were unable to replicate the military successes and fiscal stability of his reign. The emperors of this period, all of whom had only a tenuous hold on power, used law as a means of political legitimation. Thus the first phase of the prominence of a professional cadre of jurists is to be found in the later 1020s, as well as throughout the 1030s and into the first years of the 1040s, and that is precisely the period to which the present chapter is devoted. Only by understanding the changing role of the law during these decades by often insecure emperors can one understand the seeming apogee of legal studies under a second generation of jurists in the 1040s under the emperor Constantine IX Monomachos (r. 1042–55), which is examined in detail in Chapter 6. While most scholarship presents this emperor's patronage of a cadre of intellectuals and the foundation of a law school in 1047 as *ex nihilo* acts, in the following pages it will become clear that all aspects of the blossoming of legal studies under Constantine IX had deep roots in the preceding decades, and in particular in a reexamination of the legal status of heretics during the patriarchate of Alexios Stoudites (1025–43).

It was under this patriarch that a number of synodal edicts were issued against the Syrian Orthodox population in Melitene, on the empire's southeastern border, which affected the interpretation of passages dealing

[4] *Peira* 49.4: *Basil. Schol.* 60.37.79 likewise records Romanos III's admiration for Eustathios' jurisprudence. Cf. Oikonomides 1986: 172.

[5] Oikonomides 1986: 174–5.

with heretics in the *Basilika*. In particular, a provision of Justinianic law which seemingly forbade Jews from testifying in court (*Basil.* 21.1.45 = *Cod. Just.* 1.5.21) was reinterpreted as referring instead to "Nestorians", or adherents of the Church of the East.[6] By comparing provisions for Jews testifying in court in roughly contemporary sources, it can be demonstrated that a reinterpretation probably occurred around the year 1039. Exceptionally by the standards of Byzantine patriarchs, Alexios employed a commission of jurists in order to examine and redefine the legal status of heretics. The unique skills of these professional jurists, in particular their ability to consult the Greek commentaries of the *antecessores*, legal scholars of the age of Justinian and shortly afterward, allowed them to analyze and interpret difficult passages of late Roman law.

Defining Heresy in the Eleventh-Century Political Context

One of the great problems in the analysis of Byzantine law in general, as often noted in this study, is that the normative legal sources rarely reflect the political context in which they were issued or were in force. When Byzantine emperors chose to combat contemporaneous problems via the legal regime, usually they did so via the medium of imperial legislation, and only rarely did such legislation influence the normative law codes, such as the *Basilika*. With regard to heresy, the *Basilika* thus presents us with a static, sixth-century picture of anti-heretical regulations; no mention whatsoever is made in the text of the *Basilika* or its scholia of any heresy appearing after the sixth century. Thus even the Syrian Orthodox, whom in the sixth century Justinian had hoped to bring back to the Chalcedonian fold, are not directly condemned in Justinianic legislation.[7] The most egregious and noteworthy of these omissions is that of Muslims, despite the fact that they were a substantial minority of great commercial and diplomatic importance, above all in the capital city of Constantinople.[8] As Stephan Reinert notes, "conceptually, it seems that

6 Throughout this chapter the designations "Syrian Orthodox" and "Church of the East" are used rather than the older corresponding terms "Jacobite" and "Nestorian", both of which are best avoided; see Brock 1996. I use "Syrian Orthodox" and "Church of the East" throughout this chapter, except in translations when Byzantine Greek texts explicitly use the term "Jacobite" (Ἰακωβίτης) or "Nestorian" (Νεστοριανός).

7 On this relationship see especially Brock 2011; Menze 2008.

8 See especially the useful overview of the Muslim community in Constantinople in Reinert 1998, as well as Anderson 2009. The supposed construction of the mosque under Leo III at the request of the Muslim general Maslama has quite rightly been shown to be problematic by Woods 2013.

the late antique trisections of the non-Orthodox into pagans, heretics, and Jews formally persisted, but that the leaders of Byzantine society never elected to define, legally and officially, the category to which any 'Ishmaelites within' belonged."[9] In fact, in the eyes of the Byzantine jurist, not all heretics were created equal; they suffered from different degrees of legal incapacity under Byzantine law.[10]

The circumstances which prompted the edicts of Alexios Stoudites and concomitant reinterpretation of Justianianic provisions against heretics were conditioned by the empire-wide geopolitical context of the Byzantine Empire in the second quarter of the eleventh century as well as the local and regional context of the city of Melitene itself and the surrounding territory. With regard to the former, the last quarter-century of Macedonian rule after the death of Basil II represents a period of increasing dynastic instability. After the passing of Basil's aged brother Constantine VIII (r. 1025–8), the continuation of the dynasty's rule depended upon Constantine's three daughters: Eudokia, Theodora and Zoe. The next four Byzantine emperors laid claim to the Macedonian inheritance through Zoe, either via marriage (Romanos III Argyros, Michael IV Paphlagon (r. 1034–41) and Constantine IX Monomachos) or adoption (Michael V (r. 1041–2)).

The tenuousness of these rulers' claim to authority, based as it was solely on their relationship to Zoe, created a power vacuum which was filled, to a significant degree, by a resurgent patriarchate under the leadership of Alexios Stoudites.[11] The long reign of Basil II had witnessed a succession of mostly subservient patriarchs (Anthony III Stoudites (974–9), Nicholas II Chrysoberges (979–91), Sergios II (1001–19) and Eustathios (1019–25)), with the exception of Sisinnios II (996–8), who was the first layman to become patriarch since Photios. Above all, Alexios, as the arbitrator of the legitimacy of Zoe's marriages, was able to translate his authority into concessions: either on behalf of the wider church, such as the abolition during the reign of Romanos III Argyros of the *allelengyon*, the responsibility of *dynatoi* and wealthier religious houses to pay the tax arrears of the poor, which had been introduced by Basil II in 1002, or for his person in the

Though the mosque probably existed from at least the eighth century, it was likely an *ad hoc* development that had to be explained by later Byzantine writers.

[9] Reinert 1998: 149.

[10] For a recent overview of the persecution of heretics in imperial legislation, see Noethlichs 2006, for Justinian in particular Noethlichs 2006: 124–5.

[11] The importance of Alexios' patriarchate is contextualized in Lauritzen 2010; Stanković 2001–2.

form of donations to his personal monastery, for which he reputedly managed to accumulate 25 *kentinaria* of gold.[12]

In exchange for financial support and allowing the patriarchate a vastly expanded role in political affairs, Alexios offered the support of the official church to whoever sat on the imperial throne after Basil II's death. Thus another synodal edict from the year 1026, which has survived only in fragments, pronounced automatic anathema upon anyone guilty of sedition or inciting rebellion against the emperor.[13] Signed by Constantine VIII, this synodal edict signaled a remarkable shift in the balance of power in the capital, and indeed over the next fifty years the patriarchs of Constantinople enjoyed a period of unequalled influence. The oft-cited words of the later patriarch Michael Keroularious (1043–59) supposedly uttered to the usurper Isaac I Komnenos (r. 1057–9) – "I raised you up … and I can break you"[14] – certainly encapsulated the almost papal dimensions of the office's mid-eleventh-century power.

Alongside these dynastic issues, larger societal trends can be discerned as well. While scholarship over the past thirty-five years has gradually undermined notions of some of the declinist trajectories of Byzantium in the eleventh century which Paul Lemerle famously described as *une société bloquée*, this should not obscure the fact that the roughly half-century period from the end of the reign of Basil II to the ascension of Alexios I Komnenos (r. 1081–1118) represented an epoch of political instability and considerable civil strife.[15] It was in this chaotic atmosphere that a new cadre of legal professionals, including Eustathios Rhomaios and the future emperor Romanos III, found that their skills were now highly sought-after. The increasing prominence of this group of Constantinopolitan intellectuals, particularly their interest and involvement in law, can be evidenced by the anti-heretical legislation of the patriarch Alexios Stoudites.

In addition to this wider context, the local context of the city of Melitene and its hinterland is likewise important for contextualizing the edicts of Alexios Stoudites.[16] After the extensive military successes of

[12] The *typikon* for the monastery has survived only in an Old Church Slavonic translation; see the edition in Alexios Stoudites, *Typikon*, with an English summary at 423–8.

[13] Grumel 1989: n. 830; cf. Lauritzen 2010: 45–6.

[14] Cited here after Angold 1997: 73.

[15] Lemerle 1977: 249–312. Many of the assumptions concerning stagnation and decline in eleventh-century Byzantium were questioned in a collected volume devoted to answering the question of whether we can speak of a crisis during this period; see Vlysidou 2003.

[16] On the city of Melitene under Byzantine rule, see *TIB*, vol. II, 233–7; Vest 2007: vol. II, 901–vol. III, 1442.

the tenth century, beginning with the capture and razing of the city by John Kourkouas in 934 and culminating in the campaigns of the soldier-emperors Nikephoros II Phokas (r. 963–9) and John I Tzimiskes (r. 969–76), large swathes of southeastern Asia Minor and northern Syria which had not been under imperial rule since the seventh century were brought under Byzantine control once again. The ethno-religious composition of the region changed dramatically after the Byzantine conquest; the part of the population which had converted to Islam as well as Muslims who had settled in the region appear to have been driven out of Byzantine territory, particularly during the campaigns of Nikephoros Phokas. As a result of the depopulation of the area this emperor encouraged Syrian Orthodox/Jacobite settlers living in Muslim-controlled territory to resettle Melitene and its hinterland.[17] The Syrian Orthodox patriarch was invited to move his residence from Muslim- to Byzantine-controlled territory, and the region witnessed a period of extensive monastic foundation.

On the basis of the testimony of Michael the Syrian, one scholar has hypothesized, albeit somewhat speculatively, that the legal status afforded to the Syrian Orthodox community by the Byzantine state was essentially that of a *dhimmi* – i.e. conforming to the legal protections allotted to a subordinate religious grouping under Islamic rule.[18] The reasonably tolerant attitude of the Byzantine administration toward a confession which, according to Byzantine legal and political ideology, the state was obliged to persecute has a well-known precedent during the reign of Justinian himself, when Syrian Orthodox monastic communities flourished in Constantinople, at roughly the time he was limiting the legal status of heretics in the *Corpus Iuris Civilis*.[19] In short one need not search out or invent an official contemporaneous recognition of the toleration of the Syrian Orthodox community in the Byzantine Empire. As the patriarch Alexios Stoudites would later assert in his edicts, it was enough that the local administration and populace ignored already existing Justinianic provisions which had been enacted against heretics. In any case, through the end of the reign of Basil II it can be inferred that the Syrian Orthodox community in Melitene enjoyed a reasonable degree of toleration.

[17] On the migration of West-Syrians to Byzantine territory see G. Dagron 1976; Palmer 1986; Vest 2007: vol. II, 1077–93. For the history of the West Syrian Church during the brief period of Byzantine rule in the tenth and eleventh centuries, see Benner 1989.

[18] Benner 1989, 30–1, reconstruction of the supposed *chrysobullos logos* of Nikephoros Phokas at 31–3.

[19] Hatlie 2007: 143–50.

This amenable situation changed dramatically during the reign of Romanos III Argyros, as the increasing prominence of the Syrian Orthodox community in Melitene aroused the ire of the church authorities.[20] The edicts of the patriarch Alexios Stoudites against the Syrian Orthodox population in Melitene were prompted by the complaint of the Orthodox metropolitan there, John (or, according to later Syriac sources, Nikephoros) that the Syrian Orthodox patriarch, John VIII Bar Abdoun, was denigrating the Orthodox community. This complaint was initially heard by Constantine VIII shortly before his death in 1028. In 1029 Constantine's successor Romanos III summoned John VIII Bar Abdoun to Constantinople to be judged before a synodal tribunal (*synodikon dikasterion*).[21] Following an elaborate show trial John VIII Bar Abdoun was excommunicated in October 1029.[22] Shortly after the pronouncement of excommunication in May 1030 the first edict of Alexios against the Syrian Orthodox community in Melitene was issued.[23] John VIII Bar Abdoun was banished to the monastic center of Ganos in Thrace, where he died in exile.[24] The edict also relates that three Syrian Orthodox bishops, who had accompanied John Bar Abdoun to Constantinople, converted to Orthodoxy.[25] Only the signatures have survived of another edict issued in 1032 which approved the edict of 1030.[26]

Ten years later, in September 1039, Alexios Stoudites took further measures against the Syrian Orthodox community in Melitene in response to reports of illegal practices there, including: the marriage of Orthodox and non-Orthodox; the disinheritance of Orthodox by non-Orthodox; and allowing Orthodox to testify against non-Orthodox in court.[27] His edict called for the renewal of Justinianic provisions against heretics, which forbade or substantially restricted all of the aforementioned practices. Given that John Bar Abdoun, whose activity had prompted Alexios' earlier

[20] On the arrest and trial of the West Syrian Patriarch John Bar Abdoun see Benner 1989: 80–9; Dagron, 1976: 200–1; Vest 2007: vol. II, 1196–1223.

[21] Alexios Stoudites, *Edicts* 11.

[22] The text of the excommunication has not survived; see Grumel 1989: n. 838.

[23] Alexios Stoudites. *Edicts* 6–21; cf. Grumel 1989: n. 839.

[24] Mount Ganos was a major Middle and Late Byzantine monastic center, which unfortunately is not nearly as well-documented as the other primary rural monastic center in the European half of the empire, Mount Athos. For whatever reason another high-ranking West Syrian ecclesiastic, the metropolitan Igantios of Melitene, was also exiled there in 1064; Grumel 1989: n. 893; Külzer 2009: 43; Vest 2007: vol. III, 1337–41.

[25] Alexios Stoudites, *Edicts* 12–14.

[26] Alexios Stoudites, *Edicts* 25–7; Grumel 1989: n. 840.

[27] Alexios Stoudites, *Edicts* 28–42; Grumel 1989: n. 846.

measures, had died in exile in 1033, it is sensible to view this edict of 1039 as the long-term culmination of efforts to curtail the rights of the Syrian Orthodox community in Melitene and its hinterland, a process which had started in 1028. This process encompassed two parallel activities, both of which are evidenced in this edict of 1039: an exposition of the theological errors of the Syrian Orthodox as well as related heresies, and the examination of legal texts with regard to the legal status of heretics.

From the standpoint of heresiology, the edicts of Alexios Stoudites required a taxonomy of the beliefs of the Syrian Orthodox community and related heresies. Who were these "Jacobites", and why were they called so? Which of their beliefs were heretical? How did they differ from Nestorians? The manuscript from which Ficker edited the edicts of Alexios Stoudites, *Escorialiensis* R I 15, also contains a tract on heretics, *Against the Jacobites*, written by Demetrios of Kyzikos between 1026 and 1028, before he became bishop of Kyzikos.[28] Demetrios explains in this tract that, despite the appellation Jacobite, these heretics are followers of the doctrine of Eutyches, who taught that Christ, rather than having a divine and a human nature, had a combined nature that was both divine and human.[29] Moreover, Demetrios relates, the followers of Eutyches do not believe that Christ's human nature suffered on the cross and his divine nature didn't, but that Christ's divinity suffered as well on the cross, which is why the Church Fathers called them "God-sufferers" (*Theopaschitoi*).[30] While the Melkites in Syria had remained loyal to Orthodoxy, the Jacobites rejected the Council of Chalcedon, yet at the same time accepted the first three ecumenical councils.[31] In summation, Demetrios emphasizes that the Jacobites were to be treated as heretics, and they had no right to call themselves Orthodox.[32]

In addition to this heresiological exegesis a parallel examination of the legal status of heretics took place. Given the argument Demetrios had made about how the Syrian Orthodox should be classified as followers as Eutyches, despite the fact that they were better known as Jacobites in

[28] The introductory and closing paragraphs of the text are printed in Alexios Stoudites, *Edicts* 22–3, while the rest of the text corresponds to Demetrios of Kyzikos, *Against the Jacobites* 879–84, C9. On the author and text see Beck 1977: 532. The text printed in the *PG* is erroneously ascribed to "Philippus Solitarius" (better known to Byzantinists as Philip Monotropos) instead of Demetrios of Kyzikos (the likely author); see Dagron 1976: 201, n. 108; Alexios Stoudites, *Edicts* 23 There is an analysis of the text and a German translation in Benner 1989: 123–36.

[29] Demetrios of Kyzikos, *Against the Jacobites* 880, IA–IB.

[30] Ibid. 880, IC

[31] Ibid. 881, IIIA–IIIB.

[32] Alexios Stoudites, *Edicts* 22, 29–30.

his day, strongly indicates that he consulted secular jurists while composing the tract. This is because, while there are no legal prohibitions against Jacobites in the *Codex Justinianus*, this is not the case for followers of Nestorios or Eutyches. In short, this bit of heresiological genealogy supported the conclusions which the commission of jurists would eventually come to.

Reinterpreting the Justinianic Legislation

Among the signatories of the synod of 1030 were a large number of high legal officials. Eustathios Rhomaios, already a signatory of the synod of 1029, was a signatory in the following year as well.[33] Particularly prominent among the signatories were his fellow judges of the Hippodrome and Velum, positions whose activities are well-documented in the *Peira*: Constantine (judge of the Hippodrome), Michael (judge of the Velum), Nikephoros (judge of the Hippodrome), Leo (judge of the Hippodrome) and Theodore (judge of the Hippodrome), along with the rest of the "city judges" (*politikoi dikastai*).[34] The presence of these legal officials, who represented the most capable jurists in the Byzantine Empire, at an ecclesiastical synod is unusual and explains the sophisticated legal exegesis in Alexios' edict of 1039, which is by patriarchal standards extraordinary for its use of the writings of the *antecessor* Stephan to explain Justinianic legislation. Certainly the learned proclivities of the edict, which evidence a jurist of some ability, cannot be ascribed to the patriarch Alexios Stoudites himself, who, while certainly politically savvy, was to the best of our knowledge a perfectly unremarkable Stoudite monk before he was chosen as patriarch by Basil II.[35] Eustathios himself cited Stephan repeatedly in his cases.[36] Another theory is that the edict of 1039 was the work of the future director of the law school and patriarch John Xiphilinos.[37] The participation in the synod of a young John Xiphilinos need not be discounted, but the content of the edict of 1039

[33] Ibid. 11, 19; cf. Oikonomides 1986: 174.

[34] Ibid. 20–1. Unfortunately there are no numbers for these individuals in the recently completed *PmbZ*, since the edict extends beyond the work's terminus of 1025. Two plausible identifications suggested by the *PmbZ* of persons in this edict with those mentioned elsewhere are Michael (#25383), a *protospatharios* and judge of the Velum attested by his lead seal, and Nikephoros (#25681), a contemporaneous archbishop of Kios.

[35] Stanković 2001–2: 73.

[36] *Peira* 15.3, 16.9–10, 26.12, 36.15.

[37] Schminck 1986: 30–2.

was undoubtedly more the result of a long-term effort to provide a heresiological and legal basis for the state's struggle against the Syrian Orthodox population in the southeastern borderlands than the predilections of any individual jurist on the commission. In summation, the edict of 1039 amply demonstrates the increasing importance of this first generation of the legal-professional cadre in the capital, who would become even more prominent during the reign of Constantine IX.

As for the actual content of the edict of 1039, one provision in particular proved to be the most problematic for the authors of the edict: the renewal of the prohibition against heretics testifying in court against Orthodox (*Codex Justinianus* 1.5.21 = *Basil.* 21.1.45). The original constitution, issued on July 29, 531, prohibited non-Orthodox from testifying in court against an Orthodox party, regardless of whether the Orthodox party was the plaintiff or defendant.[38] Although the constitution used at first used a slightly ambiguous turn of phrase to describe Jews (*qui Iudaicam supersitionem colunt* – a phrase that, as discussed below, was applied to heretics and particularly Nestorians), there is no doubt that Jews were meant (*inter se autem haereticis vel Iudaeis*). The constitution did however allow certain heretics to testify in cases contested amongst themselves, as well as the ability to testify in cases involving testaments and contracts. At the time it was issued the constitution represented a major innovation in anti-Jewish legislation for which there was no earlier precedent.[39] Yet the *Basilika* passage cited by Alexios in the edict of 1039, which is a considerably redacted version of the Justinianic constitution, mentions only "those honoring the Judaic religion" (*hoi ten Ioudaiken threskeian sebontes*) – thus in the *Basilika*, unlike the Justinianic constitution, there is no unambiguous mention of Jews.[40]

Since the passage in the *Basilika* corresponding to the original Justinianic prohibition against Jews testifying in court does not accurately transmit the content of its prototype, it allowed some leeway for the commission of jurists mentioned in the edict of 1030. These jurists, tasked as they were with scrutinizing the legal status of heretics in general but of Syrian Orthodox in particular, interpreted this Justinianic constitution,

[38] Lounghis, Blysidu and Lampakes 2005: n. 837; *Cod. Just.* 1.5.21.

[39] Klingenberg 1998: 18–19.

[40] *Basil.* 21.1.45: "Among heretics neither Manichaeans nor Vorboritai nor pagans nor Samaritans nor Montanistai nor Taskodrougitai nor Ophitai nor those honoring the Judaic religion shall give testimony in any [court]. And all the other [heretics] shall not be received in a court having an orthodox person as the defendant, but in all other transactions or wills or legal matters having heretics as litigants they shall witness unimpeded on account of the amplitude of the evidence."

as they did with all Justinianic law, via the writings of the sixth-century *antecessores* as well as the late sixth- and early seventh-century *scholastikoi*.

First of all, it must have been immediately obvious both to the *antecessores* and to Middle Byzantine jurists reading this passage, that if Jews are included among the heretics forbidden to testify in court when an Orthodox party is present, then it appears to contradict other laws which allow suits between Christians and Jews to take place.[41] But before one can hypothesize regarding the interpretation of the passage, the question as to whether Byzantine jurists had an accurate Greek translation of the original Justinianic constitution needs to be addressed. Modern scholars know from the scholia to the *Basilika* which have survived that the writings of the *antecessor* Thalelaios constituted the principal means by which Byzantine jurists consulted the *Codex Justinianus*.[42] Thalelaios had written a commentary on the *Codex Justinianus*, to which a *kata podas* translation, an extremely literal word-for-word rendering of the original Latin, with no regard whatsoever for the syntax of Greek, was affixed later, perhaps at the start of the seventh century.[43] The *kata podas* translation affixed to Thalelaios' commentary on the passage, which is included in the scholia apparatus, renders "those honoring the [Judaic] religion" as *ton ten threskeian sebomenon* and Jews is rendered as *Ioudaioi*.[44] Problems of language thus played no role in the interpretation of this constitution, since Byzantine jurists possessed an exact Greek *ad verbum* translation of the original Justinianic constitution.

Tracking the history of the reception of this Justinianic constitution is a difficult proposition for the period from the time it was promulgated until the eleventh century, but some Byzantine canon law collections which were based on the *Corpus Iuris Civilis* allow us to glimpse how it was interpreted by jurists of the period. The *Collectio Tripartita*, a thematically organized collection of secular law covering ecclesiastical matters written between 577 and 619, contains the constitution.[45] The *Nomokanon in Fourteen Titles*, which likely was composed in the seventh century

41 *Cod. Just.* 1.9.15: "If there is a quarrel between Christians and Jews, it is not to be judged by the elders of the Jews, but by the regular judges (Si qua inter christianos et iudaeos sit contentio, non a senioribus Iudaeorum, sed ab ordinariis iudicibus dirimatur)." = *Basil.* 1.1.41.

42 See Schminck 1991c.

43 On his commentaries and the *kata podas* translation affixed to his *Codex* commentary, see van der Wal 1953: 64–104, esp. 103 (for the date that the *kata podas* translation was affixed to Thalelaios' commentary). A useful discussion of *kata podas* translations Scheltema 1970: 32–40.

44 *Basil. Schol.* 21.1.45.2.

45 *Collectio Tripartita* 1.5.22.

before undergoing revisions at the end of the ninth century and the eleventh century, constituted by far the most popular Byzantine canon law collection. It only states that heretics cannot testify against an Orthodox party in court; no mention is made in the relevant sections on Jews of the Justinianic constitution forbidding them from testifying against Orthodox.[46] It is difficult to make much of the *Nomokanon*'s omission of the constitution, but it is interesting to note that it did not make it from the *Collectio Tripartita* to the *Nomokanon in Fourteen Titles*. It at least suggests the possibility that a mere hundred years after its promulgation some Byzantine jurists were no longer interpreting the constitution as Justinian had intended; certainly the older scholia on the constitution suggest this.

Now that it has been established that our eleventh-century jurists had a correct translation of the Justinianic constitution, it remains to be seen what other commentary texts they utilized in interpreting the passage. Another scholion, taken from the *Codex* commentary of Theodore Scholastikos, interprets the passage in a way which presaged the way it would be redacted in the *Basilika*[47]. He notes that a heretic senator, for example, is still able to give testimony in court in a case involving an Orthodox party, because he is subject to the senate. Moreover, he writes, "note that Jews are not included among the miserable [sects] enumerated here." As justification for this interpretation, Theodore continues by saying that "For my own teacher, Stephan, was of this opinion." Thus although another *antecessor* read the passage as referring to Jews as well, Theodore, probably realizing that such an interpretation would contradict other laws concerning the legal status of Jews, chose to read the passage in such a way so that Jews were not prohibited from giving testimony in court when an Orthodox party was present. Of the scholia which have survived on this particular passage, only three have attributions: Theodore (*Basil. Schol.* 21.1.45.1); Thalelaios, or more accurately, the *kata podas* which was attached to Thalelaios' *Codex* commentary (*Basil. Schol.* 21.1.45.2); Thalelaios, this time from his *Codex* commentary (*Basil. Schol.* 21.1.45.9).

Before examining the remaining scholia to *Basil.* 21.1.45, which were likely the work of "new" scholiasts, that is, Byzantine jurists from the eleventh and twelfth centuries, it should be noted that the Syrian Orthodox were not the only ethno-religious minority in the Byzantine Empire to have their legal status reexamined during the Middle Byzantine

[46] *Nomokanon in Fourteen Titles* 12.2.

[47] *Basil. Schol.* 21.1.45.1. For the surviving fragments of the *Codex* commentary of Theodore Scholastikos, see Theodoros Scholastikos, *Paraphrase of the Codex Justinianus*.

period. Basil I, probably under the ideological influence of the patriarch Photios, had ordered the forced conversion of the empire's Jews in 873–4.[48] In fact the *Eigagoge* contains an interpolation on Jews with no foundation in Roman law and which was not later incorporated into the *Basilika*: "Pagans and Jews and heretics can neither serve in the army nor in public office, but are to the furthest degree dishonored."[49] Both here and in the edicts of the patriarch Alexios Stoudites the legislative impulse towards religious conformity, completely abandoning even the limited late Roman tolerance of non-Orthodox faiths, is evident.[50] Yet this regulation, if it was ever enforced, was not further pursued, as Basil's successor Leo VI does not seem to have continued the policy of forced conversion undertaken by his father.[51]

The jurists commissioned by Alexios Stoudites to investigate the legal status of heretics had at their disposal, as we have seen, the juristic works of the *antecessores*. As shown above one of these *antecessores*, Theodore, relating the opinion of Stephan, had argued that the Justinianic prohibition against heretics testifying in court did not apply to Jews. On the other hand, they had access to a *kata podas* translation of the Justinianic constitution which prohibited Jews from rendering testimony in court, period. The passage of the *Basilika* with which these jurists had to work divided heretics into two groups with two corresponding degrees of legal incapacity, at least with regard to serving as witnesses: either heretics with absolutely no legal status (e.g. Manichaeans), or heretics with restricted legal status, who could render testimony in cases involving only other heretics or in particular other circumstances, such as cases involving wills.

The work of the commission is evidenced both in the remaining scholia to the passage as well as the edict of 1039. Theodore's line of interpretation was expanded by other scholiasts – an anonymous scholiast noted that

> The constitution does not say Jews (for these ones, when there is no Orthodox opposing party, are able to render testimony legitimately, as the laws say so about them), but rather Nestorians, for like the Jews they think

48 For the context of the forced conversion and an interpretation stressing Photios as the ultimate source of this initiative, see Prieto Domínguez 2014.

49 *Eis*. 9.13; cf. Prieto Domínguez 2014: 287–8.

50 Prieto Domínguez 2014: 295–6: "The only alien element that persisted within the frontiers of the Empire was the Jewish one, and therefore Jews were declared the new objective of imperial policy. To the economic and political reasons mentioned earlier was added a theological reason: the assimilation of Judaism with Iconoclasm allowed Jews to be seen as the last remaining vestiges of the heresy."

51 Prieto Domínguez 2014: 302.

> that Christ was a mere man, believing that Christ and the divine *logos* were separated in his *hypostaseis*. That it refers to the madness of Nestorios as the "Judaic superstition" is clear from chapter 40, book 1 (*Basil.* 1.1.40).[52]

As Ficker noted in his edition of the edicts of Alexios Stoudites, with some minor deviations, the same text appears in the edict of 1039.[53] Other scholia follow this interpretation as well.[54] The consequences of this interpretation were three-fold. First, Jews were categorized as heretics with restricted legal status; second, adherents of the Church of the East ("Nestorians"), by contrast, were identified as heretics with no legal status; third, Syrian Orthodox, against whom the edict of 1039 was directed, like the Jews were classified as heretics with restricted legal status.

As the edict of 1039 attests, there had clearly been confusion regarding whether to allow heretics, in this case Syrian Orthodox, to render testimony in court; judges, at least in Melitene, had allowed this to happen. The judges mentioned in the edict were likely thematic judges, who in the late Roman tradition were primarily administrators with juridical powers as well. As these judges likely resorted not to the *Basilika* itself but rather to the one-volume *Synopsis Basilicorum Major* (*SBM*), they would have likewise seen the prohibition against heretics testifying in court, but without the explanatory scholia of Thalelaios and Theodore.[55]

In effect, the findings of the commission of jurists working under the direction of Alexios Stoudites became the official interpretation of this passage in the *Basilika*. Already by the time of the composition of the *Peira*, around the year 1050, it is stated that: "Neither a heretic nor a Jew shall witness against an Orthodox. But they can testify against one another."[56] Unlike the relevant *Basilika* passage, there is no ambiguity in the *Peira* that Jews are meant (*Hebraios*). Less straightforward is the *Legal Textbook* (*Ponema nomikon*) of Michael Attaleiates, perhaps authored in the 1070s, where it is related that heretics cannot testify against Christians.[57] It is an open question in this instance whether Jews are lumped under the term "heretics"; but this would be unusual, as Jews are almost always treated

[52] *Basil. Schol.* 21.1.45.7. The reference provided by the scholiast, so far as I can tell, does not provide support for the interpretation that this passage refers to Nestorians rather than Jews.

[53] Alexios Stoudites, *Edicts* 40, lines 8–18.

[54] *Basil. Schol.* 21.1.45.15: Οἱ Νεστοριανοὶ οἱ σέβοντες τὰ τῶν Ἰουδαίων; see also *Basil. Schol.* 21.1.45.16–17.

[55] *Synopsis Major Basilicorum* 6.29.

[56] *Peira* 30.16.

[57] Michael Attaleiates. *Legal Textbook* 429: "but neither can slaves testify against [their] masters, nor minors, nor heretics against Christians."

separately from heretics in the *CIC* and *Basilika*. A possible contributing factor to the rapid acceptance of this interpretation that most heretics and Jews were not allowed to testify against Orthodox in court could have been the authorship of new scholia and the presumed standardization of the *Basilika* apparatus after the founding of the law school of Constantine IX in 1047.[58]

The history of Jews rendering evidence in court coincides with the appearance, during roughly the same period, of formulaic oaths which Jews were required to render in court.[59] Only a little over a century after the patriarchal edict of 1039 there is mention of an oath which Jews were required to swear in court in a novel (1148) of Manuel I Komnenos (r. 1143–80). The novel was a response to the petition of a Jewish convert to Christianity who claimed that he had been promised the "Jewish house" of his parents and the property within it, which belonged to the Jewish community, by Manuel's father. When the convert requested that the *praktor* hand over the property, the Jewish community objected.[60] The *praktor* ordered that the convert swear an oath, the *sykophantikon*, which would confirm that his claim was sincere, and the Jews likewise swear the *teleion*, swearing that they would tell the truth. The Jews requested that the convert provide a form of the oath for them to swear, but after he did this they objected to it, for reasons unknown. The emperor, with the help of Basil Pekoules, judge of the Hippodrome and Velum, supplied another form of the oath which, it is claimed, was drawn from the *Book of the Eparch*.

Patlagean in her study appears to have been unaware of the Justinianic prohibition against Jews and heretics testifying against Orthodox.[61] She therefore saw the introduction of the Jewish oath in Byzantium as a degradation of Jewish legal status, which in her view had still been intact at the time of Justinian's reign in the sixth century.[62] Yet as we have seen, the tradition of Justinianic legislation concerning Jews was much more complicated than that. The fact that Manuel's novel from the year 1148 contains

[58] See Ch. 6.

[59] Among Byzantinists the study of Patlagean 1965 is the most well-known; for a comprehensive recent overview of the history of the Jewish oath, with a particular focus on the medieval West, see the impressive examination of Linder 2014.

[60] Manuel Komnenos, *De juramento Judaeorum*.

[61] Patlagean 1965: 137: "La législation justinienne reconnaît aux Juifs l'accés normal à toutes les actions en justice; ils sont même obligés de se présenter devant le tribunal ordinaire pour un litige avec un chrétien, tandis qu'ils peuvent porter devant un tribunal juif les litiges entre Juifs." See for instance Simon 1969: 239–40.

[62] Patlagean 1965: 155–6.

the text of an oath[63] which the convert to Christianity asked the Jews to swear by means that, as Patlagean theorized, there were probably unofficial forms of such oaths circulating within Byzantine society before that date. The form and content of these Byzantine Jewish oaths correspond to Jewish oaths which have survived from the Cairo Genizah.[64] Although a link cannot be proven, it is tempting to see the appearance of the first Jewish oaths in Byzantium roughly a century after the edict of 1039 as a consequence of the interpretation of the juristic commission working under Alexios Stoudites, since from 1039 onward the legal status of Jews was clearly delineated. Before that time, as the practices of the Byzantine judges of Melitene demonstrate, there was greater ambiguity or confusion regarding the degree of legal incapacity of Jews and heretics. Once it had been established which cases Jews could participate in, the procedural difficulty of determining which oath a Jew had to render in court would need to have been overcome. It appears to have been the likely period when the first Jewish oaths in Byzantium could have been authored.

Conclusion

As the edicts of the patriarch Alexios Stoudites demonstrate, Eustathios Rhomaios and the jurists of his generation found that their legal expertise was of tremendous political value during this turbulent period in Byzantine history. The ascension to the throne of Romanos Argyros, himself a judge and one-time colleague of Eustathios, was indicative of a remarkable new trend. While emperors such as Justinian in the sixth century, and then the father-son founding figures of the Isaurian dynasty (Leo III and Constantine V) in the eighth and the Macedonian dynasty (Basil I and Leo VI) in the ninth century all had employed jurists to accomplish their ideological agendas via legal codification projects, for the first time in the empire's history these jurists found themselves capable of scaling the heights of political power, even the imperial throne itself.

This first generation of politically prominent jurists took advantage of an unstable political context. The weakening of the imperial office after the death of Basil II allowed other reservoirs of power in the capital to assert their influence. Thus when the affluence and prominence of the Syrian Orthodox minority along the empire's southeastern borderlands

[63] Patlagean 1965: 138–9, Formula IA.
[64] Patlagean 1965: 151–3.

threatened the status of the state's majoritarian culture, it was not the imperial office alone, but the emperor in conjunction with the patriarch and the empire's leading jurists who attempted to address this problem.

Within this context the developments of the last decades of Macedonian rule in the 1040s and 1050s, which were dominated by the reign of the ambitious and enigmatic person of Constantine Monomachos, are better viewed as a logical next step of processes that had already been set in motion in the 1020s and 1030s. The sophisticated ways in which legal scholars approached and appropriated the Justinianic corpus were thus not a revolutionary intervention of the brilliant legal minds of Monomachos' inner circle, as some scholars have postulated. In fact, such methods are already quite evident in the edicts of Alexios Stoudites and the jurisprudence of Eustathios Rhomaios. That such scholarly approaches were not new does not undercut the revolutionary character of Monomachos' reign, as he attempted via the founding of a law school to standardize legal education and elevate the prestige of the law's practitioners. This remarkable attempt is the subject of the next chapter.

CHAPTER 6

Legal Education and the Law School of Constantinople

Introduction

The last chapter examined the political uses of the law, and particularly the way in which a new professional legal cadre exploited the political power vacuum in the capital to increase its influence. While the anti-heretical measures contained in the synodal edicts of the patriarch Alexios Stoudites (1025–43), resulting from a commission of jurists formed by the patriarch, served to consolidate the influence of this legal professional circle, the event explored in this chapter – the founding of a Constantinopolitan law school in 1047 – represented the apogee of this cadre's power. While scholars have often seen the founding of this law school as a sort of catalyst for a revival of legal education, in this chapter I will contextualize the founding of the law school amidst the momentous changes in Byzantine legal education which occurred across the period from Late Antiquity until the eleventh century. Like other aspects of Byzantine legal culture, legal education – in many respects the most stubbornly classical and Latin element of the Byzantine legal tradition – became, hardly before the ink had dried on the Justinianic legislation, rapidly Hellenized. Legal Latin, difficult even for the bilingual East Romans of the sixth century, was for later Byzantine jurists practically an impossibility. These Byzantine judges and lawyers thus approached the Roman legal tradition not by directly consulting Roman law and almost certainly never in Latin, but rather via the Greek commentaries and paraphrases of Late Antique legal scholars.

By examining the evolution of legal education from Late Antiquity to the eleventh century, it becomes clear that the new law school founded by Constantine IX. Monomachos (1042–55) did not represent any major innovation in teaching or approach to the law, as postulated in an insightful and quite influential pair of studies by Wanda Wolska-Conus.[1]

[1] Wolska-Conus 1976; 1979.

According to her reading of contemporaneous texts, John Xiphilinos introduced into the law school a curriculum emphasizing a new and highly radical approach to the law, which in effect represented "a last repetition of the scientific study of Roman law."[2] Moreover, she claims there existed two opposed schools of legal thought in the eleventh century: one, represented by Xiphilinos and his students, practiced a highly theoretical approach to the law which relied on the interpretation of legal texts of the sixth and early seventh centuries; the other represented the more established Byzantine jurists, who resented the meteoric rise of Xiphilinos and gave preference to the *Basilika* over the works of Justinianic and post-Justinianic jurists. Though Wolska-Conus' interpretation of a revolution in legal education precipitated by the law school's ambitious head and future patriarch John Xiphilinos has been influential among Byzantine historians,[3] specialists on Middle Byzantine law have come to the conclusion that the founding of the law school should not be viewed as a seminal event in legal education. Ludwig Burgmann has quite rightly remarked that the school's founding and endowment "apparently impressed the Byzantines far less than it did Byzantinists"[4]; in a similar vein Marie Theres Fögen described it as "the crowning of a flourishing science [of legal studies] rather than the cornerstone of a new science."[5]

Yet it would be a mistake to dismiss as insincere Constantine IX's attempts to standardize legal education, evident both from his founding of the law school and in his creation of the office of the *epi ton kriseon*. The ultimate failure of his reforms was certainly not due to a lack of ambition. This emperor undertook an ennoblement of secular law and the legal profession which was practically unsurpassed in Byzantine history. His reign represents the zenith of the political power and the societal cachet of professional jurists such as John Xiphilinos as well as intellectuals who dabbled in law like John Mauropous and Michael Psellos.

The development of Byzantine legal education naturally has important implications for our understanding of Byzantine legal culture. Two salient points emerge: first, that the study of Latin was absolutely vital even for the Hellenized version of Roman law which Byzantine jurists utilized, and that until the process of *exhellenismos* ("translation into Greek") was

[2] Wolska-Conus 1979: 53.

[3] Wolska-Conus' emphasis on the supposedly new teaching methods of John Xiphilinos have been incorporated in the general surveys of Byzantine history for this period: e.g. Angold 1997: 65–7.

[4] Burgmann 1999a: 603.

[5] Fögen 1996: 186.

completed over the course of the Macedonian dynasty's rule, much of the Roman legal tradition remained either nearly or practicably inaccessible; second, that legal education was not delineated as a separate course of study, as was the case in the sixth century, but rather treated as a component of advanced general education.

Legal Education in the Sixth Century

The founding of the law school, and the abuses and failures of legal education it was intended to redress, can only be understood by sketching the history of legal education from the sixth to the eleventh century. Historians fortunately know a great deal about how legal education was constituted in the sixth century, as this was one of the areas which Justinian addressed in his codification effort. Consequently, legal education in Late Antiquity is, especially in comparison with the immediately subsequent period of Byzantine history, relatively well-researched. On the other hand, from the beginning of the seventh century, during which time a number of legal teachers known as the *scholastikoi* were still active, until the time of the *Book of the Eparch*, composed during the reign of Leo VI (r. 886–912), almost nothing is known about Byzantine legal education. Thus this chapter, reflecting the relative abundance of sources describing legal education at the two termini of the period from the sixth to the eleventh century, first describes legal education in the sixth century, then briefly discusses what little is known about legal education from the seventh to the end of the ninth century before examining in detail Byzantine legal education during the time of the Macedonian dynasty.[6] Like almost any other topic within Byzantine history, it is easy to fall into the well-worn narrative of decline from a late Roman apogee to a Byzantine nadir. Indeed, it would be misleading to completely dismiss any notion of decline or decay in Middle Byzantine legal education. Knowledge of the Latin language, for instance, which was indispensable for the interpretation of Roman law even in the Hellenized form until the Macedonian recodification project[7], was certainly considerably more exceptional in the Middle Byzantine Empire than it had been under Justinian. In fact, in Justinian's time the empire still included a sizable population of Latin-speakers in

[6] For comments on jurists, lawyers and other legal professionals during the Middle Byzantine period, see Goria 2005.

[7] See Ch. 1.

the Balkan provinces and, after Belisarios' reconquests in the 530s, North Africa and Italy.

Thanks to the codification efforts of Justinian which later became known the *CIC*, much is known about legal education in Late Antiquity. The most informative document from this period concerning legal teaching is Justinian's *Constitutio omnem*, issued December 16, 533, which announced the completion of the *Digest* and outlined a new legal curriculum. The *Constitutio omnem* acknowledges the existence of law schools in Constantinople and Beirut, while at the same time censuring legal teaching in Alexandria and Caesarea.[8] According to *Cod.* 2.19.1, there were two professors of law at Constantinople in 425 and 534, teaching in public buildings, while at the same time an undetermined number taught *intra plurimorum domus*.[9] The *Constitutio omnem* itself is addressed to eight *antecessores*, an honorific term of military origin which here designates law teachers at Constantinople and Beirut.

The *Constitutio omnem* set out a new curriculum of legal education, consisting of five years of study.[10] The first year was to be devoted to the so-called "First Things" (Gr. *Prota*) (*Dig.* 1–4), because "nothing is before this, since one is unable to have a different introduction beforehand (*qua nihil est anterius, quia quod primum est aliud ante se habere non potest*)."[11] The second year covered either *Dig.* 5–11 (*De iudiciis*) or *Dig.* 12–19 (*De rebus*) in addition to *Dig.* 23, 26, 28 and 30.[12] In the third year the students were to study the *De iudiciis* or the *De rebus* (whichever of the two they had not studied the second year), as well as *Dig.* 20–2. The fourth year curriculum encompassed *Dig.* 24–5, 29, 31–6.[13] The fifth and final year the students were to read the *Codex Justinianus* in its entirety, a very difficult undertaking on which more shall be said below.[14] Sometime between the promulgation of the *Constitutio omnem* and the middle of the sixth century a sixth year of study, devoted to the *Novels*, was appended to the standard five-year legal curriculum; how precisely this happened remains poorly understood.[15]

[8] *Constitutio omnem* §7.
[9] Scheltema 1970: 4.
[10] Chart comparing the older and new curricula in Scheltema 1970: 8.
[11] *Constitutio omnem* §2.
[12] *Constitutio omnem* §3.
[13] *Constitutio omnem* §4.
[14] Ibid.
[15] Scheltema 1970: 48–9.

Already a major question in this sixth-century model of legal education, and of paramount importance for later Middle Byzantine developments, is the question of language. Bilingualism in Greek and Latin was not unusual in Late Antiquity, and some competence in both languages was necessary in order to complete the legal curriculum. Most of the *CIC* was originally in Latin, with the *Novels* constituting the only component of the *CIC* composed in both Latin and Greek.[16] Therefore a great number of Greek paraphrases, commentaries, and glosses of the Latin were made, as was a Latin translation of the *Novels*, the *Authenticum*. Justinian himself in the bilingual *Constitutio tanta/Dedoken* made allowance only for so-called *kata podas* or less commonly *kata poda* translations, namely interlinear, word-for-word translations of the Greek or Latin original.[17] Whether Justinian intended that these *kata podas* translations should be the only type of translation included in manuscripts of the *Digest* (as the *Constitutio tanta* itself is one of the introductory constitutions to the *Digest*) or whether it was a more general prohibition against *ad sensum* translations is related to the question of the validity of the so-called "Kommentarverbot" found in the same passage. Scheltema's interpretation, which is that the prohibition applied only to materials which could be included with manuscripts of the *Digest*, is the most plausible explanation.[18] Due to the bilingual nature of the *CIC* itself, commentaries and translations for the Greek-speaking students were vital tools of the legal curriculum.

While the rediscovery of Roman law in the West was accomplished through the reading of the original Latin of the *CIC*, and in particular of the *Digest*, Byzantine jurists instead utilized the extensive commentary and translation tradition in Greek of the *CIC*.[19] The late Roman legal

[16] In fact, the manuscript tradition contains no examples of empire-wide bilingual novels or novels only in Greek, yet there are enough mentions of Greek and Latin versions of the same novel in contemporaneous sources to allow the assumption that such novels were bilingual: on this question see the thorough study of Kaiser 2012.

[17] *Constitutio tanta/Dedoken* §21. For an overview of *kata podas* translations, see van der Wal 1953: 49–63.

[18] See Scheltema 1976; Simon 1991a.

[19] For many centuries it was assumed that the medieval *glossatores* had somehow been influenced by contemporaneous Byzantine law to the point that it was even conjectured that Irnerius (*c*.1050–1130), who is credited with reviving the study of Roman law in the Latin West, had studied law in Constantinople. In the twentieth century Fritz Pringsheim dismissed this notion and redefined the extent of this interaction to the idea that perhaps the *glossatores* had been influenced by the writings of the *antecessores*; see Pringsheim 1921. Despite some similarities in methodology (e.g. the discussion of imaginary cases to illustrate particular legal principles), even this relatively limited scope of interaction is no longer maintained by the majority of legal scholars; see Kaiser 2005.

scholars of the sixth century furnished the vast majority of these works.[20] From these *antecessores*, only two works have survived in their entirety: the *Paraphrase* of Theophilos and the *Epitome Novellarum* of Julian. The latter is a Latin translation of Justinian's novels, and thus not relevant to the present discussion. The *Paraphrase* of Theophilos is a free reworking of the Latin *Institutes* into Greek, characterized by a lively classroom style.[21] Its rich manuscript tradition means that it was clearly one of the most popular texts of the *antecessores*.

Among the other texts of the *antecessores* which have survived only in fragments were: for the *Digest* the translation of Dorotheos;[22] the translation of Stephan as well as his two *paragraphai*;[23] and the translation of the so-called Elder Anonymus, known as the *Summa*, from which most of the *Digest* passages in the *Basilika* are derived.[24] For the *Codex* there existed an anonymously authored *kata podas* (which was later attached to the paraphrase of the Thalelaios but was not itself authored by him)[25] and the paraphrase of Thalelaios.[26] With regard to the *Institutes*, one should mention the commentaries of Anatolios,[27] Isidoros,[28] as well as Stephan.

Most of the commentaries of the *antecessores* were structured according to how these materials would have been used in a sixth-century lecture on Roman law.[29] Each legal text was read twice. During the first reading, the legal texts themselves (Gr. *ta reta*) were translated or paraphrased line by line by the instructor. The purpose of this first reading was to ensure that the students, for the most part Greek-speaking, understood the mainly Latin legal texts they were examining. This first lecture was called the *Index*. The second lecture consisted of an elucidation of the text which had been translated or paraphrased during the first lecture. This explication of the text was conducted very much along the lines of the Socratic method,

[20] For a good overview of the various commentaries to the Justinianic corpus which stem from the sixth and seventh centuries, see Scheltema 1958a.

[21] On Theophilos see Lokin 1976; 1984; Schminck 1991e.

[22] Brandsma 1996.

[23] Scheltema 1958b; see also Hylkje de Jong 2008.

[24] Stolte 1985: 47. This Elder Anonymus is not to be confused with the Younger Anonymus/Enantiophanes (the author of the *Nomokanon in Fourteen Titles*) nor with a third Anonymus who authored the *Collectio tripartita*.

[25] Scheltema 1958a: 36–7.

[26] Van der Wal 1953: 64–79.

[27] Van der Wal 1953: 111–13. For the surviving fragments of his work see Anatolios, *Anatolius and the Excerpta Vaticana et Laurentiana*.

[28] Van der Wal 1953: 105–10.

[29] The description of the legal teaching of the *antecessores* in this paragraph is based on Scheltema 1967: 57–8.

in the form of a question-and-answer session. The comments on the text stemming from this second lecture are known in Greek as *paragraphai.*

Along with the *antecessores*, the so-called *scholastikoi*, a designation for jurists who flourished at the end of the sixth and beginning of the seventh century, also furnished a number of legal texts which were extensively consulted in the Middle Byzantine period. Theodore Scholastikos[30] composed a short paraphrase of the *Codex Justinianus*,[31] but his most important work for Byzantine jurists was an abridged version of Justinianic and a few post-Justinianic novels, with references to both the *Codex* and the *Novels*.[32] Athanasios of Emesa composed a thematically organized paraphrase of Justinian's *Novels*, a type of work which would become a model for later texts and is known as a *syntagma*.[33] In fact a tenth-century summary of the text has survived.[34] Additionally, the so-called Younger Anonymus or Enantiophanes, who also wrote the *Nomokanon in Fourteen Titles*,[35] the principal canon law collection of the Middle Byzantine period, composed *paragraphai* on the *Summa* of the aforementioned Elder Anonymus which are well-attested in the *Basilika*. Overall, for the majority of the Middle Byzantine period the work of these *antecessores* and *scholastikoi* served as the means by which Byzantine jurists examined and used the *CIC*.

Despite the fact that this commentary tradition was in Greek, it was not as accessible to Middle Byzantine scholars as it might appear at first glance. It is worth bearing in mind that, although already by the end of the sixth century the *CIC* had been Hellenized, these translations had nevertheless been intended more as aids than as replacements of their Latin prototypes. Moreover, much Latin legal terminology was either transcribed into Greek or left in the original language within the translation. As Marie Theres Fögen, who likewise has examined this phenomenon, remarked "The body of law, one could say, became Greek, but the soul remained Latin."[36]

The *Paraphrase* of Theophilos, which was the most popular introduction to secular law in the Middle Byzantine period, contains excellent examples of just how Latinized the Greek texts of the *antecessores* actually

30 Schminck 1991d; Van der Wal 1953: 119–21.
31 Theodore Scholastikos, *Paraphrase of the Codex Justinianus.*
32 Theodore Scholastikos, *Paraphrase of the Novels.*
33 Athanasios of Emssa, *Syntagma.*
34 Simon and Troianos 1979.
35 On its authorship, see Stolte 2001: 183–94.
36 Fögen 1998: 14.

were. Book I, Title 18 is a section on whether or not children who are minors require a guardian after they have been released from the power of the father, and if so, who exercises guardianship. Below is the Greek text, followed by an English translation:

Greek Text of Theophilos' Paraphrase, Book 1, Title 18
Ἐποίησα τὸν ἐμὸν υἱὸν ἢ τὴν ἐμὴν θυγατέρα ἢ ἔκγονον ἢ ἐκγόνην ἀνήβους ὄντας EMANCIPATUS. ἐπιτρόπου δέονται· τίς αὐτῶν ἐπιτροπεύσει; TESTAMENTARION οὐκ ἔστιν εἰπεῖν· τὸν γὰρ TESTAMENTARION καταλιμπάνει ὁ ἔχων τὸν ἄνηβον ὑπεξούσιον. ἀλλὰ ADGNATON; ἀλλὰ διέφθαρται τῇ EMANCIPATIONI τὰ ADGNASTICA δίκαια. τίς οὖν κληθήσεται ἐπὶ τὴν ἐπιτροπήν; καθὰ καὶ ἐν τοῖς προλαβοῦσιν εἰρήκαμεν, ὁ πατὴρ ὁ πάππος οἱ ἐλευθερώσαντες αὐτοὺς καὶ ἐπιτροπεύσουσι κατὰ μίμησιν τῶν πατρόνων, λεγόμενοι καὶ αὐτοὶ LEGITIMOI ἐπίτροποι.

English Translation
[Let's say] I have granted freedom [lit. made someone an *emancipatus*] to my underage son, daughter or offspring. They require a guardian; who shall serve as their guardian? For this is not at all a testamentary guardian. For a testamentary guardian is left by someone who has the minor under his power. But is it an agnate [i.e. a testamentary guardian of male relatives]? But the validity of *adgnastica* provisions is destroyed by the act of *emancipatio*. Then who shall inherit the guardianship? Just as we have said in the preceding [sections], the father [or] the grandfather who freed them shall also serve as a guardian in imitation of patrons. And they themselves are called the statutory guardians.

This relatively short and simple section contains a total of six Latin legal terms (*emancipatus*, *testamentarion*, *adgnaton*, *adgnastica*, *emancipatio*, *legitimoi*).[37] In fact, roughly every tenth word in the *Paraphrase* is a Latin one.[38] Although the *Paraphrase* is in Greek, without a knowledge of Latin it would be have been difficult if not impossible to use Theophilos' text effectively.[39] In modern legal cultures it is of course not unusual to have remnants of another language in legal formulae, like the Latin terms *habeas corpus* and *noli contendere* in the English common law tradition. Yet the frequency and prevalence of Latin terms in Greek did present some special problems for Byzantine jurists, and we know this because of the numerous bilingual

[37] *Legitimoi* (λεγίτιμοι) being a Hellenized form of *legitimi*.
[38] Burgmann 1999b: 62.
[39] On the Latin terms in the text see Theophilos Antecessor, *Paraphrase* xxiii–xxvi.

Latin–Greek legal lexica which were compiled in the Middle Byzantine period.[40]

The example above from the *Paraphrase* of Theophilos was a free reworking of a Latin legal textbook, the *Institutes*, included in the *CIC*. The *Paraphrase* was an immensely important text, used extensively both in the creation of the *Basilika* as well as compositions like Psellos' *Synopsis legum*. However, there also existed extremely literal *ad verbum* translations, the so-called *kata podas* translations.[41] One of the most important of these translations was affixed to Thalelaios' commentary of the *Codex Justinianus*. The *Codex* would have been, at least from a linguistic standpoint, the most difficult text to read within the *CIC*. This is because the *Codex*, as a compilation of imperial constitutions, was written in the highly recondite, flowery Latin of the imperial court. Even in Late Antiquity, at a time when bilingualism in Latin and Greek was far more common than in the Middle Byzantine period, this text would have presented considerable difficulties for Greek-speakers. Thus Thalelaios' *Codex* commentary, as well as the *kata podas* translation affixed to it, played a crucial role in the incorporation of the *Codex Justinianus* into the *Basilika*. Although the *Codex* commentary of Thalelaios with *kata podas* translation has not survived, the scholia to the *Basilika* make extensive use of it, and by referring to these scholia it is possible to see how Middle Byzantine jurists made use of both commentaries and translations in making sense of the *Codex*. The example below is of a scholion from the *Basilika* which shows how these tools were used:

> Scholion 2 to *Basil.* 29.5.31 = *Cod.* 5.14.1
> Greek Text of *Basil.* 29.5.31
> Τὰ ἐπὶ τῇ προικὶ γινόμενα σύμφωνα περὶ τῆς ἀναδόσεως ἰσχύουσιν· οὐδὲ γάρ ἐστι ψιλὸν πάκτον τὸ τοιοῦτον, ὅτε περὶ ἀναδόσεως τῶν ἐπιδιδομένων γίνεται πραγμάτων.
>
> English translation of *Basil.* 29.5.31
> Agreements which take place within the dowry about the exchange [of goods or money] are valid. For this is not some sort of open pact [i.e. a pact

[40] For an overview of the way Latin loanwords were written by the *antecessores*, see van der Wal 1983. See also the more general remarks about the presence of Latin in Byzantine juridical texts in van der Wal 1984 and especially Burgmann 1999b.

[41] On Thalelaios see Schminck 1991c. On his commentaries and the *kata podas* translation affixed to his *Codex* commentary, see van der Wal 1953: 64–104. The date that the *kata podas* commentary/translation was affixed to Thalelaios' codex commentary, was, in van der Wal's view, likely the beginning of the seventh century (van der Wal 1953: 103).

which resulted in no obligations], when [something] about the exchange of things which are given occurs.

Greek Text of Scholia 2 to *Basil.* 29.5.31

Τὸ κατὰ πόδας. Τὸ σύμφωνον, ὅπερ εἶπας, ὅτε τὴν προῖκα ὑπὲρ τῆς ἀλούμνας παρεῖχες, φυλάττεσθαι χρή, καὶ οὐκ ὀφείλει σοι ἀντικεῖσθαι ἐκεῖνο, ὅπερ εἴωθε λέγεσθαι ἀπὸ συμφώνου ἀγωγὴν μὴ τίκτεσθαι· τότε γὰρ τοῦτο λέγομεν, ἡνίκα τὸ σύμφωνον γυμνόν ἐστιν· ἐπεὶ ἡνίκα χρήματα δίδοται καὶ τίποτε περὶ τῆς τούτων ἀναδόσεως συμφωνεῖται, χρήσιμός ἐστιν ὁ κονδικτίκιος.

Ἐν τούτοις τὸ κατὰ πόδας. Ἑρμηνεύων δὲ τὸ τέλος τῆς διατάξεώς <φησιν> ὁ Θαλέλαιος· τὸ ‘χρήσιμός ἐστιν ἡ ἀπαίτησις’ εἴρηται, διότι δύναται ὡς δόσεως ἐπὶ αἰτίᾳ γενομένης τὴν πραεσκρίπτις βέρβις κινῆσαι.

English Translation of Scholia 2 to *Basil.* 29.5.31

The *kata podas* [translation]: The agreement that you mentioned, which is when you offer a dowry on behalf of a foster-daughter, it is necessary to take care, that you should not oppose it, since it is customary to say that an obligation does not arise from an agreement. For we then say this, whenever a pact is open. For since money is given and at some point an agreement is made concerning the exchange of this money, the *kondiktikios* is invoked. The *kata podas* [says this] concerning these matters. And Thalelaios, interpreting the goal of the constitution, says: "The 'demanding back' can be invoked", he states, on account of which one can sue according to the *praescriptio verbis*, because a gift took place.

Latin Text of *Cod.* 5.14.1

Legem, quam dixisti, cum dotem pro alumna dares. servari oportet, nec obesse tibi debet, quod dici solet ex pacto actionem non nasci: tunc enim hoc dicimus, cum pactum nudum est: alioquin cum pecunia datur et aliquid de reddenda ea convenit, utilis est condictio.

The scholiast to *Basil.* 29.5.31 used both a *kata podas* translation and the *Codex* commentary of Thalelaios to interpret this particular passage. No recourse to the original Latin text of *Cod.* 5.14.1 was necessary. While Latin terms remained in the mass of Greek legal commentaries and translations, Ludwig Burgmann has plausibly claimed that the last time a Byzantine jurist exclusively read a Latin section of the *CIC* was during the reign of Heraclius (610–41).[42] After the seventh century, Byzantine jurists endeavored to

[42] Burgmann 1999b: 63.

further reduce Latin's latent presence in legal texts via an important but poorly understood process by which writings of the Late Antique *antecessores* and *scholastikoi* were gradually purged of their remaining Latin content and edited into a more comprehensible and accessible, that is to say Hellenized, form: namely, the process of *exhellenismos*.

The introduction to the *Prochiron*, in detailing how this recapitulation of Justinianic law was compiled, states that "we translated the collection of Latin terms into the Greek tongue."[43] This statement describes the process to which scholars have given the ephithet *exhellenismos*. This is a term used in the secondary literature to describe how Greek commentaries and translations of the *antecessores* and *scholastikoi* were purged of their Latin legal terms and either transcribed or translated into Greek, as a designation for the "Hellenized" versions of Latin *termini technici* themselves. Evidence of the progress of *exhellenismos* can be found in the bilingual Latin–Greek legal lexica of the Middle Byzantine period,[44] with which Byzantine jurists were able to translate specialized Roman legal terms from Latin into Greek. Unfortunately, these traces of the process of *exhellenismos* do not indicate how or by whom this process was accomplished. That there was some connection between *exhellenismos* and the ongoing codification of Roman law started by Basil I (r. 867–86) and continued by his successors seems to be a valid assumption, as the latter could not have been accomplished without the former. The crowning achievement of this process was the completion of the *Basilika*, which although based on the *CIC* represented in many respects not so much a translation of Roman law as a reworking of it. Yet even the *Basilika*, especially the earliest versions of it transmitted in manuscripts, still contained a not inconsiderable number of Latin words, as did the private legal collections of the tenth century and the older scholia to the *Basilika*; it was not until 1142, when the *Ecloga Basilicorum* was authored, that the *Basilika* had been mostly shorn of its Latin legal terminology.[45]

Although *exhellenismos* allowed Byzantine jurists to fully utilize the Roman legal tradition without resorting to Latin, sometimes these *exhellenismoi* were vague or simply incorrect, and thus caused problems in legal interpretation.[46] One of the reasons that Eustathios Rhomaios was such an accomplished judge was that he appears to have been able to consult the Latin originals when there was uncertainty regarding the meaning

43 *Prochiron*, proem, lines 52–3.
44 Burgmann 1977; 1984; 1990.
45 Burgmann 1999b: 65–6.
46 Fögen 1998: 15. For examples of incorrect *exhellenismoi*, see Troianos 2001b.

of *exhellenismoi*, an extraordinarily rare ability at the time. Within *Peira* 11 "Concerning Guarantees", for example, there is some ambiguity regarding a passage which mentions two people subject to a guarantee (Lat. *stipulatio*). The *stipulatio* was part of a formulaic oral agreement, usually in the context of a gift, sale or especially loan, which obligated the person subject to the *stipulatio* to perform the deed promised.[47] Naturally, this was only a one-way obligation. In *Peira* 11.1, Eustathios is able to make sense a passage translated into Greek involving a *stipulatio* mentioning two people subject to it, which was baffling given that the *stipulatio* was only a one-way obligation.[48] Eustathios refers to the original Latin of the passage to prove that the two people supposedly subject to the *stipulatio* must in fact be both parties involved in the transaction, and not just the one subject to the *stipulatio*. He states that the translators of this passage had incorrectly translated the word for someone subject to a stipulation, and thus was apparent paradox is solved. Of course, while a jurist of Eustathios' ability was able in this instance to resolve a problem presented by the translation of the *exhellenismoi*, Eustathios himself was a judge of exceptional ability; for the typical Latin-less thematic judge, such a passage would have been almost impossible to interpret correctly.

As demonstrated in the preceding section, Roman law in its Late Antique iteration, consisting of the *CIC* as well as the numerous commentaries and translations of the so-called *antecessores*, presented considerable problems to Byzantine jurists and lawyers. Foremost among these problems was the problem of language: by the Middle Byzantine period knowledge of Latin, still vital to an understanding of Roman law, had decreased considerably. It is then unsurprising that, in the period from the beginning of the seventh century until the beginning of the "Cleansing of the Ancient Laws" under Basil I, legal collections with a complete lack of Latin legal terminology, such as the *Ecloga*, *NG*, *NM* and *NN*, came into

[47] Kaser 1971–5: vol. II (1975), 373–82.

[48] *Peira* 11.1: "The *patrikios* interpreted the aforementioned passage which mentioned two [people] subject to a guarantee [Lat. *stipulatio*] thus, saying: The Latin has two *promi[t]tendo* and two *stipoulando* and two *rheous* [for the people] subject to a guarantee. Therefore the two *rheous* does not indicate the recipients of the action alone, but also the initiators of the action, and the Latin must be interpreted this way. The two men being subject to guarantees could be either the initiators of the action or the recipients of the action. Those who translated the passages into Greek were unable to translate the term and indicate both the initiators of the action and recipients of the action alone, [but instead] they said two [people] are subject to a guarantee, which has the meaning both of requesting the guarantee and the one giving the guarantee. But others interpreted it as those seeking guarantees twice, so that if I say 'You agree to loan me something, and if you do not, it is subject to a guarantee.'"

use.[49] As argued in Chapter 4, these legal collections represented a kind of "stopgap" measure, laws which were able to be used by Byzantine legal officials before the completion of *exhellenismos* and the Macedonian codification efforts.[50] This interpretation would correspond to what little we know about Byzantine legal education from the beginning of the seventh century; namely, a long period of silence before a revival at the end of the ninth and beginning of the tenth century.

Legal Education from the End of the Sixth to the Middle of the Eleventh Century

The period of the *antecessores* is generally acknowledged to have ended in the second half of the sixth century after the death of the last jurist designated as an *antecessor*, Julian. Thereafter, jurists active at the end of the sixth and into the seventh century such as Athanasios of Emesa, Theodore Scholastikos (of Hermopolis) and Enantiophanes/the Younger Anonymous were designated as *scholastikoi*.[51] Historians of Byzantine law have characterized this period as one in which the theoretical legal teaching of the *antecessores* gave way to the more vocational and practical legal training of the *scholastikoi*.[52] The main legal textbook became Theophilos' *Paraphrase* of the *Institutes*, and while the *Novels* of Justinian were eagerly studied, the *Codex* and especially the *Digest* were largely neglected.

The great law schools of Late Antiquity at Beirut, Constantinople and Rome likely did not survive the sixth century. Beirut and its law school were devastated by the catastrophic earthquake of 551; Rome's did not outlive the sixth-century Byzantine reconquest of the city.[53] "Teachers of the civil laws" are mentioned in canon 71 of the Council in Trullo, which took

[49] Humphreys 2015 has presented a case for viewing all of these measures, as well as the *Appendix Eclogae*, as a part of an Isaurian legal reform.

[50] See Ch. 4.

[51] Scheltema 1970: 61–4. For comments about the role of law in the seventh century, including some remarks about legal education, see Haldon 1997: 254–80.

[52] Scheltema 1970: 62; Troianos 1998–9: 47–8. There is however little reason to suppose, as Scheltema does, that the educational curriculum of the *scholastikoi* somehow corresponded to the regulations for legal knowledge required of *taboullarioi* in the *BoE*. The writings of the *scholastikoi* would have likely been used mainly to train lawyers, after all, and not necessarily notaries, whereas there are no corresponding regulations in the *BoE* regarding the legal knowledge which lawyers were expected to have.

[53] Troianos 1998–9: 46–7.

place in 691–2.[54] The canon forbade them from following "pagan customs," which included going to the theater, wearing their clothes in a bizarre fashion and holding what were processions or festivals of some sort associated with the academic terms of study.[55] Similar practices in the schools of rhetoric at Antioch and Athens suggest that this was a form of student hazing which was later given the veneer of a religious procession.[56] Thus as late as the end of the seventh century there appears to have remained some vestiges of organized legal education, at least in Constantinople, and it also appears to have been taught as a separate course of study rather than as a component of a general higher level education. There is no reason to assume a radical rupture in legal education at this point.[57]

After the seventh century there is no substantive information on legal education until the end of the ninth century. The *Ecloga* contains no information on the educational background which a judge was supposed to possess; of much greater import was the moral integrity of the judge.[58] Indeed those judges who "know the law but falsify the truth" are explicitly warned against judging unjustly.[59] In any case, it is interesting to note that a half-century after the mention of the continuance of legal education in the capital, it is stated in the *Ecloga* that Roman law was difficult to interpret, particularly for those outside of Constantinople.[60]

In the ninth century, when more is known about education in general, there is no indication that law existed as a subject of study apart from a general education (*enkyklios paideia*).[61] This is true as well for what some scholars have termed a "university," but what might be better described as literary salon that also functioned as a private school with intermittent state subventions, which was founded by the caesar Bardas at the Magnaura palace in Constantinople during the reign of Michael

[54] *Canons of the Council in Trullo*, canon 71: "Those teaching the civil laws shall not follow pagan customs, neither going to the theatre, nor having so-called *kylistras*, or wear their clothes contrary to the common use, neither at the time which their studies begin nor when they bring them to their conclusion, nor are they to appear at all in the middle of the curriculum. And if someone from now on dares to do this, let him be excommunicated."

[55] Scheltema 1959, relying on the later testimony of the canonist Balsamon, notes that it possible that these *kylistrai* had been mock combats between incoming law students, which later become a lottery in which these students were divided into sections.

[56] Troianos 1998–9: 48–50.

[57] Humphreys 2015: 86, who rightly criticizes the tendency of historians of Byzantine law to assume that the seventh century was also a "Dark Age" with regard to legal education.

[58] *Ecloga*, proem, lines 52–68; cf. Humphreys 2015: 86–7.

[59] *Ecloga*, proem, lines 69–70.

[60] Ibid., lines 34–40.

[61] On the *enkyklios paideia* in the Middle Byzantine period see Kazhdan 1991c and especially Lemerle 1986: 111–17.

III (r. 842–67).[62] In the absence of any sort of evidence that a separate legal curriculum existed after the end of the seventh century, it should be assumed that the legal education became primarily vocational; in any case there is no evidence to indicate the survival of the five- and then six-year legal curriculum of the sixth century.

That legal officials acquired their offices without specialized legal training is confirmed by the description of the refounding, probably after the school had for several generations ceased to exist, of the Magnaura School by Constantine VII Porphyrogennitos (r. 945–59).[63] The school included instructors in philosophy, rhetoric, geometry and astronomy, and Constantine himself, so reports Theophanes Continuatus, dined daily with the school's students and gave them money. Even more generously, he "honored [them] by selecting from among them judges and civil servants [*antigrapheis*] and bishops [lit. metropolitans], and adorned and enriched the state of the Romans with wisdom."[64] Clearly into the tenth century legal officials had the exact same general education as other church or state functionaries.

There is no substantial information on legal education in the Byzantine Empire from the end of Late Antiquity until it is mentioned again in the *Book of the Eparch* (*BoE*). The *BoE*, authored sometime during the reign of Leo VI but probably more exactly during the first part of the tenth century, is a collection of regulations for the guilds of the imperial capital. The intended reader of this work was the eparch of Constantinople, who held the highest administrative authority in the capital outside that of the emperor himself.[65]

As a caveat to examining the information the *BoE* offers on legal education, it should be mentioned that over the last twenty-five years two scholars, Andreas Schminck and Paul Speck, have expressed weighty and as yet unrefuted concerns regarding the actual implementation of the regulations found in this text. Schmink has advanced an argument that the *BoE* is an unfinished work of the eparch Philotheos and Leo VI that stems from after the year 907, and which, following Leo's VI death, was preserved

[62] Speck 1974: 1–13 has convincingly proved that this school at Magnaura was not essentially different from other schools of higher learning in the capital; see as well the comments of Lemerle 1986: 182–5, who assigns much greater importance to the founding of these schools and the effect which they had on Byzantine intellectual life in general.

[63] Speck 1974: 22–8. He is right to call into question the continued existence of the school from the middle of the ninth century until the reign of Constantine VII (Speck 1974: 1, n. 1).

[64] *TheophCont* 446, lines 20–2.

[65] Kazhdan 1991d.

by a member of the emperor's inner circle and that it remained a literary composition rather than promulgated law.[66] Speck further advanced this line of argument, focusing on peculiarities in the manuscripts transmitting the *BoE*.[67] I share some of the skepticism of these two scholars regarding the *BoE*, though its information regarding legal education does seem to fit with the broader picture of the development of Middle Byzantine legal education.

The first section of the *BoE* is concerned with notaries (*taboullarioi*). In the Middle Byzantine period notaries were basic civil or church functionaries, and constituted a portion of the staffs which surrounded higher ranking officials like judges and military governors.[68] As such they were required to have a basic familiarity with the law.[69] More specifically, a notary "who is to be appointed should have the forty titles of the law ready-at-hand on his tongue and a knowledge of the sixty books, and have been taught a general education."[70] The "forty titles of the law ready-at-hand" refers to the *Prochiron*, while the "sixty books," which in the two main manuscripts of the *BoE* actually reads "sixty [books] of the *Basilika*", are the *Sixty Books* of Leo VI which later became known as the *Basilika*.[71] This division between active and passive knowledge of legal corpora would have been possible given the small size of the *Prochiron*, which true to its name was quite compact and could have been memorized or at the very least easily paraphrased, and the *Sixty Books/Basilika*, a massive reference work.[72] Thus while notaries were required to be familiar with Byzantine law, from the passages in the *BoE* there is no indication of any organized system of formal legal education.

We should not imagine these Constantinopolitan notaries as aloof legal scholars. The letters of Michael Psellos in particular, written well over a century after the *BoE* yet probably reflecting a broadly similar situation, are filled with petitions of this Byzantine court intellectual to civil and military officials, above all provincial judges and military governors,

[66] Schminck 1990.

[67] Speck 1991a.

[68] Regarding Byzantine notaries one should in particular consult the extensive survey of Saradi 1992, which is summarized and chronologically extended into the twentieth century in Saradi-Mendelovici 2009.

[69] *BoE* 1.1, lines 16–18.

[70] *BoE* 1.2, lines 26–28.

[71] The emendation of this passage from "the sixty [books] of the *Basilika*" to "the sixty books" by Koder in his edition of the BoE has been noted by van Bochove 2014: 71, n. 6.

[72] Troianos 1998–9: 51–2, who rightly rejects the argument of Speck 1991a that the reference to the *Sixty Books* was a later interpolation.

that they accept his students or friends as notaries on their staffs.[73] Being a *taboullarios* in the capital would have been a highly lucrative profession – the *BoE* mandates that only twenty-four such notaries were allowed in the entire city.[74] These notaries of the capital would have earned their imperially mandated legal fees (*ektagiatika*) from legal work servicing the Constantinopolitan elite; since these charges were calculated as a percentage of a case's total monetary value, their notarial work would have been among the empire's most profitable.

The *BoE* offers interesting though at times enigmatic information on who taught these notaries, and thus who conducted legal education in the capital.[75] These are the so-called "teachers of notaries" (*paidodidaskaloi nomikoi*) and a teacher *en nome archaia*. No scholar has offered a convincing explanation as to what the phrase *en nome archaia* means.[76] What the regulations of the *BoE* do indicate is that there were multiple *paidodidaskaloi nomikoi*, and thus multiple teachers of the law.[77] A regulation allowing a student of another school (*schole*) to receive instruction from the notarial guild under certain conditions with the other aspiring notaries allows for the possibility that there were several such schools.[78]

There is very little evidence in the *BoE* to contradict the general picture presented here of legal instruction being part of a general education from the end of the sixth century onwards. A notary's grasp of the law was after all confirmed by a head of the guild of the notaries, the *primikerios*, and his fellow notaries.[79] Familiarity with the law was just one of the qualifications a prospective notary was supposed to have, along with superior handwriting, good moral character, cultivated manners and

[73] See Ch. 2.

[74] *BoE* 1.23; cf. Troianos 1998–9: 51.

[75] *BoE* 1.13, 1.15 and 1.16.

[76] Discussion in Troianos 1998–9: 53. According to the interpretation of Wolska-Conus 1981, the *en nome archaia* was a privilege accorded to a particular legal teacher to teach in a public space designated for the exercise of their profession. Wolska-Conus in the same article posits an essential continuity of legal education from the disappearance of the law schools in Beirut and Constantinople until the Macedonian dynasty. The evidence on Byzantine legal education in this chapter calls into question this assumption of continuity. Moreover, her argument is based on similarities in titles and terminology more than anything else, and if Wolfram Brandes' recent work on the Byzantine administration from the seventh to ninth centuries is any indication, then this similarity could be the result of a legal educational "Proto-Renaissance" rather than actual evidence of continuity – that is, a reintroduction of Late Antique names for legal teachers around the time of the composition of the *BoE*. See Brandes 2002: 480–98.

[77] Troianos 1998–9: 52.

[78] *BoE* 1.16; cf. Troianos 1998–9: 53.

[79] *BoE* 1.1, lines 16–7.

eloquence.[80] Whatever an aspiring notary's actual qualifications might have been, this was in a sense an office he had to purchase, paying the president of the guild 3 *nomismata*, each remaining guild notary 1 *nomisma* each, as well as 6 *nomismata* to the communal fund (*trapeza*) of the guild: these customary entrance fees would have totaled thirty-one *nomismata*, a sum that can be seen, as with the purchase of many Middle Byzantine offices, as an investment. According to the *Book of Ceremonies* the notaries *tou idikou* collectively paid the treasury 55 pounds of gold for their offices, those *tou stratiotikou* 20 and those *tou sakelles* 30.[81]

The *Novella Constitutio* and the Founding of the Law School

The founding of a law school under the emperor Constantine IX Monomachos in the year 1047 is a seminal event in the history of Byzantine law and legal culture, not because (as often assumed in the older scholarship) it revolutionized legal education, but because it announced and aimed at the full restoration of late Roman law and legal studies. The establishment of the law school was viewed by Monomachos as well as by the Byzantine jurists of the period as the culmination of a process of legal reform begun by the first Macedonian dynasts, Basil I and Leo VI. It completed the process of the *anakatharsis ton palaion nomon*, the "Cleansing of the Ancient Laws," by resurrecting hitherto neglected legal education.[82] The creation of the law school reflected the political and social prominence of a Constantinopolitan cadre of jurists, who had in the previous decades had proven their usefulness by assisting in the reinterpretation of Justinianic legislation against West Syrians in the empire's southeastern borderlands. At this time the societal importance of these jurists reached its apogee, representing the last time the more secular, civil law component of the Byzantine legal tradition was revived.

Two authorities report the founding of the law school: the eleventh-century historian and judge Michael Attaleiates, as well as the greatest Byzantine canonist and titular patriarch of Antioch, Theodore Balsamon (d. *c.*1195), whose voluminous oeuvre and sharp legal and theological mind make him in the eyes of many a sort of Orthodox Thomas Aquinas.[83] Yet the most informative source regarding the law school is the so-called

80 *BoE* 1.1, lines 18–21.
81 See Ostrogorsky 1932: 306 with reference to *De cer.* 694.
82 *Novella Constitutio* §3–4.
83 Michael Attaleiates, *Historia* 17, lines 18–24; *Rh.-P.* vol. IV, 524. Cf. Dölger 2003: 15–6 (no. 863), where the former is not mentioned.

Novella constitutio, which announced the creation of the new position of *nomophylax didaskalos* along with the founding of a law school in the capital. It is important to discuss the *Novella constitutio* in the form it has been transmitted to us. There is little doubt that the author of the *Novella constitutio* was John Mauropous, the later bishop of Euchaïta, as it is included in the manuscript which contains his self-selected literary oeuvre, *Vaticanus graecus* 676.[84] As such the *Novella constitutio* is not an imperial novel, but rather a draft form of a later novel which has not come to down us but was certainly promulgated.[85] Mauropous included it along with his letters and poems as an example of his literary output, a fact which in and of itself says much about what the Byzantines thought about the law as a literary form: like other "technical" genres such as agricultural (the *Geoponika*) or military handbooks (the *Taktika*), law, if written in a high style, could be considered literature (*logoi*).

No date is attached to the *Novella constitutio*, yet Jacques Lefort convincingly argued that the novel itself was likely promulgated in March of 1047 on the occasion of the inauguration of the church of St George of Mangana, the centerpiece of an impressive monastic complex richly endowed by Monomachos himself.[86] The *Novella constitutio* is a fascinating document not only as evidence of legal education at the time of the Macedonian dynasty, but also as perhaps the most complete articulation of the justification for law, law's function and the relationship of the state and the law in the entire Middle Byzantine period. The extent to which Mauropous in the *Novella constitutio* draws upon late Roman legal texts, particularly the *Digest* and *Codex*, had not been fully appreciated by scholars until a recent study by Spyros Troianos, who has impressively demonstrated the extent to which the intellectual and future bishop invoked the Justinianic legal legacy.[87]

Though there are summaries of the *Novella constitutio* in French, German and Modern Greek, as well as a Latin translation in the most recent edition of Salač, I have included my own English translation as an

[84] Xiphilinos is almost universally acknowledged as the author of the *Novella Constitutio*, most recently by Troianos 2012c: 244, though the case also been made (less convincingly) for John Xiphilinos by Cvetler 1956.

[85] Speck 1991b: 330; Troianos 2012c: 243.

[86] Lefort 1976: 279–80. See the discussion of older literature discussing the dating of the *Novella Constitutio*, with the other possible candidates being 1043 (Follieri followed by Weiss) or 1045 (Dölger), see Troianos 2012c: 244.

[87] Lemerle 1977: 207–11; Speck 1991b: 341–7, n. 33; Troianos 2012c.

appendix to this book.[88] The first two sections of *Novella constitutio* stress the importance of law to the emperor and that it is his duty to regulate it.[89] Although law's divine origin as God's gift to mankind is mentioned, the articulation of the justification for the law and the state's relationship with it is much more philosophical than the preface to the *Ecloga*, where the law and the emperor's duty to preserve it are presented in stark biblical, and in particular Old Testament, terms.[90]

In the third section reference is made to previous emperors. They had devoted a great deal of attention to the laws

> because through [their] many pains and toils they made the laws immense, and they labored a great deal with the interpretation of the Latin, in which language the antiquity of the laws was written, and endured much hardship in making them clear, and still they thought their cleansing was worthy of much attention and effort, they transmitted this magnificent deed, most beneficial to the commonweal (I do not know whence or how) unarranged.[91]

Though the emperors in question are left unnamed, as is normally the case when critiquing past rulers in new legislation, e.g. the proem to the *Prochiron*, the reference to a "cleansing" (*anakatharsis*) of the laws points strongly to the recapitulation of Justinianic law initiated by the first two Macedonian emperors, Basil I and Leo VI.[92]

The critique of these past emperors, now centering on legal education, continues in the fourth section. Specifically, these emperors neither selected a teacher of the laws, nor did they designate a public space for legal teaching, nor did they allocate public allowances for teachers. Employing a dramatic nautical metaphor, these negligent rulers "left the divine legal education like a ship without a helmsman in the middle of the sea of life, though with it they would together be shipwrecked and perhaps wander astray and be carried off."[93]

The state of legal education is described in section five of the *Novella constitutio*. Since there was no centralized system of legal education and

[88] The best summary of the content of the *Novella constitutio* is Troianos 2012c. See Appendix.

[89] *Novella constitutio* §1–2; cf. Troianos 2012c: 245–7.

[90] Humphreys 2015: 104–5.

[91] *Novella constitutio* §3.

[92] Troianos 2012c: 249.

[93] *Novella constitutio* §4. The ship in the sea of life metaphor occurs frequently in Byzantine literature, e.g. the introduction to the *History* of Leo the Deacon.

standardized curriculum, legal teaching was conducted by individual teachers. Thus the quality of legal education was highly dependent on the knowledge of the teacher, so that "though he be more imperfect than all [others] in the practice of teaching, nonetheless what is said by him is received with certainty, [even though] it oftentimes differs from what the laws prescribe, but rather corresponds to what the teacher says, [with the student] receiving it in his memory and soul."[94] Certainly Mauropous is correct in his characterization of Byzantine legal education, and indeed Byzantine education more generally, in that it was not standardized and depended to a great extent on the competence and proclivities of the individual teacher; there existed no official, state-sanctioned legal curriculum.[95] Of the five-year course of study for law students outlined in the *Constitutio omnem* there is no trace whatsoever.

In the following sections Monomachos, through the pen of Mauropous, lays out his solution to the problem of legal education. There are numerous references in these passages of the text to the language of the Justinianic constitution *Deo auctore*, which prefaces the *Digest*: youths rushing to teachers of the law (§5), internal and external peace (§6) and the great importance attached to the study of the law over other disciplines (§7a).[96] The provisions contained in the *Novella constitutio* which were to rectify this situation included the demarcation of a school (described variously as a *didaskalia*, *paideuterion* or *phrontisterion*) and the creation of the office of *nomophylax didaskalos*.

The designation of *nomophylax didaskalos* was fitting for two reasons, according to the *Novella constitutio*: first, because he was to inculcate in his students knowledge of the law, and second, he was to have his pick of lawbooks necessary for teaching and interpretation deposited at the school by an imperial librarian, the *bibliophylax*.[97] This *bibliophylax* was likely entrusted with overseeing the legal works of the vast imperial library, a

[94] *Novella constitutio* §5. Troianos 2012c: 250–1 claims (not entirely convincingly in my opinion) that this section of the text references (without citing it directly) *Cod. Just.* 2.7.11.12, a law issued in 460 by Leo I (r. 457–74), in which jurists must swear under oath that they are learned in jurisprudence. As Troianos himself observes, while this section of the *Novella constitutio* is addressed to *symbolaiographai*, the law of Leo I concerns jurists. In addition, the corresponding Hellenized version of the law in *Basil.* 8.1.26.2 is considerably redacted and thus makes an intentional reference to the law of Leo I only possible if Mauropous was consulting a Greek commentary or translation of it in the *Basilika* or its surviving scholia which has not come to down to us. For these reasons I think an intentional reference to the constitution of Leo I by Mauropous at this point in the text is rather unlikely.

[95] Oikonomides 1986: 189.

[96] Troianos 2012c: 251–2.

[97] *Novella constitutio* §10.

collection which would have included numerous juristic books, especially those of the Late Antique *antecessores* and *scholastikoi* which were often cited by Byzantine jurists, that either have not survived or only as fragments.[98] The *nomophylax* was not to take into consideration the family background or wealth of his students, but only their ability.[99] This meritocratic stipulation plausibly refers to *Dig.* 50.13.1 (excerpted in a condensed form in *Basil.* 54.14.1), which forbids teachers of the law from accepting payment for their teaching.[100] Furthermore, he was forbidden from taking bribes, although genuine gifts were encouraged.[101] In addition to senatorial rank, the *nomophylax* himself was to be given a yearly stipend (*rhoga*) of 4 pounds of gold (*litrai*), various other allowances (*siteresia*), purple-dyed silks and a gilded staff.[102]

The future patriarch John Xiphilinos, who as we saw in the last chapter was perhaps involved in the drafting of edicts against heretics issued during the patriarchate of Alexios Stoudites, was deemed by the emperor to be the most fitting candidate for the new position of *nomophylax didaskalos*. Xiphilinos appears to have already run a school along with his friend and fellow court intellectual Michael Psellos even before his election to this position; Monomachos was thus in effect giving his school official state sponsorship and dividing this school in two, with Psellos responsible for the teaching of philosophy in one school and Xiphilinos for the teaching of the law in the other.[103]

As in the whole of the *Novella constitutio*, the Justinianic legacy is invoked in the text's discussion of the duties of the *nomophylax didaskalos*. Xiphilinos is implicitly compared to the *antecessores* Tribonian, Dorotheos and Theophilos mentioned in §3 of the constitution *Imperatoriam maiestatem*, which announced the creation of a commission to compose the *Institutes*.[104] The upshot of this invocation of the creators of the standard textbook on Roman law would have been unmistakable to the readers of the *Novella constitutio*: Xiphilinos was in effect a new *antecessor*, charged with resurrecting the glories of late Roman legal education. Like Justinian himself he was to burn the midnight oil poring over legal texts, while

98 For the likely duties of the *bibliophylax*, see Troianos 2012c: 254–5.

99 *Novella constitutio* §14.

100 Troianos 2012c: 256 speculates that Mauropous perhaps used an otherwise not transmitted Greek version of this *Digest* passage rather than the *Basilika*.

101 *Novella constitutio* §14.

102 *Novella constitutio* §11.

103 Wolska-Conus 1976: 225–7.

104 *Novella constitutio* §8; cf. Troianos 2012c: 252.

explaining them over the course of the day, conversing with his students during both periods.[105]

Another of the requirements of *nomophylax didaskalos*, that he know Latin, is likewise intended to emphasize the revival of the late Roman legal legacy.[106] Knowledge of Latin in Constantinople, particularly the sophisticated Latin necessary to read late Roman legal texts, was practically non-existent among Byzantine jurists in the eleventh century.[107] Even though many Latin words remained in the earliest versions of the *Basilika*, in private compilations of the tenth century, and in the "old scholia" to the *Basilika*, Byzantine jurists in this period had access to numerous Greek–Latin legal lexica which obviated the need for a deep knowledge of Latin. The so-called *Ecloga Basilicorum*, written in 1142, contains almost no Latin words.[108] This insistence upon expertise in Latin was thus mainly motivated by ideological as opposed to practical concerns. Just as the old *antecessores* moved easily between Greek and Latin, so would the new *antecessor* as well.

Interestingly, the *Novella constitutio* was not intended to regulate the education of all legal officials. The only two groups mentioned in the *Novella* are lawyers (*synegoroi*) and notaries (*symbolaiographoi* or *taboullarioi*). The *nomophylax* was to test each member of these groups in his knowledge of the laws, both written and oral, as well as his general moral rectitude.[109] Only with the nomophylax's approval could these lawyers and notaries be registered in their respective guilds (*systemata*).[110] Higher ranking magistrates, such as thematic judges, are not mentioned at all: a fact which testifies to the principle of late Roman legal administration, which continued throughout Byzantine history, that legal officials were usually first and foremost administrators. Of course, many high-ranking legal officials began their careers as notaries, but this certainly wasn't the case for magistrates with juridical powers, such as military governors (*strategoi*).

105 *Novella constitutio* §11; the invocation of Justinian's sleepless nights (*Nov.* 8, proem) has been pointed out by Troianos 2012c: 255.

106 *Novella constitutio* §16.

107 Van der Wal 1984: 280, among others, doubts that Byzantine jurists in the eleventh century, even the *nomophylax*, would have been able to consult juridical texts in Latin. On this question see most recently Troianos 2012c: 257.

108 Burgmann 1991c: 95–6.

109 *Novella constitutio* §20.

110 The contention of Speck 1991b: 343 that Xiphilinos became in effect the head of a new combined guild of lawyers and notaries has been rightly criticized by Troianos 2012c: 252. The text merely speaks of Xiphilinos testing their legal knowledge and moral rectitude, and does not suggest that a new guild of the sort which Speck suggests was created.

After listing these practical provisions, Mauropous closes the *Novella constiutio* with a series of exhortations to the *nomophylax* and his students.[111] Again, the evocation of the Late Antique past serves to encourage the "law-loving youth" of the present to match the wondrous jurisprudential wisdom of their predecessors. Thus Mauropous notes that while the Romans of a half millennium ago had attended schools in Beirut and "Older Rome", the hearers of the *Novella constitutio* need not leave Constantinople to quench their thirst for legal learning.[112] The students and the nomophylax were to "endeavor to run the good race, and [to be] zealots, admired champions and victors; a glory to your parents, a boast to your relatives, an ornament to the empire, and a salvation to the commonweal."[113]

The flowery language of the *Novella constitutio* unfortunately gives us no information on the legal curriculum; we know nothing about which texts were read or the style of teaching which was employed.[114] There is a vague passage in the *Novella constitutio* stating that the older laws, which were not being used, again have their validity and should be consulted.[115] This appears to merely be a general appeal to give the impression of a complete resurrection of the Justinianic legal tradition rather than a measure aimed at a specific area.[116]

Despite Monomachos' lofty ambitions for his law school, its actual impact on legal education was quite limited. One problem was its short duration: Xiphilinos was its first and only director. It lasted until perhaps 1054, and in any case was certainly no longer functioning when Xiphilinos became patriarch on January 1, 1064.[117] One should not be misled, as past scholars have been, by the impression of continuity caused by creation of the church office of *nomophylax* in the same period, which lasted into the fourteenth century.[118]

One way to ascertain Xiphilinos' activity as the *nomophylax didaskalos* is to examine his work as a scholiast to the *Basilika*. Xiphilinos is credited by scholars with some sixty-three scholia to the *Basilika*, making him

111 *Novella constitutio* §23–7.
112 *Novella constitutio* §24.
113 *Novella constitutio* §27.
114 Troianos 2012c: 262.
115 *Novella constitutio* §20.
116 *Pace* Troianos 2012c: 259, who connects this passage with his theory about Mauropous' citation of the aforementioned law of Leo I, arguing that this provision is to be interpreted as a reference to it.
117 Troianos 1998–9: 57.
118 Ibid.

one of the most productive of the "new" scholiasts of the eleventh and twelfth centuries.[119] This impressive jurisprudential output, coupled with the ambitious claims of the *Novella constitutio* itself, has given rise to two impressions regarding the impact of the law school on legal education. The first claim is that Xiphilinos and his students practiced a radical new form of legal education, championing the use of Justinianic legal texts over the *Basilika*. The second consists of the assumption that Xiphilinos and his students created a standardized scholia apparatus, in effect a *glossa ordinaria*, to the *Basilika*. There are strong reasons to doubt both claims.

The first claim is the easier of the two to refute. According to the influential view of Wanda Wolska-Conus, Xiphilinos, going against the grain of the predominant legal thinking of his day, believed in a jurisprudence based on the writings of the *antecessores* and the Justinianic corpus which served as the base of the *Basilika*. As such he and his students supposedly formed a new school of thought championing the legal writings of Justinianic jurists. Opposed to them were the older, more established legal scholars like the judge Ophrydas, mentioned in the *Peira* and appearing as the main opponent of Xiphilinos in Psellos' funeral oration for the patriarch, who clung to the narrow validity of the *Basilika*. The basis for her claim is mainly an exacting analysis of the scholia to the *Basilika* attributed to Xiphilinos, as well as inferences drawn from Psellos' funeral oration for Xiphilinos.[120]

The main problem with this theory is that it is based on a false premise: the *Basilika* were not, at least until receiving official status under Manuel I Komnenos (1143–80), conceived of as a replacement to the numerous legal writings of the Justinianic age, as Paul Speck has observed.[121] While Xiphilinos certainly showed a predilection for the writings of the *antecessores* in solving legal conundrums, the real question is whether he was any different in this respect from other Byzantine jurists of the period. One way to explore this question is to turn to the surviving works of Eustathios Rhomaios, the renowned legal scholar who some scholars think was behind the group of jurists opposed to Xiphilinos, if he was in fact still alive at all in the late 1040s.[122] Even if he was not part of this anti-Xiphilinos faction, his work was seen as exemplary by contemporary jurists and thus can be seen as representing the best of Byzantine

119 Van Bochove 2014: 84–5.
120 Wolska-Conus 1979: 14–31.
121 Speck 1991b: 322.
122 On the possibility of Eustathios still being alive in 1047, see Oikonomides 1986: 175–6.

jurisprudence in the decades before Xiphilinos and the founding of the law school.

Yet there is no evidence whatsoever for concluding that Eustathios Rhomaios had any sort of preference for the *Basilika* over other the works of the *antecessores*. On the contrary, Eustathios invokes the works of Stephan repeatedly in the *Peira*.[123] Nor is he the only *antecessor* cited: one also finds Thalelaios,[124] Theophilos[125] and Cyril.[126] Naturally, the *Basilika* are repeatedly referenced as well, but scholars agree that most of these *Basilika* citations were the work of the *Peira*'s anonymous redactor rather than that of Eustathios himself.[127] Besides the *Peira*, an eleventh-century legal treatise which was probably authored by Eustathios Rhomaios, the *Tractatus de peculiis*, likewise demonstrates that this dichotomy between pro- and anti-*Basilika* camps did not exist. In this text Eustathios makes heavy use of "old" scholia to the *Sixty Books*/*Basilika*, including possibly complete works of the *antecessores*, such as the *Codex* commentary (*Paragraphe*) of Thalelaios.[128]

A similar tendency to reference both the work of the *antecessores* as well as the *Basilika* can be found in the synodal edicts of the patriarch Alexios Stoudites discussed in the previous chapter. In seeking to bring Justinianic regulations directed against heretics back into force against the West Syrian/Jacobite population of Melitene, the commission of jurists called into action by the patriarch used both the *Basilika* and the writings of the *antecessores*, with the latter serving in the main to clarify or elucidate the former. For instance, when addressing the issue of mixed-faith marriages, i.e. between Orthodox and Jacobites or Nestorians, the writings of the *antecessor* Stephan are invoked.[129] Stephan is described as "a man being sufficiently learned in other teaching and most learned in legal matters."[130] The commission of jurists in fact included jurists on both sides of the supposed pro- and anti-*Basilika* camps: Eustathios was a signatory of the synods of 1029 and 1030, while Xiphilinos perhaps authored or helped formulate the synodal edict stemming from the year 1039.

123 *Peira* 15.3, 16.9–10, 26.12, 36.15.
124 *Peira* 7.1, 36.2, 41.23, 59.3, 56.8–10.
125 *Peira* 36.15.
126 *Peira* 26.12, 36.15, 41.15.
127 With regard to separating the jurisprudence of Eustathios from the additions of the *Peira*'s anonymous redactor, see Sirks 2010.
128 On the sources Eustathios uses in the *Tractatus de peculiis*, see Eustathios Rhomaios, *Tractatus de peculiis* 296–8.
129 Alexios Stoudites, *Edicts* 30–1.
130 Ibid., lines 28–9.

The divide between the *Basilika* and Justinianic legal texts is most apparent in an anonymous eleventh-century legal tract, the *Melete ton psilon symphonon* ("Treatise on Open Pacts"), better known by its Latin name, the *Meditatio de nudis pactis*.[131] The text concerned a case between a monastery and a *protospatharios*, and hinged around the definition of *pacta nuda*, which in Roman law denoted agreements which did not result in obligations. The *protospatharios* had donated a sum of gold to the monastery in return for an annuity; both the donor and the monastery remain unnamed in the text. Even though the annuity was paid for some years, the monks eventually found this arrangement unsatisfactory and demanded it be renegotiated, thus prompting the case. Various theories have been advanced regarding its authorship, but the best candidate is the *Basilika* scholiast Constantine of Nicaea.[132]

The author of the *Meditatio*, a member of a tribunal addressing his fellow judges, clearly champions the consultation of legal texts from Late Antiquity, particularly the writings of the sixth-century jurist Stephan and the *Digest*, over the *Basilika*. He declares at the beginning of the tract that his aim is to "follow the methods and legal writings of the great and most-renowned teacher and jurist Stephan."[133] With regard to his opponents, who only employ the *Basilika* in their argumentation, he states that "They who occupy themselves with the *Basilika* alone are hardly able to perceive what they are studying, and so one must depart from their knowledge of [the *Basilika*]."[134] He maintains the superiority of "his *Digest*" over "your *Basilika*"; the *Digest* is more praiseworthy because it "contains something more than the *Basilika*."[135] In closing, he declares that "Thus concerning these matters, I and those with me are more confident to dwell in the breadth of the ancient [legal texts] than to cast about in the confines of the *Basilika*; we are in agreement and are of the same mind concerning what I have said."[136] In terms of his reverence for Stephan as the preeminent interpreter of Roman law and predilection for the writings of the *antecessores*, the author of the *Meditatio* is very much in step with other Byzantine legal texts which have survived from the eleventh century.

[131] For general information and scholarship on the text see Troianos 2011: 292–3.
[132] Scheltema 1970a. For John Xiphilinos as the author see *Meditatio de nudis pactis* 187–236; Wolska-Conus 1979: 40–53.
[133] *Meditatio de nudis pactis*, Preface, §2.
[134] Ibid., Title 6, §27.
[135] Ibid., Title 6, §§25–6.
[136] Ibid., Title 8, §3.

The numerous references to the works of the *antecessores* in mid-eleventh-century legal sources do not fit Wolska-Conus' schema of a divide between jurists who preferred the *Basilika* over older legal writings; on the contrary, all extant texts of the Byzantine-Roman legal tradition could be validly consulted with regard to legal arguments. Though jurists might argue for the merit of one text over the other, this does not appear to have been a reflection of different schools of thought. In summation there is no compelling reason to think that law school with its director Xiphilinos introduced a new curriculum or approach to the teaching of Roman law.

The second assumption often associated with the activity of the law school is that Xiphilinos and his students created a *glossa ordinaria* of a standardized corpus of scholia for the *Basilika*, combining the "old" scholia of the sixth and seventh centuries with the "new" scholia of the Middle Byzantine period. It was long thought by many prominent legal historians of the nineteenth century (Zachariä von Lingenthal) as well as the twentieth (Leopold Wenger, Peter Pieler, Nicolaas van der Wal, J. H. A. Lokin) that this process actually took place during the reign of Constantine VII Porphyrogenntos (r. 945–59).[137] This is because the canonist Balsamon reports that a "final cleansing" of the *Basilika* took place under the emperor Constantine, though he does not specify which one.[138] Yet Andreas Schminck argued in 1986 that in fact there are good reasons for connecting this event with the reign of another Constantine, namely Constantine Monomachos, and the founding of the law school.[139]

Quite recently Thomas van Bochove has presented convincing arguments for doubting whether the process of combining old and new scholia took place in the eleventh century.[140] This is not the place to recapitulate his argument in full, but the manuscript tradition of the *Basilika* in particular validates his position. There is at least one (*cod. Paris. gr.* 1349 of the eleventh century)[141] and possibly two (the other being the *scripta inferior* of *cod. Rescr. Krakov. Jagiellońska* 28/266 of the twelfth or thirteenth century)[142] examples of manuscripts with exclusively old scholia. This demonstrates that jurists still supplied their copies of the *Basilika*

137 Summary of this debate along with references to the older literature in van Bochove 2014: 73–7.

138 *Rh.-P.* vol. I, 32, lines 5–7.

139 Schminck 1986: 33–52.

140 Van Bochove 2014: 79–86. His suggestion that it could by contrast have taken place in tenth-century Constantinople is, by his own admission, only a tentative possibility.

141 *RHBR*, no. 162.

142 *RHBR*, no. 92.

with exclusively old scholia during the eleventh century and perhaps later as well.[143] Even in the manuscripts with old and new scholia, the old scholia were not updated: they continued to refer to the laws according to where they were to be found in the *CIC* rather than the corresponding passages in the *Basilika*.[144] Thus our current understanding of the manuscript tradition of the *Basilika* casts significant doubt upon the idea that there was any standardized catena commentary of old and new scholia to the *Basilika*, least of all one created in the eleventh century by Xiphilinos and his students.

These considerations suggest the *Novella constitutio* and the founding of the law school should be interpreted primarily as an ambitious effort to complete the arc of Middle Byzantine legal reform. By attempting to regulate and standardize late Roman legal teaching, Monomachos claimed to have finished what Basil I and Leo VI had begun. This achievement was announced not only as an internal but also as an external triumph. In the words of the *Novella constitutio* "thus now may the success which has been accomplished by us, by the Grace of the Almighty endure for all time in [our] famous realm, and may no passage of time, nor any jealousy of evil ones one extinguish it, but let it shine to the end, always endeavored toward and honored by foreign peoples and presiding over an eternal justice in life."[145]

Legal Education in the Juristic Didactic Writings of Michael Psellos and Michael Attaleiates

Overall then, while the *Novella constitutio* represents an exaltation of the legal profession which enhanced the social status of mid-eleventh-century Constantinopolitan jurists, one must turn elsewhere to find out how lawyers and legal functionaries were actually educated. A valuable set of texts which reveal a great deal about legal education in the eleventh century consists of the juristic writings ascribed to Michael Psellos, who also in the 1040s was awarded the post of "president of the philosophers" (*hypatos ton philosophon*) and ran a school of rhetoric as an analogue to Xiphilinos and his school of law.[146] The major juristic text ascribed to Psellos which has

[143] Van Bochove 2014: 79–80.

[144] Van Bochove 2014: 80–1.

[145] *Novella constitutio* §22.

[146] There is a massive bibliography on Psellos studies which I won't try to cite here. An accessible introduction to Psellos as an author is Papaioannou 2013. For Psellos as a lawyer and teacher of the

survived is the *Synopsis legum*, a didactic poem written for Psellos' pupil, the emperor Michael VII Doukas (r. 1071–8). Along with the *Synopsis legum*, there are a total of eight didactic texts ascribed to Psellos, seven shorter[147] and one longer.[148] Another set of texts, perhaps the work of Psellos' students, is a collection of about forty-five commentaries of the *Synopsis legum* found in *Cod. Par. gr.* 1355.[149]

Compared to the *Novella constitutio*, these didactic juristic texts present a much clearer picture of legal education, and are invaluable in that they represent the work of a practicing lawyer. From these writings a picture of legal education emerges which is utterly different from that of Late Antiquity, at which time lawyers received five and later possibly six years of specialized legal instruction. Unlike its Late Antique forebear, Byzantine legal education appears to have been much more generalized, and advanced training in the law was merely a necessary component in the education of a highly educated person, much as Blackstone could say in the eighteenth century that no continental gentleman could consider his education complete without having attended a course or two on Justinian's *Institutes*.[150]

Employing an analysis of texts cited in the *Synopsis legum* and other works of Psellos, Günter Weiss has compiled a list of thirty-one individual juristic works to which the prolific Byzantine author had access.[151] Especially noteworthy is that Psellos himself did for the most part not directly consult the supposedly main source of law during this period – the *Basilika* or any of its various antecedents.[152] Indeed, Psellos himself says as much in his *Synopsis legum*, describing Leo VI's *Sixty Books*, the predecessor to the *Basilika*, as follows: "Then [comes] the summary book of [the emperor] Leo, / So that the entire sixty-book [compendium] contained all the laws, / The *Codex*, the *Digest*, and the *Novels*, / They are related and breathe together the different laws, / Thoroughly examined,

law the most useful studies are those of Dennis 1994; Fisher 2012; Fögen 1982; Weiss 1977; Wolska-Conus 1979: 55–97.

147 Michael Psellos, *Brevis Divisio Novellarum Iustiniani* and *Minor legal texts.*

148 Michael Psellos, *To his Students on the Names of Suits.*

149 Fögen 1982.

150 Blackstone 1765–9: vol. I, 4: "In most of the nations on the continent, where the civil or imperial law under different modifications is closely interwoven with the municipal laws of the land, no gentleman, or at least no scholar, thinks his education is completed, till he has attended a course or two of lectures, both upon the institutes of Justinian and the local constitutions of his native soil, under the very eminent professors that abound in their several universities."

151 Weiss 1977.

152 Weiss 1977: 101.

indexed properly and legitimately; / But it is difficult to interpret, and extremely unclear."[153] Instead, he relied almost exclusively on commentaries, lexica and paraphrases. The importance of the *antecessor* Theophilos' *Paraphrase* is especially noticeable, as Psellos cribbed extensively from it in the *Synopsis legum*.[154] As noted above, the *Paraphrase* seems to have served as the standard Byzantine legal textbook, given its collection of legal norms and concise explanations of legal terminology.

With regard to subject matter, the *Synopsis legum* and the other juristic didactic writings of Psellos are an admixture of practical legal material and antiquarianism. One of the primary and apparently most difficult tasks of the Byzantine jurist was the categorization of a suit (*dike*). This necessitated identification of an action (Gr. *agoge*, Lat. *actio*) under which the suit was brought forward by the plaintiff and then its corresponding obligation(s) (Gr. *enoche*, Lat. *obligatio*). Thus a number of treatises on actions from the Middle Byzantine period have survived.[155] One of the most prominent jurists of the eleventh century, Garidas, authored a treatise on actions which has not survived but traces of which can be found in scholia to the *Basilika*.[156] In the *Synopsis legum* Psellos describes this process by using a metaphor, likening actions to mothers and their attendant obligations to daughters: it fell to the student to correctly match the two.[157] Many of Psellos' smaller juristic didactic texts are likewise devoted to correctly naming actions and their obligations. One of the reasons that the actions/obligations identification process was difficult for students is again the problem of the legacy of Latin in Byzantine law. The names of actions and obligations in the Middle Byzantine period remained in Latin, although transliterated into Greek. Thus much ink was spilled in explaining what these Latin legal terms meant in Greek.[158]

Yet this quite practical training came side-by-side with obscure antiquarian quiddities. In his text "To his Students on the Names of Suits", Psellos remarks that he has noticed that his students have trouble identifying the Greek and Latin names of suits. He then states that "For though the Greek [legal terms] are mentioned with Greek words, unless one untangles the intention and shall proclaim the cause of the placement of

153 Michael Psellos, *Synopsis legum*, lines 44–9.
154 Weiss 1977: 102.
155 Edited in Meijering 1990, with a legal-historical analysis of the two texts later in the same volume by Fögen, 1990.
156 On Garidas see Fögen 1990: 244–6.
157 Michael Psellos, *Synopsis legum*, lines 96, 124.
158 E.g. Michael Psellos, *Synopsis legum*, lines 106–7.

[these terms] through etymology, in which they dwell, then they won't be well-understood by the readers."[159] Psellos then proposes to compile a lexicon of Latin legal terms set alongside their Greek equivalents for the benefit of his students. Instead of completing what he suggests be done, this serves as a point of departure for a discussion of the offices and legal institutions of ancient Athens, with the original problem, of the students incorrectly identifying suits, probably unsolved. An emphasis on antiquarian and peripheral information is evident as well in the commentaries on the *Synopsis legum*, perhaps written by Psellos' students. This confirms the notion that Byzantine legal education was merely a part of a more advanced schooling and did not constitute a specialized field of study in and of itself.[160]

Finally, these juristic didactic texts shed some light on what exactly was considered law in this period. While the *Basilika* as a reappropriation of Justinianic law assured that Roman law up until the time of Justinian was enforced and valid, these texts of Psellos demonstrate which legal texts from the seventh to the eleventh centuries were incorporated into legal teaching. Conspicuously absent are any of the more important legal texts, at least in terms of manuscripts, from that period of time, including the *Ecloga*, *NG*, *NM* and *NN*. Post-Justinianic imperial legislation is only haphazardly referenced: the most prolific legislator after Justinian, Leo VI, seems to have had only a mixed impact on the legal curriculum: Leo VI's novels are the basis for thirty-four lines of the *Synopsis legum*.[161]

Legal education of a different sort is evident in the *Legal Textbook* of Michael Attaleiates. Attaleiates had extensive legal experience as a judge, including occupying the somewhat-mysterious position of *krites tou stratopedou*.[162] His *Legal Textbook*, issued in 1073/4, is of a very different character than the didactic juristic writings of Psellos.[163] After a brief survey of Roman law from its origins to the time of the composition of the

159 Michael Psellos, *To his Students on the Names of Suits* 196.

160 Fögen 1982: 300.

161 Michael Psellos, *Synopsis legum*, lines 839–72.

162 On Attaleiates see now especially Krallis 2012, who does not really delve into his activity as a judge and legal scholar. For the position of *krites tou stratopedou* see Haldon 2002; Gkoutzioukostas 2006.

163 Wolska-Conus 1997: 97–101 has advanced the thesis that the *Legal Textbook* of Attaleiates was written in response to the *Synopsis legum* of Psellos. This would fit her notion of an eleventh-century dichotomy of Byzantine legal teaching, with one camp representing Xiphilinos and Psellos, who advocated a more "philosophical" form of legal teaching and reference to the Late Antique legal commentary tradition, and another camp which promoted the exclusive use of the *Basilika*. As I have argued above, I don't think there is a compelling case for postulating such a binary division of eleventh-century legal education.

Sixty Books,[164] the majority of the *Legal Textbook* consists of thematically grouped quotations from the *Basilika*. Toward the end of the work there is a brief description of some post-Macedonian legislation as well as a reproduction of Leo VI's Novel 116.[165] Thus it appears as though at least some of the more recent legislation was taught to Byzantine jurists, judging from the educational texts of the period. A caveat to this statement is that Attaleiates himself states in the *Legal Textbook* that a great deal of Leo VI's legislation was no longer in force: "The blessed lord emperor Leo issued many novels, but they were not in use, excepting only those which were written without other laws already in existence, or which were a supplement to the novels enacted by Justinian."[166]

Conclusion

Though legal education changed substantially from the specialized five- or six-year program of legal studies in Late Antiquity, its basis remained, well into the eleventh century, the didactic works and commentaries of the premier jurists of the Justinianic age, the *antecessores*. A specialized legal course of study was never realized in the Middle Byzantine period: instead, instruction in the law was a part of an advanced general education. This tendency is even more striking in the Late Byzantine period.[167]

A number of eleventh-century events lend credence to the supposition that there was a renaissance in legal education: the founding of the law school of Constantine IX Monomachos, the composition of numerous special-subject legal treatises, the quantity and quality of scholia to the *Basilika*,[168] and the number of Byzantine intellectuals, such as Michael Attaleiates, Michael Psellos, and John Xiphilinos who were interested in legal teaching. In summation, there is no reason to doubt the occurrence of a considerable revival of legal studies under the Macedonian dynasty.

The signal event in the history of legal education in this period was the founding of the law school in 1047 under the auspices of the emperor Constantine IX Monomachos. Even though its founding reflected rather than initiated a revival in the study of secular law, the grandiose

164 Michael Attaleiates, *Legal Textbook* 415–17.

165 Ibid. 491–3, 497.

166 Ibid. 491.

167 Troianos 1998–9: 58.

168 The prominent eleventh-century scholiasts included John Xiphilinos, Constantine of Nicaea, Kalokyros "Sextos," Gregory Doxapatres and Michael Agiotheodorites; see Troianos 2011: 282–4; Burgmann 1989.

pretensions to the resurrection of late Roman legal education expressed in the *Novella constitutio* should be taken seriously. The study of the law was given the solemnest sanction of the state; likewise the monastic setting of the school and strong religious language of the *Novella constitutio* gave the pursuit of legal studies divine overtones.

From the standpoint of Byzantine legal culture, the creation of the law school and the ennoblement of jurists represented a final rapprochement with the Roman political legacy. Even though the manuscripts of the period clearly show that Byzantine legal scholars were hurriedly excising and Hellenizing the last vestiges of Latin from their legal tradition, Xiphilinos as well as any future director of the school was supposed to have mastered the language. The numerous intertextual references in the *Novella constitutio* strongly indicate that Xiphilinos was thought of as a new *antecessor*. While the law schools of Rome and Beirut had passed away, the legal legacy of the Justinianic age flowered anew in Constantinople.

Conclusions
The End of Secular Law in Byzantium?

Over the course of the two concluding chapters of this study a narrative of the increasing prominence of a cadre of legal specialists has taken shape. In contrast to the mostly anonymous or shadowy figures who carried out the "Cleansing of the Ancient Laws" ordered by the first Macedonian dynasts, Basil I (r. 867–86) and Leo VI (r. 886–912), these jurists stood at the center of the chaotic middle decades of the eleventh century. Their elder statesman, Eustathios Rhomaios, saw his one-time colleague Romanos III Argyros (r. 1028–34) attain the imperial throne. As we saw in Chapter 5, the emperors after Basil II (r. 967–1025) found the legal expertise these jurists possessed of great value in addressing political concerns, like the problem of minority populations in the empire's southeastern borderlands. The creation of a Constantinopoltian law school in 1047 represented the apogee of these jurists' power and societal influence. The school's founding document, the *Novella constitutio*, elevated and ennobled legal education to an extent not seen since Justinian's day. With the school's president John Xiphilinos acting as a new *antecessor*, the Middle Byzantine revival of the Late Antique Roman legal tradition was complete. By the middle of the eleventh century the study of Roman law was flourishing: numerous commentaries, scholia and treatises were being written; not just Xiphilinos, but the other great intellectuals of the day like Michael Attaleiates and Michael Psellos also studied and wrote on the law; and the maintenance of secular law had become a cornerstone of Middle Byzantine political ideology.

From the standpoint of the *longue durée*, it is worth contemplating the transformation of the Roman legal tradition achieved under the Macedonian dynasty. Of the three threads of Byzantine legal culture employed throughout this book – the Roman political heritage, Orthodox Christianity and Hellenic cultural orientation – the empire of the crisis-ridden sixth and recovering seventh centuries had turned to the second of these in order to survive. Though the state was already thoroughly

Christianized by the sixth century, Justinian I (r. 527–65) still thought of himself and his subjects mainly as Romans, emphasizing the first component of Byzantine legal culture. The seventh-century shock of the rise of Islam and the loss of the eastern provinces caused a reevaluation of both Byzantine identity and the way in which law was conceived of and used. Justinian II (r. 685–95, 705–11) seems to have seen canon law as a more useful means of political legitimation than secular law.[1] The promulgators of the *Ecloga*, the emperors Leo III (r. 717–41) and Constantine V (r. 741–75), described their subjects not as "Romans" but rather "marked as Christians" (*christosemeiotoi*).[2] Even if the *Ecloga* brought about little actual substantive changes to Roman law, its presentation of the law was a significant innovation: "It posited Roman law as not just ultimately emanating from God, but in fact a continuation of the same law given through the prophets. Similarly, emperors were not part of a separate narrative, but the heir to the apostles and prophets, Moses and Solomon."[3]

The more stable and economically vibrant empire of the Macedonian dynasty did not express the law in these extreme Christian terms. By this time Christianity had become an accepted and stable element of Byzantine legal culture. Thus a judge like Michael Attaleiates could casually comment that the churches, monasteries and venerable houses of his day had the same *res sacrae* status as the temples and religious sanctuaries of his pagan Roman forebears, an analogy that would have horrified a jurist of the Isaurian age.[4] Law continued to be further Christianized from the ninth to the eleventh centuries, but more in the Justinianic rather than the Isaurian mold. Gone was the radical imperial self-presentation as Maccabean priest-kings in the *Ecloga*; instead Leo VI in his *Novels* intervened as necessary in areas of Roman legislation where he thought the law was not quite Christian enough.

More relevant to the empire's identity was the pan-Mediterranean process, which began around the year 800, of the reappropriation of the Roman heritage by the Byzantine, Carolingian and Caliphal polities.[5] The program of the "Cleansing of the Ancient Laws" undertaken in the second half of the ninth century was a major part of the Byzantine response to this project. On a practical level, the Roman legal tradition was Hellenized.

[1] Humphreys 2015: 37–80, esp. 79.
[2] Humphreys 2015: 255.
[3] Humphreys 2015: 128.
[4] Michael Attaleiates, *Legal Textbook* 420; cf. Stolte 2007: 126–7.
[5] Speck 1991b: 312–16.

Latin words were gradually purged from Byzantine law and replaced with *exhellenismoi*. Yet the Byzantine jurists of the time at the same time benefitted from the social prestige of having mastered the Latin language, the key to unlocking the "The Wisdom of the Italians."

Perplexingly, this remarkable revival of secular law in Byzantium, which seemed by the middle of the eleventh century to be still in its incipient stages, was extinguished by the 1080s almost as quickly as it had appeared.[6] In fact, the end of the eleventh century is the last time one can speak of Byzantine secular law without qualification. As yet there is no convincing explanation as to why this happened. Certainly the political turmoil associated with the end of the Macedonian dynasty, which had at first enhanced the status of secular law and in particular a Constantinopolitan cadre of jurists, played a role in disrupting the revival of secular law. Constantine IX Monomachos (1042–55), who invested so much political capital in the creation of his law school, quarreled with the intellectuals he had so lavishly supported at the start of his reign, and was not able to establish a stable succession. His creation of the offices of the *epi ton kriseon* and the *nomophylax didaskalos* thus did not achieve the effects in legal education and practice which he had hoped for.

An explanation for the end of the secular legal tradition in Byzantium must take into account the gradual blurring of Byzantine secular and canon law. In the first five hundred years of its existence Byzantine canon law, starting with the Nicaean corpus of canons and ending with second revision of the *Nomokanon in Fourteen Titles*, had mostly played second fiddle to secular law.[7] Already in this period there was certainly an awareness that canon law, that is the corpus of *kanones*, was a coherent and separate tradition outside of secular law.[8] Yet there never developed, and this is a clue to the fate of secular law in Byzantium, a separate class of canon lawyers. Instead, via a phenomenon which David Wagschal has termed "borrowed specialization," the holders of certain church offices had to acquire and exercise expertise in both canon and secular law.[9] It is precisely officials of this sort – figures like Balsamon (d. after 1195), Alexios Aristenos (fl. mid twelfth century) and John Zonaras (fl. mid twelfth

[6] Burgmann 1999a: 603–5.

[7] The language and content of the Byzantine canon law tradition in this era has been recently examined in detail by Wagschal 2015.

[8] Wagschal 2015: 62–3, 219.

[9] Wagschal 2015: 80–3.

century) – who are the towering legal scholars of the twelfth century, without contemporary secular analogues.

In the context of the end of the Byzantine secular law tradition, there is also something to the observation of Ludwig Burgmann that, especially when looking at the manuscript tradition, canon law was a steady presence while secular law required *Vergegenwärtigung*, an active effort to recall or resurrect the Roman legal tradition.[10] The emperors of the Macedonian dynasty were the last Byzantine emperors to do this; a hearkening to the Roman legal tradition was not part of the political agenda of the Komnenoi or Palaiologoi. Nor did later dynasties embark on the same ambitious codification projects. The outstanding monuments of the Byzantine law after the 1080s were due to the Herculean efforts of individual canonists rather than the state-sponsored initiatives of earlier centuries.

A final factor in the rapid disappearance of secular Byzantine law was its close relationship and dependence upon the Byzantine state itself. Of the outstanding legal achievements produced during the time of the Macedonian dynasty, only the *Prochiron* found a reception outside of a Byzantine Greek context.[11] The *leges speciales* and Isaurian *Ecloga*, by contrast, could be adapted more easily to circumstances within the various polities of the Byzantine Commonwealth.[12] The gradual decline of the Byzantine Empire entailed a correspondingly shrinking number of scholars interesting in the secular legal heritage of the Roman state.

Tradition and Transformation: Byzantine Legal Culture under the Macedonian Dynasty

By defining Byzantine legal culture as the interplay between the Roman political legacy, Orthodox Christianity and Hellenic culture, I hoped to create a definition that would not only apply to all periods of Byzantine history, but would also allow one to follow the strands of continuity and change in its Middle Byzantine iteration. In this book I have advanced a number of arguments regarding these three components of Byzantine legal culture, and it is worthwhile to here summarize these points as well as their broader implications.

10 Burgmann 1999a: 612.
11 Burgmann 2005c: 49–50.
12 See Ch. 4.

Byzantinists, much more so than other pre-modern historians, have always struggled with the issue of continuity of the Byzantine state and society. While rupture and transformation stand at the heart of Western medieval studies (the collapse of the western half of the Roman Empire) or Islamic history (the rise of Islam), the Byzantine Empire, which witnessed and survived both of these epochal events, did not outwardly change to the same degree. The transformation wrought by the seventh century has only in the last twenty-five years come to be appreciated to the extent it deserves.[13] Yet recently there have emerged strong voices in favor of the continuity of Roman political institutions and Hellenic culture, and one thinks here in particular of Anthony Kaldellis.[14] The findings of this monograph certainly inform this essential debate concerning continuity and transformation.

With regard to the Roman political and institutional heritage, law and legal culture from the ninth to the eleventh century certainly show some strong elements of continuity. Yet the leitmotif of legal reform in this period, the program of the "Cleansing of the Ancient Laws" which was examined in Chapter 1, betrays that this outward stasis was achieved via tremendous internal effort and transformation. The renewal and reworking of Justinianic law was accomplished according to Giuseppe Tomasi di Lampedusa's maxim, expressed in *The Leopard*, that "everything needs to change so everything can stay the same." This brief but brilliant resuscitation of secular law was prompted and carried out for reasons of external (the pan-Mediterranean competition to claim the Roman political legacy) and internal (dynastic legitimation) exigencies. The institutions of secular law were likewise fitted to a Middle Byzantine context: the courts, like the empire itself, were highly centralized, with a sharp divide between center and periphery. These courts, staffed and used for the most part by the elite, came to reflect the aristocracy's penchant for patronage and influence-peddling, as outlined in Chapter 2.

While in law and legal culture the Roman political legacy was recast in a Middle Byzantine context, the role of Orthodox Christianity in Byzantine legal culture grew steadily but inexorably in importance. In Chapter 3 I explored the growing importance in Byzantine legal thought of terms imported from theology, that triad of *kainotomia*, *oikonomia* and

[13] See especially Haldon 1997; and now Haldon 2016.

[14] Kaldellis 2007; 2015.

philanthropia. This process, though slow and gradual, was perhaps the most momentous of all the transformations taking place during this period. It signaled the metamorphosis of the guiding principle of the Roman legal tradition, from a system which sought the objective discernment of truth to one which reenacted Orthodox Christianity's narrative of humankind's attainment of salvation, which in the courtroom saw the judge (consciously) imitating God's mercy towards the guilty (sinners). The centrality of Orthodoxy to the empire's identity had a more persecutory side as well, as for instance in the frequent attempts at the forced conversion of Jews in this epoch or the effort, narrated in Chapter 5, to exclude non-Orthodox from the legal system in empire's southeastern borderland. The growing prominence of Orthodox Christianity in law and legal culture both facilitated and foreshadowed the inevitable joining of Byzantine canon and civil law.

The relationship between Hellenism and law and legal thought in this period is perhaps the most straightforward of the three components of Byzantine legal culture. The cleansing or *anakatharis* of the Roman legal tradition was first and foremost a process of Hellenization. Though knowledge of Latin was still treasured by some jurists of the period, the law lost its last vestiges of Latin. In fact, as I demonstrated in in Chapter 6, Byzantine law had long been, perhaps as early as the seventh century, a predominately Greek affair. Yet as the process of *exhellenismos* or "translating into Greek" began at the end of the ninth century, at least a superficial familiarity with Latin would still have been necessary for the Byzantine jurist. By the middle of the eleventh century, as the commentary tradition to the *Basilika* was in full bloom and, according to some views, perhaps standardized, even the need for this cursory knowledge of Latin had disappeared. Moreover, from the standpoint of later impact, the most important legal works produced during this period – the *leges speciales* – were utterly Latinless compositions, a fact which at least partially accounts for their popularity in the Byzantine Commonwealth.

While this study was concerned exclusively with the period of Macedonian rule, there is certainly scope for examinations of Byzantine legal culture both before and after this epoch. M. T. G. Humphreys' thoughtful reevaluation[15] of the Isaurian dynasty's legal achievements is certainly a promising start, while the comparatively rich source

[15] Humphreys 2015.

material for last centuries of the Byzantine Empire would pay rich dividends to someone willing to investigate it. As such I hope that this study might serve as a guide to scholars examining periods both before and after it.

Considerations for Future Research

As I stressed at the start of this study, my goal was not to write Kazhdan's proposed "New History of Byzantine Law," that is, an examination of the evolution of Byzantine legal institutions. Instead, I have aimed to present a framework for further inquiry on Byzantine law via the heuristic device of Byzantine legal culture – the complex interplay of the Roman political legacy, Orthodox Christianity and Hellenic cultural orientation. Although utilizing a different methodology than the one Kazhdan proposed, my goal is in the end the same as his was: to move beyond *Quellenkritik* and towards a social history of Byzantine law.

At the same time, the examination of the diachronic development of certain legal institutions in Byzantium is certainly more possible than some scholars have allowed.[16] An excellent example is John Thomas' largely legal-historical study of the evolution of private religious foundations, a groundbreaking work that has never received the attention it deserves.[17] His monograph shows that the lack of archival documents outside of the Middle and Late Byzantine periods is hardly an insurmountable problem. In fact it is the systematic editing and publication of this archival material, above all in the excellent Archives de l'Athos series, which urgently calls for the reevaluation of our understanding of Byzantine legal institutions.

One can also still profit from careful readings of normative legal sources, as M. T. G. Humphreys' aforementioned reevaluation of the *Ecloga* and other "Dark Age" legislation demonstrates.[18] Scholars have still barely scratched the surface of the *Basilika*, above all their rich scholia tradition, even though they have now been scrupulously edited. There are few studies of individual scholiasts, despite the abundance of material at hand.[19]

[16] See in particular the objections of Burgmann 1991: 198–200; Simon 2005 1–4.
[17] Thomas 1987.
[18] Humphreys 2015.
[19] Two noteworthy exceptions are Burgmann 1989 for Kalokyros Sextos and Penna 2014 for Hagiotheodorites.

Yet perhaps the greatest area of need, particularly for Anglophone Byzantine Studies, is for more research on canon law. Both the Frankfurt and Groningen Schools of Byzantine Law are concerned first and foremost with secular law.[20] Byzantine canon law has simply not received the attention it deserves outside of the Orthodox cultural sphere. Emblematic of this sorry state of affairs is the fact that the most recent monograph of arguably the most important Byzantine canonist, Theodore Balsamon, is written in Latin.[21] A rich pre-Revolutionary tradition of Byzantine canon law research in Russian is virtually unknown in Western Byzantine Studies, while contemporary scholarship in Modern Greek is ignored almost to the same degree. The latter has produced some good historical analyses of canon law that could serve as models for future work. One thinks of Soterios Varnalides' treatment of *charistike* as an institution of canon law; I. M. Konidares' study of monastic *typika* as legal texts; or Eleutheria Papagianne's examination of the treatment of property law in ecclesiastical courts.[22]

A final consideration regarding the future direction of scholarship on Byzantine law is one of audience. Like Byzantine Studies in general, scholars of Byzantine law need to address questions of common interest among pre-modern historians in general, above all medievalists. I have endeavored with this monograph to show that Byzantine legal culture is not some *sui generis* phenomenon, but rather the engagement with the Roman legal tradition in a medieval Eastern Mediterranean context. The Byzantine case differs in details rather than essentials from this process elsewhere in the medieval world.

In closing, scholars could do worse than to follow the exhortation of Constantine IX Monomachos to the *nomophylax*'s students, that

> with discerning interpretation, a bold tongue, and holding to truth and certainty in all respects, you shall recognize the wholesome logic of the laws, and you shall heed the living voice of the laws even in the letters of lifeless books … you shall imitate the good and sensible farmers, who always deem the nourishment of the soil worthy of an abundant love of beauty (*philokalia*), who take the fruits of the soil not just one time, and after awhile leave it thorny and overgrown, but they perform a careful deed, and how useful it shall perpetually be as it continually bears the same crop

[20] There are some exceptions to this tendency, such as Bernard Stolte's studies and edition (in preparation) of the *Nomokanon in Fourteen Titles.*

[21] Stevens 1969.

[22] Konidares 1984; Papagianne 1992–2010; Varnalides 1985.

> for themselves and those who come after them, all of them always reaping a harvest from it.[23]

With this thought in mind I now take leave of my own small plot of land, in which I have invested much of my own *philokalia*, and hope that it bears fruit for others.

[23] *Novella constitutio* §23.

APPENDIX

Translation of the Novella constitutio

Editorial insertions are indicated by brackets [], while Greek words are affixed after their translated English equivalents by parentheses, e.g. (*proedria*). Page numbers in brackets, such as [p. 19], indicate the page of the text in Salač's edition. I would here like to heartily thank Andreas Schminck for sharing with me his own soon to be published German translation of the *Novella constitutio*, from which my translation below into English greatly benefitted.

Text

A novel pronounced by the Christ-loving emperor, Constantine Monomachos, on the declaration and proposal for a teacher of the laws.

1. And what concern, what manner of work or endeavor, is more fitting to His Majesty than concern for the laws? For the honor of an emperor is, according to the saying, to love judgment. Both righteousness and discernment are the foundation of his throne. These are entirely impossible to accrue to an emperor, except from and through the law. It is through it that emperors rule; so it is also for both princes and potentates lording over the earth. For although through these very laws themselves both imperial and divine power is freed from legitimate authority, since it [this power] rules over everything, it itself is not subject to anything else on earth.
2. But we pay heed to those very emperors who, by seeking the grace of just prudence and by rendering this [grace] as a sort of recompense to the laws, exercise their power over those living under their rule through the laws, and prefer to reign kindly and justly through them rather than tyrannize violently and unlawfully without them, thinking it wiser that they rule in this way [through the laws] than against the subjects they rule. For the tyrant and emperor differ in

this respect, that the former (as it is said) possesses the law as a means to an end, but the emperor by contrast possesses the law as his end, understanding [his] rule as legitimate authority, and gladly accepting the law as the wise helmsman of [his] rule. It [the law] is an invention and gift of God, it is both called and viewed as the art of the good and equal, and it sets aright all of mortal life and obtains a wondrous order for affairs. And order is the chief component of good things (as the saying goes), encompassing the temporal as well as the divine.

3. Therefore the pious emperors who came before us recognized the innate power in the laws, and did not pay less attention to laws than to arms. They held back the vicissitudes of war with noble stratagems or rather with succor from Above, and beautified the rectitude of peace with the best legislation, showing through both [means] [p. 19] the dignity and greatness of imperial wisdom. Although they thus concerned themselves with the honor of the laws, much of what they introduced was only partially useful, because through [their] many pains and toils they reduced the boundlessness of the laws, and they labored a great deal with the interpretation of the Latin, in which language the antiquity of the laws was written, and endured much hardship in making them clear, and still they thought their cleansing was worthy of much attention and effort, yet something which was most excellent and beneficial to the commonweal (I do not know whence or how) they left unarranged.

4. For though they honored the usefulness of the laws, they overlooked their practice, and though they especially reverenced them, they did not find a teacher for them, but when they tested notaries (*symbolaiographoi*) and examined lawyers (*synegoroi*), they ascertained from where and how [they acquired knowledge about] legal matters, and formerly they did not appoint any of those either counted among the guilds or to those registered as the most knowledgeable rhetoricians, before they identified their teachers and made known how much time they had spent in the learning of the laws. They passed over he who taught these things diligently and transmitted accurate knowledge of the laws to them accurately, with great enthusiasm and purpose; they did not select a single man able to do this, nor did they set aside some place of assembly for lovers of the law, nor did they allocate public allowances, nor did they deign to establish or organize anything which became a school, but they left the divine legal education like a ship without a helmsman in the middle of the sea of life, though with it

they would together be shipwrecked and perhaps wander astray and be carried off.

5. For we know of almost no one among those who have been recently called to public service, who due to his trustworthy learning, as though from an anchorage or well-suited port, sets sail upon the affairs and matters of state, but to whose knowledge such a part of the youth rushes, and seeks him especially fervently as a teacher, and since we see no one who excels either in this [regard] or is acknowledged by imperial judgment and opinion, each person who happened to rush to him is carried away by greater confusion, and every other person trusts himself as a teacher, and though he be more imperfect than all [others] in the practice of teaching, nonetheless what is said by him is received with certainty, [even though] it oftentimes differs from what the laws prescribe, but rather corresponds to what the teacher says, [with the student] receiving it in his memory and soul. Therefore much vexation and confusion has arisen concerning judgments on every occasion in these matters; inasmuch as those to whom it has fallen to judge, except in a very few instances of those well-versed in most of the books of the laws, they do not consider or utter the same things about the same matters, but from various [degrees] of learning introduce different opinions (as it seems) and most of them are in disagreement and clash with each other, so that they create terrible confusion for those who [are attempting to] investigate the laws thoroughly for the resolution of pressing matters. Since no one can bear to suffer a slight by any of his opponents in these matters, but instead everyone endeavors on behalf of excessive ambition and juvenile thirst for fame to seem to be thought of as somehow thinking better than others, he does not shrink from dissent and quarreling with everyone. What could possibly be more despicable than this, that when they who are called by others to resolve doubts, they do not themselves seem to differ with one another in the least?
6. Therefore Our Pious Power did not suffer to overlook these developments, but since our Emperor of the Heavens, who shatters wars in His Powerful Hand and Heavenly Arm, who opposes the arrogant, yet who gives grace to the humble, has put a stop to both foreign wars and domestic insurrections, and now the enemy is quiet, and the populace is peaceable, and a tremendous peace holds in the [domains] of the Romans, and nothing pulls our intentions in a different direction, [but] through the goodwill of the Almighty we turn all of our attention toward the further correction of our state.

7. Indeed, of those things which are for the commonweal we have already, with God, enacted much, and if something has been left undone, then it shall come to pass entirely at the proper time of appropriate dispensation, should God approve of it. 7a. At the present time Our Serenity deems the misuse of the laws worthy of attention, considering it the greatest of injustices that that which in life frees us from injustice is taken no notice of and subjected to still more injustices, as well as to consider that which establishes order and beauty for all others is led astray by such disorder, and no word is uttered about such a great good – that is the teaching of the laws, which govern our empire gloriously and our state blamelessly with the hands of God. For in fact it is terrible and abominable that [in comparison with] other disciplines and arts, such as logic and in some of the arts of craftsmen, that they have their own places set aside and leaders designated, receive chairs (*proedriai*) and are apportioned public maintenances, yet why was nothing good given for the encouragement of the pursuers [of] the most necessary of all disciplines, the most beneficial of all studies, without which all things are superfluous and inane (for of what benefit are these things, if good order is absent?). Indeed, this in all respects has become foreign to our commonwealth and departed, so that there is neither a known house in it to be its own in it nor some rule, nor a rank (*bathmos*), nor a privilege, but it was entirely neglected and rejected, just as any base craft, as completely useless for human life, and remained unregulated and uncorrected, to be commiserated rather than admired, to be thought as worthy of lament rather than of zeal.
8. But these are the matters up to this point, and what sort of thing [it shall be] henceforth, the deed itself (as they say) shall demonstrate. For Our Majesty, considering this pious deed exceedingly useful and fitting in its time, and which shall be counted a gain for [our] common state and at the same time for [our] good repute and benefit, [Our Majesty] having considered this well, has become more enthusiastic for legal study, and makes good what seems to be a deficiency for the correct functioning of the commonwealth. [Our Majesty] nominates the most learned *illoustrios* John, surnamed Xiphilinos, a judge of the Hippodrome and an *exaktor*, as an exegete and teacher of the laws. He has demonstrated his profound learning neither obscurely, without mark, or faintly, but has manifestly and publicly shone in his experience of affairs. Likewise, he has adorned himself with the arts both of

eloquence and of his knowledge of the laws, and no one has ever been more favored by our commands.

9. Therefore this [man], with good esteem and judgment, shall start a select and approved school (*didaskalia*) of the laws, since he has been honored with a worthy and enviable chair (*proedria*), receiving as resources for its functioning from Our Munificence, and it shall not be a school small and unworthy, but on the contrary most glorious, famous, and worthy of such a great matter [i.e. the teaching of the laws].

10. From this moment on, with the help and cooperation of Heaven, practically the most beautiful and most pleasing building from our illustrious household is to be left [as a] school (*paideuterion*) for the laws, which we have been preparing with the greatest of expectations, [and which] we have dedicated to our God, the Giver of all good things [p. 25], and we have gloriously established the famous among martyrs, the triumphant in name and deed George, as its great patron of the house, founder, and guardian, who also has a church there – [we would not want a school] without his martyrly succor and supplication (I think) – [thus] we have had it rebuilt and prepared the building to be a holy monastery (*phrontisterion*). 10a. Therefore it shall be as it has already been stated, a place set aside there for lovers of legal learning, which Our Power has granted to them, in which [Our Power] also established a didactic chair, and this glorious building shall be called the school of law, and the teacher the *nomophylax didaskalos*, [and he does not receive this title] for the sake of convenience or without reason, but because he teaches the laws and it falls to him to protect the laws – the former [because] he shall inculcate in his students the protection and preservation of the will of the laws, making all of them very clear and transmitting legal education intact as much as he is able, and the latter [because] he shall guard the books of the laws, which shall be deposited by the reverend librarian there [in the school] for free use and for however he sees fit to manage them, especially the necessary [books] and the more useful [books] for the teaching of the laws. 10b. Indeed, Our Pious Power has arranged this beneficially, so that the one selected to this [post] by [Our] Majesty should always have all the tools of his trade in house and that he should not have to borrow these things from others or ask for something else from elsewhere and be compelled to collect [these things] on each [occasion], if he should happen to lack them because of his poverty.

11. And the one called *nomophylax* shall persist in the following way, and he shall exercise the following rights and privileges. He shall be counted among the most glorious senators, and he shall at once have the seat after the *epi ton kriseon*, with whom he shall also be introduced to Our Power on the same days as he does, and he shall be honored with our company and appearance in a like manner, so that he then might be more eager, especially taking pride in the abundance of his honor. And a *rhoga* of four *litrai*, purple-dyed silks, and a staff [gilded or silvered] shall be accorded to him every year from our hands, and he shall also have this or that for the sake of his public allowances (*siteresia*).
12. We have already finished and polished the illustrious *nomophylax*, just like a new statue, with the unutterable mercies of the Providence who guides all, who brought this divine and most-fitting work to our attention and who guarded such a thing in the days of Our Power.
13. [p. 27] Therefore according to our selection of so great a rank, and since you have merited divine approval to occupy it, o most noble *nomophylax*, never suffer to be seen as ignorant of so much favor, nor endeavor toward having our hopes in you proved false, but bring all zeal and all eagerness in revealing the knowledge of the laws to the youth, both clearly and especially with much accuracy, busying yourself unceasingly and perpetually with this work alone and spending your whole life [doing] this, by night studying the matters which lead to interpretation, and by day interpreting them, and during both [periods] unhesitatingly conversing with students. It is clear that the only days which have been set aside for you are those on which it is customary for grammarians to have leisure.
14. You shall not discriminate against those who come to the hearing [of your lectures] on the laws according to lineage, nor according to wealth, but according to excellence, as is necessary, you shall choose by lot the class of your chair. You shall deign to receive and spend time with all without envy, and have dealings with all without money or pay, and you shall use a clean hand [i.e. not be bribed] and a clean tongue and opinion of the laws; those who defile other offices through bribes with such austerities, you above all know well, [as] the exegete of the laws. Except perhaps if one of those stemmed from a favored house, then he would nobly want to show favor to the teacher. For then we would not somehow forbid the gift of the donor, but indeed we would encourage it, as we ourselves think that it is in accordance with the pious laws and condemn as misanthropy the utter abstention

[from gift-giving], as simply an un-charitableness to the tradition of all.

15. Be mindful especially of the good conduct of your hearers, with the atmosphere of a reverend monastery pervading the school, since it is necessary that the one striving to attain a true education is to have been taught to have character and rectitude before knowledge.

16. If you do these things thusly, and you endeavor to show to us what sort of person you are by [your] deeds, both you yourself above all, as well as those who succeed to this rank in the future, then you shall receive other useful things from Our Majesty according to your aim, and this most-fitting chair, which for the moment is entrusted to you, you shall have for life, and it cannot be revoked or given in succession, unless someone somehow shows himself to be unworthy of such an honor, suffering either from laziness or ignorance, or otherwise being unfit morally and not useful to this good circle of students. [p. 29] The one who regards this chair should be on his utmost guard for this and tremble at the danger above his head, if some wrong be uncovered or if he dares to entirely transgress one of the regulations specified by us, neither letting his mind be diverted by some other matter nor taking such a gamble at all, unless he is conscious of the most important things of all – that he has much experience in the laws with [his] knowledge, and he speaks each of the two languages with complete accuracy – I mean Greek and Romaïc [Latin] – he acts boldly against the exercise of labors and the ill effects of sleeplessness, which necessarily are present for a man laboring in the office of so great a rank and profession. And do not allow some pungent and terrible malice to lie in your heart, or such a person shall escape notice [of this malice] in all his manners, and if the one suspected of this should first commit some criminal act, then a more worthy and powerful person shall take his chair.

17. But now this is testimony for those who come later. Our Power is not minimally, but rather entirely eager, in our ordination of the *nomophylax*, and if it should be needed again, [Our Power] commends similar matters to the emperors [reigning] after us. May the sun never look down upon such an outrage [i.e. not approving a new *nomophylax*], even if this has sometimes happened to other disciplines, of which I would rather not say anything further, I do not praise many of them.

18. Therefore we do not at all suffer that any of the things wrought through neglect or any deviation in this matter at any time or in any

way, but we call him to this chair (*proedria*), and we admit him to the height of his enviable throne, from where he has there exercised sufficiently the matters of the laws, and from where he has acquitted himself and excelled his fellow students by the greatest measure both in the amplitude of his character and in the vigor of his diligence, even in the eloquence of his tongue and the superabundance of his sagacity, and – most importantly of all – in the rectitude of his morals. Combining [all these traits] so to say, he, is seen by us as the first, having a blamelessness in other [matters] and being the most experienced in his knowledge of the laws no less than of other subjects. For we desire that our holy laws be used like famous bodyguards in speeches, and that everywhere, like emperors, [p. 31] that entire matters are defended by them and that they are in the vanguard of a procession for honor and at the same time for safety against those who do not shrink from threatening them with most bold sophistry. Would that the rhetorical art did not render the plausible unpersuasive and the implausible persuasive!

19. But earlier that which almost eluded us is at hand: For since at one point we mentioned the notaries (*symbolaiographoi*) and lawyers (*synegoroi*), we thought it necessary to impress upon them, that in every respect this, our endeavor for the laws, is sound and not in any respect lacking, something of the greatest common benefit.

20. Therefore we ordain that what is stated explicitly in the old laws about them [the notaries and lawyers], the lack of use of which has already rendered them to be thought of as almost having never been written, that they have their own validity once again, and not only that they take great pains and diligently learn the [content] of the laws from the most wise *nomophylax*, but that they not be registered in such guilds (*systemata*), before this very teacher [i.e. the *nomophylax*] confirms them, and before he validates their aptitude in both the knowledge of the laws and in their general correctness – both in the sound of the tongue [orally] and in the writing of the hand [written].

21. Anyone who dares to insert himself either among the lawyers or among those called *taboullarioi* contrary to this rule [ought] not to profit a single time from his own rashness, but at once let him be banished from there with the greatest of urgency, so that by his fate he recognizes that the indifference hitherto does pervade among those here, but rather that most ancient accuracy of the laws, recently [re] introduced in matters, and that such [things are] neither a gift of fate

nor a fortuitous windfall, instead of a reward of diligence and hard work now set before only those who are worthy.

22. Thus now may the success which has been accomplished by us, by the Grace of the Almighty endure for all time in [our] famous realm, and may no passage of time, nor any jealousy of evil ones extinguish it, but let it shine to the end, always endeavored toward and honored by foreign peoples and presiding over an eternal justice in life.

23. These things we have both enacted and written for the glory of God and the undying memory of Our Serenity, and they shall be a great component of the world of good order and shall effect a much more beautiful and harmonious concord of the state. These matters which have been granted by us to you, in receiving [them] in the honor and glory of your youth, o young lovers of learning, render the greatest thanks to the Divinity above, [p. 33] which granted so much of His Providence to you and to those coming after you. For such things were not granted to anyone of those before you, and they have now been magnanimously bestowed upon you by the divine Beneficence, so that you might thus easily and painlessly possess the quite vexing and painstaking tradition of the laws, and may you receive it as a nourishment which cultivates teaching. For no longer like those before you shall you chance upon an exegesis through bare enigmas and riddles (I mean with legal terminology), as though you heeded certain ambiguous oracles, requiring a further oracle to interpret, nor shall you prophesy ambivalently concerning their [the laws'] intent, you who distrust yourselves even more than others concerning that which you think to understand among them. Instead, with discerning interpretation, a bold tongue, and holding to truth and certainty in all respects, you shall recognize the wholesome logic of the laws, and you shall heed the living voice of the laws even in the letters of lifeless books, [the living voice of the laws] which Our Serenity has set before all in the middle, as a sounding which must be heeded, which shuts the side-doors and opens for you one wide and imperial gate, through which you may enter and exit as you desire, unimpeded, and you shall find the pasturage of the laws you seek in this most reverend and divine monastery of the Victor. To whom you shall fittingly also give many thanks, and just as to a mother so you shall render the praise and honor befitting the nourisher of your education, and you shall imitate the good and sensible farmers, who always deem the nourishment of the soil worthy of an abundant love of beauty [*philokalia*], who take the fruits of the soil not just one time, and after awhile leave

it thorny and overgrown, but they perform a careful deed, and how useful it shall perpetually be as it continually bears the same crop for themselves and those who come after them, all of them always reaping a harvest from it. 23a. And so in the same way you, o well-born, shall be able to tenderly love this which has become an affectionate nourisher to you and likewise a leader of much better nourishment, and you should endeavor to offer to it worthy donations for its maintenance (*tropheia*) as well as worthy donations for its teaching (*didaskalia*), and that with all your works and words you laboriously bring about for it permanence and structure and a greater yield, and that as faithful pupils you remain absolutely true to it, so that with your support it will be able to yield such things and more for all time, with the eyes of God gazing down upon it well-disposed from above.

24. [p. 35] But we are especially able to take heart in this and to hope that in all the time afterward, that you would desire to do something worthy, acceptable and pleasing to both God and men. If matters happen to happily exceed our expectations, putting away all hesitation and no longer losing one's head at the difficulty of the enterprise and not despairing that the great and most divine education [of the laws] is entirely uncorrectable or correctable only with difficulty, you shall bear on toward this [learning] with a certain wise inspiration and mania (as the wise among you say), and you shall consider it most outlandish that the hardworking and law-loving youths of long ago set out on distant journeys for the sake of this [legal learning], some of whom departed to Older Rome by their love of the hearing of the Roman laws, and others settled in Beirut, where the most prominent of men in the legal profession taught the laws and were heard in the past. Yet you yourselves would not want to enjoy such good at home because of a most wicked silliness (for why would someone request something else?), instead experiencing that myth [of Tantalus] as your very own, being punished with terrible thirst in the middle of a spring.

25. And in no way shall you suffer any longer to waste your prime in less useful matters or entirely indolently and lazily, but rather strive toward good contention with one another, and make much great effort for the good reputation of the laws, knowing the greatest prize, and receiving an especially good recompense. 25a. For indeed if you should more zealously hold to the learning [of the laws], and you should stretch yourselves out completely toward its success, you shall comfort and nourish our best hopes, that your zeal was not for naught

or in vain, but you shall seek a more glorious life, and you shall administer many parts of our state. For it is clear that Our Majesty, as well as those always reigning after us for the rest of time, shall prize you, who acquired a glorious name and reputation by your legal education, before others in the distribution of offices. We shall render a fitting recompense for [your] good decision.

26. In running toward such a prize and end, be strong and brave. Beautify [your] fatherland with these most beautiful of deeds. All Our Power prays for all of you, both the teachers and students, all that which is most powerful. [Our Power] is moved to its core, and thirsts after your repute in good things.

27. [p. 37] Therefore may you receive the contents of our prayer as an auspicious end, o beneficent Providence, and my most beloved children. As long as both heaven and earth remain, may this, your wondrous circle, be preserved, always much and greatly praised. And [may] none of you [be] unsuccessful. And may none of you turn out useless or inglorious. But may all of you be [as follows]: Endeavor to run the good race, and [to be] zealots, admired champions and victors; a glory to your parents, a boast to your relatives, an ornament to the empire, and a salvation to the commonweal, and the greatest dignity among the ranks of the offices. We ask by the glory of God, to whom we entrust all things, that you be conspicuous among them at all times, and that you be supplied abundantly and richly with every other bounty of good things through the mercy and grace of His Goodness.

Bibliography

PRIMARY SOURCES

Agapetos the Deacon, *Mirror of Princes* = R. Riedinger (ed. and trans.) (1995) *Agapetos Diakonos, Der Fürstenspiegel für Kaiser Iustinianos*. Etaireia philon tou laou. Kentron ereunes Byzantiou 4. Athens.

Alexios Stoudites, *Edicts* = G. Ficker (ed.) (1911) *Erlasse des Patriarchen von Konstantinopel Alexios Stoudites*. Kiel.

Typikon = A. M. Pentkovskiĭ (ed.) (2001). *Типикон патриарха Алексия Студита в Византии и на Руси*. Moscow.

Apocalypse of Anastasia = Homburg, R. (ed.) (1903) *Apocalypsis Anastasiae. Ad trium codicum auctoritatem Panormitani Ambrosiani Parisini*. Leipzig.

Appendix Eclogae = L. Burgmann and S. Troianos (eds.) (1979) "Appendix Eclogae," *FM* 3: 24–125.

Arabic Ecloga = S. Leder (ed.) (1985) *Die arabische Ecloga: Das vierte Buch der Kanones der Könige aus der Sammlung des Makarios*. Forschungen zur byzantinischen Rechtsgeschichte 12. Frankfurt.

Arabic Prochiron = J. Pahlitzsch (ed.) (2014) *Der arabische Procheiros Nomos. Untersuchung und Edition der Übersetzung eines byzantinischen Rechtstextes*. Forschungen zur byzantinischen Rechtsgeschichte 30. Frankfurt.

Athanasios of Athos, *Testament* = P. Meyer (ed.) (1894) *Die Haupturkunden für die Geschichte der Athosklöster: Grösstentheils zum ersten Male*. Leipzig: 130–140.

Athanasios of Emesa, *Syntagma* = D. Simon and S. Troianos (eds. and trans.) (1989) *Das Novellensyntagma des Athanasios von Emesa*. Forschungen zur byzantinischen Rechtsgeschichte 16. Frankfurt.

Attaleiates, Michael, *Legal Textbook (Ponema nomikon)* = L. Sigoutas (ed.) (1861) "Μιχαὴλ Ἀνθυπάτου καὶ Κριτοῦ τοῦ Ἀτταλειώτου. Ποίημα νομικὸν ἤτοι Πραγματεῖα ποιηθεῖσα κατὰ κέλευσιν τοῦ Βασιλέως Μιχαὴλ τοῦ Δούκα," *ΘΕΜΙΣ* 8, 47–155. Reprinted in *JGR*, vol. VII: 409–97.

Diataxis = P. Gautier (ed.) (1981) "La diataxis de Michael Attaliate," *REByz* 39: 5–143.

Historia = I. Pérez Martín (ed. and trans.) (2002) *Historia/Miguel Ataliates; introducción, edición,traducción del griego y commentario de Inmaculada Pérez Martín*. Neuva Roma 15. Madrid.

Basil., *Basil. Schol.* = H. J. Scheltema and N. van der Wal (1953–88) *Basilicorum libri LX.* (17 vols. Series A = Text, 8 vols.; Series B = Scholia, 9 vols.) Groningen. *Basilika (Scholia)* contained in Series B (vols. 9–17) of the Groningen edition cited above; also D. Holwerda (ed.).

BMFD = J. P. Thomas and A. C. Hero. (eds) (2000) *Byzantine Monastic Foundation Documents* (5 vols.) Washington, DC.

BoE = J. Koder (ed. and trans.) (1991) *Das Eparchenbuch Leons des Weisen. CFHB* 23; Series Vindobonensis. Vienna.

Burgmann, L. (ed.) (1984) "Das Lexikon ἄδετ – ein Theophilosglossar," *FM* 6: 19–61.

(ed.) (1990) "Das Lexikon αὐσηθ," *FM* 8: 249–337.

Burgmann, L., and M. T. Fögen (eds) (1982) "Florilegium Lesbiacum," *FM* 5: 107–78.

Canons of the Council in Trullo = J. D. Mansi (ed.) (1901–27) *Sacrorum conciliorum nova et amplissima collection.* (59 vols.) Paris: vol. XI, 929–1006.

Chronographia brevis (e cod. Coislin. 193) = C. de Boor (ed.) (1880) *Nicephori archiepiscopi Constantinopolitani opuscula historica.* Leipzig: 218–26.

CIC = P. Krueger, T. Mommsen and R. Schoell (eds) (1970–2) *Corpus Iuris Civilis*, 21st edn. (3 vols.) Dublin.

Cod. Just. = P. Krueger (ed.) (1970) *Codex Justinianus*, 15th edn. Dublin in *CIC*, vol. II.

Cod. Theod. = P. Krueger and P. M. Meyer (1905) *Codex Theodosianus.* (2 vols.) Berlin.

Collectio Tripartita = N. van der Wal and B. H. Stolte (eds.) (1994) *Collectio Tripartita, Justinian on Religious and Ecclesiastical Affairs.* Groningen.

Constantine VII, *Novel I on Legal Fees* = *JGR*, vol. I, col. 3, n. 7, 218–21.

Novel II on Legal Fees = *JGR*, vol. I, col. 3, n. 9, 227–9.

Constitutio omnem = *CIC*, vol. I, part 2, 10–12.

Constitutio tanta/Dedoken = *CIC*, vol. I, part 2, 13–24.

De cer. = J. J. Reiske (ed.) (1829) *De ceremoniis aulae Byzantinae libri 2, graece et latine. CSHB* 5. (2 vols.). Bonn.

Demetrios of Kyzikos, *Against the Jacobites* = *PG*, vol. CXXVII, 879–85.

Digest = T. Mommsen (ed.) (1970) *Digesta*, 21st edn. Dublin in *CIC*, vol. I, part 2.

Dittrich, J. (ed.) (1993) "Die Scholien des Cod. Taur. B.I.20," *FM* 9: 181–298.

Ecloga = L. Burgmann (ed. and trans.) (1983) *Ecloga: das Gesetzbuch Leons III. und Konstantinos' V.* Forschungen zur byzantinischen Rechtsgeschichte 10. Frankfurt.

Eisagoge = K. E. Zachariä von Lingenthal (ed.) (1852) *Collectio librorum juris graeco-romani ineditorum Ecloga Leonis et Constantini, epanagoge Basilii Leonis et Alexandri.* Leipzig: 61–235. Reprinted in *JGR*, vol. II: 229–368, 410–27. Newer edition and German translation of the proem in Schminck 1986: 4–11.

Epitome (legum) = K. E. Zachariä von Lingenthal (ed.) (1856) *Liber juridicus alphabeticus sive Synopsis minor et Ecloga legum in epitome expositarum.* Leipzig: 277–431. Reprinted in *JGR*, vol. IV: 261–585, 596–619. Newer edition and German translation of the proem in Schminck 1986: 112–19.

Freshfield, E. H. (trans.) (1926) *A Manual of Roman Law: The Ecloga*. Cambridge.
(trans.) (1928) *A Manual of Eastern Roman Law: The Procheiros Nomos*. Cambridge.

Gosh, Mkit'ar, *Datastanagirk'* = R. W. Thomson (ed.) (2000) *The Lawcode [Datastanagirk'] of Mxit'ar Gōs*. Dutch studies in Armenian language and literature 6. Amsterdam and Atlanta, GA.

Gregentios of Taphar, *Nomoi* = A. Berger (ed. and trans.) (2006) *Life and Works of Saint Gregentios, Archbishop of Taphar*. Millenium-Studien 7. Berlin; New York: 410–48.

Ivir. = J. Lefort, N. Oikonomidès and D. Papachryssanthou and the collaboration of H. Métrévéli (eds.) (1985-) *Actes d'Iviron*. Archives de l'Athos 14, 16, 18–19. (4 vols.) Paris.

John of Rila, *Testament* = I. Ivanov (ed.) (1917) *Sv. Ivan Rilski I negoviyat monastir*. Sofia: 125–34.

Jus graecoromanum. I. and P. Zepos (eds.) (1962) (8 vols.) Aalen. Reprint of the 1931 edition.

Kekaumenos, *Strategikon*. C. Roueché (ed. and trans.) (2013) *Kekaumenos, Consilia et Narrationes*. SAWS edition. Published online at: www.ancientwisdoms.ac.uk/library/kekaumenos-consilia-et-narrationes/

Komnenos, Manuel, *De juramento Judaeorum* = *JGR*, vol. III, 440–2.

Land Legislation of the Macedonian Emperors = Svoronos, N. G. (ed.) (1994) *Les novelles des empereurs macédoniens concernant la terre et les stratiotes: introduction, édition, commentaires*. Bibliothèque byzantine; Études 4. Athens.

Lavra = P. Lemerle, A. Guillou, N. Svoronos and the collaboration of D. Papachryssanthou (eds) (1970–82) *Actes de Lavra*. Archives de l'Athos 5, 11. (2 vols.). Paris.

Law for Judging the People = H. W. Dewey and A. M. Kleimola (ed. and trans.) (1977) *Zakon sudnyj ljudem = Court Law for the People*. Ann Arbor, MI.

Legal History Treatise = A. Schmink (1993) "Ein rechtshistorischer 'Traktat' im Cod. Mosq. gr. 445," *FM* 9: 81–96.

Leo VI, *Novels* = S. N. Troianos (ed. and trans.) (2007) Οι Νεαρές Λέοντος ς' του Σοφού. Athens.
Taktika = G. Dennis (ed. and trans.) (2010) *The Taktika of Leo VI*. *CFHB* 49; Series Washingtonensis. Washington, DC.

Life of Saint Basil the Younger = D. F. Sullivan, A.-M. Talbot and S. McGrath (ed. and trans.) (2014) *The Life of Saint Basil the Younger. Critical Edition and Annotated Translation of the Moscow Version*. Dumbarton Oaks Studies 45. Washington, DC.

Life of Nikon Metanoeite = O. Lampsides (ed.) (1982) Ο εκ Πόντου όσιος Νίκων ο μετανοείτε: Κείμενα, σχόλια. Pegai tes historias ton Hellenon tou Pontou 4. Athens.

Lokin, J. H. A., and R. Meijering (eds.) (1999) *Anatolius and the Excerpta Vaticana et Laurentiana*. Groningen.

Louis II, *Letter to Basil I* = W. Henze (ed.) (1928) *Epistolae karolini aevi*. MGH Epistolarum 7. Berlin: 385–94.

McGeer, E. (trans.) (2000) *The Land Legislation of the Macedonian Emperors.* Mediaeval Sources in Translation 38. Toronto.

Mauropous, John, *Letters*. A. Karpozilos (ed. and trans.) (1990) *The Letters of Ioannes Mauropus Metropolitan of Euchaita. CFHB* 34; Series Thessalonicensis. Thessaloniki.

Meditatio de nudis pactis = H. Monnier and G. Platon (ed. and trans.) (1974) *Études de droit byzantine.* London: part III, 2–246.

Meijering, R. (ed.) (1990) "Ῥωμαϊκαὶ ἀγωγαί. Two Byzantine treatises on legal actions," *FM* 8: 1–152.

Metanoite, Nikon, *Testament* = O. Lampsides (ed.) (1982) Ο εκ Πόντου όσιος Νίκων ο μετανοείτε: Κείμενα, σχόλια. Pegai tes historias ton Hellenon tou Pontou 4. Athens: 252–6.

Meyer, P. (ed.) (1894) *Die Haupturkunden für die Geschichte der Athosklöster: Grösstentheils zum ersten Male.* Leipzig.

Nicholas I, *Letter to Michael III* = E. Perels (ed.) (1925) *Nicolai I. papae Epistolae.* MGH Epistolarum 6. Berlin: Letter 88, 454–87.

Nicholas I Mystikos, *Miscellaneous Writings* = L. G. Westerink (ed. and trans.) (1981) *Nicholas I, Patriarch of Constantinople, Miscellaneous Writings. CFHB* 6. Washington, DC.

Nikodemos, *Testament* = D. Feissel and A. Philippidis-Braat (eds.) (1985) "Inventaires en vue d'un recueil des inscriptions historiques de Byzance. III. Inscriptions du Péloponnèse (à l'exception de Mistra)," TM 9: 267–396, here 301–2.

Nomokanon in Fourteen Titles = J. B. Pitra (ed.) (1864–8) *Iuris ecclesiastici Graecorum historia et monumenta iussu Pii IX. Pont. Max.* (2 vols.) Rome: vol. II, 433–640.

Nomos Georgikos. E. E. Lipshits, I. P. Medvedev, E. K. Piotrovskaia (eds and trans) (1984) Византийский земледельческий закон. Leningrad.

Nomos Mosaikos = L. Burgmann and S. Troianos (eds) (1979) "Nomos Mosaïkos," *FM* 3: 126–67

Nomos Nautikos = W. Ashburner (ed. and trans.) (1909) *The Rhodian Sea-Law.* Oxford.

Nomos Stratiotikos = P. Verri (ed.) (1978) *Le leggi penali militari dell'impero bizantino nell'alto Medioevo.* Rome.

Novella constitutio = A. Salač (1954) *Novella constitutio saec. XI medii: quae est de schola iuris Constantinopoli constituenda et legum custode creando.* Textes breves graeci et latini 1. Prague.

Pakourianos, Gregory, *Typikon* = P. Gautier (ed. and trans.) (1984), "Le typikon du sébaste Grégoire Pakourianos," *REByz* 42: 5–145

Patzes, *Tipoukeitos* = C. Ferrini et al. (eds.) (1914–57) *M. Kritou tou Patze Tipoukeitos: sive librorum LX Basilicorum summarium.* (5 vols.) Rome.

Photios, *Bib.* = R. Henry (ed. and trans.) (1959–91) *Bibliothèque/Photius.* (9 vols.) Paris.

Letters = B. Laourdas and L. G. Westerink (eds.) (1983–8) *Photii patriarchae Constantinopolitani Epistulae et Amphilochia.* Bibliotheca scriptorum Graecorum et Romanorum Teubneriana. (6 vols.) Leipzig.

Prochiron = K. E. Zachariä von Lingenthal (ed.) (1837) *Ὁ Πρόχειρος Νόμος. Imperatorum Basilii, Constantini et Leonis prochiron*. Leipzig. Reprinted in *JGR*, vol. II: 107–228, 395–410. Newer edition and German translation of the proem in Schminck 1986: 55–61.

Psellos, Michael, *Brevis Divisio Novellarum Iustiniani* = G. E. Heimbach, K. Witte and K. E. Zachariä von Lingenthal (eds.) (1838–43) *Anekdota*. (3 vols.) Aalen: vol. II, 234–7.

Letters of Psellos KD = E. Kurtz and F. Drexl (eds.) (1936–41) *Michaelis Pselli scripta minora*. (2 vols.) Milan: vol. II.

Letters of Psellos S = K. N. Sathas (ed.) (1872–94) Μεσαιωνική Βιβλιοθήκη. (7 vols.) Venice: vol. V, 219–523.

Minor legal texts. Texts I–VI in Weiss 1973b.

Orationes forenses et acta. G. T. Dennis (ed.) (1994) Stuttgart.

Orationes hagiographicae. E. A. Fisher (ed.) (1994) Stuttgart.

Synopsis legum = G. Weiss (1977) "Die 'Synopsis legum' des Michael Psellos," *FM* 2: 147–214.

To his Students on the Names of Suits = J. R. Boissonade (ed.) (1838) *De operatione daemonum: accedunt inedita opuscula Pselli*. Nuremburg: 95–110.

The Usual Miracle at Blachernai = E. A. Fisher (ed.) (1994) *Orationes hagiographicae*. Stuttgart and Leipzig: 200–29.

Rhomaios, Eustathios. *De hypobolo* = D. R. Reinsch (ed.) (1986) "Eustathios Rhomaios' Opusculum über das Hypobolon," *FM* 7: 239–52.

Hyponemata on Marriage Law = A. Schminck (ed.) (1979) "Vier eherechtliche Entscheidungen aus dem 11. Jahrhundert," *FM* 3: 221–79.

Tractatus de peculiis = M. Th. Fögen and D. Simon (eds.) (1998) "Tractatus de peculiis," *FM* 10: 261–318.

Russo-Byzantine Treaties = D. H. Kaiser (ed. and trans.) (1992) *The Laws of Rus': Tenth to Fifteenth Centuries*. The Laws of Russia; Series 1, Medieval Russia 1. Salt Lake City, UT.

Simon, D., and S. Troianos (eds) (1979) "Die Epitome zum Novellensyntagma des Athanasios," *FM* 3: 280–315.

Sixty Books, proem = Schminck 1986: 17–24.

Syrianos Magistros, *De re strategica* = G. T. Dennis (ed. and trans.) (1990) *Three Byzantine Military Treatises*. *CFHB* 25; Series Washingtoniensis. Washington, DC: 1–135.

Synopsis Basilicorum Major = K. E. Zachariä von Lingenthal (ed.) (1869) *Synopsis Basilicorum*. Reprinted in *JGR*, vol. V.

Syro-Roman Lawbook = W. Selb and H. Kaufhold (ed. and trans.) (2002) *Das syrisch-römische Rechtsbuch*. Veröffentlichungen der Kommission für Antike Rechtsgeschichte 9. (3 vols.) Vienna.

Taktikon Uspenskij = N. Oikonomidès (ed.) (1972) *Les listes de préséance byzantines des IXe et Xe siècles*. Paris: 41–63.

Theodore Balsamon, *Canonical Responses to Mark, the Patriarch of Alexandria* = *Rh.-P.* vol. IV, 447–496. English translation: P. D. Viscuso (trans.) (2014) *Theodoros Balsamon, Guide for a Church under Islām: The*

Sixty-Six Canonical Questions Attributed to Theodōros Balsamōn: A Translation of the Ecumenical Patriarchate's Twelfth-Century Guidance to the Patriarchate of Alexandria. Brookline, MA.

Theodore Scholastikos, *Paraphrase of the Codex Justinianus* = H. J. Scheltema (ed.) (1972) "Fragmenta breviarii Codicis a Theodoro Hermopolitano confecti," *Byzantina Neerlandica* 3: 9–35 and H. R. Lug (ed.) (1976) "Ein Bruchstück des Codex-Kommentars des Theodoros," *FM* 1: 1–15.

Paraphrase of the Novels = G. E. Heimbach, K. Witte and K. E. Zachariä von Lingenthal (eds) (1838–43) *Anekdota*. (3 vols.) Aalen: vol. III, 1–165.

TheophCont = I. Bekker (ed.) (1838) *Theophanes Continuatus*. Bonn.

Theophilos Antecessor, *Paraphrase of the Institutes* = J. H. A. Lokin, R. Meijering, B. H. Stolte and N. van der Wal (eds) (2010) *Theophili antecessoris paraphrasis institutionum. With a translation by A. F. Murison*. Groningen.

Tiftixoglu, V., and S. Troianos (eds.) (1993) "Unbekannte Kaiserurkunden und Basilikentestimonia," *FM* 9: 137–79.

Treu, M. (ed.) (1893) "Ein byzantinisches Schulgespräch," *ByzZ* 2: 96–105.

Vita Basilii = I. Ševčenko (ed. and trans.) (2011) *Chronographiae quae Theophanis Continuati nomine fertur liber quo Vita Basilii Imperatoris amplectitur*. CFHB 42; Series Berolinensis. Berlin.

SECONDARY SOURCES

Aerts, W. J. et al. (2001) "The prooimion of the Eisagoge: Translation and commentary," *SG* 7: 91–155.

Anderson, G. D. (2009) "Islamic spaces and diplomacy in Constantinople (tenth to thirteenth centuries C.E.)," *Medieval Encounters* 15: 86–113.

Angold, M. (1997) *The Byzantine Empire, 1025–1204: A Political History*. 2nd edn. London and New York.

Ashburner, W. (1910) "The Farmer's Law," *JHS* 30: 85–108.

(1912) "The Farmer's Law (continued)," *JHS* 32: 68–95.

Baun, J. (2007) *Tales from Another Byzantium: Celestial Journey and Local Community in the Medieval Greek Apocrypha*. Cambridge and New York.

(2008) "Last things," in *The Cambridg;e History of Christianity*, ed. T. F. Noble and J. H. M. Smith. New York: vol. III, 606–24.

Beck, H.-G. (1965) *Byzantinisches Gefolgschaftswesen*. Bayerische Akademie der Wissenschaften. Philosophisch-Historische Klasse. Sitzungsberichte, Jahrg. 1965, 5. Munich.

(1977) *Kirche und theologische Literatur im Byzantinischen Reich*. Handbuch der Altertumwissenschaft 12. Abt., 2. T., 1., Bd. 2nd edn. Munich.

(1979) *Die Byzantiner und ihr Jenseits: Zur Entstehungsgeschichte einer Mentalität*. Bayerische Akademie der Wissenschaften. Philosophisch-historische Klasse. Sitzungsberichte 6. Munich.

Bell, J. (2001) *French Legal Cultures*. London.

Benner, Th. H. (1989) *Die syrisch-jakobitische Kirche unter byzantinischer Herrschaft im 10. und 11. Jahrhundert*. Marburg.

Berger, A. (1954) "Studi sui Basilici IV: La legislazione di Giustiniano ed I Basilici," *Jura* 5: 87–122.

(2001) "Das Dossier des Heiligen Gregentios. Ein Werk der Makedonenzeit," Βυζαντινά 22: 53–65.

Bernard, F. (2011) "'Greet me with words': Gifts and intellectual friendship in eleventh-century Byzantium," in *Geschenke erhalten die Freundschaft: Gabentausch und Netzwerkpflege im europäischen Mittelalter. Akten des Internationalen Kolloquiums Münster, 19.-20. November 2009*, ed. M. Grünbart. Byzantinistische Studien und Texte 1. Berlin: 1–11.

Bibikov, M. (2007) "La legislazione romana penale nell'Ecloga bizantina e slava," in *Problemi della traduzione dei Digesta giustinianei nelle lingue europee*. Atti del Seminario internazionale di Diritto romano, Caserta 13–14 June 2005. Naples: 79–92.

Blackstone, W. (1765–9) *Commentaries on the Laws of England*. (4 vols.) Oxford.

Blankenburg, E., and F. Bruinsma (1994) *Dutch Legal Culture*. 2nd edn. Deventer and Boston.

Bourdara, Kalliopē A. (1987) *Το δίκαιο στα αγιολογικά κείμενα*. Athens.

(2000) "Η λαϊκή αντίδραση στην έναρξη της εικονομαχικής πολιτικής του Λέοντος Γ'. Νομική θεώρηση των αγιολογικών," *Βυζαντινά* 21: 459–73

(2004) *Εικονομαχία και Δίκαιο. Νομική θεώρηση των αγιολογικών κειμένων*. Athens.

Brand, C. M. (1991) "Leo Tornikios," In *The Oxford Dictionary of Byzantium*, ed. A. P. Kazhdan et al. (3 vols.) New York: vol. II, 1216.

Brandes, W. (2002) *Finanzverwaltung in Krisenzeiten: Untersuchungen zur byzantinischen Administration im 6.-9. Jahrhundert*. Forschungen zur byzantinischen Rechtsgeschichte 25. Frankfurt.

(2010) "Review of B. Jokisch, Islamic imperial law: Harun-Al-Rashid's codification project. Berlin/New York 2007," *ByzZ* 103: 216–30.

Brandileone, F. (1886) *Il diritto bizantino nell'Italia meridionale: dall'VIII ad XII secolo*. Naples, reprinted (1987) in Bologna.

Brock, S. P. (1996) "The 'Nestorian' Church: A lamentable misnomer," *Bulletin of the John Rylands Library* 78: 23–35.

(2011) "The conversations with the Syrian Orthodox under Justinian (532)" in *Doctrine and Debate in the East Christian World*, ed. A. M. Cameron and R. G. Hoyland. Burlington, VT: 49–84.

Brandsma, F. (1996) *Dorotheus and his Digest Translation*. Groningen.

Brubaker, L. (ed.) (1998) *Byzantium in the Ninth Century: Dead or Alive? Papers from the Thirtieth Spring Symposium of Byzantine Studies, Birmingham, March 1996*. Publications/Society for the Promotion of Byzantine Studies 5. Aldershot.

(2009) "Byzantine visions of the end," in *The Church, the Afterlife and the Fate of the Soul*, ed. P. Clarke and T. Claydon. Studies in Church History 45. Woodbridge: 97–119.

Brubaker, L. and J. Haldon (2001) *Byzantium in the Iconoclast Era (ca 680–850): The Sources, an Annotated Survey*. Birmingham Byzantine and Ottoman Monographs 7. Aldershot.

(2011). *Byzantium in the Iconoclast Era, c. 680–850: A History*. Cambridge and New York.

Burgmann, L. (1977) "Byzantinische Rechtslexika," *FM* 2: 87–146.

(1982) "Ist der Nomos Georgikos vorjustinianisch?" *RJ* 1: 36–9.

(1989) "Kalokyros 'Sextos'. Anmerkungen zu einem Basilikenscholiasten," *SG* 3: 11–21.

(1991a) "Ansinnen an byzantinische Rechtshistoriker," *RJ* 10: 193–200.

(1991b) "Kormčaja Kniga," in *The Oxford Dictionary of Byzantium*, ed. A. P. Kazhdan et al. (3 vols.) New York: vol. II, 1149.

(1991c) "Λέξεις ῥωμαϊκαί. Lateinische Wörter in byzantinischen juristischen Texten," in *Lexicographica Byzantina: Beiträge zum Symposion zur byzantinischen Lexikographie (Wien, 1.–4.3.1989)*, ed. W. Hörandner and E. Trapp. Byzantina Vindobonensia Band 20. Vienna: 61–79.

(1991d) "Oath," in *The Oxford Dictionary of Byzantium*, ed. A. P. Kazhdan et al. (3 vols.) New York: vol. II, 1509.

(1991e) "Tipoukeitos," in *The Oxford Dictionary of Byzantium*, ed. A. P. Kazhdan et al. (3 vols.) New York: vol. III, 2088.

(1991f) "Zakon Sudnyj Ljudem," in *The Oxford Dictionary of Byzantium*, ed. A. P. Kazhdan et al. (3 vols.) New York: vol. III, 2219.

(1994) "Editio per testamentum (with: N. Svoronos, Les novelles des empereurs macédoniens concernant la terre et les stratiotes, Athen 1994)," *RJ* 13: 455–79.

(1997) "Zur Organisation der Rechtsprechung in Byzanz (Mittelbyzantinische Epoche)," in *La giustizia nell'alto Medioevo secoli IX-XI: 11–17 aprile 1996*. Settimane di studio del Centro italiano di studi sull'alto Medioevo XLIV. (2 vols.) Spoleto: vol. II, 905–30.

(1999a) "Die Gegenwart der Vergangenheit im byzantinischen Recht," in *Ideologie e pratiche del reimpiego nell'alto medioevo, 16–21 aprile 1998*. Settimane di studio del centro italiano di studi sull'alto medioevo 156. Spoleto: 591–612.

(1999b) "Λέξεις ῥωμαϊκαί. Lateinische Wörter in byzantinischen juristischen Texten," in *Lexicographica Byzantina. Beiträge zum Symposion zur byzantinischen Lexikographie (Wien, 1.–4.3.1989)*, ed. W. Hörandner and E. Trapp. Byzantina Vindobonensia 20. Vienna: 61–79.

(2002) "Juristische Buchproduktion in Byzanz," in *Juristische Buchproduktion im Mittelalter*, ed. V. Colli. Studien zur europäischen Rechtsgeschichte 155. Frankfurt: 247–67.

(2003) "Turning Sisinnios against the Sisinnians: Eustathios Romaios on a disputed marriage," in *Byzantium in the Year 1000*, ed. Paul Magdalino. Leiden and Boston: 161–81.

(2005a) "Die Gesetze der byzantinischen Kaiser," FM 11: 77–132.

(2005b) "Zur diplomatischen Terminologie in der Peira," in *Zwischen Polis, Provinz und Peripherie: Beiträge zur byzantinischen Geschichte und Kultur*, ed. L. M. Hoffmann. Wiesbaden: 457–67.

(2005c) "Mittelalterliche Übersetzungen byzantinischer Rechtstexte," in *Antike Rechtsgeschichte: Einheit und Vielfalt*, ed. G. Thür. Veröffentlichungen der Kommission für antike Rechtsgeschichte 11. Vienna: 43–66.

(2008) "Peira 51. Übersetzung und Kommentar," in Troianos 2008: 5–26.

(2009) "Die Nomoi Stratiotikos, Georgikos und Nautikos," *ZRVI* 46: 53–64.

(2011). "The production of law books in Byzantium," in Lokin and Stolte 2011: 79–96.

(1992) *Bibliographie zur Rezeption des byzantinischen Rechts im alten Rußland sowie zur Geschichte des armenischen und georgischen Rechts*. Forschungen zur byzantinischen Rechtsgeschichte 18. Frankfurt.

(1991) "*Nomos Stratiotikos*," in *The Oxford Dictionary of Byzantium*, ed. A. P. Kazhdan et al. (3 vols.) New York: vol. III, 1492.

Bury, J. B. (1911) *The Imperial Administrative System in the Ninth Century: With a Revised Text of the Kletorologion of Philotheos*. British Academy; Supplemental Papers 1. London.

Cappel, A. J. (1991a) "Dynatoi," in *The Oxford Dictionary of Byzantium*, ed. A. P. Kazhdan et al. (3 vols.) New York: vol. I, 667–8.

(1991b) "Poor," in *The Oxford Dictionary of Byzantium*, ed. A. P. Kazhdan et al. (3 vols.) New York: vol. III, 1697–8.

Cappel, A. J. and A. P. Kazhdan (1991c) "Patronage, social," in *The Oxford Dictionary of Byzantium*, ed. A. P. Kazhdan et al. (3 vols.) New York: vol. III, 1602.

Chitwood, Z. (2013) "At the origins of *ephoreia*," *BMGS* 37.1: 53–62.

(2014) "The patriarch Alexios Stoudites and the reinterpretation of justinianic legislation against heretics," *GRBS* 54.2: 293–312.

Clark, D. S. (ed.) (2007) *Encyclopedia of Law and Society: American and Global Perspectives*. (3 vols.) Los Angeles.

Constantelos, D. J. (1991) *Byzantine Philanthropy and Social Welfare*. 2nd edn. Rutgers Byzantine Series 4. New Rochelle, NY.

Constas, N. (2001) "'To sleep, perchance to dream.' The middle state of souls in patristic and Byzantine literature," DOP 55: 91–124.

Cosentino, S. (2000) "The Syrianos's 'Strategikon': a 9th century source?" *Bizantinistica* 2: 243–80.

Crawford, M. H. (2012) "Twelve Tables," in *The Oxford Classical Dictionary*, ed. S. Hornblower and A. Spawforth. 4th edn. New York: 1521.

Cupane, C. (1988) "Appunti per uno studio dell'oikonomia ecclesiastica a Bisanzio," *JÖByz* 38: 53–73.

Cvetler, J. (1956) "The authorship of the novel on the reform of legal education at Constantinople (about 1045 A.D.)," *Eos* 48.2: 297–328.

Dagron, G. (1976) "Minorités ethniques et religieuses dans l'Orient byzantin à la fin du Xe et au XIe siècle: l'immigration syrienne," *TM* 6: 177–216

(1980) "La perception d'une différence: Les débuts de la 'Querelle du Purgatoire,'" in *Actes du XVe Congrès International d'Études Byzantines*. (4 vols.) Athens: vol. IV, 84–92.

(1990). "La règle et l'exception. Analyse de la notion d'économie," in *Religiöse Devianz: Untersuchungen zu sozialen, rechtlichen und theologischen Reaktionen auf religiöse Abweichung im westlichen und östlichen Mittelalter*, ed. D. Simon. Studien zur europäischen Rechtsgeschichte 48. Frankfurt: 1–18.

(2003) *Emperor and Priest: The Imperial Office in Byzantium*, trans. Jean Birrell. Cambridge and New York. Originally appeared in French as G. Dagron, *Empereur et prêtre: étude sur le "césaropapsime" byzantin*. Paris, 1996.

de Jong, Hylkje (2008) *Stephanus en zijn Digestenonderwijs*. The Hague.

Deles, D. (2005) Η αρπαγή γυναίκας στο Βυζαντινό δίκαιο. Forschungen zur byzantinischen Rechtsgeschichte 16; Athener Reihe. Athens.

d'Emilia, A. (1965–6) "L'applicazione pratica del diritto bizantino secondo il titolo della Πεῖρα Εὐσταθίου τοῦ Ρωμαίου relativa alla compravendita," *RSBN* n.s. 2–3[12–13]: 33–80.

(1967) "L'applicazione pratica del diritto ereditario bizantino secondo la c.d. 'Peira d'Eustazio Romano'," *RSBN* n.s. 4[14]: 71–94.

Dennis, G. T. (1994) "A rhetorician practices law: Michael Psellos," in *Law and Society in Byzantium: Ninth-Twelfth Centuries*, ed. A. E. Laiou and D. Simon. Washington, DC: 187–97.

Dölger, F. (1940) "Zum Gebührenwesen der Byzantiner," in *Études dédiées à la mémoire d'André Andréadès*. Athens: 35–59.

(1945) "Ist der Nomos Georgikos ein Gesetz des Kaisers Justinian II.?," in *Festschrift für Leopold Wenger zu seinem 70. Geburtstag, dargebracht von Freunden, Fachgenossen und Schülern*. Münchener Beiträge zur Papyrusforschung und antiken Rechtsgeschichte 35. (2 vols.) Munich: vol. II, 18–48, reprinted in Dölger 1961: 241–62.

(1961) *Paraspora: 30 Aufsätze zur Geschichte, Kultur und Sprache des byzantinischen Reichs*. Munich.

(1964) *Byzanz und die europäische Staatenwelt: Ausgewählte Vorträge und Aufsätze*. Darmstadt: 232–60.

(2003) *Regesten des Kaiserurkunden des oströmischen Reiches. 1. Teil, 2. Halbband: Regesten von 867–1025. Zweite Auflage neu bearbeitet von Andreas E. Müller unter verantwortlicher Mitarbeit von Alexander Beihammer*. Corpus der griechischen Urkunden des Mittelalters und der neueren Zeit. Reihe A: Regesten. Abteilung 1: Regesten des Kaiserurkunden des oströmischen Reiches. Munich.

Efthymiades, E. (ed.) (2011–14) *The Ashgate Research Companion to Byzantine Hagiography*. (2 vols.) Farnham and Burlington, VT.

Erickson, J. H. (1977) "Oikonomia in Byzantine canon law," in *Law, Church, and Society: Essays in Honor of Stephan Kuttner*, ed. K. Pennington and R. Somerville. Philadelphia: 225–36.

Evangelatou-Notara, F. (2005) "Ἀδελφᾶτον. Ψυχικόν. Evidence from notes on manuscripts," *Byzantion* 75, 164–70.

Feldbrugge, F. J. M. (2009) *Law in Medieval Russia*. Law in Eastern Europe 59. Leiden and Boston.

Fisher, E. A. (2012) "Michael Psellos on the 'usual' miracle at Blachernae, the law, and neoplatonism," in *Byzantine Religious Culture: Studies in Honor of Alice-Mary Talbot*, ed. D. Sullivan, E. Fisher and S. Papaioannou. The Medieval Mediterranean: Peoples, Economies and Cultures, 400–1500 92. Boston and Leiden: 187–204

Flogaitism, S., and A. Pantélis (eds) (2005) *The Eastern Roman Empire and the Birth of the Idea of the State in Europe*. European Public Law Series 80. London.

Fögen, M.-Th. (1979) "Zur Restitution von B. 37.1 und 2," *FM* 3: 178–93.

(1982) "Zum Rechtsunterricht des Michael Psellos," *JÖByz* 32.2: 291–302.

(1987) "Gesetz and Gesetzgebung in Byzanz. Versuch einer Funktionsanalyse," *Ius Commune* 14: 137–58.

(1989) "Legislation und Kodifikation des Kaisers Leon VI," *SG* 3: 23–35.

(1990) "Byzantinische Kommentare zu römischen Aktionen," *FM* 8: 215–48.

(1991a). "Law in Italy, Byzantine," in *The Oxford Dictionary of Byzantium*, ed. A. P. Kazhdan et al. (3 vols.) New York: vol. II, 1195.

(1991b). "Longi Temporis Praescriptio," in *The Oxford Dictionary of Byzantium*, ed. A. P. Kazhdan et al. (3 vols.) New York: vol. II, 1249.

(1994) "Legislation in Byzantium: a political and bureaucratic technique," in *Law and Society in Byzantium, Ninth–Twelfth Centuries*, ed. A. Laiou and D. Simon. Washington, DC: 53–70.

(1996) "Modell und Mythos: die Rechtsfakultäten von Konstantinopel, Neapel und Bologna im Mittelatler," *RJ* 15: 181–204.

(1998) "Reanimation of Roman law in the ninth century: remarks on reasons and results," in *Byzantium in the Ninth Century: Dead or Alive/Papers from the Thirtieth Spring Symposium of Byzantine Studies, Birmingham, March 1996*, ed. Leslie Brubaker. Publications/Society for the Promotion of Byzantine Studies 5. Aldershot: 11–22.

Fowden, G. (1993) *Empire to Commonwealth: Consequences of Monotheism in Late Antiquity*. Princeton.

Galatariotou, C. (1987) "Byzantine ktetorika typika: a comparative study," *REByz* 45: 77–138.

Georgesco, V. A. (1969) "Contribution à l'étude de la reception du 'Nomos Georgikos' dans les principautés danubiennes," *Byzantina* 1: 81–134.

Gibson, J. L., and G. A. Caldeira (1996) "The legal cultures of Europe," *Law and Society Review* 30.1: 55–86.

Gkoutzioukostas, A. E. (2004) *Η απονομή δικαιοσύνης στο Βυζάντιο (9ος-12ος αιώνες). Τα κοσμικά δικαοδοτικά όργανα και δικαστήρια της πρωτεύουσας*. Βυζαντινά Κείμενα και Μελέται *37*. Thessaloniki.

(2006) "Ο κριτής του στρατοπέδου και ο κριτής του φοσσάτου," *Βυζαντινά* 26: 79–99.

Glykatzi-Ahrweiler, H. (1960) *Recherches sur l'administration de l'empire byzantin aux IXe–XIe siècles*. Paris.

Goodale, M., and E. Mertz (2007) "Anthropology of law," in *Encyclopedia of Law and Society: American and Global Perspectives*, ed. D. S. Clark. (3 vols.) Los Angeles: vol. I, 69–78.

Górecki, D. M. (1998) "Fiscal control of unproductive land in tenth century Byzantium: policies and politics," *FM* 10: 239–60.

(2009) "Constantine VII's *peri ton stratioton*," *GRBS* 49.1: 135–54.

Goria, F. (2005) "Il giurista nell'impero romano d'Oriente (da Giustiniano agli inizi del secolo XI)," *FM* 11: 147–211.

Granić, B. (1931) "Das Klosterwesen in der Novellengesetzgebung Kaiser Leons des Weisen," *ByzZ* 31: 61–9.

Gregory, T. E. (2010) *A History of Byzantium*. 2nd edn. Chichester und Malden, MA.

Grumel, V. (1989) *Les Regestes des actes du patriarchat de Constantinople*. Vol. I: *Les actes des patriarches*. Fasc. II et III: *Les regestes de 715 à 1206*. 2nd edn. Paris.

Grünbart, M. (2015) *Inszenierung und Repräsentation der byzantinischen Aristokratie vom 10. bis zum 13. Jahrhundert*. Münstersche Mittelalter-Schriften 82. Paderborn.

Gutas, D. (1998) *Greek Thought, Arabic Culture: The Graeco-Arabic Translation Movement in Early 'Abbāsid Society (2nd–4th/8th–10th Centuries)*. London and New York.

Haldon, J. F. (1993) "Military service, military lands, and the status of soldiers: current problems and interpretations," *DOP* 47: 1–67.

(1997) *Byzantium in the Seventh Century: The Transformation of a Culture*. Revised edn. Cambridge and New York.

(2002) "The *krites tou stratopedou*: a new office for a new situation?," *TM* 14: 279–86.

(2009a) *The Social History of Byzantium*. Chichester.

(2009b) "Social élites, wealth, and power," in Haldon 2009a: 168–212.

(2009c) "Towards a social history of Byzantium," in Haldon 2009a: 1–30.

(2016) *The Empire that Would Not Die: The Paradox of Eastern Roman Survival, 640–740*. (Carl Newell Jackson Lectures.) Cambridge, MA, and London.

Hanson. J. (2010) "The rise and fall of the Macedonian renaissance," in *A Companion to Byzantium*, ed. L. James. Chichester: 338–50.

Harries, J. D. (1999) *Law and Empire in Late Anitquity*. Cambridge and New York.

Harvey, A. (1989) *Economic Expansion in the Byzantine Empire, 900–1200*. Cambridge and New York.

Hatlie, P. (2007) *The Monks and Monasteries of Constantinople, ca. 350–850*. Cambridge.

Hendy, M. F. (1985) *Studies in the Byzantine Monetary Economy, c. 300–1450*. Cambridge and New York.

Herrin, J. (2013a) *Margins and Metropolis: Authority across the Byzantine Empire*. Princeton.

(2013b) "From bread and circuses to soup and salvation: the origins of Byzantine charity," in Herrin 2013a, 267–98.

Holmes, C. (2005) *Basil II and the Governance of Empire (976–1025)*. Oxford Studies in Byzantium. Oxford and New York.

Howard-Johnston, J. D. (1984) "Thema," in *Maistor: Classical, Byzantine, and Renaissance Studies for Robert Browning*, ed. A. Moffatt. Byzantina Australiensia 5: 189–97. Canberra.

Humfress, C. (2007) *Orthodoxy and the Courts in Late Antiquity*. Oxford and New York.

Humphreys, M. T. G. (2015) *Law, Power, and Ideology in the Iconoclast Era, c. 680–850*. Oxford Studies in Byzantium. Oxford.

Hunger, H. (1963) "Φιλανθρωπία: eine griechische Wortprägung auf ihrem Wege von Aischylos bis Theodoros Metochites," *Anzeiger der österreichischen Akademie der Wissenschaften Philosophisch-historische Klasse* 100.1: 1–21.

(1964) *Prooimion: Elemente der byzantinischen Kaiseridee in den Arengen der Urkunden.* Wiener byzantinische Studien 1. Vienna.

Jokisch, B. (2007) *Islamic Imperial Law: Harun-al-Rashid's Codification Project.* Studien zur Geschichte und Kultur des islamischens Orients n.s. 19. Berlin and New York.

Jones, A. H. M. (1964) *The Later Roman Empire, 284–602: A Social, Economic, and Administrative Survey.* (2 vols.) Oxford.

Kaiser, D. H. (1980) *The Growth of the Law in Medieval Russia.* Princeton.

Kaiser, W. (2005) "Berytos and Bologna: some remarks on Fritz Pringsheim," in *The Eastern Roman Empire and the Birth of the Idea of the State in Europe*, ed. S. Flogaitis and A. Pantélis. European Public Law Series 80. London: 344–52.

(2012) "Die Zweisprachigkeit reichsweiter Novellen unter Justinian: Studien zu den Novellen Justinians (I)," *ZRG* 129: 392–474.

Kaldellis, A. (ed. and trans.) (2006) *Mothers and Sons, Fathers and Daughters: The Byzantine Family of Michael Psellos.* Notre Dame, IN.

(2007) *Hellenism in Byzantium: The Transformations of Greek Identity and the Reception of the Classical Tradition.* Cambridge.

(2015) *The Byzantine Republic: People and Power in New Rome.* Cambridge, MA, and London.

Kaplan, M. (1992) *Les hommes et la terre à Byzance du VIe au XIe siècle: Propriété et exploitation du sol.* Publications de la Sorbonne. Série Byzantina Sorbonensia 10. Paris.

(1993). "Les moines et leurs biens fonciers à Byzance du VIIIe au Xe siècle: acquisition, conservation et mise en valuer," *Revue bénédictine* 103: 209–23, reprinted in Kaplan 2011: 479–95.

(2011) *Pouvoirs, Église et sainteté:. Essais sur la société byzantine.* Les classiques de la Sorbonne 3. Paris.

Kapoian-Kouymjian, A. (1974) "Le Catholicos Grégoire II le Martyrophile (Vkayasēr) et ses pérégrinations," *Bazmavep* 132: 306–25.

Karayannopulos, I.E. (1958) "Entstehung und Bedeutung des Nomos Georgikos," *ByzZ* 51: 357–71.

(1959) *Die Entstehung der byzantinischen Themenordnung.* Byzantinisches Archiv 10. Munich.

Kaser, M. (1971–5) *Das römische Privatrecht*, 2nd edn. (2 vols.) Munich.

Kaufhold, H. (1976) "Zur Übernahme byzantinischer Rechtsbücher durch die Armenier," *Handēs Amsōreay* 90: 592–614.

(2012) "Sources of canon law in the eastern churches," in *The History of Byzantine Canon Law to 1500*, ed. W. Hartmann and K. Pennington. Washington, DC: 215–342.

Kazhdan, A. P. (1988) "Che cosa chiede lo storico di bisanzio allo storico del diritto?," Κοινωνία 12: 129–44.

(1989) "Do we need a new history of Byzantine law?," *JÖByz* 39: 1–28.

(1991a) "Alexios Stoudites," in *The Oxford Dictionary of Byzantium*, ed. A. P. Kazhdan et al. (3 vols.) New York: vol. I, 67.

(1991b) "The *Basilika* as a source," in *The Oxford Dictionary of Byzantium*, ed. A. P. Kazhdan et al. (3 vols.) New York: vol. I, 265–6.

(1991c) "Curriculum," in *The Oxford Dictionary of Byzantium*, ed. A. P. Kazhdan et al. (3 vols.) New York: vol. I, 564–5.

(1991d) "Eparch of the city," in *The Oxford Dictionary of Byzantium*, ed. A. P. Kazhdan et al. (3 vols.) New York: vol. I, 705.

(1991e) "Farmer's Law," in *The Oxford Dictionary of Byzantium*, ed. A. P. Kazhdan et al. (3 vols.) New York: vol. I, 778.

(1991f) "Leo the Mathematician," in *The Oxford Dictionary of Byzantium*, ed. A. P. Kazhdan et al. (3 vols.) New York: vol. II, 1217.

(1991g) "Symeon of Bulgaria," in *The Oxford Dictionary of Byzantium*, ed. A. P. Kazhdan et al. (3 vols.) New York: vol. III, 1984.

(1994) "Some observations on the Byzantine concept of law: three authors of the ninth through the twelfth centuries," in *Law and Society in Byzantium, Ninth–Twelfth Centuries*, ed. A. Laiou and D. Simon. Washington, DC: 199–216.

Kazhdan, A. P. and M. C. Bartusis (1991) "Custom," in *The Oxford Dictionary of Byzantium*, ed. A. P. Kazhdan et al. (3 vols.) New York: vol. I, 565–6.

Kazhdan, A. P. and M. C. Bartusis , and A. W. Epstein (1985) *Change in Byzantine Culture in the Eleventh and Twelfth Centuries*. The transformation of the classical heritage 7. Berkeley, CA.

Kazhdan, A. P. (1997) "The social world of the Byzantine court," in Maguire 1997: 167–97.

Kelly, C. (2004) *Ruling the Later Roman Empire*. Revealing antiquity 15. Cambridge, MA.

Klingenberg, E. (1998) "Justinians Novellen zur Judengesetzgebung," *Aschkenas* 8: 7–27.

Koder, Johannes. "Zur Bedeutungsentwicklung des byzantinischen Terminus *Thema*." *JÖB* 40 (1990): 155–65.

Konidares, I. (trans.) (1982) Ἡ εὕρεση τοῦ δικαίου στὸ ἀνώτατο Βυζαντινὸ δικαστήριο. Athens: a modern Greek translation of Simon 1973.

(1984) Νομική θεώρηση των μοναστηριακών τυπικών. Athens.

Köpstein, Helga (1993) "Sklaven in der 'Peira'," *FM* 9: 1–33.

(1995) "Thessaloniki: Wiege des Nomos Georgikos," in Διεθνές Σύμποσιο "Βυζαντινή Μακεδονία", *324–1430 μ.Χ., Θεσσαλονίκη 29–31 Ὀκτωβρίου 1992*. Thessaloniki: 157–64.

Krallis, D. (2012) *Michael Attaleiates and the Politics of Imperial Decline in Eleventh-Century Byzantium*. Medieval and Renaissance Texts and Studies, Arizona Centre for Medieval and Renaissance Studies 422. Tempe, AZ.

Kresten, O. (2002) "Ἄρκλαι τριμίσια. Lexikalisches zu den sozialen Maßnahmen des Kaisers Rhomanos I. Lapapenos im 'Katastrophenwinter' 927/928," *Anzeiger der philosophisch-historischen Klasse* 137.2: 35–52.

Külzer, A. (2009) "Das Ganos-Gebirge in Ostthrakien (Işılar Daği)," in *Heilige Berge und Wüsten. Byzanz und sein Umfeld. Referate auf dem 21.*

Internationalen Kongress für Byzantinistik. London, 21.–26. August 2006, Österreichische Akademie der Wissenschaften. Philosophisch-historische Klasse. Denkschriften, 379. Vienna: 42–51.

Laiou, A. E. (1971) "A note on the Farmer's Law, chapter 67," *Byzantion* 41: 197–204.

(1994a) "L'étranger de passage de l'étranger privilégié à Byzance, XIe-XIIe siècles," in *Identité et droit de l'autre*, ed. Laurent Mayali. Berkeley, CA: 69–88.

(1994b) "Law, justice, and the Byzantine historians: ninth to twelfth centuries," in *Law and Society in Byzantium: Ninth–Twelfth Centuries*, ed. A. E. Laiou and D. Simon. Washington, DC: 151–85.

(editor-in-chief) (2002) *The Economic History of Byzantium: From the Seventh through the Fifteenth Century*. Dumbarton Oaks studies 39. (3 vols.) Washington, DC.

(2003) "Οικονομικά ζητήματα στη 'Πείρα' Ευσταθίου του Ρωμαίου," in *Η αυτοκρατορία σε κρίση? Το Βυζάντιο τον 11ο αιώνα, 1025–81*, ed. V. N. Vlysidou. Διεθνή συμπόσια 11. Athens: 179–89.

Laiou, A. E. and C. Morrisson (2007) *The Byzantine Economy*. Cambridge and New York.

Laiou, A. E. and C. Morrisson and D. Simon (eds) (1994) *Law and Society in Byzantium: Ninth–Twelfth Centuries*. Washington, DC.

Lampe, G. W. H. (ed.) (1961), *A Patristic Greek Lexicon*. Oxford.

Lauritzen, F. (2010) "Against the enemies of tradition: Alexios Studites and the Synodikon of Orthodoxy," in *Orthodoxy and Heresy in Byzantium: The Defintion and the Notion of Orthodoxy and Some Other Studies on the Heresies and the Non-Christian Religions*,Quaderni di Nea Rome 4, ed. A. Rigo and P. V. Ermilov. Rome: 41–8.

Lefort, J. (1976) "Rhétorique et politique: trois discours de Jean Mauropous en 1047," *TM* 6: 265–303.

Lemerle, P. (1977) *Cinq études sur le XIe siècle byzantin*. Paris.

(1986) *Byzantine Humanism: The First Phase: Notes and Remarks on Education and Culture in Byzantium from its Origins to the 10th Century*. Byzantina Australiensia 3, trans. H. Lindsay and A. Moffatt. Canberra. Originally appeared in French as *Le premier humanisme byzantin: Notes et remarques sur enseignement et culture à Byzance des origins au Xe siècle*. Paris, 1971.

Letsios, D. G. (1996) *Νόμος Ῥωδίων Ναυτικός; Das Seegesetz der Rhodier, Untersuchungen zu Seerecht und Handelsschiffahrt in Byzanz*. Δημοσιεύματα ναυτικού δικαίου 1. Rhodes.

Lilie, R. J. (1984) "Die zweihundertjährige Reform," *ByzSlav* 45: 27–39, 190–201.

Linder, A. (2014) "The Jewry-oath in Christian Europe," in *Jews in Early Christian Law: Byzantium and the Latin West, 6th–11th Centuries*, ed. J. V. Tolan and N. R. M. de Lange, Religion and Law in Medieval Christian and Muslim Societies 2. Turnhout: 311–58.

Lipshits, E. E. (1981) Законодательсво и юриспруденция в Византии в IX-XI вв. историко-юридические этюды. Leningrad.

Lokin, J.H.A. (1976) "Theophilus Antecessor," *Tijdschrift* 44: 337–44.

(1984) "Die Karriere des Theophilus Antecessor: Rang und Titel im Zeitalter Justinians," *SG* 1: 43–68.

(1989) "Habent sua fata Basilica," *SG* 3: 1–10.

(1993) "The study of Byzantine law in the Netherlands," *Tijdschrift* 61: 325–33.

(1997) "The novels of Leo and the decisions of Justinian," in Troianos 1997a: 131–40.

(2010) "Wills in Byzantine law," in J. H. A. Lokin, *Analecta Groningana ad ius graeco-romanum pertinentia*, ed. Th. E. van Bochove. Groningen: 225–242.

Lokin, J.H.A. and B. H. Stolte (2011) *Introduzione al diritto bizantino: Da Giustiniano ai Basilici*. Pubblicazioni del CEDANT 8. Pavia.

Lounghis, T. C., B. Blysidu and S. Lampakes (2005) *Regesten der Kaiserurkunden des oströmischen Reiches von 476 bis 565*. Zyprisches Forschungszentrum; Quellen und Studien zur Geschichte Zyperns 52. Nicosia.

McCormick, M. (2001) *Origins of the European Economy: Communications and Commerce, A.D. 300–900*. Cambridge and New York.

Macrides, R. J. (1999) *Kinship and Justice in Byzantium, 11th–15th Centuries*. Aldershot and Brookfield, VT.

(2005) "The law outside the lawbooks: law and literature," *FM* 11: 133–45.

Magdalino, P. (1987) "Observations on the Nea Ekklesia of Basil I," *JÖByz* 37: 51–64.

(1989) "Honour among Rhomaioi: the framework of social values in the work of Digenes Akrites and Kekaumenos," *BMGS* 13: 183–218.

(1994) "Justice and finance in the Byzantine state, ninth to twelfth centuries," in Laiou and Simon 1994: 93–115.

(1999) "The distance of the past in early medieval Byzantium (VII–X centuries)," in *Ideologie e pratiche del reimpiego nell'alto medioevo, 16–21 aprile 1998*. 2 vols. Spoleto: vol. I, 115–46.

(ed.) (2003) *Byzantium in the Year 1000*. Medieval Mediterranean Peoples, Economies and Cultures, 400–1500 45. Leiden and Boston.

(2009) "Court society and aristocracy," in Haldon 2009a: 212–32.

Maguire, H. (ed.) (1997) *Byzantine Court Culture from 829 to 1204*. Washington, DC, and Cambridge, MA.

Mardirossian, A. (2004) *Le livre des canons arméniens (Kanonagirk' Hayoc') de Yovhannēs Awjnec'i: église, droit et société en Arménie du IVe au VIIIe siècle*. Corpus scriptorum Christianorum orientalium 606. Leuven.

Margetić, L. (1985): "La Legge Agraria: Accenni ad alcuni problemi della storia del diritto," *Rivista di studi bizantini e slavi* 5: 103–35.

Mathews, Th. F., (1982) "'Private' liturgy in Byzantine architecture: towards a re-appraisal," *CArch* 30: 125–38.

Medvedev, I. P. (2001) Правовая культура Византийской империи. St Petersburg.

Menze, V. L. (2008) *Justianian and the Making of the Syrian Orthodox Church*. Oxford and New York.

Merry, S. E. (2012) "What is legal culture? An anthropological perspective," in Nelken 2012a: 52–76.

Messis, C. (2012) "La famille et ses enjeux dans l'organisation de la cité idéale chrétienne: le cas des Lois des 'Homérites'," in *Les réseaux familiaux: Antiquité tardive et moyen âge in memoriam A. Laiou et É. Patlagean*, ed. B. Caseau. Collège de France – CNRS Centre de Recherche d'Histoire et Civilisation de Byzance, Monographies 37. Paris: 207–40.

Michel, A. (1949) "Sprache und Schisma," in *Festschrift Kardinal Faulhaber zum achtzigsten Geburtstag, dargebracht vom Professorenkollegium der Philosophisch-theologischen Hochschule Freising*. Munich: 37–59.

Mitteis, L. (1891) *Reichsrecht und Volksrecht in den östlichen Provinzen des römischen Kaiserreichs: Mit Beiträgen zur Kenntniss des griechischen Rechts und der spätrömischen Rechtsentwicklung*. Leipzig.

Monnier, H. (1923) *Les Novelles de Léon le Sage*. Bordeaux.

Morris, R. (1976) "The poor and the powerful in tenth-century Byzantium," *Past and Present* 73: 3–27.

(1986) "Dispute settlement in the Byzantine provinces in the tenth century," in *The Settlement of Disputes in Early Medieval Europe*, ed. W. Davies and P. Fouracre. Cambridge: 125–47.

(1995) *Monks and Laymen in Byzantium, 843–1118*. Cambridge and New York.

(2008) "Documents: Athos," in *The Oxford Handbook of Byzantine Studies*, ed. R. Cormack, J. Haldon and E. Jeffreys. Oxford and New York: 136–43.

(2010) "Reciprocal gifts on Mount Athos in the tenth and eleventh centuries," in *The Languages of the Gift in the Early Middle Ages*, ed. W. Davies and P. Fouracre. Cambridge and New York: 171–92.

(2011) "Communal legal activity in the Athos region in the tenth century," in *Law, Custom, and Justice in Late Antiquity and the Early Middle Ages: Proceedings of the 2008 Byzantine Colloquium*, ed. A. Rio. London: 63–76.

(2013) "Travelling judges in Byzantine Macedonia (10–11th c.)," *ZRVI* 50: 335–45.

Mortreuil, J. A. B. (1843–6) *Histoire du droit byzantin: Ou du droit dans l'Empire d'Orient, depuis la mort de Justinien jusqu'à la prise de Constantinople en 1453*. (3 vols.) Paris.

Moulakis, C. M. (1963) *Studien zur Epitome Legum*. Munich.

Nelken, D. (2007) "Culture, legal," in *Encyclopedia of Law and Society: American and Global Perspectives*, ed. D. S. Clark. (3 vols.) Los Angeles: vol. I, 370–6.

(ed.) (2012a) *Using Legal Culture*. JCL Studies in Comparative Law 6. London.

(2012b) "Using legal culture: purposes and problems," in Nelken 2012a: 1–51.

Neville, L. (2004) *Authority in Byzantine Provincial Society, 950–1100*. Cambridge and New York.

Noethlichs, K. L. (2006) "Revolution from the top? <Orthodoxy > and the persecution of heretics in legislation from Constantine to Justinian," in *Religion and Law in Classical and Christian Rome*, Potsdamer Altertumswissenschaftliche Beiträge (PAwB) 15, ed. C. Ando and J. Rüpke. Stuttgart: 115–25.

Nörr, D. (1969) *Die Entstehung der longi temporis praescriptio. Studien zum Einfluß der Zeit im Recht und zur Rechtspolitik in der Kaiserzeit*. Arbeitsgemeinschaft

für Forschung des Landes Nordrhein-Westfalen. Geisteswissenschaften 156. Cologne.
Obolensky, D. (1971) *The Byzantine Commonwealth; Eastern Europe, 500–1453*. New York.
Oikonomides, N. (1976) "L'evolution de l'organisation administrative de l'empire byzantin au XIe siècle," *TM* 6: 125–52.
(1986) "The 'Peira' of Eustathios Rhomaios: an abortive attempt to innovate in Byzantine law," *FM* 7: 169–92.
(1997) "Title and income at the Byzantine court," in Maguire 1997: 199–215.
Ombres, R. (1984) "Latin and Greeks in debate over purgatory, 1230–1439," *JEH* 35.1: 1–14.
Ostrogorsky, G. (1932) "Löhne und Preise in Byzanz," ByzZ 32: 293–333.
(1980) *History of the Byzantine State*, trans. from the German by J. Hussey. 2nd edn. Oxford.
Palmer, A. (1986) "Charting undercurrents in the history of the West-Syrian people: the resettlement of Byzantine Melitene after 934," *Oriens Christianus* 70: 37–69.
Pantazopoulos, N. J. (1971) "Peculiar institutions of Byzantine law in the Georgikos Nomos," *Revue des études sud-est européenes* 9: 541–7.
Papagianne, E. S. (1992–2010) Η νομολογία των εκκλησιαστικών δικαστηρίων της βυζαντινής και μεταβυζαντινής περιόδου σε θέματα περιουσιακού δικαίου. Forschungen zur byzantinischen Rechtsgeschichte; Athener Reihe 6, 11 and 18. (3 vols.) Athens.
(2008) "Το έγκλημα της 'φθοράς' και η αγωγή 'περί ύβρεως' στο χωρίο 49.4 της Πείρας," in Troianos 2008: 81–106.
Papaioannou, S. (1998) "Das Briefcorpus des Michael Psellos: Vorarbeiten zu einer kritischen Neuedition. Mit einem Anhang: Edition eines unbekannten Briefes," *JÖByz* 48: 67–117.
(2001) "The 'usual miracle' and an unusual image: Psellos and the icons of Blachernai," *JÖByz* 51: 187–98.
(2010) "Letter-writing," in *The Byzantine World*, ed. Paul Stephenson. London and New York: 188–99.
(2013) *Michael Psellos: Rhetoric and Authorship in Byzantium*. Cambridge.
Papastathes, C. K. (1978) *Το νομοθετικόν έργον της Κυριλλομεθοδιανης Ιεραποστολής εν Μεγάλη Μοραβία*. Ελληνική Εταιρεία Σλαβικών Μελετών 2. Thessaloniki.
Patlagean, E. (1965) "Contribution juridique à l'histoire des juifs dans la Méditerranée médiévale: les formules grecques de serment," *Revue des études juives* 124: 137–56.
Patlagean, E. (1977) *Pauvreté économique et pauvreté sociale à Byzance, 4e–7e siècles*. Civilisations et sociétés 48. Paris and The Hague.
Penna, D. (2014) "Hagiotheodorites: the last antecessor? Some remarks on one of the 'new' Basilica scholiasts," *SG* 9: 399–427.
Pentcheva, B. V. (2000) "Rhetorical images of the Virgin: the icon of the 'usual miracle' at the Blachernai," *Res: Journal of Anthropology and Aesthetics* 38: 34–55.
(2006) *Icons and Power: The Mother of God in Byzantium*. University Park, PA.

Pertusi, A. (1958) *La formation des thèmes byzantins*. Berichte zum XI. Internationalen Byzantinisten-Kongress, 1. Munich.

Pieler, P. E. (1978) "Byzantinische Rechtswissenschaft," in *Die hochsprachliche profane Literatur der Byzantiner*. Handbuch der Altertumswissenschaft 12.5, ed. H. Hunger. (2 vols.) Munich: vol. II, 343–480. Revised Modern Greek version in "Νομική φιλολογία" (trans. E. Papagianne and Sp. Troianos) in *Βυζαντινή λογοτεχνία. Ἡ λόγια κοσμική γραμματεία τῶν Βυζαντινῶν*, ed. H. Hunger. (3 vols.) Athens, 1994: III, pp. 183–379.

(1987) "Lex Christiana," in *Akten des 26. Deutschen Rechtshistorikertages. Frankfurt am Main, 22. bis 26. September 1986*, ed. D. Simon. Studien zur europäischen Rechtsgeschichte, Veröffentlichungen des Max-Planck-Instituts für Europäische Rechtsgeschichte 30. Frankfurt: 485–503.

(1989) "'Ανακάθαρσις τῶν παλαιῶν νόμων und makedonische Renaissance," *SG* 3: 61–77.

(1997) "Das Alte Testament im Rechtsdenken der Byzantiner," in Troianos 1997b: 81–113.

(2007) "Neue Überlegungen zum byzantinischen 'Bauerngesetz'," in *Festschrift für Bruno Huwiler zum 65. Geburtstag*, ed. P. Pichonnaz, N. P. Vogt and S. Wolf. Bern: 489–97.

(2008) "Die Bauführung auf fremden Grund nach § 21 NG," in Troianos 2008: 107–25.

Pitsakes, K. G. (2000), "Ἡ ἱστορία τῆς Ρώμης καὶ τοῦ Ρωμαϊκου Δικαίου στὰ βυζαντικὰ καὶ μεταβυζαντικὰ νομιικὰ ἐγχειρίδια," in *ΤΙΜΑΙ Ιωάννου Τριανταφυλλοπούλου*. Athens-Komotene: 399–436.

(2003) "Μήπως 'Le grand siècle de la science du droit canonique' στο βυζάντιο είναι στην πραγματικότητα ο 11ος αιώνας," in Η αυτοκρατορία σε κρίση? Το Βυζάντιο τον 11ο αιώνα, *1025–81*, ed. V. N. Vlysidou. Διεθνή συμπόσια 11. Athens: 231–66.

(2005) "Byzantine law: a constituent of European legal tradition," in *The Eastern Roman Empire and the Birth of the Idea of State in Europe*, ed. S. Flogaitis and A. Pantélis. European Public Law Series 80. London: 251–89.

Pratsch, Th. (2001). "Ἡ ἀρχαία τοῦ πολιτεύματος δικαιοδοσία. Überlegungen zur Ecloga," *JÖBzy* 51: 133–58.

Prieto Domínguez, O. (2014) "The mass conversion of Jews decreed by Emperor Basil I in 873–4: its reflection in contemporary legal codes and its underlying reasons," in *Jews in Early Christian Law: Byzantium and the Latin West, 6th–11th Centuries*, ed. J. V. Tolan and N. R. M. De Lange. Religion and Law in Medieval Christian and Muslim Societies 2. Turnhout, 283–310.

Pringsheim, F. (1921) *Beryt und Bologna*. Leipzig.

(1963) "Über die Basiliken-Scholien," *ZRG* 80: 287–341.

Puliatti, S. (2011) "L'organizzazione della giustizia dal V al IX secolo," in Lokin and Stolte 2011: 381–465.

Ramelli, I. (2006) *Il basileus come nomos empsychos tra diritto naturale e diritto divino. Spunti platonici del concetto e sviluppi di età imperiale e tardo-antica*. Naples.

Rance, P. (2007) "The date of the military compendium of Syrianus Magister (formerly the sixth-century Anonymus Byzantinus)," *ByzZ* 100.2: 701–37.

Rapp, C. (2008). "Hellenism and identiy in Byzantium," in *Hellenisms. Culture, Identity, and Ethnicity from Antiquity to Modernity*, ed. K. Zacharia. Aldershot and Burlington, VT: 127–48.

(2009) "Charity and piety as episcopal and imperial virtues in late antiquity," in *Charity and Giving in Monotheistic Religions*, ed. M. Frenkel and Y. Lev. Studien zur Geschichte und Kultur des islamischen Orients. Beihefte zur Zeitschrift "Der Islam", n.s. 22. Berlin and New York: 75–87.

Rapp, S. (2013) "Caucasia and the making of the second Byzantine Commonwealth: Byzantinization, cosmopolitanism, and the Georgian Athonites," in *Georgian Athonites and Christian Civilization*, ed. D. Muskhelishvili. New York: 57–62.

Reinert, S. (1998), "The Muslim presence in Constantinople, 9th–15th centuries: some preliminary observations," in *Studies on the Internal Diaspora of the Byzantine Empire*, ed. H. Ahrweiler and A. Laiou. Washington, DC: 125–50.

Richter, G. (2005) *Oikonomia: Der Gebrauch des Wortes Oikonomia im Neuen Testament, bei den Kirchenvätern und in der theologischen Literatur bis ins 20. Jahrhundert*. Berlin and New York.

Rodolakes, G. E. (2007) Από το Νόμο Ροδίων στο 530 βιβλίο των Βασιλικών. Συμβολή στη μελέτη του βυζαντινού δικαίου. Academy of Athens, Yearbook of the Research Centre for the History of Greek Law 40, supp. 8. Athens.

Saradi, H. (1992) *Le notariat byzantin du IXe au XVe siècles*. Athens.

(1994) "On the 'archontike' and 'ekklesiastike dynasteia' and 'protasia' in Byzantium with particular attention to the legal sources: a study in social history of Byzantium," *Byzantion* 64: 69–117, 314–51.

(1995) "The Byzantine tribunals: problems in the application of justice and state policy (9th–12th c.)," *REByz* 53: 165–204.

Saradi-Mendelovici, H. (2009) "A history of the Greek notarial system," in *Handbuch zur Geschichte des Notariats der europäischen Traditionen*, ed. M. Schmoeckel and W. Schubert. Rheinische Schriften zur Rechtsgeschichte 9. Baden-Baden: 523–58.

Sarris, P. (2011) "Law and custom in the Byzantine countryside from Justinian to Basil II (c. 500–1000)," in *Law, Custom, and Justice in Late Antiquity and the Early Middle Ages: Proceedings of the 2008 Byzantine Colloquium*, ed. A. Rio. London: 49–62.

Scharf, J. (1956) "Photios und die Epanagoge," *ByzZ* 49: 385–400.

(1959) "Quellenstudien zum Prooimion der Epanagoge," *ByzZ* 52: 68–81.

Scheltema, H. J. (1935) "Probleme der Basiliken," *Tijdschrift* 16.3: 320–46.

(1942) "Ueber die Natur der Basiliken," *Tijdschrift* 23.3: 287–310.

(1958a) "Korreferat zu P. Zepos, Die byzantinische Jurisprudenz zwischen Justinian und den Basiliken," in *Berichte zum XI. internationalen Byzantinistenkongress, München, 1958*. Munich: 35–41, reprinted in Scheltema 2004: 338–44 (B16).

(1958b) "Über die Werke des Stephanus," *Tijdschrift* 26: 5–14, reprinted in Scheltema 2004: 331–7 (B15).
(1959) "Κυλίστρα," *EESB* 29: 78–80, reprinted in Scheltema 2004: 345–6 (B17).
(1960) "Über die Scholienapparate der Basiliken," in *Mnemosynon Bizoukidès*. Thessaloniki: 139–45, reprinted in Scheltema 2004: 359–64 (B20).
(1967) "Byzantine law," in *The Cambridge Medieval History*, 2nd edn, vol. IV, ed. J. M. Hussey: pt. 2, 55–77, reprinted in Scheltema 2004: 38–87 (A2).
(1970a) "L'auteur de la méditation de nudis pactis," in *Études offertes à Jean Macqueron*. Aix-en-Provence: 595–7.
(1970b). *L'enseignement de droit des antécesseurs*. Leiden, reprinted in Scheltema 2004: 58–110 (A3).
(1976) "Das Kommentarverbot Justinians." *Tijdschrift* 44: 307–31.
(2004) *Opera minora ad iuris historiam pertinentia*. Groningen.
Schiemann, G. (2001) "Tabulae duodecim," in *Der neue Pauly: Enzyklopädie der Antike*, ed. H. Cancik and H. Schneider. Stuttgart and Weimar: vol. XI, 1200–1.
Schminck, A. (1985) "'Rota tu volubilis.' Kaisermacht und Patriarchenmacht in Mosaiken," in *Cupido legum*, ed. L. Burgmann, M. T. Fögen and A. Schminck. Frankfurt: 211–34.
(1986). *Studien zu mittelbyzantinischen Rechtsbüchern*. Forschungen zur byzantinischen Rechtsgeschichte 13. Frankfurt am Main.
(1989). "'Frömmigkeit ziere das Werk': Zur Datierung der 60 Bücher Leons VI.," *SG* 3: 79–114.
(1990). "'Novellae extravagantes' Leons VI," *SG* 4: 195–209.
(1991a) "The *Basilika* as a source," in *The Oxford Dictionary of Byzantium*, ed. A. P. Kazhdan et al. (3 vols.) New York: vol. I, 265–6.
(1991b) "Epitome legum," in *The Oxford Dictionary of Byzantium*, ed. A. P. Kazhdan et al. (3 vols.) New York: vol. I, 724.
(1991c) "Thalelaios," in *The Oxford Dictionary of Byzantium*, ed. A. P. Kazhdan et al. (3 vols.) New York: vol. III, 2030.
(1991d) "Theodore Scholastikos," in *The Oxford Dictionary of Byzantium*, ed. A. P. Kazhdan et al. (3 vols.) New York: vol. III, 2046.
(1991e) "Theophilos," in *The Oxford Dictionary of Byzantium*, ed. A. P. Kazhdan et al. (3 vols.) New York: vol. III, 2065–6.
(1999) "Probleme des sog. 'Νόμος Ῥοδίων ναυτικός'," in *Griechenland und das Meer: Beiträge eines Symposions in Frankfurt im Dezember 1996*, ed. E. Chrysos, D. Letsios, H. A. Richter and R. Stupperich. Mannheim: 171–8.
(2001) "The beginnings and origins of the 'Macedonian' dynasty," in *Byzantine Macedonia, Identity Image and History: Papers from the Melbourne Conference July 1995*, ed. J. Burke and R. Scott. Byzantina Australiensia 13. Melbourne: 61–8.
(2005a) "Bermerkungen zum sog. 'Nomos Mosaïkos'," *FM* 11: 249–68.
(2005b) "Zur Einzelgesetzgebung der 'makedonischen' Kaiser," *FM* 11: 269–323.
(2005c) "*Leges* ou Nomoi? Le choix des princes slaves à le'époque de Photius et les débuts de la'ἀνακάθαρσις τῶν παλαιῶν νόμων," in *The Eastern Roman*

Empire and the Birth of the Idea of the State in Europe. European Public Law Series 80, ed. S. Flogaitis and A. Pantélis. London: 309–16.
(2015a) "Minima Byzantina," *ZRG* 132: 469–83.
(2015b) "Subsiciva Byzantina," *Tijdschrift* 83: 126–44.
Schubart, W. (1937) "Das hellenistische Königsideal nach Inschriften und Papyri," *APF* 12: 1–26.
Sergheraert, G. (1960) *Syméon le Grand (893–927)*. Paris.
Ševčenko, I. (1981) "Levels of style in Byzantine literature," *JÖBzy* 31.1: 289–312.
Shepard, J. (ed.) (2007) *The expansion of Orthodox Europe: Byzantium, the Balkans, and Russia*. Aldershot and Burlington, VT.
Signes Codoñer, J. (2009) "The corpus of Leo's novels: some suggestions concerning their date and promulgation," *SG* 8: 1–34.
(2011) "Las Novelas de León el Sabio," in Lokin and Stolte 2011: 267–321.
Signes Codoñer, J., and F. J. Andrés Santos (2007) *La introducción al derecho (eisagoge) del patriarcha Focio*. Nueva Roma 28. Madrid.
Silvestrova, E. (2011) "Fishing rights and the problem of συνήθεια in the novels of Leo the Wise," in Lokin and Stolte 2011: 601–15.
Simon, D. (1969) *Untersuchungen zum Justinianischen Zivilprozess*. Münchener Beiträge zur Papyrusforschung und antiken Rechtsgeschichte 54. Munich.
(1973) *Rechtsfindung am byzantinischen Reichsgericht*. Frankfurt am Main. Modern Greek translation in Konidares 1982.
(1976) "Provinzialrecht und Volksrecht," *FM* 1: 102–16.
(1978a) "Handschriftenstudien zur Byzantinischen Rechtsgeschichte," *ByzZ* 71: 332–48.
(1978b) "Marginalien zur Vulgarismusdiskussion," in *Festschrift für Franz Wieacker zum 70. Geburtstag*, ed. Okko Behrends et al. Göttingen: 154–74.
(1987) "Das Ehegüterrecht der Pira. Ein systematischer Versuch," *FM* 7: 193–238.
(1988) "Die Epochen der byzantinischen Rechtsgeschichte," *Ius commune* 15: 73–106.
(ed.) (1990) *Religiöse Devianz: Untersuchungen zu sozialen, rechtlichen und theologischen Reaktionen auf religiöse Abweichung im westlichen und östlichen Mittelalter*. Studien zur europäischen Rechtsgeschichte 48. Frankfurt.
(1991a) "Corpus Juris Civilis, Commentaries on the," in *The Oxford Dictionary of Byzantium*, ed. A. P. Kazhdan et al. (3 vols.) New York: vol. I, 535.
(1991b) "Intestate succession," in *The Oxford Dictionary of Byzantium*, ed. A. P. Kazhdan et al. (3 vols.) New York: vol. II, 1004.
(2005) "Wozu?," *FM* 11: 1–4
Sinogowitz, B. (1956) *Studien zum Strafrecht der Ekloge*. Athens.
Sirks, B. (2009) "The Peira: Roman law in Greek setting," in *Studi in onore di Remo Martini III*. Facoltà di Giusprudenzia e di scienze politiche collana di studi "Pietro Rossi" n.s. 23. Milan: 583–91.
(2010) "Peira 45.11, a presumed succession pact, and the Peira as legal source," in *Quellen zur byzantinischen Rechtspraxis; Aspekte der Textüberlieferung,*

Paläographie und Diplomatik, Akten des internationalen Symposiums, Wien, 5.-7.11.2007, ed. C. Gastgeber. Vienna: 189–99.

Smyrlis, K. (2006) *La fortune des grands monastères byzantins: fin du Xe–milieu du XIVe siècle*. Centre de recherche d'histoire et civilisation de Byzance, Monographies 21. Paris.

Speck, P. (1974) *Die Kaiserliche Universität von Konstantinopel*. Byzantinisches Archiv 14. Munich.

(1991a) "(Erlassenes?) Gesetz oder ein weiteres Schulbuch? Überlegungen zur Entstehung des Eparchenbuchs," *Varia* III. Poikilia Byzantina 11, ed. P. Speck et al. Bonn: 292–306.

(1991b) "Konstantinopel – ein Modell für Bologna? Zur Gründung einer Rechtsschule durch Irnerius," in *Varia* III. Poikilia Byzantina 11, ed. P. Speck et al. Bonn: 307–48.

Stanković, V. (2001–2) "The Alexios Stoudites' patriarchate (1025–1043): a developmental stage in patriarchal power," *ZRVI* 39: 69–87.

Steinwenter, A. (1930) "Die Rechtsstellung der Kirchen und Klöster nach den Papyri," *Zeitschrift der Savigny-Stiftung für Rechtsgeschichte: Kanonistische Abteilung* 19: 1–50.

(1932) "Byzantinische Mönchstestamente," *Aegyptus* 12, 55–64.

(1958) "Aus dem kirchlichen Vermögensrecht der Papyri," *Zeitschrift der Savigny-Stiftung für Rechtsgeschichte: Kanonistische Abteilung* 44: 1–34.

Stephenson, P. (2000) *Byzantium's Balkan Frontier: A Political Study of the Northern Balkans, 900–1204*. Cambridge and New York.

(ed.) (2010) *The Byzantine World*. London and New York.

Stevens, G. P. (1969) *De Theodoro Balsamone. Analysis operum ac mentis iuridicae*. Coronoa Lateranensis 16. Rome.

Stolte, B. H. (1985) "The Digest Summa of the Anonymus and the Collectio Tripartita, or the case of the elusive Anonymi," *SG* 2: 47–58.

(1998) "Not new but novel: notes on the historiography of Byzantine law," *BMGS* 22: 264–79.

(2001) "In search of the origins of the Nomocanon of the Fourteen Titles," in *Byzantine Law: Proceedings of the International Symposium of Jurists, Thessaloniki, 10–13 December 1998*, ed. C. Papastathis. Thessaloniki: 183–94.

(2003–4) "Is Byzantine law Roman law?," *Acta Byzantina Fennica* n.s. 2: 112–25.

(2005) "Balancing Byzantine law," *FM* 11: 57–75.

(2007) "Law for founders," in *Founders and Refounders of Byzantine Monasteries*, ed. Margaret Mullett. Belfast Byzantine Texts and Translations 6.3. Belfast: 121–39.

(2008) "Justice: legal literature," in *The Oxford Handbook of Byzantine Studies*, ed. E. Jeffreys, J. Haldon and R. Cormack. Oxford: 691–8.

(2009) "The social function of the law," in J. Haldon (ed.), *The Social History of Byzantium*. Chichester and Malden, MA: 76–91.

(2010) "Zwei neue Basiliken-Handschriften in der Österreichischen Nationalbibliothek II: Rechtshistorische Analyse," in *Quellen zur byzantinischen Rechtspraxis; Aspekte der Textüberlieferung, Paläographie und*

Diplomatik, Akten des internationalen Symposiums, Wien, 5.-7.11.2007, ed. C. Gastgeber. Vienna: 139–51.

Stouraitis, I. (2014) "Roman identity in Byzantium: a critical approach." *ByzZ* 107: 175–220.

Svoronos, N. G. (1964a) *Recherches sur la tradition à Byzance: la Synopsis major des basiliques et ses appendices*. Paris.

(1964b) "Remarques sur la tradition du texte de la novelle de Basile II concernant les puissants," *ZRVI* 8: 427–34.

(1981) "Notes sur l'origine et la date du Code rural," *TM* 8: 487–500.

Thomas, J. Ph. (1984) "A Byzantine ecclesiastical reform movement," *Medievalia et humanistica* n.s. 12: 1–16.

(1986) "The crisis of Byzantine ecclesiastical foundations," *ByzF* 9: 255–73.

(1987) *Private Religious Foundations in the Byzantine Empire*. Dumbarton Oaks Studies 24. Washington, DC.

Thomson, R. (1991a) "Ananias of Širak," in *The Oxford Dictionary of Byzantium*, ed. A. P. Kazhdan et al. (3 vols.) New York: vol. I, 84–5.

(1991b) "Nersēs of Lambron," in *The Oxford Dictionary of Byzantium*, ed. A. P. Kazhdan et al. (3 vols.) New York: vol. II, 1457.

(1995) *A Bibliography of Classical Armenian Literature to 1500*. Turnhout.

(2007) "Supplement to a *Bibliography of Classical Armenian Literature to 1500 AD*: Publications 1993–2005," *Le Muséon* 120: 163–223.

Tobias, N. (2007) *Basil I, Founder of the Macedonian Dynasty: A Study of the Political and Military History of the Byzantine Empire in the Ninth Century*. Lewiston, NY.

Tougher, S. (1997) *The Reign of Leo VI (886–912): Politics and People*. Medieval Mediterranean 15. Leiden and New York.

Trapp, E. (1994–) *Lexikon zur byzantinischen Gräzität: besonders des 9.-12. Jahrhunderts*. Veröffentlichungen der Kommission für Byzantinistik 6. Vienna.

Treadgold, W. (1984) "The Macedonian renaissance," in *Renaissances before the Renaissance: Cultural Revivals of Late Antiquity and the Middle Ages*, ed. W. Treadgold. Stanford, CA: 75–98.

(1988) *The Byzantine Revival, 780–842*. Stanford, CA.

(1997) *A History of the Byzantine State and Society*. Stanford, CA.

Troianos, S. N. (1980) *Ὁ «Ποινάλιος» τοῦ Ἐκλογαδίου. Συμβολὴ εἰς τὴν ἱστορίαν τῆς ἐξελίξεως τοῦ ποινικοῦ δικαίου ἀπὸ τοῦ Corpus Iuris Civilis μέχρι τῶν Βασιλικῶν*. Forschungen zur byzantinischen Rechtsgeschichte 6. Frankfurt.

Troianos, S. N. (1986) "Μοιχεία και περιουσιακές συνέπειες. Μία παρερμηνεία στη βυζαντινή νομολογία του 11ου αιώνα," in *Μνήμη Ν. Χωραφά, Η. Γάφου, και Κ. Γαρδίκα*. Athens: 283–9.

Troianos, S. N. (1990) "Die kirchenrechtlichen Novellen Leons VI. und ihre Quellen," *SG* 4: 233–47.

Troianos, S. N. (1997a) "Die Novellen Leons VI," in Troianos 1997b: 141–54.

Troianos, S. N. (1997b) *Analecta Atheniensia ad ius Byzantium spectantia*. Forschungen zur byzantinischen Rechtsgeschichte 10. Athens-Komotini.

Troianos, S. N. (1998–9) "Rechtsunterricht und Honorar der Professoren in byzantinischer Zeit," *Bullettino dell'istituto di diritto romano "Vittoria Scialoga"* 40–1: 41–59.

Troianos, S. N. (2001a) "Δίκαιο και ιδεολογία στα χρόνια των Μακεδόνων," Βυζαντινά 22: 239–61.

Troianos, S. N. (2001b) "Römisches Recht und byzantinisches Recht. Juristische Kuriosa bei den 'Exhellenismoi'," in *Byzantine Law: Proceedings of the International Symposium of Jurists, Thessaloniki, 10–13 December 1998*, ed. C. Papastathis. Thessaloniki: 15–20.

Troianos, S. N. (ed.) (2008), *Κατευόδιον: in memoriam Nikos Oikonomides*. Athens-Komotene.

Troianos, S. N. (2011) Οι πηγές του Βυζαντινού Δικαίου. 3rd edn. Athens.

Troianos, S. N. (2012a) "Byzantine canon law to 1100," in *The History of Byzantine and Eastern Canon Law to 1500*, ed. W. Hartmann and K. Pennington. Washington, DC: 115–69.

Troianos, S. N. (2012b) "Byzantine canon law from the twelfth to the fifteenth centuries," in *The History of Byzantine and Eastern Canon Law to 1500*, ed. W. Hartmann and K. Pennington. Washington, DC: 170–214.

Troianos, S. N. (2012c) "Η Νεαρά Κωνσταντίνου του Μονομάχου ἐπὶ τῇ ἀναδείξει καὶ προβολῇ τοῦ διδασκάλου τῶν νόμων," *Byzantina Symmeikta* 22: 243–63.

Troje, H. E. (1971) *Graeca leguntur: Die Aneignung des byzantinischen Rechts und die Entstehung eines humanistischen Corpus iuris civilis in der Jurisprudenz des 16. Jahrhunderts*. Forschungen zur neueren Privatrechtsgeschichte 18. Cologne and Böhlau.

Tsourka-Papasthathe, D. (2001) "Vente d'office: observations sur la Πεῖρα Ευσταθίου του Ρωμαίου 38.74," in *Byzantine Law: Proceedings of the International Symposium of Jurists, Thessaloniki, 10–13 December 1998*, ed. C. Papastathis. Thessaloniki: 229–34. A French version of (2002) "Πώληση οφφικίου. Παρατηρήσεις στην 'Πείρα' Ευσταθίου του Ρωμαίου 38.74," *Επιστημονική Επετηρίδα Δικηγορικού Συλλόγου Θεσσαλονίκης «Αρμενόπουλος»* 23: 13–30.

van Bochove, T. E. (1996) *To Date and Not to Date: On the Date and Status of Byzantine Law Books*. Groningen.

(2011) "Some Byzantine law books: introducing the continuous debate concerning their status and their date," in Lokin and Stolte 2011: 239–66.

(2014) "Tenth century Constantinople: centre of legal learning? Second thoughts concerning the addition of *older scholia* to the Basilica," *FM* 12: 67–96.

van der Wal, N. (1953) *Les commentaires grecs du code de Justinien*. The Hague.

(1983) "Die Schreibweise der dem Lateinischen entlehnten Fachworte in der frühbyzantinischen Juristensprache," *Scriptorium* 37: 29–53.

(1984) "Problèmes linguistiques recontrés par les juristes byzantins," in *Non nova, sed nove: Mélanges de civilisation médiévale dédiés à Willem Noomen*, ed. M. Gosman and J. van Os. Groningen: 279–83.

(1989) "Probleme bei der Restitution verlorengegangener Basilikenbücher," *SG* 3: 143–54.

van der Wal, N. and J. H. A. Lokin (1985). *Historiae iuris graeco-romani delineatio: les sources du droit byzantin de 300 à 1453*. Groningen.

Varnalides, S. (1985) Ο θεσμός της χαριστικής (δωρεάς) των μοναστηρίων εις τους Βυζαντινούς. Byzantina keimena kai meletai 21. Thessaloniki.

Vasiliev, A. A. (1961) *History of the Byzantine Empire, 324–1453*, 2nd edn. (2 vols.) Madison, WI.

Vernadsky, G. (1925) "Sur l'orgine de la loi agraire." *Byzantion* 2: 169–80.

Vest, B. A. (2007) *Geschichte der Stadt Melitene und der umliegenden Gebiete: Vom Vorabend der arabischen bis zum Abschluss der türkischen Eroberung (um 600–1124)*. (3 vols.) Hamburg.

Vlysidou, V. N. (ed.) (2003) *Η αυτοκρατορία σε κρίση? Το Βυζάντιο τον 11ο αιώνα, 1025–81*. Διεθνή συμπόσια 11. Athens: 179–89.

Von Benda-Beckmann, F. and K. von Benda-Beckmann (2012) "Why not legal culture?," in Nelken 2012a: 86–103.

von Falkenhausen, V. (2007). "The South Italian sources," in *Byzantines and Crusaders in Non-Greek Sources, 1025–1204*, ed. Mary Whitby. Oxford: 95–121.

Vryonis, Jr., S. (1974) "The *Peira* as a source for the history of Byzantine aristocratic society in the first half of the eleventh century," in *Near Eastern Numismatics, Iconography, Epigraphy and History: Studies in Honor of George C. Miles*, ed. Dickran K. Kouymjian, Beirut: 279–84.

Wagschal, D. (2015) *Law and Legality in the Greek East: The Byzantine Canonical Tradition, 381–883*. Oxford Early Christian Studies. Oxford.

Weiss, G. (1973a) "Hohe Richter in Konstantinopel. Eustathios Rhomaios und seine Kollegen," *JÖB* 22: 117–43.

(1973b) *Oströmische Beamte im Spiegel der Schriften des Michael Psellos*. Miscellanea Byzantina Monacensia 16. Munich.

(1977) "Die juristische Bibliothek des Michael Psellos." *JÖB* 26: 79–102.

Wenger, L. (1953) *Die Quellen des römischen Rechts*. Österreichische Akademie der Wissenschaften; Denkschriften der Gesamtakademie 2. Vienna.

Wieacker, F. (1955) *Vulgarismus und Klassizismus im Recht der Spätantike*. Sitzungsberichte der Heidelberger Akademie der Wissenschaften, philosophisch-historische Klasse 3. Heidelberg.

Wilson, N. G. (1983) *Scholars of Byzantium*. Baltimore.

Woods, D. (2013) "Maslama and the alleged construction of the first mosque in Constantinople c. 718," in *Negotiating Co-Existence: Communities, Cultures and Convivencia in Byzantine Society*, ed. B. Crostini and S. La Porta. Bochumer Altertumwissenschaftliches Colloquium 96. Trier: 19–30.

Wolska-Conus, W. (1976) "Les écoles de Psellos et de Xiphilin sous Constantin IX Monomaque," *TM* 6: 223–43.

(1979) "L'école de droit et l'enseignement du droit à Byzance au XIe siècle: Xiphilin et Psellos," *TM* 7: 1–107.

(1981) "Les termes νομη et παιδοδιδασκαλος νομικος du 'Livre de l'éparque'," *TM* 8: 531–41.

Zachariä von Lingenthal, K. E. (1892) *Geschichte des griechisch-römischen Rechts*, 3rd edn. Berlin.
(1839) *Historiae juris graeco-romani delineatio. Cum appendice ineditorum*. Heidelberg.
Zepos, P. (1981) "«Ψυχάριον», «Ψυχικά», «Ψυχοπαίδι»," Δελτίον της Χριστιανικής Αρχαιολογικής Εταιρείας 10: 17–28.
Živkovič, T. (2005) "Uspenskij's Taktikon and the Theme of Dalmatia," *Σύμμεικτα* 17: 49–85.
Zuckerman, C. (1990) "The military compendium of Syrianus Magister," *JÖByz* 40: 209–24.
Žužek, I. (1964) *Kormčaja Kniga: Studies on the Chief Code of Russian Canon Law*. Orientalia Christiana Analecta 168. Rome.

Index

Abbasid Caliphate, 19, 20, 132
Abū l-Barakāt, 127
actions, names of, 180
Africa, 91–92
afterlife, conceptions of the, 93–94
Against the Jacobites, 140
agape, 87
Agapetos the Deacon, 87
akroatai, 50–51, 113
Alexios Stoudites, Patriarch, 136–37, 141, 175
allelengyon, 136
Amorian dynasty, 25
Anakatharsis ton palaion nomon. See "Cleansing of the Ancient Laws"
Ananias of Shirak, 129
Anastasius Bibliothecarius, 21
Anatolikon, judge of, 68
Anatolios, 155
Ani, 18
antecessores, 23, 23n. 27, 155–56
  in the *Peira*, 175
anthypatoi, 51
antigrapheis, 55, 164
Antioch, 18
antiquarianism
  in the legal works of Psellos, 180–81
Antonius, Emperor, 119
Apocalypse of Anastasia, 93–94
Appendix Eclogae, 117, 118
archontes, 50, 56
Armeno-Georgian Chalcedonians, 106–07
Ashburner, Walter, 120, 121
Asia Minor, 18, 19, 110, 138
assarion, 98
asylum, 90
Athanasios of Athos, 74
Athanasios of Emesa, 22, 156, 162
Athonite monasteries, 19, 39, 74
  archives, 11, 23, 23n. 26, 190
Authenticum, 154
Balkans, 19, 20
  transmission of Byzantine law, 124–25
Basil I, Emperor, 20
  ethnic origin, 18n. 8
  exchange of letters with Louis II, 20–21
  forced conversion of Jews, 145
Basil Pekoules, 147
Basil, quaestor, 66
Basilika, 32–35
  availability of, 35
  in the *Book of the Eparch*, 165
  as official law, 35
  scholia, 10–11, 33, 177–78
  unwieldliness of, 179–80
bia, 57
biblia, 34
bibliophylax, 171
Blackstone, William, 78
Boleron, judge of, 68
Book of the Eparch, 28, 164–67
  as the purported origin of the Jewish oath, 147
Breadth of the Laws, 27, 79, 113
bribery
  definition of, 54
  in the *Ecloga*, 56
  in the *Eisagoge*, 56
  in the letters of Psellos, 69
  in the *Novels of Leo VI*, 57
  in the *Strategikon* of Kekaumenos, 64–65
Bulgarian Empire, 18, 19, 20
Burgmann, Ludwig, 151
Byzantine Commonwealth, 103, 124
Byzantine law
  as a codified legal system, 78–80
Byzantine legal culture, definition, 2–3, 4–7

canon law, 13, 15, 22, 22n. 24, 41, 191
  merging with secular law, 186–87
canons of church councils
  validity as secular law, 40–41
Canons of the Emperors, 126

Carolingian Empire, 19, 20, 21
christosemeiotoi, 24, 185
Cicero, 16
"Cleansing of the Ancient Laws", 44
Codex Justinianus, 33
  as a component of legal education, 153
  on Jews and heretics testifying in court, 142
  paraphrases of, 142
  use of Thalelaios' commentary, 158–59
Collatio legum Mosaicarum et Romanarum, 115
Collectio Tripartita, 143
common law system, 3
Constantine of Nicaea, 176
Constantine V, Emperor
  as promulgator of the *Ecloga*, 23–25
Constantine VII, Emperor
  novels on legal fees, 60
Constantine/Cyril, 124
Constitutio Omnem, 153
Constitutio tanta/Dedoken, 154
Council in Trullo, 162–63
Crete, 18
customs, 80–81
  foreign, 106
Cyclades Islands, 119
Cyprus, 18

Datastanagirk', 125
David the Iberian, 106–07
de Tocqueville, Alexis, 12
defensor civitatis, 84
Demetrios of Kyzikos, 140
Deo auctore, 170
derogation, 113–14
Digest, 16, 33
  as a component of legal education, 153
  completion of, 153
  on the *Rhodian Sea-law*, 119
  translations of, 155
  use of Greek paraphrases, 154
Dionysios of Halikarnassos, 98
diptychs, 73
divine dispute resolution, 99–102
dowry, 158–59
dynatoi. See powerful

ecclesiastical property, 3–4
Ecloga
  criticism of, 28
  on the qualifications of judges, 163
  translation of, 24
Ecloga Basilicorum, 160, 172
Egypt, 35, 106
Eisagoge
  authorship, 29, 29n. 57
  criticism of, 28
  dating of, 29, 29n. 56
  on Jews and heretics, 145
ektagiatika, 53–60
Elder Anonymus, 155, 156
elite, 83
Elpidios, 70
emperor
  challenge to his legal authority, 82
  as the *empsychos nomos*, 81–82
  transmission of oral opinion, 82–83
empsychos nomos, 81–82
en nome archaia, 166
Enantiophanes, 156, 162
encyclopedism, 12, 17n. 5
endowments, 98
enkyklios paideia, 163
Epanagoge. See Eisagoge
eparch, 53, 73–74
ephoros, 74
epi ton kriseon, 53
epidiorthosis eis to philanthropoteron, 24, 40, 86
epistolography, 66
Epitome, 42–43
  synopsis of Roman legal history, 43
Epitome Novellarum, 155
epitropos, 74
Euchaïta, bishop of, 66, 88, 168
Eurotas River, 72
Eustathios Rhomaios
  on adultery, 1–2
  as the basis of *Rechtsfindung*, 77
  citation of legal works, 175
  on endowments, 98
  on grounds for divorce, 94–95
  on the legality of foreign customs, 106–07
  on the presumption of guilt, 95–96
  on punishment, 88
  relationship with Romanos III Argyros, 133–34
  review of a bequest, 74
  as a signatory of the *Edicts* of Alexios Stoudites, 141
  use of Latin, 160–61
  on wards with dispersed estates, 91–92
  works of, 8–10
Eutyches, 140–41
eviction, 82–83
exhellenismos, 27, 160–61

Farmer's Law. See Nomos Georgikos
Ficker, Gerhard, 140
Fögen, Marie Theres, 151
Friedman, Lawrence, 5

Gaius, 16
Ganos, 139
Gregentios of Taphar. *See Nomoi* of Gregentios of Taphar
Gregory Pakourianos, 107
Gregory Vkayaser, 128
guardianship, 156–58

Haldon, John, 83
Harmenopoulos, Constantine, 112
Hellenic culture, Hellenism, 97–102, 189
Heraclius, Emperor, 22, 23
heretics
  legal status, 142–48
Hermodorus, 16
Hexabiblos, 112
Homer, 1
Homerites, 115–17
Humphreys, M. T. G., 50, 111, 120, 189, 190
hypatos ton philosophon, 178
hypobolon, 9
hypomnema, 8, 99, 100

ibn al-'Assāl, 126
illustris, 91
Imperatoriam maiestatem, 171
imperial title, 21
Index, 155
inheritance, 106–07
Institutes, 33
  commentaries on, 155
Institutionengeschichte, 4
Isaurian dynasty, 18, 24
  criticism of, 40
  as legislators, 23–25
Isidoros, 155
Italy, 16, 18, 110
ius civile, 16

Jacobites. *See* Syrian Orthodox
Jewish oath, 147–48
Jews
  forced conversion by Basil I, 145
  legal status, 142–48
John I Tzimiskes, Emperor, 94
John Mauropous, 67
  as the author of the *Novella constitutio*, 168
  on *philanthropia*, 88
John of Odzun, 125
John of Rila, 71
John VIII Bar Abdoun, Patriarch, 137–40
John Xiphilinos, 171
  as a new *antecessor*, 172
  as a supposed advocate of Late Antique legal works, 174
John, *droungarios*, 85
John, Orthodox metropolitan of Melitene, 139
Jones, A.H.M., 54
judges
  city (*politikoi*), 53, 55, 60
  of the Hippodrome, 53, 70, 71, 98, 99, 130, 141, 147
  provincial, 28, 52–53, 57, 59, 69, 146
  of the Velum, 53, 90, 98, 99, 130, 141, 147
judicial impartiality, 62
Julian, 155, 162
Justinian I, Emperor
  criticism of, 37–38
  Novels of, 22, 33, 38, 153

kagkellarios, 51
kainotomia, 35, 92–93
Karayannopulos, Johannes, 112
kata podas, 154
kathismata, 61
Kazhdan, Alexander, 4, 105, 190
Kekaumenos
  on *philanthropia*, 88
  on provinical justice, 65
Kelly, Chistopher, 54
kephalaia, 34, 114
klasma land, 39
Knigi Zakonnye, 125
Kommentarverbot, 154
Komnenian Revolution, 15
Konidares, I. M., 191
Kormčaya Kniga, 125
krites tou stratopedou, 181
ktetorika typika, 70

Land, Jan Pieter Nicolaas, 103
Latin
  lack thereof in the transmission of Byzantine legal texts, 127–29
  as language of the Twelve Tables, 16–17
  in legal education, 154
  mistranslations of, 21
  as a prerequisite for the *nomophylax didaskalos*, 172
  superiority over Greek, 20–21
  in the works of the *antecessores* and *scholastikoi*, 156–60
Law for Judging the People, 124
law school
  of Beirut, 153, 162
  of Constantinople, 153, 162–63, 167–78
  of Rome, 162

lawyers, 172
legal collections
  private, 8, 14
legal curriculum
  disappearance of Late Antique model, 163–64
  in Late Antiquity, 153
  lecture style, 155–56
legal sources
  official, 7–8
  unofficial, 11
legal system
  in Constantinople, 53
  in the provinces, 50–53
legal texts, cost and availability of, 129
leges speciales, 109
length of legal texts, 129–30
Leo III, Emperor
  as promulgator of the *Ecloga*, 23–25
Leo the Mathematician, 129
Leo VI, Emperor
  monastic legislation of, 39
  novels of, 22
Leo, *strategos*, 99–102
literary references, 98
liturgical commemoration, 72, 73
Lokin, J. H. A., 120, 177
longi temporis praescriptio, 85
Louis II, Emperor
  letter to Basil I, 20–21

Macedonia, 61
Macedonian Renaissance, 12, 32, 122
Magdalino, Paul, 47
Magnaura School, 163–64
Makarios, 127
Manuel I Komnenos, Emperor, 35, 147–48
Marie Theres Fögen, 156
Mark III, Patriarch of Alexandria, 35, 130
marriage law, 24
Medidatio de nudis pactis, 80, 176
Medvedev, I. P., 7n. 20
Melitene, 137–40
Methodios, 124
Michael Attaleiates, 181–82
  description of the Phokades' forged lineage, 122
  on the founding of the law school, 167
  on Jews and heretics, 146
  monastery and poorhouse of, 73–74
  on *res sacrae*, 97
  on the status of religious institutions, 185
Michael I Keroularios, Patriarch, 1n. 2
Michael III, Emperor, 25
  exchange of letters with Pope Nicholas I, 20–21
Michael Psellos, 77, 171
  antiquarianism, 180–81
  letters of, 67–70
  as a teacher of the law, 178–81
  on the unwieldliness of the *Basilika*, 179–80
  The Usual Miracle, 99–102
Michael VII Doukas, Emperor, 99
military governor, 51–52, 57, 59
military lands, 13
Mitteis, Ludwig, 103–05
Mkit'ar Gosh, 125
monastery
  of the Great Lavra, 74
  mentioned in the *Meditatio de nudis pactis*, 176
  of Nikon Metanoeite, 72
  of Peristerai, 85
  Rila, 71
  of Stoudion, 73
  Tou Kalliou, 99–102
  Tou Piperatou, 71
monastic acts, 105
Moravia, 124
Morris, Rosemary, 61
Mosaic Law. *See Nomos Mosaikos*
Moses, 24
murder
  in the *Peira*, 90
Muslims, 108, 136
mutilation, 116

Nea Ekklesia, 32
Neoplatonism, 99–102
Nerses of Lambron, 126
Neville, Leonora, 48
New History of Byzantine Law, 3–4, 190
Nicholas I Mystikos, Patriarch, 71
  on access to patriarchal letters, 61
Nicholas I, Pope
  letter to Michael III, 20–21
Nicholas Serblias, 98
Nikephoritzes, judge, 69
Nikephoros I, Emperor
  as founder of the theme system, 51
Nikon Metanoeite, 72
Nomoi of Gregentios of Taphar, 115–17
Nomokanon
  Georgian translations, 126
Nomokanon in Fourteen Titles, 156
Nomokanon in Fourteen Titles
  on Jews and heretics testifying in court, 143–44
Nomokanon of St. Sava, 124
nomophylax didaskalos, 170–72
Nomos Georgikos, 110–14

date of composition, 110–11
geographic origin, 110
manuscript tradition, 111–13
perceived validity, 113
Nomos Mosaikos, 114–18
manuscript tradition, 117–18
Nomos Nautikos, 118–23
date of composition, 121
prologue, 121–23
structure, 121
notaries, 64, 165–67, 172
Novella constitutio, 167–73
Numidia, 54

Obolensky, Dimitry, 124
oikoi, 48
oikonomia, 89–92
Oikonomides, Nicholas, 90, 105
oikoumene, 41
Orthodox Christianity, 86–96, 189
ostiarios, 61
Ostrogorsky, Georg, 51, 111

Papacy, 19, 20
Papagianne, Eleutheria, 191
paragraphai, 156
Paraphrase of Theophilos, 155, 156–58
use by Psellos, 180
paroikoi, 82–83
Patlagean, Évelyne, 147, 148
patronage
in the legal system, 69–70
in monastic foundation charters, 70–74
patronage, private, 47
patronage, state, 47
Patzes, 105
Paulicians, 18
Paulus, 119
peculium, 9
Peira, 8–10
as the basis of *Rechtsfindung*, 77
challenge to imperial authority, 82
on Jews and heretics, 146
on the number of witnesses needed for a will, 92–93
Peloponnese, 72–73
judge of the, 72–73
military governor of the, 72–73
penal law, 24, 86
in the *Peira*, 89–90
Peter of Corinth, 94
Philadelphia, judge of, 68
philanthropia, 63, 87–88
Phokades
forged lineage, 122
Photios, Patriarch, 29
as author of the *Eisagoge*, 29–32
on the ideal judge, 62–63
on judicial corruption, 66
Pieler, Peter, 77, 177
Plutarch, 98
Pomponius, 16
poor, 12, 57–58, 83
definition of, 84–85
power elite, 83
powerful, 12, 57–58, 83
praitor, 51
presumption of guilt, 95–96
private legal collections
definition, 109–10
Prochiron, 25–29
in the *Book of the Eparch*, 165
dating of, 26, 26n. 41
professional jurists
as collaborators in the *Edicts* of Alexios Stoudites, 141–42
prolepsis, 95–96
protonotarios, 51
protospatharios
mentioned in the *Meditatio de nudis pactis*, 176
psychikon, 98

quaestor, 55

Reichsrecht, 103–05
Reinert, Stephan, 135
res sacrae, 97
Rhodes, 118–23
Rhodian Sea-Law. *See Nomos Nautikos*
Roman law
as the basis of Byzantine law, 78–80
Romanitas, 19, 20, 21, 29, 41, 43, 44
Romanos I Lekapenos, Emperor
legislation on the powerful, 83
Romanos III Argyros, Emperor
challenge to his legal authority, 82
patronage of Eustathios Rhomaios, 133–34
Romanos Skleros, 86, 95–96
Rus', 125
Russian Primary Chronicle, 107
Russo-Byzantine Treaties, 107

Samonas, 85
Saradi, Helen, 60
Sarris, Peter, 105
Scheltema, H. J., 154
Schminck, Andreas, 120, 164, 177
scholastikoi, 23, 23n. 27, 156

sekreta, 129
semeioma, 9
Sententiae Syriacae, 126
Simon, Dieter, 77, 104
Sixty Books. See Basilika
Skeuenas, *magklabites*, 90
social class, 83
Solomon, 24
Sozopolis, bishop of, 68
Speck, Paul, 164, 174
sportulae. See ektagiatika
St. Basil the Younger, 94
Stefan Dušan, 124
Steinwenter, Artur, 3–4
Stephan, 80, 155
  in the *Edicts* of Alexios Stoudites, 175
  in the *Meditatio de nudis pactis*, 176
  in the *Peira*, 175
stipulatio, 160–61
Stolte, Bernard, 76, 113
strategos. See military governor
suits, names of, 180
sykophantikon, 147
Symbatios, 16–17, 42–43
Symeon of Bulgaria, Tsar, 20, 20n. 14
sympatheia, 63
symponoi, 6, 52
Synopsis Basilicorum Major, 121, 146
Synopsis legum, 178–81
syntagma, 156
Syria, 18, 91–92, 138
Syrian Orthodox, 137–40
  in the taxonomy of Byzantine heresey, 140–41
Syrianos Magistros
  on the ideal judge, 64
Syro-Roman Lawbook, 103–04, 126

Taktikon Uspenskij, 52
teachers of notaries, 166
teleion, 147
Thalelaios, 143, 155, 158–59
theme system
  development of, 50–51
Theodora, 94
Theodore Balsamon, 35, 130, 167, 177, 191
  on the founding of the law school, 167
Theodore Scholastikos, 156, 162
  on Jews and heretics testifying in
    court, 144
Theodore the Stoudite, 89
Theopaschitoi, 140
Theophanes Continuatus, 164
Thessaloniki, 18, 110
Thrakesion, 100
Tipoukeitos, 105
titloi, 34
Topoisammlungen, 77
transmission of Byzantine legal texts, 127
  in Arabic and Syriac, 126–27
  in Armenian and Georgian, 126
  in Slavic languages, 125
Troianos, Spyros, 168
Twelve Tables, 16–17, 97
Tychikos, 129

Umayyad Caliphate, 19, 20
Usual Miracle, The, 99–102

Vakhtang VI of Kartli, King, 126
van Bochove, Thomas, 177
van der Wal, Nicolaas, 120, 121, 177
Varnalides, Soterios, 191
Vaspurakan, 18
Vernadsky, George, 111
Virgin, the, 99–102
Vita Basilii
  description of legal reform, 25
Vladimir, Prince of Kiev, 125
Volksrecht, 103–05
Volusius Maecianus, 119

Wagschal, David, 186
watermill, 99–102
Wenger, Leopold, 177
will
  number of witnesses needed, 92–93
Wolska-Conus, Wanda, 150–51, 174

Xenophon, 98

Yemen, 115–17
Younger Anonymus, 156,
    see also Enantiophanes

Zachariä von Lingenthal, Karl
    Eduard, 5n. 12, 110, 120,
    121, 177
Zakon gradskii, 125